Memories of Lotsane:
The Chronicles of An African Boarding School.

By Sebati Edward Mafate

Aventine Press

© 2012, Sebati Edward Mafate
First Edition

No part of this book may be reproduced or transmitted in any form or by any means, electronic, or mechanical, including photocopying, recording, or by any information storage, and retrieval system without written permission from both the copyright owner and the publisher of this book.

Published by Aventine Press
55 E. Emerson St.
Chula Vista
www.aventinepress.com

ISBN: 1-59330-764-0

Library of Congress Control Number: 2012904193
Library of Congress Cataloging-in-Publication Data
Memories of Lotsane / Sebati Edward Mafate

Printed in the United States of America
ALL RIGHTS RESERVED

Forward

 Contradicting social, psychological, and ambitious forces acting on a growing teenager's mind, more often than not, become too much to bear. It is only those determined characters like **MAFATE SEBATI**, *whom I have known for a period of three years, who manage to overcome pressures caused by those forces, and come out with a career that is consonant with their ability. Otherwise, many people find themselves struggling in life just to manage, without enjoying what they do, because of failure to overcome those pressures at that tender age.*
 One of the challenges that face teachers in schools is to give an appropriate orientation to their students at that age because of the above mentioned forces. It is only when a teacher puts down his/her foot that, at a later date, when a student is settled in a career that is in line with his/her ability, that you may, as a teacher, get compliments for your insistence on the appropriate direction that led them to that career.
 Peer pressure is one of the forces that sometimes disorient teenagers, and in most cases, in the form of distraction, and hence their performance. Sebati details these pressures vividly in **Memories of Lotsane**.
 Psychological forces destabilize teenagers by drawing their efforts to their dreams rather than realities of what they are capable of doing. This is aggravated by parents' ambitions for their children who sometimes get them off the course of what they can do best, and hamper their achievements. All these forces come out very clearly in **Memories of Lotsane**, *as Sebati was subjected to all these forces, but being a well-focused young man, he managed to overcome them.*
 It was obvious to all who taught him that he was stronger in Art subjects than Natural Sciences, and I was delighted that he finally pursued the area where he was most talented.
 In his **Memories of Lotsane**, *Sebati, who was known by his teachers as energetic, well behaved, and endowed with many abilities, describes how he performed on the stage and the compliments he got*

from various people. As the director of interschool drama competition, in a nutshell, I would say that he was marvelous on stage, and it would have been a waste if he did not secure an opportunity to enter the film industry for a career.

What Sebati does not spell out, but comes out clearly in his writing is his positive approach to life in general. At no time does he look at other people, be it his peers, or his superiors at Lotsane from a negative angle. He always has nice words to say about even those we know no one else could find anything good to say about them.

The truthful approach with which the book is written, and the minute details that are covered reawakened the memories of Lotsane that were dying in me, and I could not help but to feel that I miss it.

Emmanuel Mudidi, Former Lotsane teacher, Member of Parliament, Minister of Education, Rwanda, and Rector of the Kigali Institute of Technology.

Authors note

This book tells of my experiences at Lotsane Senior Secondary School, at a time when I was privileged to be a part of that great institution. The events described henceforth happened from January 1985 to December 1987. In some instances, people's names have been changed or omitted altogether for obvious reasons. I also want to make it clear that this was not an attempt to besmirch anyone's good name, but instead to share pleasant and at times, not so pleasant memories of our youth. For me personally it was a wonderful journey, as I hope it will be for you, the reader, whether you are an ex Lotsane student or just a citizen of this beautiful universe who enjoys a true, and I hope, entertaining narrative. Thank you very much.

Acknowledgements

A lot of people have been instrumental in making this book a reality. First and foremost, I would like to thank God Almighty for putting me on this earth, and for blessing me with my wife and cherished companion, Vivian Lorena Mafate, who always, over the years, encouraged me to share these experiences with my fellow men; and Gina Law Aguirre, who, after I told her the story of Lepholeta 'City' Senne and the great Lotsane soccer team of 1986, sparked something in me which got me to start writing the very next day. I also want to thank Sethunyiwe Oitsile, Adam 'Mastermind' Masebola, Mbako 'Rams' Ramashaba, Cross Kgosidiile, Betty Bolaane Mathiba, Tiny Diswai-Moremi, John 'Buddha John' Monyai, uncle Vincent 'Rizzah' Malepa (who made my dream scholarship to the U.S. a reality), and many others for providing timely and invaluable information during my research. And really, where would I be without John Max Moreti and Allim '48 Hrs' Milazi? I am indebted to each and every single one of you.

For my children: Amantle, Sennuwy, Uri Sebati, Ulani, and Tladi. For I remind you to ...

"Rejoice, O young man, in thy youth; and let thy heart cheer thee in the days of thy youth ..." Ecclesiastes 11:9.

Introduction

I have heard someone in a song say '*I cannot hide from my memory*', and with someone who has been blessed with a memory like mine; one finds out more often than not that that saying is absolutely true. Many of my memories are from my days at boarding school in Botswana. This was from 1982 through 1987. However, the period that stands out is from 1985 to 1987 – that was during my stay at Lotsane Senior Secondary School. Those years there rank up as among the happiest in my life; although, like everyone else, I hope many more are still to come.

A lot of things happened during that time. I have told of the many escapades of boarding life to friends and strangers alike in Africa and the United States, and the reaction has always been the same – '*why don't you write about these experiences and share them with the world?*' Truth be told, the thought had occurred to me; but I always wondered where I would begin, and what I would say. Will I offend anybody? Will people find this funny? Is it really worth my time ... etc ... etc ... Then I thought, why not? If these experiences were memorable to me, then why not write about them?

I know at least someone will find it funny that a certain Blackie (and that was his name given at birth) or Davis (a name he gave himself), when as a goal keeper, walked out on his team during a football game (soccer), knowing fully well that he was indispensable. As he walked out of the field, Blackie was declaring his undying love to his one and only. Or that another fellow named Andries 'Hotstix' Ryan single-handedly demoralized an entire soccer team by shouting all kinds of obscenities at them in his broken Setswana? What about if I told you of the wildest things you would hear if you put 14 adolescent boys to live together in one room for a year? I hope this book will answer many of those questions and more, and that with me, you will relive the moments of my life, many of which have been very impactful. Even though I am just an ordinary Joe like everyone else, but just like you, I do have a story to tell.

BOOK ONE: 1985

'May you live in interesting times.'
An ancient Chinese curse.

Chapter 1

I had always heard of Lotsane Senior Secondary School. After all, it was, at the time, the only school of its kind; by that I mean that it was the only school that offered only forms four and five (an equivalent of 11th and 12th grade). Plus, to be accepted at Lotsane, or at any other school that offered senior secondary education, you had to pass the national examination at the end of form three, known as the Junior Certificate (JC), with a minimum passing grade of a high division three – Third. The highest grade one could get was Merit, followed by First, Second, Third, and an outright Fail. I got in with a high third, and how I got in with such a low passing grade is something we will save perhaps for my memoires.

However, I remember vividly the day I was told that I had been accepted at Lotsane. I can still feel that late summer breeze on my face that mid-January early evening of 1985. You see, a high third class pass did not necessarily guarantee admission at senior secondary school. So, from the moment I learned about my grade I was (with the help of my dad) contemplating other options, like repeating my form three at an adult night school in the city where we lived – Gaborone.

The possibility of returning to my old school, Itireleng Secondary School was discussed, because repeating at that school had been done before. There was only one catch though, and that being going back all the way to form two. Even my father - a staunch believer in a strong and/or good education, and that the process alone, he believed, was similar to a marathon race, being that it was not who won, but who finished the race that mattered - agreed that such a move would be a complete waste of time, and I agreed. Although, later on, I did find out that my former beloved school did, in fact, review their policy that same year, allowing the not-so- successful students to repeat form three after all.

en hoping that if I were to proceed to form four, as planned in 1985, my school of choice would be Lobatse Secondary School (Lobsec), or Moeding College, and at the very least, St. Joseph's college. The term 'college' here is used loosely, and should not be confused with the term 'college' as it applies in the United States. The two aforementioned schools are secondary schools, which ranked among the oldest in the country; and were opened at a time when a high school certificate was almost equivalent to what a college degree is today.

The point I am trying to make here is that I desperately wanted to head back South. South is where Lobatse was, and Lobatse is where I practically grew up from my early to mid-teens – from a child to an adolescent. Lobatse is where I knew about true friendship, life, happiness, and the pursuit of *girls*.

That is why when my step mother said to me, on that mid-January early evening, that I had been accepted at Lotsane Senior Secondary School for my form four, I had just cause to be apprehensive, and even a bit disappointed. Nevertheless, I was not going to complain. I mean, how dare would I? After all, there were many who were ready to kill for what I had.

What made me a bit concerned was that Lotsane was up North, unknown territory, and compared to where I had really wanted to go, I might as well be headed to the boondocks. But, don't get me wrong, I was grateful that at least I was going to be completing my form four after all. The talk of night school was dead and buried. After form four, then form five, and after that, University – just the thought that University was somewhat within reach was enough to give me the chills.

Lotsane is situated near the Lotsane River, thus the name. At the time, it seemed to be in the middle of nowhere. The campus was surrounded by bush, mostly *mophane* and had earned the nickname 'Robben Island' from the students back in those days. The closest to civilization was a village called Palapye or *'Sphala'*, as it was affectionately known by the students; and as of this writing, it is said to be the fastest growing town in Africa. The village was a little over five Kilometers (three miles) north of the school. There were several ways to get to Palapye for a student; by bus, train, hitch hiking, and for the privileged few, their parents dropped them off.

I was scheduled to travel by train, but a few days before my departure, my aunty Dikeledi, a Lotsane alumnus herself (class of 1982), told me that I could actually catch a bus headed to Francistown (the second largest city after Gaborone, which is north of the country). Additionally, she mentioned that the bus would drop me off right at the gate, and this seemed a far better option than the train.

I remember packing all my clothes and other belongings in a big metal case called a trunk, and that thing was heavy. I also had provision; my mother had prepared my most favorite dish, chicken and dumplings. I boarded the bus with the understanding that the journey would take at least five hours, not knowing that the real journey, to my other self, had also begun in earnest.

Perhaps now is the time to divert a little and explain how the educational system in Botswana worked at that time. I have stated earlier that, at the time, Lotsane Senior Secondary School was the only school of its kind. The rest of the schools in the country were either standalone junior secondary schools (offering forms one through three), like the one I had left, or they offered both junior and senior levels, like the school I had desperately wanted to attend – Lobsec.

Now, because Lotsane only offered forms four and five, that meant that the entire form four student body, set to graduate in 1986, was going to be a bunch of newbies or *'manyewane'* (the new ones), as we were later called - among many other nick names. Perhaps, that was comforting because that meant I was not going to be the only new one, but I and I suspect, the rest of us *manyewane* had absolutely no idea what awaited us.

The second I arrived at my new school I did, for a brief moment, feel pangs of nostalgia. I missed my old school and my friends terribly; I wondered what they were doing at that very moment. I suppose that was only normal, but that feeling was quickly subdued as fast as it came. I was moving forward in life, not backward. The campus was one of the most beautiful I had ever seen. The fact that there were staff houses on the premises revealed that Lotsane was self-contained.

These were my feelings and observations as I was being led to the boys' dormitories by the kind security guard who was helping me carry my very heavy trunk. When I arrived at what would be my new home, all 20 dormitories (or dorms) in an 'E' shape without the middle bar, I sat in front of dorm 20 wondering what my next move would be. The guard parted with the words 'watch your back son', and I was soon alone questioning which ancestors I had wronged to end up at this school. There was a lot of activity going on as everyone was adjusting to their new environment.

Dormitory number one through 11 housed the form fives (the seniors). Dorm 12 I –would very soon find out – was a mixture of forms four and five. Each dormitory had seven metal bunk beds, meaning that each housed 14 students. Dorms 13 through 20 were entirely for the form fours, with a prefect (all of them were seniors) assigned to every dormitory. There were five blocks in all with a common room in between, and each block comprised of four dormitories. These were blocks 'A' through 'E'.

As I sat there, ignoring the mild taunts from some of the '*manyewane*', it did not take long before I started to notice some familiar faces – much to my greatest relief. I saw from a distance (even though he did not see me), a guy I knew from Primary School called Ramodimo Mariri, who we used to call 'Breke' or 'Blue Kop', because someone had remarked that he somehow resembled a lizard with a blue head. I was going to walk up to him, but then at that moment, I noticed an even closer ally.

Festus Lejowa was like me – an ex Itireleng student. As a matter of fact, we were in the same class from form one to form three. So, it is safe to say we knew each other very well. He was also crippled on one leg, and thus walked with a very noticeable gimp. I had no idea that he had also been accepted at Lotsane and at seeing him I was very pleased, because that meant settling in would be much easier than I had at first imagined. I went up to him, and through him I realized that there were also two other Itireleng alumni at Lotsane: a fellow named Olefhile 'Chamzen' Thelo and another chap who like Festus walked with a perceptible gimp, named Okgabile, but was better known to everyone as 'Da Quanch'. I can bet that four out of five people who knew him never got to know his real name. Da Quanch was a very interesting fellow, but we will get to him later.

Festus then introduced me to a friend he had just met from Kanye called Alfred Ntseane who we later called 'Tonkana ya lebowa' (a little donkey from lebowa), how and why they called him that I have to this day absolutely no idea. We hung out for a while talking about what we anticipated life would be like at the new school. We all talked about the University being our next step and how we all wished it would be. Alfred and Festus had both indicated that the school had many beautiful girls, but Alfred suspected there could be much more than what he had observed, and as he was saying that the bell rang for our very first lunch at the school.

We waited for the form fives to go first. Then, we soon followed the moment we felt they had settled down. Upon arriving at the dining hall, all two to three hundred of us newbies, including the girls, were made to line up and walk into the dining hall. The minute we did it there was sheer bedlam. What the form fives decided to do was to sit at the very back of the dining hall – that place was huge. The moment we entered the hall there were all kinds of jeers from them, *"form four, form four, form four ..."* they screamed, boys and girls alike; hitting their metal plates with their spoons, producing a deafening din that would not go away.

Festus tried to sneak back out of the hall as the abuse was unbearable. But, just as he was about to step out he came face to face with the boarding master. The man who was hired by the school to take care of the boys, and to make sure that the school regulations were strictly adhered to – a fierce looking man everyone called 'Boarding Master', 'Bongo Man' or 'BM'; though, his given name was Mr. Molefi. Upon seeing Festus' bid for freedom Mr. Molefi emphatically said to him, "Hey, where do you think you are going? Back inside!"

The pandemonium had hardly ceased when taunts began to be mainly directed at a guy named Tlhase Malope Tlhase. You see, Tlhase stood out like a sore thumb, because he was skinny and over six feet tall, actually closer to six feet five inches. In Southern Africa, at that height, you are looked upon like a freak of nature. And boy did Tlhase stand out! He was among the last people to be served when everyone else had sat down. I believe the food supply was running low, because he was given a small amount of mealie rice and meat. To make matters worse, instead of holding his plate at chest level at least, Tlhase held it almost knee high. For the life of me, I still cannot to this day comprehend why he did that; was he trying to hide his plate out of embarrassment? Because if that was his intention he did a very poor job at it, as everyone could see that he had been short changed.

In the midst of the noise, one form five girl shouted with a distinct voice, "People, how could you be so cruel giving this gentleman so little food when you can tell that he has a *very elongated stomach*?" Laughter and more laughter followed. It did not end until Tlhase and the rest of us were finally seated and ate our food with a somewhat ruined appetite. All of us had thought such behavior was not expected from senior students, but we were mistaken. It turned out that this kind of treatment was tradition, it was a baptism of fire, and we could not wait to be seniors so that we too could dish out the same to the newbies the following year.

Chapter 2

The first night I spent in dorm 15, Festus' dorm, the others where I was to be assigned to were full. And as luck would have it, one of the prefects who I knew from way back when, Solomon 'Solly' Maswabi, whose parents were friends of the family, assured me that I would be assigned to my new dormitory the next morning, which happened to be Sunday.

Three things happened on Sunday without fail: general cleaning, inspection, and the interminable church services. Of course, the other two chores were disliked, but church service took the cake. That is why Sundays were kind of a drag in a boarding student's life.

That morning at breakfast, we were seated at the assigned tables per dormitory where we intermingled freely with the seniors. The jeers that had happened less than 24 hours earlier at the same venue were now a thing of the past. Later, after breakfast, as I was standing in front of dorm 15 wondering what my cleaning assignment would be, I noticed a form five fellow gesturing at me to come to him. He was standing in front of dorm 12. I wondered what he wanted from me. When I got to him he said, "Hi, what is your name?"

"Sebati."

"I am Fungwa. I understand you will be living with us."

"Living with you?"

"Yes, in dorm 12." *The most coveted dorm in the boys' boarding house!* Solly had definitely pulled some strings. It helps to know someone at the top.

Just at that moment, a good looking light skinned athletic fellow came up to us, and immediately started telling me what my cleaning assignment would be. I soon realized that he was a prefect.

"There are a couple of guys already scrubbing the floor in the dormitory, and you can help them out, because that will be your duty from now on." That was the day I was introduced to John 'Max' Moreti. He looked to me too young to be a prefect. Nonetheless, I was pleased

I would be under him for I liked him instantly. I believe that was the time we began to bond, because we have been more than friends ever since, and the many intervening years have done nothing to diminish that brotherly bond.

I also noticed that as he was talking he kept doing the back glide, known universally as the moonwalk. This meant only one thing, Max had been bitten by the breakdance bug. The hip hop craze had hit the country in 1984, and had spread like wildfire. Everyone who could was doing it. Like any other teenager at that time, I wanted to learn the dance, but was a bit shy and too self-conscious at the time to share my desire with anyone. Breakdance was so fascinating. It seemed to be a dance that was associated with the cool guys in Botswana back in the day. The girls loved it, which in itself was motivation enough; even though, it looked very difficult to learn. Seeing that Max was into the dance too, and that I was going to be living with him, it was only a matter of time before I too would become a part of the hip hop craze.

Soon, I was slowly introduced to my dormitory mates, all 13 of them. There was Johane Mooketsi from Francistown Secondary known also as 'Jugi' (pronounced 'jury') Mmabaledi Sefako, the staunch believer from Moshupa who later became a full-time ordained Minister; he slept on the bed above me. Pema Dibotelo was also from Moshupa, who also took great pride in speaking the Setswana language like a cultured elder; deliberately polishing each word before it came out of his mouth. Thuso Godson Ramodimoosi was a form four like me from Kagiso Secondary school in Ramotswa. Albert Lekobe Mochotlhi was also From Ramotswa, a form five and a Kagiso alumnus. Gilbert Kabelo Sebei Gaboutloeloe, a form five, was a Kagiso alumnus as well, but hailed from the Barolong Farms – Hebron to be exact, in the South close to the border with South Africa. Alfred 'Tonkana Ya Lebowa' Ntseane also attended Kagiso Secondary School. Bernard Mathabathi Mokotedi, a form four (also my class mate as it turned out), came from Kagiso Secondary school. Katu Phori, a form five, came from Macha Secondary School in the Kalahari region. Fungwa Gochane, whose roots were like mine, South African, came from Mater Spei College in Francistown, one hell of a character. Mater Spei offered senior secondary education which Fungwa completed. He had passed his junior certificate exams with flying colors, but rumor had it that upon finishing his exams he set a locker on fire, thus his transfer to Lotsane. There was Cromwell Sibanda from Francistown Secondary school, a math whiz and a very gifted artist. Cromwell could draw anything to almost picturesque perfection.

There was one member of dorm 12 missing who none of the form fours had met, because he was serving out a 20 school day suspension that had begun effectively at the end of the last academic year (December 1984), and would run to an end about two to three weeks after our arrival. This was none other than the charismatic and flamboyant Joshua 'Big Joe' Ntsuke.

The story behind his suspension took place during the previous term (semester) that coincided with the then seniors writing and completing their final exams; these were international examinations under the auspices of the University Of Cambridge in England that determined whether or not a student could proceed to University. As always, after taking these exams the students did not feel that the school rules applied to them anymore. Some would go around campus smoking in public, and as in this particular instance, others pushed the envelope even further by purchasing beer and bringing it to the boarding house.

Big Joe, I am told, got one of the unopened beer cans and took it to class with him. End of term combined in this case with end of year, was an exciting time at Lotsane and I would not be surprised if the same held true with the other schools around the country. At this time, exams have been taken, teachers are not as strict, the rules are somewhat relaxed and most importantly, at the back of everyone's mind is the fact that the long December break combined with the festive season is around the corner. Many times regular class periods are 'kickback' time. One could bring a book or even a comic to read during what would be normal school periods. I believe this had to be one of those moments, because when the coast was clear with no teacher in sight Big Joe stood in front of his class, pulled out the unopened can of beer that he had hidden and said, much to everyone's utter amazement (I am certain):

"Ladies and gentlemen ... may I have your undivided attention please ... this is a beer."

"Ooooo!" I'm sure was the reaction.

"... this is how you pop it open." He opened the can, and to his disbelieving audience who were now spellbound, he lifted the opened can to his mouth and pronounced, "... and this, this is how you drink a beer." He concluded as he started to swallow the contents to a now applauding audience. This was incredible!

As fate would have it, right at that moment a handsome young teacher, Mr. Zwide Mbulawa, walked into the class. Big Joe was caught with the gun not smoking, but actually discharging the bullet.

"By all means, continue ..." Mr. Mbulawa said, "... don't let me interrupt. When you are done, let's take a short trip to Mr. Mahole's office.

Mr. Victor Isaac Mahole was the principal of the school from its inception in 1980. A South African who had lived through the struggle during the dark days of apartheid; a man who had seen a lot during his lifetime – in short Mr. Mahole or 'Legoro', as he was known among the students, was not a man to be trifled with. I am quite sure Big Joe immediately knew the imminent danger he was in, because I heard he broke down and wept while he was being led to Legoro's office. He must have realized that his fate was sealed.

One thing I never publicly announced while at Lotsane was that my father and Mr. Mahole were personal friends, and that they knew each other since they were kids. Festus heard this from my dad not too long after our arrival, and was to use that knowledge in a way that was to haunt him in the most humiliating way, but then again I am getting ahead of myself.

Since Big Joe was serving out his suspension a chap named Shadrack Fologang, also a form five, lived with us during that time, but his stay was short. He was dark as night, very loud to a point of being a bit obnoxious. He was holding on for as long as he could because one form five had to move to make way for me. Since no one really wanted to move, all the names of the form fives living in dorm 12 were put in a hat. Unfortunately for him his name was picked out. Shadrack ended up moving to Dorm Three, I think, but was a regular visitor.

I pretty much kept to myself that very first day, scrubbing the floor with Thuso, Katu, and Bernard, getting the dormitory ready for inspection; which did happen later on that morning, and I fast realized what a big deal it was. It was conducted by one of the teachers accompanied by the head boy and his two assistants. Sometimes, even the head girl would be present, and if a girl was going to see your dormitory it was really in your best interest to have the place immaculate. If it was not, you were going to hear about it from the other girls. The very first inspection was headed by Legoro himself.

First and foremost, dormitories were judged on their overall cleanliness. Personal lockers had to stay wide open and neatly arranged. Beds had to be made and you had to have your uniform on, cleaned and ironed. Points were awarded or subtracted on all these categories. At the end of the year, a prize was awarded to the dormitory with the most points. The winning dorm would be announced at the annual prize giving ceremony.

After inspection we attended church service. This was conducted by students who belonged to the Scripture Union (SU); for the most part, these students were despised because a number of them were seen as hypocrites. They always tried to 'convert' anyone they came in contact with, and were thus avoided at all costs. Nevertheless, since church service was their stage and attending was mandatory, we were compelled to sit and listen to what they had to say whether we liked it or not. And they took full advantage of the opportunity. To put it bluntly, these services were long and boring; of course, this had no bearing on being a Christian or not.

The rest of that very first Sunday afternoon was spent exploring the vast campus. I was with Festus for the most part, meeting and making new friends. There were some faces of people I had known yet had not seen for years, like Sefako Molomo who we called 'Cracker', a fellow by the name of Tebogo Maruping; even some girls I went to primary school with, like Lingani Tafa and Nthepha Raditladi. It seemed to me that Lotsane was a place of reuniting. Also, that was the day when I found out (because Max was a member) that there was a ballroom dance club at the school that practiced in the dining hall, before they moved to a classroom, which happened to be Room Five. I went just to see what it was all about. The country music was enticing to the ear, but I did not intend to stick around that long. In all honesty, only one dance had captured my imagination – breakdance. However, just as I was about to leave, I laid eyes on her for the first time. My heart skipped a beat. From that moment on, I just knew she had to be mine.

Chapter 3

Her name was Alice Mukokomani. We maintained eye contact for the briefest of moments. She was checking me out, I could tell, because I was doing the same thing. I thought she was a form four because to me, she looked too young to be a senior. I thought at the time that in my 16 years of living that had to be the most beautiful girl I had ever laid eyes on. But then, we guys always have a knack for saying that every time we are hit by a thunderbolt. In Lobatse I had a long time loyal girlfriend named Joyce Sebolao. Unfortunately, the memory of Joyce started to fade almost immediately when Alice came into the picture. I reasoned that with my killer good looks and charm (vanity is one deadly sin many adolescents, myself included, are guilty of at one point or another without being aware of it) winning her heart was going to be a walk in the park. Even today, I just cannot help chuckling at how naïve I was back then. I left the dining hall just as I had come. The thunderbolt that had struck me had seemingly vanished.

One other thing I found that was so great about Lotsane was the wide variety of clubs. There were even four soccer clubs known as sub teams. These were: Callies, Chiefs, Santos, and Executive Cosmos. The seniors who belonged to these clubs recruited heavily. It turned out that at the end of the year there was a tournament that was staged by these clubs with prize money to be won. The competition was fierce, and thus the recruiting of members and players alike. I joined Callies because most of the members were like me, from the south.

My greatest joy of those first few days was joining the Karate club. It just so happened that as I was leaving the dining hall, a big guy named Molefi Sanoto was standing on one of the permanent benches that were nearby. As I passed by him he said, "Hey man, don't you want to join the Karate club?"

"Yes."

"Go to that classroom over there, form four, Room One." He pointed at a nearby class as he immediately turned his attention to fishing for more new recruits among the newbies.

I had first been introduced to Karate at the age of 11 in 1979. This was at my father's insistence, since he never intervened in my or my siblings' quarrels, letting us fight it out on the streets. At Itireleng Secondary School we did not have a Karate club, but there was a *dojo* at the local movie theatre. I had joined the club at some point, even bought a *gi* (Karate uniform); much to the amazement of my fellow Karatekas at the club – such a thing was almost unheard of at the time. My stay at the club did not last, as it was hard to train at an off campus site and keep up with my studies at the same time.

That is why I was thrilled when I heard that there was a club right at the school. Room one was filled, as many form fours were eager to join as well. That is the thing about Karate, the very thought of being able to perform like the people seen in movies has a tendency of attracting people who believe such feats can be reached with ease; forgetting that the fancy moves they see are a finished product and overlooking the actuality that many hours, days, and even years were put into it.

We were introduced to the great Mmolawa Roukes 'Leruga' Edmund Nokane, who was the *Sensei* or teacher, and our leader. The way it worked was that the club was run by students. In this case, Roukes, a form five student, was chosen by the previous instructor to be *sensei*. This was done by identifying the best student among the form fours at the end of the year to become the next year's *sensei*. Roukes advised us of this at our very first meeting. I had a strong feeling that I would be the next *sensei* come 1986. Max was a martial artist too and a great one at that. He had to be because he was Roukes's deputy or *sempai*. There was just no escaping this guy.

Roukes was also from Ramotswa and like Max, attended Kagiso Secondary School. As a matter of fact, I recently found out that the two are distantly related. Little wonder they were, and are still, so close. He took his art very seriously. In the gym he was a no nonsense instructor, and took no prisoners. Like any great teacher he could immediately discern his students' strengths and weaknesses. Upon pointing that out, he would quickly bring you up to speed in the area you were lacking. Throughout my life as a student of the art, I have studied under many instructors. To this day, Roukes Nokane ranks up there among the best. To my knowledge, I am talking about a man who never officially got his black belt; which justifies the great Bruce Lee's philosophy that belts were meant to hold your pants in place – nothing more.

Furthermore, Roukes was a very able fighter; so too was John Max Moreti, and another senior Karateka named Khudzani Gaaboipiwe. I do believe that, had this trio stuck to the art with the dedication and zeal they showed in high school, and had the facilities and resources in the country not been lacking at the time, these three gentlemen would have been counted among the best fighters in the world today, hands down.

Outside the gym Roukes was an entirely different person: funny, loud, and jolly. There was never a dull moment around him. He had a way of describing events; and his was always a spellbinding performance, given off the cuff with the skill of a gifted storyteller. What is more, Roukes was always eager to instigate a fight when one was about to brew. He lived in dorm 11, right next to us. Once in a while, after lights off, my dorm mates and I would hear laughter coming from his dormitory. At times, we were privileged to catch one of his few jawbreakers; like one where he talked about a petty thief who stole a local bishop's cassock and gown, and in turn, tried to sell it back to him. We also heard him tell stories about a land far off where the flies were as big as a fully grown chicken.

***

We were assigned temporary classes during those first couple of weeks at Lotsane. This was done on a first-come-first-serve basis. The first group was temporarily assigned to class one or T1, the second group to T2, and so forth. I was in T6. This was done, I soon found out, because the administration was busy getting all our junior certificate grades sorted out to later determine which classes we were going to be assigned to.

There were two main categories that students were divided into. Those good at math and science were put in classes whose emphases were in math, physics and chemistry. But those, like me, for whom math was not their strong point, were put in classes whose core was humanities. This came as a huge blow since I had been brainwashed by my father from childhood that either I become an engineer or perish. The reason for my downfall had been a poor grade in math; even though, my science was good. Had my grade been a little higher, I would have been put in the science classes, and still be on course to becoming an engineer. But then I was not going to let that temporary setback deter me from my given destiny – I was to later find a way.

During that time, when we were placed in temporary classes, we were told that, once again, according to tradition, the following Saturday (our second one there) was set aside for a 'Beginners Concert'. By now, we were all familiar with the school's strict routine that almost never varied from Monday through Friday:

4:55 a.m. Warning Bell
5:00 a.m. Rise, Wash and Dress
6:00 a.m. Breakfast
7:00 a.m. Warning Bell
7:10 a.m. Classes Begin
10:30 a.m. Assembly and Tea Break
11:00 a.m. Classes Resume
1:00 p.m. End of Classes
1:10 p.m. Lunch
2:00 p.m. Afternoon Prep
4:00 p.m. End of Afternoon Prep and Beginning of Extra-Curricular Activities
6:00 p.m. Supper
7:00 p.m. Evening Prep
9:00 p.m. Warning Bell (At this time, girls always left first — for obvious reasons.)
9:10 p.m. End of Prep (This was the scheduled time for the boys to leave.)
9:30 p.m. Lights Off

Lights off meant silence, no one was supposed to talk at that time because it was time to sleep; as we were expected to be in bed. The boarding master would patrol in silence all the dormitories from one

(1) through twenty (20) to make sure that this rule was adhered to at all times. The prefects were expected to help in enforcing the rule, but then again, rules are meant to be broken and this particular one was the easiest to break.

Saturday was the day we lived for. We did not have to wake up early. We could sleep in if we so wished, and not even make our beds after getting up. Additionally, Saturday was that one day in the week where we were not required to wear our uniform. Most importantly, Saturday night, from 7 p.m. to 10 p.m., was allotted for entertainment; although, we were to provide the entertainment in the form of the 'Beginners Concert' on the second Saturday.

Earlier during the week, the seniors had been going from class to class to notify us that each class would have to do some type of performance, and that it was mandatory. Many, including myself, were too shy to participate, and with good reason: the jeers at our first lunch were still fresh in our minds. Besides, I had decided that they would rather kill me first than to have me do any kind of performance. Fortunately, there were quite a few who were eager to be a part of it. That saved my skin and many others. There was the dorm 16 boys' choir among others, the two Pantsulas (the beautiful 'ghetto' dance), and the highlight of the night: breakdance.

There was a fellow I knew by the name of Marios Dakune Rakgwasi, who I had known from Lobatse. As a matter of fact, he attended Lobsec for his junior certificate. I was pleasantly surprised that he had been accepted at Lotsane for his form four. This was rare because Lobsec had senior secondary school. In any case, I knew Dakune to be a very gifted soccer player in Lobatse. We even played for a team that I formed with my boarding house colleagues at Itireleng. Dakune lost interest in soccer after watching Lionel Richie's *'All Night Long'* video when it came out toward the end of 1984.

Dakune went to great lengths to describe this 'revolutionary and phenomenal dance'. He was trying very hard to replicate the moves, but could not. However, when we reunited in 1985, I noticed that the guy had been practicing and had, in fact, become a great dancer. Hence, that night he wowed the audience, the girls in particular — whose appreciation, in all honesty, was something we all coveted. Dakune was instantly popular. That fueled my desire even more to be not just a breakdancer, but a darn good one at that. I had no illusions as to what it would take to achieve that feat during my time at Lotsane.

***

Allim '48 Hrs.' Milazi arrived about a week and a half after we were settled in. He was not the only one, as we were seeing late arrivals every day. Some unlucky ones' arrival coincided with tea break, right when we were getting ready to resume class. They were subjected to the jeers of *'form four, form four, form four ....'* This time, the noise was all the more loud because there were more percussion instruments at the form fives' disposal. Fungwa, for one, had a lid from a garbage can and hit it with a stick repeatedly to enhance the sound effects.

Since I had been one of the last to be assigned a dormitory, the late arrivals were put in the common room between block D and E. This soon filled up and the block C common room was soon occupied, as well. Unlike the dormitories, common rooms did not have lockers because they were meant to be recreational rooms for an entire block; but with the growing demand for form four vacancies, these common rooms had to make way for 30 plus steel bunk beds.

Allim was one of the late arrivals who, compared to the rest of us in the student body, looked like a youngster fresh out of elementary school. Extremely bright, and judging by the manner with which he spoke English, he immediately gave one the impression that he had attended good schools in the past and was well brought up. Allim was one of those privileged few, who were dropped off by their parents, and got picked up when schools closed at the end of the term.

He adapted very quickly. The form fives took an immediate liking to the cool and devilishly handsome youngster; and thus, gave him the nickname '48 Hrs.' Originally, the moniker was 'Two Hrs.' but that name quickly changed, because of the popular buddy-cop movie starring Eddie Murphy and Nick Nolte. Allim earned that name after someone had observed that that's how long it took for him to adapt, when many of us *manyewane* were still trying to find ourselves. In time, Max, Allim, and I became inseparable.

Chapter 4

Over the next few weeks, we were finally put in our permanent classes. As the days went by, I began to see more and more of Alice. Each day, my feelings for her grew stronger and stronger to the point where they could not be contained any longer. I had to make contact, putting her on notice that I was the most suitable guy for her in the whole school. At this point in time, the only person I could trust with such inner feelings was Festus; and so I confided in him. I told him that there was a girl I wanted for my girlfriend, a senior.

As days went by, I got to know more and more about her. Not only was she very pretty, she was also a very gifted student. I was told she had attended a junior high school in the northern part of the country. I was also informed that she had a boyfriend the previous year (a senior who had already graduated), but that did not matter to me. She was beautiful, classy, and as far as I was concerned, single. In retrospect, I wonder why I was the only guy who had the guts to approach her.

I was counting on Festus to help me win her heart. He was to be the go-between. This meant that he would be the person relaying the messages to her to set up the first appointment (not to be confused with a first date) — things worked differently in boarding school. You asked to meet the girl so that you could persuade her to be your girlfriend.

The initial news Festus brought was disheartening. The girl was not interested in meeting me, because she had no intention of going out with me or of being in a relationship whatsoever. Further attempts by Festus proved to be all the more disconcerting. If anything, the messages were becoming nasty. This went on for over a month and a half; so long that even some of my dorm mates were starting to feel my anguish.

One day, Sebei came up to me and said, "Sebati, are you sure Festus is relaying your messages?"

"Yes ... why do you ask?'

"Okay, tell me this, why are you sending him to deliver your messages?" was Sebei's answering question.

"What do you mean?"

"What I mean, Sebati, is that the girl probably does not even know you. My suggestion is that you talk to the girl yourself. Then, get rejection, if there ever was one to begin with, straight from her — not from a third party." Well, the more I thought about this, the more it made sense. There is a saying in Setswana that says a rock-rabbit has no tail because it sent other animals to get one for it. Alice was a beautiful and attractive girl; what would stop Festus from making his own move? After all, the temptation would have been there (this last thought I quickly discarded). Festus was a personal friend who would never stab me in the *'heart'*. Still, I never really liked the way he always looked at her, and why she seemed to always be the subject of his conversation.

For instance, entertainment often alternated from dance night (record night) one Saturday, to movie night the next. This particular Saturday was movie night. Max, Festus, Allim, and I were seated together watching John Sturges' 1960 classic *'The Magnificent Seven'* when, all of a sudden, a beautiful woman (the actress Rosenda Monteros) appeared. Festus almost jumped to his feet.

"Man, she looks very much like Alice. Goodness gracious! The resemblance is so uncanny and distinct, don't you guys see that?" No one responded. We were into the movie; but I think everyone else, just like me, drew the same conclusion. The truth was that there was not even one iota of resemblance we could see. One would say it was like comparing apples to oranges, but in this case, it was like comparing apples to potatoes; that's how far off Festus was. It seemed as if he was seeing Alice in every woman.

***

Life on the academic end was moving according to plan; as far as the administration was concerned. All of us *manyewane* were quickly adapting. We found out that senior high school or Cambridge, as it was known, was a whole different ball game. The workload was more than we could have ever imagined, and the grading system was much different to the one we were accustomed to. I hated the subject combination I was given — thanks to my poor math grade. Nonetheless, I did my best, with the belief that I would change my course to Science when the time came.

My class was form Four-Seven (classes were listed not in alphabetic, but numerical order). There were eight form four classes in all: form Four-Zero (the pure science class), form Four-One through form Four-Seven. My old school friends, Da Quanch and Olefhile, were also assigned to the same class.

I made new friends quickly, among them, Thuto Tomeletso (who has the memory of an elephant), Benjamin 'Body Roc' Thupe, Shia Cheno, Tlhalefang Tebele, Moletlanyi 'Pro' Nthobatsang, Joseph Thupe, and Jewawa Febion Khembo, to mention but a few. Out of the aforementioned, Jewawa was a character. Now, the way Benjamin came to earn his nickname was as follows: someone at school had seen the breakdance movie, *'Body Rock'*. This chap mentioned that in the movie was a dancer who performed a style called 'the windmill' on *a ball*; an almost impossible feat if you ask me. We all believed that account to be true until Benjamin, who turned out to be the only other person to have seen the film, disputed that by just simply saying, "Now, as for that one fellas ... I did not see him ... I did not see him!" He even struck both hands in a sweeping motion as an added emphasis, as though getting rid of dust. We all laughed.

We also had in our class a tall, ungainly-looking fellow who was cross-eyed, named Tshimologo Oageng. Now, because Da Quanch walked with a perceptible gimp, Jewawa said that when he walked he looked as though he was constantly falling into ditches. Tshimologo went further on to say that Da Quanch actually walked as though he was dancing 'the robot'. Tshimologo would live to regret having made that remark, because if there was something Da Quanch was gifted with, besides gab, it was wit and a loud mouth. Instead of taking offence to what Tshimologo said, he somehow turned it around and actually nicknamed Tshimologo 'Robot' - the name stuck to this day.

As if that was not enough, Robot became the constant target of Jewawa's jokes. Jewawa was just as witty and humorous to a fault as Da Quanch (the two were good friends), especially at Robot's expense. This barrage of jokes reached a frenzy after one side-splitting incident.

For some reason, our class teacher (advisory), who also doubled as our History instructor, a wonderful but firm English woman named Miss Demetrio, appointed me and a girl named Kgomotso class monitors. Normally, to be a class monitor you had to be elected by your peers; but in this case, much to my surprise, Miss Demetrio informed the class that Kgomotso and I were the monitors from that point on. The class voiced their displeasure, of course, but Miss Demetrio would hear none of it. As far as she was concerned, the matter was settled and she brooked no discussion or debate.

As a monitor, you were trusted upon to see to it that order was maintained. You were like a prefect, but on a very low scale because you were in charge of a class. Noise makers during evening and afternoon prep were to be reported by jotting down their names and handing them to the teacher on duty. This is because during afternoon and evening prep, students were unsupervised; nonetheless, they were expected to be quietly studying or doing their assignments. The administration was very strict when it came to that. That is why teachers were always around to make sure that students were doing exactly that – studying and doing their assignments.

Noise making was obviously common place, because students left in a classroom unsupervised found it too tempting an opportunity not to stay quiet. So when that happened, as a monitor, you were expected to write the names of the perpetrators; since the first thing that a teacher said when he or she came to a class that had been making noise, but was miraculously silent upon their arrival was, "Monitor, let me have the list of names of all the people who were making noise."

Failure to produce the list meant that you did not do your job, and not doing your job meant that you would be the one punished, which in most cases meant corporal. I had experienced that once before, making me determined not to be the "good guy" anymore, and left to suffer like Jesus for everyone else's sins. So I made it a habit to keep a list of trouble makers at all times. In some cases, the noise would be so out of hand that I would, at my own initiative, deliver the names to a teacher on duty without being asked. I must say that I was not a very popular dude those first few months.

However, one day, during evening prep, the noise had started a bit low key. As a joke, I began writing down the names of the noisemakers.

Tshimologo was among the first batch of noisemakers as usual. Initially, this list was not intended to be given to the teacher on duty. So, instead of writing the name 'Tshimologo', I wrote in its place his nickname 'Robot'.

Then, things quickly escalated; my pleas to the culprits to stop making noise fell on deaf ears. As a matter of fact, every time I asked them to be quiet just made matters worse. So I continued writing the name, this time with impunity. I was not going to be flogged for not having the list of names.

In the end, I had a long list that, among others, included Da Quanch, Jewawa, Tlhalefang, and Chamzen – there were even some girls' names on it. I did not wait for the teacher on duty to come and demand to know who the noisemakers were. In this instance, the teacher was Mr. Irvine, a plump Chemistry instructor from England who was very liberal with his cane. He was in the staff room when I handed him the list, and he promised to attend to the matter immediately. No sooner had I gotten back to class when Mr. Irvine arrived, list in hand.

He stood at the door and calmly said, "If I call your name please wait for me outside ..." I had never seen such a bunch of nervous people, but please believe me when I say I was taking no joy out of this. It was either I did my duty or I would be the one to bear the consequences, me and me alone.

"Tlhalefang ..." suspect number one got up and, as instructed, waited outside. "Barbara ... Okgabile ... Abel ... Ditlalelo ...." One at a time, they left the class and waited outside. "*Jewana* ..." he meant to say 'Jewawa'; nonetheless, we all knew who he intended to call. Jewawa left the room with a murderous frown on his face, in agreement with the prevailing view of everyone else who had been called that he was wrongly accused.

And now for the classic: "Robot ..." At first, I thought my ears were playing tricks on me. Did Mr. Irvine just say what I thought he said? To my horror, I then realized my indiscretion. *I had forgotten to get rid of the moniker on the list and write his real name!*

"Robot ..." Mr. Irvine called again. This time, he looked up upon realizing that there was no immediate response the first time around. Everyone naturally looked at Tshimologo who was squirming on his chair like a caged animal.

"Robot ..." with his English accent, it sounded more like 'Robert'. Again, Tshimologo hesitated but then got up at last. At that moment, another classmate seated next to him, named Jabulisani Butale, tried to pull him back into his seat saying, "Hey, sit down...you are *not* Robot." He was right. On the other hand, Tshimologo thought it would be best if he heeded to the call. Then with everyone else whose names had been called, he followed Mr. Irvine to the staff room. At that point, I heaved a long sigh of relief, because by actually going to the staff room, Tshimologo was acknowledging that he was Robot and thus sparing me from chastisement. I would have been punished for writing down his nickname since the school frowned upon making fun of other students.

Apparently, I sighed too soon because some 15 minutes later, Jewawa came to the class room alone - that murderous frown still on his face. Without so much as a word, he looked at me and gestured to follow him to the staffroom. He was pissed! For me this could mean only one thing – trouble. I was not quite certain why I was being called, but I had a vague feeling that it had something to do with Robot.

Upon arriving at the crowded staffroom (it seemed there were many more names on the list than I had perceived), Mr. Irvine came up to me and asked, "Sir, who is Robot?"

Without hesitation I pointed at Tshimologo. "It is this man," I said, expecting trouble.

"Hey! No...that's not his name!" some girls in the group said in Setswana. However, Mr. Irvine was not about to listen to them, neither would he have understood them anyway. At that moment, Tshimologo protested vehemently. With his crossed eye, he looked an even more nervous wreck.

"T-that is not my name," he said.

"If you are not Robot then why are you here?" Mr. Irvine retorted. Tshimologo had no immediate answer to that, neither was Mr. Irvine expecting one, because he then said to me, "Thank you, you're free to go."

As I was leaving, Mr. Irvine turned to the suspect, cane in hand, and said, "Okay, touch your toes Robot. Next time, you should know better than to lie to me." Tshimologo, like everyone else, was whipped on his backside; but of all the people, he got the worst of the canning for giving Mr. Irvine a hard time.

Now, upon returning to class, some very furious people voiced their belief that they had been wrongly accused. Top on that list was Jewawa Khembo, to a point that he and I almost got involved in a physical altercation. I was training regularly. As a result, my reflexes were razor sharp. Jewawa was not a fighter but a lover, so I pretty much fancied my chances of winning. Nevertheless, I did not underestimate him. Looking back, it is a good thing that we did not get into a fight, as future events would dictate.

On the other hand, Robot, the guy who really had every right to be mad, was more mellow and diplomatic about the whole situation, which made me feel bad. He did not deny the fact that he deserved to be on the list among the noisemakers since he came up to me quietly and said, "Man, why did you write the name Robot when you fully know that that's not my name?" I could understand his gripe. I had humiliated him and thus had no answer. That's when he turned around and made an announcement to the whole class.

"From now on, whoever calls me Robot must go and say that to his father... and I mean it!"

No one took him seriously. The damage had already been done. From that time on, he was known to everyone as 'Robot'. Notwithstanding, that night, I was the most hated person in my class. Had it not been for the fact that I was a Karateka (everyone knew who the martial artists were), I would have been mugged. So, for many, including the girls, their anger was expressed only in words and diluted at that. Even Da Quanch made an underhanded comment as he gimped around the class toward his desk.

"People, don't worry, this is typical of people who have never in their lives had any kind of power given to them, however infinitesimal that power is." None of these silly remarks got to me, because I was doing what I was supposed to do, seeing to it that order was maintained at all times. Again, it was either me or them, and you best believe it was not going to be me – no sir.

∗∗∗

The next day, all was forgiven and forgotten, but not for Robot – did he hear about it! Jewawa mercilessly barraged us with jokes at Robot's expense; mimicking how Robot talked and acted when confronted by Mr. Irvine about his identity. The fact that he was cross-eyed did not help matters either. Students could be cruel like that.

Jewawa was not the only mischief-maker though. I remember one incident in which I was a party in making fun of Robot. This was during our English period. Our teacher, Miss Esplin, also from England, had us read a passage from our text book about a boy trespassing in a park after hours, and his encounter with the night watchman. Since English was the most important subject in our course (to obtain a passing grade you had to pass English), all aspects of the English language were drilled into us students, which included speech and writing. In this instance, we were to practice our speaking skills. Miss Esplin had us pair up. Out of each pair, one was to play the trespasser and the other, the night watchman. There was no script to follow. It was all improv and it had to be done in English.

I teamed up with Jewawa. Initially we went through the whole act over and over again, but after a while it became boring, so we decided to spice it up a little. As the trespasser, he acted like Robot and I as the watchman, played Mr. Irvine. Now, whenever Mr. Irvine spoke, his stomach shook, and to recreate that, I was compelled to use my palm to make my 16-year-old-flat-belly move up and down. Jewawa imitated Robot to a tee. Our act was so unique and hilarious that the rest of the class, including Miss Esplin, stopped to watch us. Now, as for Robot, the poor fellow was facing the wall as if captivated by it.

Alas, this was only the beginning because Jewawa was relentless, and laughter was always sure to follow thereafter. It got to a point that, whenever Jewawa was about to perform one of his acts, Robot would sense what was coming and then simply drop his head in embarrassment, and only to raise it after the storm had subsided.

Chapter 5

I trained nonstop after school. It was hard at first, but my body began to respond rapidly by growing stronger. Since I had been introduced to Karate at an early age, it helped me catch on very fast. In time, I was one of the best new recruits; even though Roukes had remarked that I was good but was troubled by the exercises, which was true at the time.

One of the rules we had to adhere to as a club was: no fighting outside the gym. As a school rule fighting was strictly prohibited, period. But then again, in many instances, fights could not be avoided, especially among teenage boys. As Karatekas our behavior was to be exemplary; we were expected to be self-disciplined, exercising control, even when provoked. There was, however, one member of our club who found this rule very hard to follow. His name was Nelson Moselane who we later nicknamed '*Mashi*' or 'Milk" behind his back, this, after a funny incident that I will get into later.

Like Roukes, Nelson was always serious in the gym to a point of being a bit overzealous, always with a frown on his face. With him in the midst, there was no goofing around. Nelson was like a self-appointed gym policeman. I was later shocked and pleasantly surprised to find out that Nelson was actually a fun-loving-jolly-fellow who, like Roukes, could be the life of a party.

One night, just after evening study, we heard a commotion at the entrance of our dormitory and all of a sudden the room was filled with a lot of the form five student body; they were all talking at once. In the midst of this commotion were Nelson and Shadrack. A fight was brewing between the two. Some mischievous boys among the crowd eager for a treat decided to egg them on.

"Seconds away, round one ... fight guys," someone quipped.

"It's Gerrie Coetzee versus Greg Page," remarked Michael Balebetsi, who had a trademark Afro at the time. Greg Page and Gerrie Coetzee were two heavyweight boxers who had just battled for the WBA

(World Boxing Association) championship, with the former emerging victorious.

"You know, if it were me, I would have connected a couple of punches by now," said Tiroyamodimo whom we called Tiro.

By this time, the two would-be combatants were ready to get it on. Of the two, it seemed obvious to everyone that Nelson was more than eager for the fight. At that point, Shadrack decided that the wise thing to do was to walk away. As he turned to do just that, Nelson instantaneously gave him a vicious shove that almost knocked him over.

"Don't turn your back on me!" He shouted.

Shadrack reacted by throwing his books aside and charged at Nelson with what looked like great fury. A fight now seemed inevitable and for a moment, the whole dormitory was silent as it appeared that the audience had finally been granted their wish. Nelson was ready for him, because he immediately clapped his hands once and had his fists in position. For a person who was about to be engaged in what, for all intents and purposes, looked like a brutal fight, he seemed very confident, overly relaxed, and happy that the fight was finally on.

On the other hand, Shadrack looked tense. Since Nelson had initiated the aggression by shoving him, naturally, we all expected Shadrack to retaliate in kind and quickly, either with a punch or, at the very least, a vicious shove of his own. Instead, Shadrack looked a bit scared to do either. I think that fear had a lot to do with the fact that he appeared paralyzed at the prospect of crossing swords with a student of the martial arts. This would be a fight where, in theory, he would be at a complete disadvantage.

Upon sensing the fear in Shadrack, Nelson became more and more bold and confident that, in the end, he did something that nobody had seen before – he started to whistle. And just at that point, Max intervened and separated the two guys, much to Shadrack's relief, given that his initial fury had been faked.

Shortly thereafter, the whole episode soon turned humorous as everyone was trying to reenact the whole scenario that had just taken place. However, it was particularly difficult to imitate Nelson's whistling while laughing at the same time.

***

It seemed as if there was no convincing Alice to be my girlfriend; let alone, meet me in person so that I may persuade her that I and only I was the right guy for her on this God's green earth. It was also becoming remarkably obvious that Festus's involvement was detrimental to the whole cause. I remember even writing a letter to her describing what a great guy I was, how my heart skipped a beat every time I saw her, and all that puppy-dog-romance-talk that a teenager with a huge crush comes up with. I even went on to tell her that I was not one of those guys who wanted a woman just for sex; I was looking for true love, commitment and all that good stuff that I thought a girl would like to hear. Max delivered the letter on my behalf – and I waited anxiously for her response.

The response did come a day or two later, and I received the news after lights off. Max came up to my bed and said to me in confidence, "Man the prognosis is bad ..." I could feel my bowels turning to water.

"What did she say man, I mean d-did she respond to the letter?"

"Actually, she said there was no need to reply as she is not interested in having a boyfriend. Believe me Sebati, I tried to make her see the light, but it was useless." Every word was like a mule kick in the stomach.

"So, do you suggest that I throw in the towel?"

"I hate to be the one to say it man, but yes. Remember she is not the only pebble on the seashore; she's the one who has missed out. You are a great guy Sebati and don't ever forget that." The words came from a place of love, but they did little to ease my pain. She *was* the only pebble on the seashore, and I did *not* want her to miss out. Not surprising, sleep was as elusive as Alice that night.

Aside from my Karate, breakdance was fast becoming my other passion. I was slowly picking up moves on my own. I was determined to learn the dance despite the constant comments from Albert Lekobe Mochotlhi that I looked very funny trying to do breakdance, and that I would look better opting for another type of dance. He suggested the 'ghetto dance' Pantsula, but I was not to be swayed. The hip hop craze was too good and too cool to let it pass by.

The breakdancers had a class where they normally practiced after school. Music was always blasting from the omnipresent 'boom boxes' of the 1980's; these guys took their art very seriously and practiced hard. Besides Max, Dakune, and Ramodimo 'Breke' Mariri I did not know anyone else in the crew. They had even attracted some beautiful girls like Motshidisi Mosidila who, like me, were determined to learn the dance. One day, I decided to go to the dance room on my own initiative. My three allies were not present at the time.

Instead of observing what the others (who were hard at practice) were doing I decided, without thinking, to throw myself into the fire, and at the mercy of the criticism of the pros. In this instance, the jibe came from a guy I just knew by sight, who was a form 4 like me. His name was Patrick Moemedi 'Two-Two' Raperekisi. I must admit that at first I did not quite like Moemedi at all. To me he seemed too full of himself and cocky. When I tried to make a certain move that was out of my depth, causing me to almost fall flat on my face, he said softly in his raspy voice as he was performing the 'waves', "amateurs will just put us in trouble." It was a stinging remark and I had no choice but to leave with my head hanging. Later on, we were to laugh about that; even though he admitted that he did not quite recall the incident in question.

I continued practicing moves on my own and started befriending a few of the other breakdancers like Letsogile 'Tso' Lekgaotswe, Noble Katse, Maulter, and David Makuni. In time, 'Two-Two' and I became really good friends. Living with Max helped a lot because we were able to exchange ideas and moves; soon thereafter, to my surprise, I actually began to get good. I think being in shape because of Karate helped quite a bit.

The first term also meant that it was the season for track and field events. We were divided into houses as participating in track and field events was mandatory, that is if you were physically able. I have always been a fast runner, maybe not the fastest, but my speed was above average. The four houses were named Buffalo, Zebra, Impala, and Kudu. I was a buffalo. Tryouts in each house meant that the fastest runners and those good at field events were to be identified to represent their respective houses; then, at a set date, which was a Friday, there would be an inter house competition. This is when the houses competed against each other, and the best athletes to represent the school were picked from there to later compete in the inter school competitions in the region.

Since at the time I was a bit too bashful and self-conscious I pretended not to be a fast runner (I was to keep up that charade, as it turned out, until 1987). Consequently, I did not qualify to be a part of the team that represented our house. During the tryouts, I remember merely throwing one leg in front of the other. It must have looked funny for someone my height (I was already over 6 feet tall) because Mmabaledi, my Christian dorm mate who slept in the bed above me, remarked later how hilarious my running looked. I was to have the last laugh not too long after.

Sports day was always a day that we looked forward to. It would normally happen on a Friday and all classes were cancelled that day. It was a bright sunny morning that found us at the football field that day, teachers and students alike. On that day, even teachers would behave like school kids as they cheered for their respective houses, and at times get into heated arguments in front of students – a sight no one had ever witnessed until it came to such events.

The first event, as was always the case, was the 5000 meters. This was running 12 laps around the field; kind of a mini marathon of some sort. This race was open to anyone. Since this was a race of endurance and stamina, it was common to see a lot of the participants drop out during the race. By the 9th lap you clearly had an idea of who the favorites on winning the race were going to be.

Leading the pack that day was a form 5 named Andrew Botlhole, otherwise known as 'Devil'. How and why he got that nickname I have no clue, but I suspect it must have been for his soccer prowess. In any case, Devil was in front closely followed by another chap whose name eludes me; and just when it seemed as if Devil had won the race, a runner who had been lagging behind within striking distance came out of nowhere and sprinted to the finish line beating Devil by a heartbeat. We were all stunned by this spectacular finish but no one was more bewildered than Devil himself.

Someone later said that that race, much to the amusement of many, was symbolic of the notion between good and evil. The devil, he said, made the world believe that evil will triumph; but just when victory seemed a foregone conclusion, good would out of nowhere, snatch victory from the jaws of defeat. This was a low blow because Andrew was a great guy and nowhere near that judgment of who he was. That guy who won the race was bitter when he was defeated by a better athlete in the long jump; that athlete was none other than the grand Diirilwe 'D-One' Matoto who was to later do the seemingly impossible for Lotsane in a way that was to be remembered for a generation.

Meanwhile all this time as the events were going on, I could not help but notice Alice wherever she was, and no matter how hard I tried I could not avoid her. I was with Max all this time and was forced to confide in him even though we had both agreed that pursuing her further was a lost cause, and would just succeed in causing more pain. I don't know but the girl was just enchanting if not irresistible.

A little later was the 4 X 400 Meter relay race an event where the athletes ran their entire lap and handed the baton to his teammate. Mmabaledi's team looked to be the clear cut winners, because when Mmabaledi took over as anchor his closest rival had a handicap of more than five seconds. It seemed to all of us too much of a gap to overcome, and Mmabaledi appeared to be a little over confident as he ran, more like jog trotting rather, and he was constantly facing the ground as he ran.

Then something short of amazing started to unfold right before our eyes. Mmabaledi's rival was gaining on him with remarkable consistency, so much such that on the last bend when Mmabaledi seemed to be tiring this fellow hurtled passed him at incredible speed, and won the race in dramatic fashion. That week as a member of the SU it had been Mmabaledi's turn to read the bible at the school assembly. After the race someone said that Mmabaledi lost because as he kept looking at the ground he would occasionally catch glimpses of some of his favorite verses from the bible, and as such was busy trying to discern the scripture in question which was why he lost. It was my turn to laugh at Mmabaledi when I heard that.

When the event ended it was time to head back to the dormitories, and then soon after it would be lunch time. As we were heading back Max suddenly grabbed my arm and said, "Sebati look ..."

My heart skipped a beat yet again. Alice and her friend (who I later found out to be her cousin) had walked right by us. I could have easily bumped into her - that's how close she was.

"What do you make of this?" Max asked.

"I have no idea Man."

"Look at this, there is so much space. They could have taken a much less conspicuous route why did they just walk past us?"

"Beats me."

"No, I think we need a second round all is not lost the girl is still interested in you."

Max's words were like an oasis in the vastness of the Sahara. I was rejuvenated once more. To this day I still wonder how I could have been that persistent over a girl who clearly had no interest in me.

***

One thing the school frowned upon was fraternizing with members of the opposite sex in dark corners. Girls were dropping out of high schools left right and center due to unwanted pregnancies, and this was a serious violation of the school rules that could get you suspended and in extreme cases expelled. So, if you were with a girl at night and at the wrong side of the campus you had to make sure you were inconspicuous, because teachers were always patrolling the academic area and the surroundings at night.

One Saturday night after a movie, Festus was chatting with a girl he had befriended. Her name was Avriel Stoneham, she was mixed with Scottish blood I am told, and she also had a beautiful sister who also was a student at Lotsane named Cassandra. Festus was conversing with this girl in an area that was considered out of bounds, and given that it was night time this was a violation, and unfortunately Festus was caught before he could run away (not that it mattered because he could not really run due to his condition) by the headmaster Mr. Mahole himself. It just so happened that that was one of those very rare nights when Legoro himself walked the beat. All Mr. Mahole did was ask for his name, and told Festus to come to his office Monday morning promptly after assembly. In most cases the boy would be the one whose fat would be in the fire, because we were looked on as the hunters, and the women the hunted.

Now instead of doing what he had been told Festus sought to follow the misguided counsel from some other students, many of them form 5's including one Clement Pholo, also an ex Itireleng student, and another named Lopang, but known to the rest of us as Rabbie, who said, "Man don't go, the chap was drunk and by Monday he will have forgotten." Festus believed this to be true, and did not honor the appointment with Legoro as he had been told. Monday came and went by with no incident, and it seemed as if Festus's gurus had been right after all.

Tuesday during assembly, after the regular routine of prayer, singing, and announcements, Mr. Mahole stepped forward and consulted a piece of paper he was holding and said, "I would like to see Festus immediately after assembly please."

I think sometimes we forget that teachers had been students before, and that they are familiar with all the tricks in the book. Mr. Mahole, I am certain, knew that Festus was counting on him to forget. We all held our breaths, I was particularly afraid for my friend. Mr. Mahole was known to be ruthless to students who deliberately defied him.

I watched Festus as he headed to Mr. Mahole's office, wondering if he was going to come out of the office crying because a suspension had been handed down. Speaking of suspension, Joshua 'Big Joe' Ntsuke had already served his, and we were all formally introduced.

When Festus got to Legoro's office, I think the latter saw fear in Festus's eyes, because having known the guy for quite a few years now, I knew he could give that sad puppy dog look that was hard to ignore. Mr. Mahole simply told him, "Listen, next time if I tell you to come obey, and don't think I have forgotten. It is in your best interest that you heed to my call. I could suspend you right here and now, but I won't, just don't do that again you hear?"

"Yes sir."

"Okay let it be the last time. You can go now."

A relieved Festus was scot free, and the matter should have rested right there and then, but then Festus went out of his way to embellish the reason why Mr. Mahole let him go with not so much as a slap on the wrist. No, Festus actually told everyone who would listen that the reason was because Mr. Mahole and his father attended school together. This was just the first of a series of untruths that came from him, and would land him in very humiliating situations. Little did I know that another bombshell was forthcoming.

Finally my long awaited chance to speak to Alice in person arrived. It happened one Saturday afternoon after lunch. I remember that day Max was in a particularly jolly mood, so without thinking much about it I looked at him, and popped the question.

"Hey do you think you can ask Alice to meet me after lunch?"

"Sure why not?" was his immediate response. God bless him, because under normal circumstances he would have reminded me that we had both agreed that this was a lost cause.

I immediately rushed back to the dormitories convinced that she was going to turn me down again. No sooner was I approaching the dormitories did I hear Max from a distance calling out excitedly, "Hey guys where is Sebati, has anyone seen him?" At that moment my heartbeat accelerated for I knew the moment had finally come.

I don't quite recall exactly what I said that day, but all of it was in English. For some unknown reason when asking a girl out guys always resorted to speaking in English. I do remember feeling unusually at ease though; she looked a little different up close and personal, and seemed a tad nervous. She was to tell me much later that my eyes were a bit scary that first meeting – she was not the first or the last person to have said that about me.

She did not agree to be my girlfriend on our very first meeting (I did not expect her to), nor did she agree on the second. She just kept saying that she did not want to be in a relationship, and even though I respected her decision I was not prepared to accept it. I was trying to get her to change her mind, to convince her that actually being in a relationship with me would not be such a bad idea, I knew as a form 5 she was preparing for the big exam at the end of the year, and I was not going to be in her way when it came to studying, and there was no way I was going to let her grades slip on my account.

What struck me as odd during that first encounter was the fact that Alice seemed to be seeing me for the first time, and looked a bit surprised that I had been asking her out to begin with. The third or fourth time when we met, and seemed a little bit more comfortable around each other I then asked her:

"Alice, I am curious didn't you get any of my messages?"

"What messages?"

"I had been sending messages to you through Festus to ask you to meet me, and this started back in early February." We were in late March now less than a month before the end of the term.

"Festus?!?"

"Yeah ... him."

"Festus came up to me the very first time and said, '*I have a message for you from someone*'. And then he said he would deliver the message the next day. The next day when he came he said, '*actually the message is from me*' and he started asking me out, and has been doing that ever since."

This was unbelievable. I was shocked and dumbfounded. Festus!

That was when the words of Sebei echoed in my ears '*... the girl probably does not even know you ...*'

Although the thought did cross my mind, because Alice was beautiful, and like I believed earlier temptation could never be ruled out, and even though the warning signs had been there; I never really expected treachery to such a scale. I looked at her and said, "No Alice you're joking ... please tell me you are joking."

"*Sebati* I'm not joking." My heart soared. She called me by name, she knew my name. It was very flattering I must admit, because I did not recall ever telling her my given name, and my imagination became further inflamed into thinking that she had done some background check on me, which meant she was interested, why else? This was a teenager's inflamed imagination at full throttle.

Seeing us together that day talking anyone would have assumed that we were an item. So much such that when we were done talking as she mentioned that she had to plait someone's hair (she was still adamant that she did not want to have a boyfriend), Max came up to me immediately thereafter and said, "Everything went well right?"

"No ... she's still refusing man." I could feel Max deflating.

"No man ... seriously? Seeing you guys talking I was delighted thinking that things were great between the two of you."

"Yes, I know, but I am all the more hopeful now."

Later that day, even a fellow martial artist named Class came up to me after dinner as we were heading back to the dormitories and asked, "Hey man, are you and Alice boyfriend and girlfriend?"

Being the eternal optimist that I am I was tempted to say yes, but lying about something like that could prove to be very harmful. I was evasive in my response and then smiled without really giving an answer leaving Class to draw his own conclusion for I lived to fight another day.

Chapter 6

Andries 'Hotstix' Ryan was a colored from the very southern tip of the country, a place called Bokspits. People of mixed blood origin in Southern Africa are called 'coloreds,' and the term in this instance is never meant to be derogatory. They are mainly Afrikaans speakers as they are originally from South Africa. In Bokspits, there is a large population of these colored people who moved across the border from South Africa and into Botswana, and became, for the most part, very successful cattle ranchers. Hotstix was a part of these people.

He was very light skinned, and a sharp dresser, who took great pride in his personal appearance. Hotstix even looked great in a school uniform. He is one person every Lotsane student during our tenure will always remember fondly. Loud, and at times a bit brash, he was also someone who was not shy to speak his mind. What was worse was that he could not speak Setswana very well, and many times when he did he transposed words, and whatever he wanted say would come out differently and the meaning would be way off, which would always invite laughter, and you would think that would make him shy or self-conscious, on the contrary, you had to be Hotstix not to care.

Somehow Hotstix found out about my issue with Festus. To this day I have no idea exactly how he did, because at the time Hotstix and I hardly spoke, we only knew each other by sight. I suppose I should not have been surprised because in boarding school juicy gossips spread like wild fire. I must have confided in someone besides Max, and all it would have taken was for that person to tell someone else, and in no time the news reached Hotstix – the very wrong person it turned out.

On very rare occasions the rules during Friday evening prep would be relaxed somewhat. Teachers would not be as vigilant as usual (now that I think of it this was perhaps payday), and as such the mood in every classroom was jolly. And at times a student would stroll to a friend's classroom and have a good time. This was done not with impunity, because much as we enjoyed this rare treat we were eager not to abuse the privilege. This Friday happened to be one of those rare ones. Hotstix and a few of his friends were hanging out in the Technical Drawing (TD) room. This was because one of Hotstix's closest friends, a form 4 named Atang Makgekgenene (who later became a renowned race car driver), also a TD student, was busy with his drawings and Hotstix was busy running his mouth with his tall tales.

The story is that during this time while the guys were in the TD room, Festus happened to pass by and Hotstix called him in, and immediately took him to task.

"Festus tell us what happened," Hotstix is said to have begun his onslaught.

"What are you talking about?"

"I am talking about what happened between you and Sebati."

"Me and Sebati?"

"Yes, Sebati sent you to go and speak to a girl on his behalf, basically to set up an appointment to meet the girl and ask her out. What did you end up doing?" Hotstix wanted to know. I could only imagine the very familiar sly grin that was playing on his face at that moment.

And to this Festus is said to have replied, "Yes Sebati sent me to be his go between, basically play matchmaker and then ..."

They say he barely finished what he was saying when everyone in the room, including the usually conservative Atang, who was still busy with his drawings, burst out into a long and loud chaotic laughter.

"No, no, Festus," Hotstix said amidst laughter. "We asked for the true version of events – *not* your version."

"What are you talking about?"

"Sebati sent you to talk to the girl to set up an appointment for him. You on the other hand decided to ask the girl out yourself, and when the girl turned you down you went and told Sebati that things were bad, when the truth of the matter was that your little ploy had backfired - deny that?" Hotstix had scored a complete victory. Festus was dumbfounded for he could not dispute the veracity of these allegations.

"Why did you have to do that to a friend who trusted you with his life?" Hotstix pressed on mercilessly, but the onslaught got even more vicious. "Being handicap does not mean the rules change to suit you, or give you the right to steal other people's girls." More laughter followed. I was to hear all about this the next morning after breakfast.

Even though I felt that Festus needed a slap on the wrist for what he had done, and he got more than that, he was still my friend, and I thought Hotstix's remarks were a little below the belt especially on a matter that, and let truth be told, was really none of his business. To me at least that was inexcusable, but then again that was Hotstix being Hotstix.

***

The great thing about joining the right club was the field trips. The ingredients for that were a strong product, and a very good coordinator. A coordinator was a teacher whom the club asked to be just that – the coordinator, between the club and the administration. The main objective for every club was to raise money for the end of year party. This also served as a handover from the old committee to the new one.

The more money a club raised the merrier the party would be. Thus funds were raised during the course of the year, and every member was expected to participate in one way or the other. This was done by selling candy, cream donuts, buns, and fat cakes to arranging trips where a club would perform at say another school, and collect proceeds from the cover charge.

It was easy for the Karate club to secure such fund raising trips because first, we had a very powerful committee led by Roukes, Max, Ambi Sebataladi, Monosi, and Khudzani. Second, in Mr. Mothei, who was also our Setswana teacher, and a very likeable man, we had a very able coordinator, and on such trips a teacher was expected to accompany the students. Mr. Mothei always had time for us and never once did he let the club down or say he was too busy. Prior to teaching at Lotsane Mr. Mothei had been teaching at Kagiso Secondary School, Roukes and Max's alma mater so he was a natural choice to be coordinator for the club.

To make the club even more palatable Roukes was to prove his genius and business acumen that was to serve him well in years to come. He got the breakdancers and Pantsulas and incorporated them into the Karate club. This was done to entertain the audience after the usual demonstration of brick breaking, *katas*, and sparring. We even had a small self-defense skit between Daisy Alexander (a female member of the club) and I that showed women how to thwart a would be mugger or rapist. This performance I must say always got rave wherever we performed.

Our very first trip that year was to Serowe, the fabled village of the rain wind, as described in the late Bessie Head's book that is situated less than 30 miles west of Palapye. We were scheduled to perform at the Teachers Training College that happened to be all girls. Travelling from school for any field trip was done in the school's own open 5 ton truck driven by the ever reliable Kabelo 'KB' Moroka. The school also had a smaller van with a canopy that was used for much smaller groups.

Since these kinds of trips were fun, it was not uncommon to see many students accompanying us who were not members of the club, especially students from the female populace. None of us ever made a big deal about it, and it did help that most of the girls who came along were pretty, and the company of comely damsels was always most welcome.

That very first field trip was on a Friday, and we left the campus just before sunset, and heading west that day the sight was breathtaking. The mountains, the scenery, the fresh air, the yonder horizon where the sun was setting, the country side breeze, and the moment was something that has stayed with me ever since - it was pure magic.

We gave a great performance that night capped with the Pantsula and Breakdancers' show we raked in a lot of money, but most importantly word spread in the region, and it was not long before we started getting invitations from all the secondary schools in the district to come and perform during their entertainment nights, which like ours were on Saturday.

A few weeks later we were invited to perform at a school in Mahalapye about 45 miles south of Palapye named Madiba Secondary. This school was a bitter rival and old foe when it came to sports or any kind of competition. This night was no different, because when it was time for our breakdancers to perform, breakdancers from Madiba not to be bested decided to crash the party, and instantly a battle was on.

Cheered on by their home crowd the Madiba break dancers went into a frenzy so much such that the decibel level rose to an almost deafening height. Our dancers led by Dakune, Tso, Two-Two, and Cracker (he was outstanding that night) were itching to match their rivals pound for pound, but they bid their time because they had an 'Ace' up their sleeve. The song playing was one our break dancers practiced to everyday and was more than 15 minutes long.

The Madiba dancers had no way of knowing this, because by the sixth or seventh minute just as they were getting spent after starting like a house on fire, was when our dancers seized the moment and took the dance to their opponents. When finally the Madiba dancers could hardly lift their arms due to fatigue our dancers made them look like a bunch of amateurs, and in the end even the girls from the rival school wanted to know more about our dancers' personal lives. My breakdance skills were still rudimentary at the time, and I could not wait for the day when I could finally be a part of this fun.

During these trips Max and I befriended two girls namely Nametsegang Puni Sennanyana and Esther. They were both knockouts particularly Nametsegang who liked me, and Esther I believe had the hots for Max. I was attracted to her as well and thought of making my move, especially after she won the 'Miss Form 4' beauty pageant, but then like rainfall after a long and never ending dry season, the thought would be replaced by the smiling face of Alice. So nothing happened that should have between us and the girls, and I suspect much to their disappointment, but we have always remained great friends to this day. Maybe it is true that some things are not meant to be, but at least I should have tried and found out if that saying was spot on. I really should have as time would tell.

At this time Max introduced me to one of his best friends, a handsome clean cut gentleman from Francistown Secondary School, but hailing from Marobela village. Our lives were to cross paths much later in a very big way. His name was Balisi Bonyongo, a form 5 student, and one of the most brilliant minds I have ever met. He was also very good friends with Alice since they were classmates, and they sat together during afternoon and evening prep.

I found out later on that Balisi had on numerous times, on his own accord, also tried to convince Alice to go out with me, but of course she would not budge. Now that I think of it, all this pursuing convinced her that I only had her in my cross hairs and no other girl, and the chase must have been some sort of natural high for her, because I had made it too easy for her to think that she was the beginning and the end, which sadly I must admit was true at the time.

Days were also flying like doves in the sky. Already we were approaching the end of the term which was in mid April. Botswana being a Christian country celebrates Easter, meaning that when Good Friday came, we had a four day weekend. Some students would go home during this brief break, and this happened when a parent specifically asked for permission either by a phone call or by writing a letter to the headmaster. This led to a funny incident involving none other than my very good friend Jewawa Febion Khembo.

The rules were very clear. On a long weekend like Easter if a student wished to be with his or her family at that time the school had to have the parents' permission. Jewawa wrote a letter to the headmaster pretending to be his dad, and thereafter dropped the letter in the school's mail box.

Unfortunately for Jewawa, the school messenger (whose name was Notice believe or not) always scanned through the mail it turns out, before he took it to the main post office in Palapye as he always did. So when he saw a letter addressed to the headmaster, he felt that it was prudent to save the postal service the trouble of sorting, and then routing the mail back to Mr. Mahole, when he could deliver it to the man himself, who at that moment was in his office which happened to be just down the hallway.

The next morning at assembly Mr. Mahole said, "I would like to see *Sewawa* Khembo immediately after assembly, who on his own behalf wrote a letter to me pretending to be his father so that he could be granted permission to go home for the Easter weekend," laughter followed. "So will *Sewawa* Khembo, please come to my office and pick up his stamp and envelope," more laughter.

As for me I was very worried for my friend and partner in crime. But to be quite honest, I was not totally surprised that Jewawa would pull a stunt like that; he was that brazen. And that is an understatement. Later on, he was to relate the whole episode to me word for word.

The moment when he walked into Mr. Mahole's office, the headmaster burst out with laughter, and then just as sudden assumed a frighteningly sinister demeanor. That was classic Victor Isaac Mahole, because when he did that you knew you were in deep trouble. Also present was the vice headmaster Mr. Maganu, and the head of the disciplinary committee Mr. Felix Mhuriro (the 'h' in his name is silent) an imposing, tough, no nonsense big man, who was feared and respected by all.

"What were you thinking when you wrote this letter?" Mr. Mahole wanted to know.

"Sir, I did not write the letter."

"Young man you are in enough trouble as it is, and lying to us will just make matters worse for you. Now I'll ask you one more time what were you thinking when you wrote this letter?"

"But sir, I am telling you that I did not write this letter."

"Who did then?" This time it was Mr. Maganu who asked.

"I have no idea sir."

"Okay, there's only one way to find out, and son pray to God that all you are telling us is the truth," Mr. Maganu warned. "Go and get your notebooks right at this instant." They wanted to do a handwriting analysis.

With his heartbeat running at what I would assume 110 miles per hour Jewawa got his notebooks. He told me that he had gone to great lengths to change his handwriting, and since he was left handed; he did tell me that in some instances to appear more convincing he had used his right hand.

Upon comparing the notes Mr. Maganu looked at him and said, "*Monna* (man), you wrote this letter." It was a statement.

"No sir I didn't."

"Do you know that we can take this letter to the police right this instant and have their trained handwriting experts decipher that it was you who wrote this letter?" Mr. Mhuriro who was quiet all this time declared. It was a bluff of course, and I don't know if Jewawa bought it or had just gone too far in his denial to admit now.

"Stop playing with us, you wrote this letter," Mr. Maganu insisted. At this point Jewawa said he had had enough, and then was just about to confess, when out of nowhere Mr. Maganu unwittingly came to his rescue by saying, "Okay tell your friend with whom you are in cahoots that if you two nimrods try to pull a stunt like this again both of you will be severely punished." It turns out that that was their suspicion all along that there was another party involved, and were hoping that under duress Jewawa would name his accomplice. Of course no such party existed. "Now hand me the stick and bend over," Mr. Maganu said.

Jewawa was whipped several times on his backside, and then the headmaster did an amazing thing.

"Make sure you tell your friend not to do that again," he said. "Also you have been granted permission to go home," he continued. Maybe these people were not quite the monsters we had made them out to be.

Jewawa did go home to Mahalapye that long Easter weekend so did a lot other students. To my knowledge he never tempted fate twice. Me, Max, Festus, and a few other friends decided to stay at school.

By this time though, Festus's reputation of untruths had reached an alarming height of epic proportions. For instance, one day a fellow form 4 named Lucky came to our dormitory as he sometimes did since he was from Ramotswa, and an ex Kagiso Secondary School student, and mentioned that Festus had told them that whenever the president of Botswana came to Lobatse (his home town), he almost always had lunch at his house, and that he had even served him personally. Lucky was not making this up, because I did hear Festus say that on one or two occasions, but then again I had no idea that he would spread it around.

The situation came to a head during that long weekend after tea break (a lot of extra food went around because many students were gone); we were relaxed on the beautiful lawn in the academic area. There were a few of us including Roukes that bright and sunny April morning when suddenly out of the blue Roukes blurted out: "Festus, you know it has come to everyone's attention that almost every word that comes out of your mouth is a lie. You know to be known for lying is not a very good thing at all, you must stop it, and soon." Being the loud talker that he was Roukes suddenly got everyone's attention. Festus could barely hide his embarrassment, and whenever he was put on the spot like that he would always smile nervously.

"I have no idea what you are talking about Roukes."

"Take for instance the other day," Roukes continued in a way that made Festus's denial seem irrelevant if not trivial. "You were caught with a girl right? And then the headmaster had you come to his office. After forgiving you for your slight what did you do? You went about telling people that the reason why he forgave you was because he went to school with your dad." It was a fact and thus indefensible. What amazed me was how on earth Roukes had found out what Festus had said; again one could place the blame squarely on the Lotsane rumor mill that some people had dubbed *'Radio Lotsane.'*

And Lucky who was not too far off playing with a soccer ball with undivided attention said, "There's also this thing of President Masire having lunch at your home."

"Listen to that …" Roukes said.

This was followed by another allegation, and another, and another, and yet another. To all this Roukes kept saying, "Listen to that, and that … goodness when does this end?"

Always the dramatic, Roukes heaved a long and heavy comical sigh and said, "Festus, I'll ask you one simple question and please answer it truthfully … okay?"

"Okay …"

"The truth and nothing else Festus."

"Agreed."

"Alright, there is cracking jokes, pulling people's legs and bold face lying, tell us which category you fall under."

To this Festus smiled and said, "Well I do sometimes pull people's legs."

In response, Roukes threw his hands in the air, and looked at that serene blue African summer morning sky as though appealing to the high heavens, and said, *"Akere la utlwa, waaka gape!"* "You see, he's lying again!" All except Festus laughed. And really I felt bad for him later.

But most importantly, I think that episode went far in helping Festus realize the harm he was causing not only to others but to himself, because I thought he took a dramatic turn for the better after that.

Chapter 7

Nelson continued getting into fights outside the club. Later, as I got to know him better, I could not help but wonder why a person who was seemingly jolly and playful would always get into altercations. One day in dorm 10 he faced off with a fellow named Nicassen Tau. In a fair fight I don't think Nicassen would have stood a fighting chance, literally, and he knew it, which is why he resorted to a broomstick as his primary weapon as opposed to his fists.

Nicassen also got help from his dormitory mates like Willington and Senwelo. What they would do is that whenever Nelson launched an attack, they would hold him, but no one would hold Nicassen, and unimpeded the latter would take advantage and put the broomstick to full use. Again John Max Moreti came to the rescue, and Nicassen was saved. No one would save Nelson though. The club got tired of his shenanigans and was thus unceremoniously booted out.

Nelson vehemently protested the committee's decision. "What do I do if someone calls my mother a disparaging name?" he asked, "just turn back and swallow the insult?"

"What happened to just walking away?" Someone from the committee responded. "You of all people should be fully aware of our creed Nelson; what example are you setting for the youngsters?" The youngsters in this case was us the form 4's – *manyewane*.

In the end the committee's decision was final, and thereafter Nelson was not a member of the Karate club anymore. That never dampened his spirits though; he remained the same jolly and fun loving guy, sometimes to a fault, that I would soon get to know.

Every week a prefect was assigned the duty of making sure that the breakfast, lunch, and supper time bell was rung on time. In addition to that he was to make the announcements during lunch time about club meetings and also read the 'receipt list'. The receipt list call, if your name was on it, meant that your parents, a close relative, or a friend had sent you money. Thereafter you would go to the office and claim your receipt, and permission was almost automatically granted to go to the post office in Palapye to get your cash. This was because money set via the postal service was done so through registered mail.

The majority of prefects were not comfortable making public announcements. Such duties it seemed were left to the head boy at the time. A towering, very affable, and at times unyielding gentleman when the situation called for it, named Polite Mabalane. He was known to everyone as 'head boy', and when he spoke everyone listened, and we all liked him.

Sometimes a prefect on duty would have a regular student, in most cases his dorm mate, do the honors of ringing the bell at the times given, and even make announcements. A lot of the students took this assignment with great enthusiasm – none more than Nelson, and later it was a fellow named Blackie Davis Kealotswe who we will get to later.

One weekday morning Nelson had that opportunity. Excited as usual, he went through the announcements in rapid succession. That particular morning he was exceptionally jazzed, even to an extent of running from one end of the dining hall to another. We did not pay him much attention at our table as we ate our breakfast, this was until one incident changed things, and we were to remember it for years to come.

All of a sudden when we looked up and saw Nelson again he looked like a ghost! There was milk splashed all over his face, and what a contrast it looked against his dark skin. And he kept saying to someone repeatedly: "*O irang*? ... *O irang?* ... *O irang*?" "What are you doing? ... What are you doing? ... What are you doing?" The funny thing about all this was that Nelson was making no attempt to wipe the milk off his face – none whatsoever, which made the whole scene all the more hilarious.

The perpetrator in this case was a fellow I had not known up until that moment, because he was a quiet and unassuming gentleman; the type you knew better not to mess with. His name was Mbako 'Rams' Ramashaba. The two faced off with Nelson still asking the question. A few people jumped in to separate them, but Nelson was not done and followed Rams outside as the latter was being led away, and at one time he tried on several attempts to shove Rams with the bell he had in his hand.

Someone in the small crowd that had gathered said, "*Nelson baya bele hatshe o mo iteye ka matsogo.*" "Nelson put the bell down and hit him with your hands."

In the end a fight did not happen just as we had thought. Nelson wiped the milk off his face finally and everyone went their separate ways. I wondered to myself, who was this fearless guy who had humiliated Nelson in public? And just at that moment, I overheard a form 5 who like Hotstix was from the Bokspits area, and a colored like him, named Harimanz Titus explain the whole episode to a few curious individuals who were anxious to know what had triggered the spat.

"Oh man Rams just slowly, carefully, and in a very dignified manner turned around and in an instant, taking us all by surprise, splashed the milk on Nelson's face," he said.

For the time being the incident was forgotten until not too long thereafter when it was revived.

As boys we loved football (soccer), and listening to games involving our favorite teams was the norm, you had those who pledged their loyalty to either Orlando Pirates or Kaizer Chiefs. These are professional teams in South Africa and their bitter rivalry is legendary. Reception over the radio was good, and the closer to South Africa you were the better the signal. In Gaborone and Ramotswa the commentator on the radio sounded like he was speaking from a room next door.

At Lotsane however it was an entirely different story. To be able to even minutely hear the game; we would go to the bushy area at the south side of the school behind the staff houses (this was a practice that was later forbidden). This was because out here there was a huge water tank that was situated on a surface about 30 feet high. It was here where we were able to catch a very weak signal of Radio Tswana; the station in South Africa that broadcasted the games live. In order to follow the action we had to be totally silent. At times the signal would disappear entirely for up to 10 minutes, and on some days it would be longer than that.

One day we were at this area trying to listen to the game, and had to be silent as usual. It was me, Sebei, a form 5 named Laolang 'Lali' Sebogiso, Nelson, a few other guys including a scary looking form 5 who was big in stature, and very dark skinned named John Kagiso Obuseng from Mmadinare, but he was known to the whole school as 'Bull', and was often serenaded when he made a public appearance especially on the soccer field. Everyone feared him, and years later he was to tell me that he never understood why, because unbeknownst to many though he was a devout Christian in his own quiet way.

On that particular day the reception was terrible. Dead airs were continuous and not too far in between, and it was not long before we got bored by the silence – ours and that from the radio. I kept glancing at Nelson and then at Sebei; then I picked up a white piece of paper and placed it on my forehead. I looked at Sebei again and then at Nelson, and he immediately got the joke. The white paper represented the milk, and then Sebei did something that scared me half to death.

He looked up at Nelson, and with no hesitation said, "By the way Nelson, what happened between you and Rams, what was up with all that milk?"

I was shaking in my boots; certain that I was about to witness something bad taking into account the Nelson I knew from the gym, and the Nelson who seemed to be engaged in fights more often than not. I feared for my friend. Instead, Nelson did something that earned my utmost respect, which has not diminished to this day. He smiled comically.

"Man can you believe that guy?" and then he started to demonstrate how Rams turned around, and splashed him with the milk complete with the expression that apparently was on Rams's face. Now since we had to be silent because of the reception issues, Nelson gestured about the way he and Rams were acting, and was mouthing the words.

"I said to him *o irang, o irang.*" He was even gesticulating with both arms.

I had never seen this side of Nelson. Since we could not laugh loudly, suppressing the laughter was almost killing us, but Nelson would not stop, he kept poking fun at himself and the whole episode. So much such that Lali went on to ask, *"Monna Nelson, a go lo mole e ne e le mashi kana starch water?"* "Man Nelson, was that milk or starch water?"

Starch water was the sweet mixture of milk and water that was a substitute for students who did not drink tea or coffee. I drank starch water because it was sweet nothing more. Lali went on to say that he was asking him that, because he thought he saw Nelson sticking his tongue out at the corner of his mouth to lick some of the milk that was dripping. That is why he questioned if the content was in fact starch water. By this time we were all in stitches that Bull had to intervene in his soft and matter of fact way.

"*Eh banna, go lo ha re tlile go reetsa match, gara tlela go goga letlhaku.*" "Eh guys, we are here to listen to the match, and we did not come here to crack jokes." Instead of shutting us up that just made matters worse, and the purpose of why we were all there to begin with was now a distant memory. Some chap that Nelson was.

Many years later I was to catch up with Rams and asked him what really happened that day, and he told me that Nelson had bumped into him, causing him to spill some of the milk from his cup onto his uniform, now instead of apologizing Nelson just pretended like the incident never happened, and instead gave Rams the middle finger and to this the latter responded in kind. The two are still great friends even to this day.

***

Finally the first term came to an end. That morning I was summoned to the school accountant's office, and was given my holiday allowance of about sixty Pula. At the time that kind of money to a young teenager was like a million dollars. It happened this way because my schooling was being paid for by the United Nations due to the fact that my father was a political refugee. It was a very exciting moment. Max, Sebei, Albert, and myself had long decided that we were going to go back home by train. Allim was to be picked up by his parents as usual.

There were two types of trains every time schools closed, there was the 'special' and the 'mixed'. The special usually arrived around 8:30pm at the Palapye station, and was meant for students picked up not only from Lotsane but all the schools along the way. The mixed was for everyone. Unlike the special, the mixed train was the favorite among students because it was basically public transportation and had a buffet car that served alcohol – no such thing was allowed on the special. In short really the mix was more fun, and this train arrived at 10:30pm.

That morning we cleaned our classrooms and dormitories, and later we took pictures, Allim, Max, and I, and since Allim and I were going to be in Gaborone, and Max not too far off in Ramotswa, the possibility of meeting during the three and a half week break was discussed, and we all agreed that that would be a great idea. That end of the term also marked the beginning of a new chapter in my life. My martial arts had improved tremendously, and I was skilled enough to call myself a breakdancer at last. I even had a street name (all break dancers had one), and mine was 'Jones'. Even to this day many of my friends who knew me then still call me by my street name.

Even though I was not the best dancer on the crew (a breakdance team) I could hold my own against the seasoned veterans. Hanging out together was a now a norm among us break dancers when opportunity allowed, and we were known as 'the cool cats'. We even resorted to training on Saturday and Sunday mornings, but mostly Saturdays as early as 5:00am so that we could not be seen by the general population; as now our practice sessions began attracting spectators particularly the girls.

At the level that I was at as far as the breakdance was concerned, I knew that heading back home for the holidays to the city would only help me get better. Gaborone was where it all happened, where the main crews were. The break dancers in Gaborone were more advanced because they had the privilege of getting the latest moves and songs from TV. The main crews came from Gaborone Secondary School (GSS). These were *Jammers Beyond Control* (JBC) and *Magnificent Beat Riders* (MBR) there were many more like Midnight City Breakers (MCB), but these two, JBC and MBR, were the main ones and the best.

JBC it turned out was founded by an African American who went to school at GSS named Ali Eric Barr. He was straight from Harlem New York, where the hip hop craze is said to have begun. His parents had come to Botswana to work as expatriates. A breakdancer himself and a great one at that, Ali Eric Barr gave that crew a clout that was priceless, and boy how the girls loved them! This crew had other great dancers like William Ferguson, Peter 'Jam' Masie, and Brian Letsididi. They were treated like rock stars wherever they went. And with the diversity that GSS had in as far as its student population I am talking about fans from all races: Black, White, Latina, and Asian. There was also another crew named 'Stellafunk' whose members were well-known to be tough and muscular, and among them were Benjamin Tjindu Maekopo, who later became a very good friend of mine, and Christian Hansley Gaiqui. My hope was that getting back to Gaborone; I would at least meet some of these guys and learn more from them. My teachings instead came from an entirely different and unexpected source it turned out.

That last day of school was surreal. By late afternoon the campus was almost empty as most of the students, including Alice, I was quick to notice, had left. After supper at 6pm we were shuttled in the school truck and taken to the Palapye station. At night the Palapye station feels and looks magical because of the orange lights that burn all night until dawn. In those days students like us from the south, waited for either the south bound special or mixed, and the ones headed north waited for the north bound train. The mixed northbound arrived at around midnight after we were long gone, and would reach Francistown the next morning between 7 and 8am.

Boys being boys, the moment we were cut loose at the station, Max, Lekobe, Sebei, and I headed to the nearest bottle store (liquor store). Asking for identification from teenagers was a practice that was unheard of at the time. Drinking did happen at school when opportunity allowed, but it was a very serious offence, and the consequences were dire. Prior to heading to the bottle store Lekobe had been dutifully munching on some green apples. At the time I was a teetotaler so I bought two soft drinks, which for a boarding student were a treat. I had not tasted one of these in three months so the first one really hit the spot.

The guys got two bottles of a sweet alcoholic drink that tasted almost like apple cider called *'Autumn Harvest'*, which they took in very generous proportions, and as a result everyone was cheerful as we headed back to the station. Even though we were off campus, and the rules did not exactly apply, my friends were prudent in as far as their indulgence was concerned, and behaved extremely well under the circumstances.

There were only two mishaps that night. The first being that when the first train arrived, the special train only for students, Sebei mistook it for the mixed, which we had all agreed to take when it arrived a bit later, and thus we were separated. The second was when the southbound mixed train finally arrived, and the throng of passengers began boarding the train, I noticed that the line split in a loop very close to the entrance like the passengers were avoiding something or someone. I went to investigate, as I got closer I smelt a strong stench of apples in the air, only to find that it was Lekobe right in the midst of the crowd puking his guts out with big pieces of the apples he was eating earlier coming out. Apparently, he had taken a little more of the *Autumn Harvest* than was good for him. Max, Two-Two, and I came to the rescue, and the rest of the journey was pleasant and uneventful.

We arrived in Gaborone the next morning around 6am. Max, Lekobe, and a few others proceeded further south to Ramotswa. This after we bade our farewells, and promised to meet at an event that was to be held in a week or so at the national stadium; this event was the Botswana Defense Force day or BDF day, where the army always made their annual spectacular show for the public.

At the station in Gaborone I ran into my other dormitory mate who was waiting for a connecting bus to his home village Moshupa. This was none other than Pema Dibotelo. The morning was a bit chilly for him I think, because he was wearing his black school blazer. He was clean cut and proper as always. I had not seen him on the train so I asked him, "Pema, did you come on the special?"

"I suppose that's what I ought to be telling myself," he replied in his rich Setswana. That response would become a personal inside joke between us.

I went home feeling invigorated. It was just three months earlier when I was headed to Lotsane, a brand new one, uncertain of what lay ahead. Now I had made many more new friends than I would have thought possible, I was a martial artist and a breakdancer, and had learned more about life those first three months at Lotsane than I would have expected. I was also in love, and could not wait to go back and finish what I had started.

My family was thrilled to see me again, especially my two little brothers Sekobileng and Ronnie who were seven and five years old respectively at the time. The first thing I showed my immediate junior brother Ramasupologo, or Rama, as he is known, was the fact that I could do the breakdance moves – he was impressed. And this was huge coming from him because he has always been my eternal critic.

I had a heart to heart talk with my father about what had transpired this past term. How I had wanted to be in the science classes but had been disappointed. I laid out my plans for the future and he was supportive and agreeable. The plan was that I would rewrite the math paper I had failed at junior certificate, and with a better grade I would change my course to study science, which would mean repeating my form 4; a decision which to this day I still believe is one of the best I have ever made in my life.

During the break I also took the time to visit my friends at my old school in Lobatse, among them was Abram Thekiso, Tlhaloso Semausu, and Thabo 'Amajoni' Sebataladi. It was a wonderful and exciting reunion. Amazingly word had reached my friends that I was among other things a breakdancer.

"How did you guys find out?" my mouth must have been agape.

"Oh Dakune told us," Tlhaloso said.

Dakune, of course, I should have known. After all Lobatse was like Festus his home town, and he was a frequent visitor of the boarders at Itireleng Secondary School, even during the time that I was there. Nothing major had changed during my absence, except that many of my friends it seemed had grown up a little since the last time I saw them, and I would think that was the same reflection they had about me. The only thing I regret even to this day about that break, and that visit is that I completely and totally snubbed Joyce; the one and only girl who truly loved me. I did apologize to her many years later, but that did little to ease the guilt I felt, because the truth of the matter is that she did not deserve it. I was living in a fool's paradise at the time, because Alice was not my girlfriend even though in my mind I thought she was. Nonetheless, I could have been more civil to a girl who loved me like no other ever did at the time.

I did meet up with Max as arranged, and a few other guys from Lotsane like Ephraim 'Sputla' Moikabinyane at the national stadium. It was a mini reunion of some sort and we all had a great time. Since Max and I could barely stay away from each other for a long time it seemed, we agreed to meet the very next Saturday at the Capitol Cinema at the main mall, which we did, and as usual we had a blast. After the movie, we took a walk to the station where he caught the bus back to Ramotswa, and I went back home. That walk on that day as we headed westwards watching the sunset was a beauty. It would only be a few weeks that we would be back to school.

During those holidays we had a guest at our house who was a friend of my father, a young man in his early 30's at the time, and also like my father at the time a political refugee from South Africa named Manqoba Ngubeka. Small in stature, but with the heart of a lion, he had aspirations of becoming a journalist, and the fact that I was a martial artist interested him immensely, because according to him he said he wanted to be able to sneak into apartheid South Africa, and gather information to bring to the outside world, but he said he would have to be skilled in unarmed combat to be able to achieve such a feat, so buoyed by my passion for the art, I would imagine, we trained regularly. The regimen included strenuous exercises and roadwork, and I was surprised to realize later how great in shape I was.

My brother Rama though not a bonafide break dancer per se, knew many moves and he was really good even though his style was the Pantsula dance. At night before bed we would go over his moves and how I would incorporate them with mine. The thing with breakdance I found out was just like Karate – to be good you had to practice every day.

I also found my long ago packed Karate uniform (called a *gi*), the *matushi* brand that I had bought back in 1982 when I joined the club in Lobatse. The texture of that *gi* was tough and rough such that when you punched it gave an accompanying motivating sound, which is why it was dubbed *'the greatest Karate suit in the world.'* When I showed it to Max later he just said to me, "Man Sebati let's say we exchange, I give you my *gi* (which was made of regular cloth) and I get yours?" I was more than willing to oblige, because to me it made no difference, I loved that *gi*, but I loved my brothers John Max Moreti and Rama even more.

Chapter 8

I arrived at school two days late, but it really was not a big deal as far as the administration was concerned, because some students like Hotstix who lived in the Bokspits area were always expected to arrive late that first week – the school made that exception. Max, Two-Two, Allim, and a few of my friends were worried thinking that I had perhaps been transferred to another school, and most likely in Zimbabwe (that possibility had been discussed), but their fears were put to rest when I arrived.

It felt good to be back, and most of all I had some unfinished business with Alice. What was more was that I had sought the help of a lady friend of mine whom I had met through Sebei since they were very close friends, and also from Kagiso Secondary School named Keorapetse Cisky Keakile. To this day I regard meeting this woman as one of the best things to have happened in my life. Her friendship and her warmth were real. What I thought was a great advantage was that Cisky was Alice's dorm mate. In fact Cisky was more than willing to play the 'number nine'. In soccer that's the striker, in boarding school colloquial that meant someone who had your interests at heart, and would do anything in their power to make sure that that you won the girl of your dreams' heart. A number five on the other hand was the opposite; so one could say Festus was at some point a 'number five'.

Cisky's prognoses when Sebei approached her for the job was that I should not have a problem, because of the way the girls in her dormitory, and I would assume Alice too, talked about me. Just as the girls were a constant point of discussion after lights off with us the same was true with the girls. Cisky's optimism was contagious even though the reality of things was bleak, and it would only get worse.

The second term ran from mid May to the first week of August. This was known as the winter term not by mistake, because in June and July Palapye has very cold winters. I would think the cold air comes mostly from the east where in the distance the beautiful Tswapong foothills are visible. Although they are never snowcapped, as snow is something you never see in Botswana, the breeze from these mountains is acrimoniously cold.

We did not have hot water for our showers (we all showered together in one big area, just like in the prison movies), and very early in the morning the pipes would be frozen, and when you turned on the water you would hear the water battling to surge through the pipes. The trick was to wait for a good five minutes, letting the water run through the pipes for as long as possible to flush the ice out, because that is what was impeding the water to flow. Now if you walked into the shower right before the pipes were flushed; you would feel as though a brick had landed right on top of your head - that's how cold the water was. As a result taking a shower was not among the most favorite things to do in the second term.

Not taking a shower in dorm 12 was something that you would hear about, especially if a few days went by without visiting the spell of rain. Chief among the people who would remind you of this deliberate oversight were Big Joe, and Alfred 'Tonkana Ya Lebowa' Ntseane; the 'little donkey from lebowa'. They called it *'go latsa'* or 'sleeping it over without a bath.' Very often it would be Cromwell who would bear the brunt of these criticisms, and to his credit he did not care, because he would often say, "*Ee ke a latsa jaanong?*" "Yes, I let it sleep over without a bath so what?"

Nevertheless Big Joe would not let him off that easy. Cromwell, by nature was very aloof, and a constant whiner especially towards guys from Ramotswa, something I never understood, part of this I would attribute to his ailment, he was an epileptic and would go into fits at the spare of the moment, be it in class, in the dormitory, the dining hall, the showers – everywhere. And these attacks would be sudden, and come without warning, especially on overcast days it seemed. And I think that made him very self-conscious.

In addition to that Cromwell had a prodigious appetite. We had three square meals a day, well four if you included tea break, but for any active teenager this was never enough. Thus it was always a good idea to augment that with a food supply of your own. This would be mainly canned food like fish, beans, beef, archer (vegetable or mango), and bottles of tomato sauce (ketchup), orange juice, and mayonnaise. These were the most popular food groups among boarding students.

At lunch time what Cromwell would do was pour a generous amount of ketchup into his cup, then add fish, mayonnaise, archer, and beans then mix it up with whatever was served at lunch, and asking him to share his food would be like asking a crab to walk straight so no one bothered him. After lunch he would lie down on his bed, and stay that way until afternoon prep. Big Joe once remarked that he behaved like a python after a hearty meal.

"*Monna* Cromwell," he said one day. "All the time whenever we come back from lunch you lie down like you don't know what. You're like a python. I mean I could slap you silly right now, and there is not a thing that you can do to me because your stomach is full." This was always followed by laughter.

However Big Joe was far from done. One time Cromwell bent over to pick something up and Big Joe said, "Man why don't you bend elsewhere? Show your butt to the wall or something because we have no idea what it is you've eaten, whether it was tomato sauce, archer or mayonnaise." This was a direct jibe at Cromwell's lunch concoction.

In spite of all this there always was a sense of unity and camaraderie in our dormitory, but then this would be sullied for the most part by Fungwa, and this always happened when it was his turn to set our table in the dining hall before our meals. The way it worked was in pairs and this went by beds. Since Big Joe and Johane's bed was the first they would be the setters that first week of the term followed by me and Mmabaledi, and it went in that order until the process repeated itself. You always knew that the term was coming to an end when it was your turn to set the table for the second time during that period. Whenever it was Fungwa's turn that week would be a nightmare for all of us.

What this guy would do was always get more on his plate than anyone else. This of course meant someone was getting the leanest share, and in many cases that would be me since I never had the guts to complain openly fearing reprisal. When his week ended he would even have the vile to ask, "Does anyone think I was unfair?"

This was done in a threatening tone, meaning that if you answered truthfully he was going to deal with you when his turn came up again.

To this I remember not being candid, and said, "Oh yeah, yeah you were fair Fungwa." It galled me to say that because that was cowardice on my part.

Then John 'Max' Moreti, my friend, my brother, said something that day that fluffed my feathers.

"Some people will say Fungwa was fair for fear of being given little food."

I felt it in the pit of my stomach, not because he looked at me after he said that, but because it was true. It was there and then that I swore to myself that if the subject came up again, I would be more than forthright and not be intimidated like before. I had my opportunity when Fungwa's turn came up. He asked the question again, and I told him straight up what I thought.

"I say you were not fair."

"I was not fair?"

"Yes, do you think when you get more and everyone else gets less that's fair?"

He had no immediate answer to that, and when he finally did his response was that of a man mortified by the truth.

"You will starve when my turn comes."

"I'll have my turn too Fungwa, and just know that your evil deeds will not go unpunished," I retorted.

"Go unpunished? You are very superstitious."

"We shall see." And I let the matter rest right there for now. I knew on any given day I could take Fungwa one on one despite this rumor that he never fought fair, and that if you beat him up in a fight, he would come after you at night and attack you while you were asleep. This particular rumor was never really proven, and I've always thought it was a travesty. That and the fact that he had numerous weapons hidden in his locker, I personally have seen a stick and a pair of sling shots nothing more, but all in all it takes a lot more to get me into a fist fight with someone.

This story about Fungwa having an entire arsenal in his locker led to two separate funny incidents. The first involved Max. One day he and Fungwa got into an argument that escalated, but Fungwa was smart to know how far he could go with Max, because he knew what the latter was capable of.

"Yeah, I know you Karate guys think that you can beat up everybody," was Fungwa's parting shot as Max and I were leaving for class, since this was just after tea break.

"You know what Fungwa I'm glad you pointed that out," Max retorted. "Because that saves me the trouble of me telling you that, and worse still actually demonstrating it. So I'd advise you to shut up right this instant or you'll be seeking your weapons in your locker, and on me it would take much, much more than that."

Fungwa did the wise thing and heeded to Max's advice. It was the first time I had seen him subdued in such a manner, and as for me I was never so proud. It just felt great standing next to my friend as he cut Fungwa down to size, and this done with precise and deliberate calm, a skill in martial arts known as 'the art of fighting without fighting'. It takes a true martial arts champion to master that technique. And I was seeing one that day.

The second happened one Sunday afternoon when I walked into our dormitory and into a heated argument between Festus and Fungwa.

"Hey keep talking smack and I'll slap you boy," Fungwa threatened.

"I don't think so man," Festus said. They were seated on the bottom part of one of the bunk beds, and Max was seated right there in between them to intervene if things got ugly, which would probably explain Festus's bravado that day. Then soon after Fungwa said something disparaging to Festus, and the latter responded by mimicking Fungwa in a very funny way, at this Fungwa became very upset and said, "Go and say that to your father."

"Hey man don't involve parents," Festus protested. It was typical of Fungwa bringing in parents when it came to personal clashes. The standoff continued unabated until Fungwa felt he had enough.

"Man Festus if you don't stop with this nonsense right now, I'll make you defecate in your pants, and that' a promise."

"Everyone defecates."

"Oh, I suppose that would mean every single person in the world right?"

"Yes."

"Even those you said not to include right?"

"Yes," Festus replied without realizing the full import of Fungwa's words, because what he meant by *'even those you said not to include right?'* meant the parents, a subject that was supposedly out of bounds. In the end Max called the two to order. This was after Fungwa became really vexed and all but slapped Festus.

A little later Festus said to Max in confidence, "You know it's not like I'm scared of this dude. The only reason I don't want to fight him is because I'm afraid he will resort to weapons."

Fungwa, resorting to weapons when fighting Festus? Even I could not believe my ears. To say that was absurd would be a gross understatement - it was an insult if you ask me. The next day after lunch we were back in the dormitory as usual, and as we were getting ready for afternoon prep Max, said very casually, "Oh by the way Fungwa, Festus says he is not scared of you. The only reason why he won't fight you he says is because you use weapons when you fight, and you'd use them on him, and so he wants no part of it."

Fungwa was taken aback by this revelation.

"What? Festus actually said that?"

"Yep."

Now his fists were smoking. Without another word, he stormed out of the dormitory, and headed toward dorm 15 almost at full trot. I think in his mind he had had enough of this tomfoolery with Festus, and was going to end it right there and then, perhaps with a few slaps to the face. I felt bad for Festus, but said nothing. A few of our dormitory mates including Sebei and Mathabathi followed suit. After a brief pause Big Joe rushed after Fungwa and his entourage.

"I'm going to put off the fire with petrol," he said as he left.

Max and I stayed put. For me I just did not want to witness Festus being slapped silly, because by the look of things that seemed very possible judging by Fungwa's reaction. A while later the group came back with Sebei saying to Big Joe, "Man I was expecting you to fan the flames far more than you did." He was laughing as he said this, and I then realized that once again Fungwa had probably let Festus off the hook. I was glad.

The episode I heard played out like this: when Fungwa entered dorm 15 he went up to Festus who was relaxed on his bed, which happened to be the top bed on the metal bunk bed. It happened so quick that Festus was taken by surprise.

"Yah sonny," Fungwa said as he shook him violently by his collar. "I hear that you say you are not scared of me, and the reason that you will not fight me is because I use weapons?"

"Fungwa, you use weapons? Man you try that on people like me I will make you pee in your pants, and that's the truth." It was Big Joe being impish as usual and inciting Fungwa.

"W-who said that?" Festus was panicked. Max was not there this time so save him. "I n-never said t-that."

"Never mind who did. I'm here and as you can see no weapons, now get off your bed and let's put them up, because I want to make sure that *after* you beat me up I'll just walk away and not use weapons like you say I do. Now come on let's put them up."

This of course was a proposition Festus could not accept.

"Now that," Big Joe said as he looked around at everyone, "is a darn good idea don't you think?"

In the end nothing happened, thankfully, even though the likes of Sebei and Mathabathi were saying that Big Joe did not really instigate a beating like he would normally do. I would think Fungwa felt sorry for Festus, and decided not to whack him as he would have done, this judging by the way he had stormed out of the dormitory.

***

The beginning of the second term meant a second attempt at winning Alice's heart. I was certain that during the three and a half week break she had had enough time to think and realize what a great guy I was. This especially after the encouraging signs I saw on our last meeting. Little did I know that disaster waited in a way I would never have imagined.

It happened on the second Saturday of the term. This was during dance night, otherwise known to us as 'Record Night'. I immediately spotted her, and asked Max to let her know that I wished to speak to her. As I waited, I remember my palms sweating profusely and I was shivering nervously. This is something that had never happened before – it was a premonition of what was about to happen. When she finally came she casually took a seat opposite me.

"Hi Alice ... how are you doing?" I tried very much not to sound nervous.

"I'm fine ... what do you want?" She was cold and cutthroat. This took me by surprise, and I immediately realized that I had my work cut out for me.

"Oh, I just thought me and you ..."

"Me and you could be what? ... Boyfriend and girlfriend? Are you kidding me? Didn't I give you the boot?" I could not believe it; where was this hostility coming from?

"My goodness Alice, I didn't know you too could speak like the other uncouth girls in this school. I thought that type of talk was beneath you." I really meant it. That slight rebuke I think kind of softened her up a little, and I mean *just* a little.

"So? In any case I'm going to tell you here and now that you won't succeed in convincing me to be your girlfriend."

"Alice this is not a test, it's not about me trying to prove to the world that I can succeed. It is just my love for you," I said.

"Be that as it may but you won't succeed," she insisted with affected unconcern.

"Alice, what is it about me that's so repugnant that you have to treat me like this?" I think now I was in desperate earnest.

"Nothing. I've told you again and again that I do not want to be in a relationship." It was true.

"Yes I know, but I just can't get over loving you, and that's the truth." Guys do lie sometimes to get what they want I know, but I was not lying that night.

"You know what; I don't want to argue with you anymore." It was a dismissal, and every further attempt was thwarted unceremoniously. I remember even trying to hold her hands in mine so she could feel my soft warm palms, but she gently untangled my fingers, stood up, and with not so much as a goodbye she left me with a huge lump in my throat. I went outside for some fresh air wondering what had just happened. The night was ruined.

"So what happened?" Max wanted to know, also present was Allim and Sebei as this apparently was supposed to have been my coronation. Therefore they were understandably anxious to know what had transpired.

"Man Max she was vicious." I then went on to relate the whole scenario word for word, as they listened in stunned silence. They all agreed that the enmity was totally unnecessary.

"You know I had a feeling that something was not right," Max said. "Because when I came up to her and told her that you wished to speak to her, her initial response was *'No tell him I won't speak to him,'* and then after a brief pause she said, *'Okay tell him I'm coming'* and she had said that in a non-committal way." That now familiar feeling of my bowels turning to water returned. Perhaps had she stuck to her first decision she would have spared me the humiliation.

I felt sick for the rest of that weekend. Even the next morning, when Roukes had the whole 'Block C' entertained with some of his famous tall tales after general cleaning, did absolutely nothing to cheer me up. I was drowned in my sorrow that even a concerned dorm mate Mathabathi asked me, "Are you alright man?"

"Yeah," I fibbed, with not much conviction in my voice, as I was in no mood to relive that nasty experience by relating over and again to anyone who cared to listen about what had happened.

Later, even Max had to concede that pursuing this girl was officially a lost cause. There are some girls who deserved to be chased, but in the end one has just got to accept when he's been defeated, and I was. As a result, I accepted that bitter reality even though it was not the easiest thing in the world to do. Even with powerful allies like the divine Keorapetse Cisky Keakile, her dorm mate, it was just plain useless to pursue her any further. Normally such a thought would be liberating, but not in this case. The more I tried to forget her, the harder it was to do; hence I made no further attempts to try. So I left it up to nature, and time to take its course whatever and whenever that may be. In the end, I had to admit the bitter, ugly, and messy truth – the girl was *not* and was *never* meant for me. There was nothing else left to do but to piece together the bits of my broken heart.

As the month of June was getting closer Fungwa was thinking of putting a play together commemorating the June 16, 1976 Soweto uprisings. He was determined to make this happen, because he brought with him all the necessary memorabilia and a skit he had written. In addition to that he also brought a large and expensive looking boom box, which he used to play all the revolutionary songs and speeches. By all accounts it seemed as if a humongous performance was in the books. At some point he initiated a meeting with everyone who was interested in the play. I attended, but was ruled out of any participation because according to Fungwa I was 'too shy.'

Now during this time as Fungwa was preparing for his play, he kept playing the boom box every morning after rising bell until it was time to go to school. The only problem was that in doing so he would connect the tape player to the power outlet in the laundry room not far from the dormitory, meaning that he was using the school's electricity; something that was strictly forbidden, because if you were caught using electricity for anything other than ironing and I'd think also boiling water in a kettle, that item, whatever it was, was immediately confiscated, and the rule was that you could only get it back a year from the date it was appropriated, and for a form 5 that was more like never.

One morning just as we were getting dressed and ready for school, the radio that was already part of our early morning ritual suddenly went dead, and before we could make sense of what was happening we saw the boarding master, Mr. Molefi, walking into the dormitory casually rolling the long electric cable that was connected to the boom box. At that moment we all knew that Fungwa's most valued possession was gone, and could only be claimed back in a year if ever.

We watched helplessly as BM picked up the gigantic radio, and with not so much as a word to anybody began walking away. Someone must have alerted Fungwa as to what was happening, because he came rushing into the dormitory, and confronted BM demanding his radio back. I could not quite tell what he was saying from where I was standing, but he had his hand on the handle of the radio as he tried to stop BM from taking it away.

"Let go," BM said softly, but Fungwa kept trying to pull it away. "Let go I said," BM said again, but Fungwa would not, and the situation was getting tenser by the minute, because this was outright defiance toward an authoritative figure, and BM was not someone to be trifled with. Then at that moment Big Joe stepped in, and advised Fungwa to let go of the radio; it was no use getting into more trouble over it. We all heaved a sigh of relief, because I was certain, and so was everyone else; that had Fungwa continued to resist the consequences would have been dismal. The play that he had planned went ahead as scheduled, and Big Joe put on a great performance, but without the boom box the desired sound effects were lost, and that took a lot of the luster from the play.

And then something happened that was to drastically change the course of events in my life. The form 5's at the time studied a Setswana novel entitled *'Omphile, Umphi Modise'* as part of their syllabus, and a senior secondary school in the northern part of the country named Tutume McConnell College, came to Lotsane in early June to perform a play based on this novel.

Since this was an educational event, evening prep was cancelled that Friday, and we all assembled at the dining hall where the play was performed. The play for us form 4's was endless and boring as we were not familiar with the book or the story. In great anticipation, since the play was very long, the Tutume administration organized some entertainment that was scheduled to take place right after the play. They brought along acrobats, a magician, and the cream of the night - two break dancers!

These two dancers they had picked up on their way to Lotsane were from Francistown, and attended a secondary school called Mater-Spei College. The two dancers were Mbiganyi 'B-Coll' Butale, and Oggie 'Double G' Joseph. They were part of the crew MBR, and were of course very good and advanced dancers. We met and welcomed them at the parking lot after they arrived with the Tutume students. The two were met by me, Max, Two-Two, and Dakune. The rest of the dancers from our Lotsane crew like, Tso, Noble, David, and Maulter were nowhere in sight. My guess is that they felt intimidated by the presence of these two very advanced dancers, and thus made themselves scarce.

B-Coll, with whom our paths were to cross much later in life in the United States, looked the typical breakdancer, cap backwards with his street name printed on it, carrying the ubiquitous boom box on his shoulders as he played the very latest break dance songs that we were hearing for the very first time. I remember his big eyes shining in the dark, and one of the first things he said to Dakune and Two-Two after the formal introductions was, "Guys, there's only two of us, would you mind joining us, because the more dancers the merrier."

"Sure thing," Two-Two said excitedly. That was the thing with Two-Two when it came to performing in public - he needed no second invitation. Even Benjamin 'Body-Roc' Thupe once remarked that Two-Two just 'loved' the fans a little too much.

We then went to dorm 9 where B-Coll had a relative who lived there named Brian Butale, and watched the guys get ready for their performance. They also wore matching cotton sweat pants and sweaters (track suits). Two-Two and Dakune were holding a discussion between themselves, and one of the things they decided was that *'Sebati should be a part of the dance too!'*

"Yes, I agree, he's skilled enough, he can hang," Two-Two confirmed.

I started to shake from head to toe at the thought of performing under those bright florescent lights, and in front of all those people. I wanted to appear calm, but already I began to sweat that cold winter evening. The first question that came to my mind was: in doing this am I not going to make a fool of myself? Just that thought alone was scarier than anything else in my life at the time. So my very first instinct was to decline the offer.

But then again, girls liked breakdancers. And desperate moments call for desperate measures. I had long ago spotted Alice in the audience like I always did for some reason. I knew exactly where she was seated with her friends, and if I performed she would most certainly see me. I was also almost 100% certain that she was not aware that I was in fact a breakdancer, and that held true for the majority of the school, but I was not too concerned about any of them. My main mission was to electrify that one person in the crowd.

Since my skills were not quite there yet, I told the guys that what I could do was open up the stage for them. That meant I would be the first dancer on the floor to perform my routine, leave, and then the rest would take over. As the time drew all the more closer I was getting more and more nervous. Since I was not feeling cold anymore after the decision for me to participate was reached; I handed my sweater to Breke with instructions to gauge Alice's reaction the moment I appeared on the dance floor.

As soon as the acrobats and the magician were done; it was at last announced that the breakdance performance would soon begin. The anticipation from the audience was palpable, and felt as if one could reach out in the air and touch it. By this time I was a nervous wreck, especially when someone peeked inside the hall and declared that the space where we were to dance was a bit too small, and then promptly Polite, the head boy, made the announcement.

"They say the space is a little too small, and ask if you would kindly move backwards." Immediately thereafter we could hear the sound of the chairs scrapping against the cement floor as they moved backwards. At that moment, I was looking at the numerous routes that led to the boys' dormitories. It was not too late to run for it now I thought to myself. And in an instant the place was quiet as the music had started. It was one of the latest breakdance songs I had heard earlier when the two MBR dancers were warming up. I have never been able to track that song, as I have never known the name of it, but it still plays in my mind once in a while, and I've given it the name *'Universal Countdown.'*

"...*what I want you to do is to begin the countdown* ..." The metallic voice from the song blasted through the very powerful stereo system that seemed to make the very walls of the hall vibrate. In an instant, Cracker, who had been operating the stereo, as he was the school's deejay at the time came rushing outside and said with a sense of urgency: "Guys, guys, people are waiting are you ready?"

"Yes," Two-Two said confidently as he gently grabbed me by the shoulders and guided me to the entrance.

"... *five, four, three, two, one, zero ...zero...zero...*" the song continued followed by its superlative beat.

"This is it Jones, go get them." Two-Two's words were more than motivating. What happened next just flashes through my mind. However, I do remember distinctly a scream from one of the girls as she anticipated what was to come. Now that I look back, I think the girl was Mable Maphane, who was like me a form 4 at the time, and I saw a girl named Cecilia Madi, who happened to be Alice's classmate. I had not planned on what moves to perform, I just reacted on instinct, but I was later told that the feat was magnificent. So much such that I heard cheers coming from the crowd as some girls shouted my name, one of whom I recognized as Chedza, my classmate. I did my thing and thereafter back glided outside.

"That was excellent Jones," Two-Two patted me on the back. And then it happened - there was a loud applause! "Listen to that," Two-Two was ecstatic. "They are applauding for you man!" That was the thing about those great Lotsane students, if they appreciated something they made sure you knew about it, but the opposite was unfortunately true. That is why the applause went far in reassuring me that my performance had been great. Max told me, many years later, that he too had been pleasantly surprised and impressed at my performance and bravery that night. It was not only him it seemed – I had taken everyone by surprise as I would later find out. Even to this day I still get chills whenever I think of that night.

The rest of the performance was simply magical. The two MBR dancers put on a great show to a point where our star dancer Dakune was reluctant to compete, but Two-Two stood up to the challenge, and matched the seemingly more superior dancers pound for pound. That night Moemedi Patrick 'Two-Two' Raperekisi was simply brilliant, and his girlfriend Sinah, who was also among the audience, could not help but feel proud of her man, and it showed.

After it all ended I went up to Breke to get my sweater, but most importantly to find out about Alice's reaction, because really the truth of the matter is that I could have gotten it from him anytime, even the next morning if I so wished since I really did not need it, but I was anxious for the verdict, and that more than anything else. My performance had all been for her.

"So?" I asked. "What was her reaction?"

"Huh?"

At that moment I could tell that Breke had no idea what I what I was talking about. And right there and then I had this distinct feeling that Breke had been caught up in the moment like everyone else, and had forgotten his 'assignment'.

"Alice ... did you get her reaction when I was dancing?"

"Oh ... oh that? Y-yes. Well she was cool and showed no reaction." Breke did not want to admit that he had forgotten, and I did not blame him. I mean really how did I expect that she would react? Smile and run across the room and declare her undying love? Well Maybe.

That night sleep did not come easy, the song I danced to seemed to be playing over and over in my ears as questions were going through my head, and the one I could not get past that bothered me the most all night seemingly, was the one I was afraid to answer: *'Did I make a fool of myself in Alice's eyes?'* I would not know the answer to that until the next morning.

That Saturday morning was bright and sunny. At breakfast I could hardly look around as all eyes were on me, principally from Alice's table, and others in the vicinity. I could almost hear the whispers from the girls followed by their smiles and furtive glances – even from Alice. But I was under no illusion that I had swept her off her feet. Nonetheless, I must say it felt great even though I tried to appear as nonchalant as possible.

After breakfast, Big Joe asked me to accompany him to one of the form 5 dormitories in 'Block A'. A block I hardly ever visited; that dormitory (dorm 3) was crowded, and everyone was speaking Kalanga, a dialect I did not understand as it is spoken mainly by people from the northern part of Botswana. I was instantly the topic of their discussion I could tell, and they were making no attempt to hide the fact whatsoever, because whatever they were saying was not anything conniving or malicious. Among them was a chap I later came to know as Bakani Bagwisanyi and another named Sethunyiwe Oitsile; they were both like Balisi brilliant guys from Francistown Secondary School.

"What were they saying?" I asked Big Joe as soon as we left.

"They were all saying how amazed they were by you. None of them ever thought you were a breakdancer, and a great one at that."

I had a smile on my face that whole weekend.

***

Not too long afterwards, news spread around the boys' dormitories that the boarding master's house had been attacked. What had happened was that one Friday night after lights off, someone went to the BM's house which was located just next to 'Block A'. Whoever it was had from a vantage point fired a few stones shattering several of the Boarding Master's windows.

This had been a brazen attack. Who could have done it and why? That was the question on everyone's mind when the news reached us. When it came to motive, I believe quite a few of us had our own suspicions, but wisely kept our mouths shut. This however was a serious offense. A crime if you ask me, because a man's family had been exposed to danger, and if it was not dealt with who was to say such a thing would not escalate?

The next morning BM called an urgent meeting of all the prefects to launch a quick investigation and identify the culprit. The night before,

Friday June 14th 1985, was the day that would forever live in infamy for that was the day when commandos of the then South African regime crossed the border into Botswana, defying international sovereignty, and brutally killed 14 people who they accused of being ANC (African National Congress) terrorists. Among those murdered were two Batswana women and a little boy.

Sunday afternoon June 16th was an overcast day, and we were hanging out in the academic area. Among us that day was a joyful gentleman from Bobonong, a form 4 like us, and a fellow with whom I had become fast friends with named Cross Kgosidiile. We were discussing among other things the attack on the BM's house; when out of nowhere Fungwa appeared. He seemed very interested in the conversation at hand; since Max was giving us feedback of what had transpired during the prefects' meeting, and the subsequent investigation.

"Apparently, there was a witness to all this who ..." Max said.

"A witness?" Fungwa interrupted. He seemed troubled by this revelation.

"Yes, the BM's daughter saw someone wearing a white T-Shirt. That person was seen running away soon after the windows were broken, and disappeared around the 'Block C' area." Dorm 12 was of course in 'Block C'.

"B-block C?" Fungwa stammered.

"Yes, and when we were sent to investigate we realized that the perpetrator was wearing boots, and when we followed the boot prints, they faded behind the 'Block C' area, because the people assigned to clean the surroundings swept the prints clean."

"B-boots ... d-did you say the perpetrator was wearing boots ... a-as in military boots?" I had never seen him so spooked.

Fungwa owned a pair of military boots, and before Max could answer, he said something almost in soliloquy that, to me at least, sounded strange for a man who was supposed to be innocent.

"I know they will make me step on the dirt so that they can see the print mark left by my boots. What I'll do is put a false bottom on the soles of the boots, or better yet just hide them at the river. Yeah that's what I'll probably end up doing." The river in question was the nearby seasonal Lotsane River from which our school got its name.

The question I had, and I am sure everyone else did that day, as Fungwa mumbled on was: Why go through all this trouble of hiding boots, worried about prints, and concerned that a witness had said the perpetrator had vanished around 'Block C' if you are in fact innocent? It then dawned on me that BM had just recently confiscated Fungwa's beloved boom box, and if he was to get it back, if it all, would be in a year. That to me was a clear cut motive to get even. In addition to that, seeing a visibly panicked Fungwa at Max's revelations made me believe that something was definitely afoot. After he left, Cross laughed long and hard.

"No guys, he did it, it was him. He's the one who broke the BM's windows."

All this time I was willing to give Fungwa the benefit of the doubt, but in light of what had just transpired right before my eyes, I was inclined to agree with my pal Cross Kgosidiile, and I know everyone else did. I mean seriously, and in all fairness, who else could it have been?

Our conversation soon diverted to other things, and not too long afterwards Roukes came by and sat with us. After a while he looked at me and said, "Sebati, tell me something why don't you have a girlfriend? You think you're too good looking and that the girls will practically throw themselves at your feet? You better think again, this is Lotsane my boy that kind of thing only happens in fairy tales."

I heaved a long and heavy sigh.

"Man Roukes, if only you knew what I've been through you would not be saying that," I said.

"What are you talking about?"

"There's this girl I've been chasing for months that in the end I had to give up and let her go."

"Who's this girl?"

"Alice ... Alice Mukokomani."

Roukes thought about this for a moment as he kept saying to himself repeatedly 'Alice, Alice, Alice ...' this was amazing to me at least; for I expected everyone to know her the instant I mentioned her name. I guess there were some people who just did not see her in quite the same eminence as I did, and Roukes just so happened to be one of them.

"What class is she in?" *Are you kidding me*?!

I told him, to which he smiled and said, "Just give her to me, and I'll set her straight. All I have to tell her is how lucky she is to have a guy like you pursuing her with single minded fortitude as you've been."

"Be my guest," I said, without giving what I said much thought. Her dorm mates (Cisky in particular) had tried, friends had tried, and a beautiful girl with a heart of gold named Sepankinyana (SP) on her own had tried - even Fungwa of all people. I heard from someone that he had on his own volition approached Alice, and asked her why she would not go out with me, and that she was making a big mistake. I asked Fungwa about this one day, he was busy fixing a pair of sling shots as he was trying to explain to me when and why he had talked to her, but he kept rumbling, and I could not quite understand what he was trying to say as he was too busy with his sling shot, so I decided not to pursue the matter, because he had obviously failed like all others before. What then could Roukes say or do that would make this girl change her mind?

Moreover, Roukes could be playful at times so there was no telling if he was serious or not; after all practical jokes were also his stock in trade. That is why I did not give the matter too much thought afterwards. We continued our discussions about current events and the like. Then a little later Two-Two asked me to accompany him to speak to some girl, him and Sinah were having some problems, but I was not too worried as I knew they would sort them out.

We were headed back to rejoin the rest of the gang when I was suddenly horrified by what I saw. The ballroom dancers were practicing in a class nearby (room 5), and Roukes went there called Alice outside, and was actually speaking to her as he said he would. I was almost instantly paralyzed with dread. My first instinct I remember was to flee as far away from the scene as possible. Suddenly, the pain and frustrations of the past months that I was miraculously getting good at keeping at bay came back now with a vengeance. I was literally sick to the stomach as I felt old wounds re open.

"Man, I can't be anywhere near this," I told Two-Two, as I was about to skedaddle, but Two-Two would hear none of it.

"Hey Jones you're *not* going anywhere, what's the farce about? You don't have to be scared you know."

Back among the friends it was hard now to hear what anyone was saying. I tried very hard to say anything that would ease my nervousness, but it was useless, and from my peripheral view I could see Roukes still speaking to Alice. And what struck me as odd though was that she was actually smiling all throughout, but then of course I was not buying into all that. Looks can be deceiving I knew only too well, and I had vowed never to be as naïve as I was in the past.

A little later Roukes came to us with a big smile planted on his face. What on earth was going on? He looked at me and said, "Sebati, send someone to call that girl and have her tell you what she just told me." Suddenly everything started spinning full force.

"No way." I was not about to suffer another humiliation.

He looked at me again and smiled, and secretly gave me the thumbs up sign. My heart jumped to my throat – this could only mean one thing, but I dared not hope. I looked at Cross who immediately smiled and shrugged his bony shoulders.

"Come with me," he said. "Let's head to the dormitories." I walked beside him with a racing heart. All this was happening way too fast.

"Man, I promise you this - that girl is going to crown you *today*." It was a statement. Somehow I believed him, but still I could not get my heart to accept the same thing.

"Roukes please don't play with me. This has been a long and painful process." I could hardly breathe. If Roukes had at that moment asked me to part with everything that I would *ever* own and give it to him - even a kidney, I would have readily agreed.

We got to his dormitory, dorm 11, and he said to me, "Sebati, listen … I would never mislead you or say or do anything that would hurt you. You're my student, but most importantly my boy so my word counts. Listen I would go into detail, but bottom line is I fixed everything the girl is yours. Now we're going to head back, I'll have you wait someplace and I'll call her, and you'll hear it right from her mouth. I swear to you Sebati this is it."

Was all this happening really? I wondered as we headed back to the academic area. For a teenager such things can be real hard to grasp all at once. The academic area on a Sunday afternoon, especially on an overcast day, was pretty much a very quiet place as there was not much activity going on. Roukes had me wait in front of the Biology laboratory and went to fetch her. I waited anxiously – not for an instant deluding myself as to what was about to happen. Soon thereafter I could hear the 'click-clock' sound in the corridor created by the Biology lab and one of the classes, which in this case was room 8. This was a 'click-clock' sound made by a female's shoes, and in an instant Roukes and Alice appeared, the former then dramatically presented her to me; that classic million dollar smile unabated as he left.

She walked slowly over to me, we said our 'hi's', I recall that the atmosphere this time was more relaxed compared to our previous encounter. However, I was extremely nervous this time around, and then to my horror I went on babbling inanely about how even if the world ended tomorrow kind of thing how my love would never die blah, blah, blah, and when I was done with my Don Juan Demarco speech she simply asked me in a soft voice, "So what do we do now?" *'We'?'* This was very encouraging.

"I just want to know Alice; I just want to know finally at this instant what you think of me."

"Well, I just came to tell you that *I love you Sebati!*"

I had to make her repeat that at least three times before it actually hit me like a ton of bricks. And just like that we were boyfriend and girlfriend - we were an item. *God bless Roukes a million times over and forever* I remember saying that to myself. I held her hand for a moment before letting go, and she walked across to a classroom with a big smile on her face. It was the start of a romance I would never forget. A dream had come true.

I walked away stunned and dizzy, and what Roukes did next was classic. He got Max and Two-Two, the two of my closest friends he could find at short notice, and had them sit at an area where they would have a perfect view of me the moment I emerged so they could be the first in this world, besides Alice, to witness my initial reaction. My reaction must have been a sight because they all smiled, and I ran around the nearest classroom and then toward them. By the time I got to them, my legs failed me, and the guys almost literally had to carry me to the dormitory.

This was before Max said to me in slight rebuke, "Come on Sebati, the girl is watching you behave yourself man." He was joking of course, but that quickly brought me back to my senses. It took a while for everything to sink in, just imagine a teenager realizing his very first crush and you will know what I am talking about. I was so excited that even at supper as we were heading to the dining hall Roukes (he was always a sharp dresser) was standing at the door, and munching on his bread and tea nonchalantly as if he had no idea that he had impacted a life said, "Sebati, are you even going to be able to eat?" he smiled mischievously.

    Max smiled too and even said, "Hey we may even have breakdance to thank." I must have fallen asleep with a big smile planted on my face that night.

Chapter 9

The administration finally zeroed in on their chief suspect regarding the broken windows incident. One day when we were away for afternoon prep the boarding master, the deputy headmaster Mr. Maganu, and Mr. Mhuriro came to our dormitory, and raided Fungwa's locker. In it they found assorted items like condoms (that were never ever used), sticks, and most incriminating of all a pair of sling shots and the military boots. Further investigations, were to confirm their suspicions that Fungwa was the person responsible for breaking the BM's windows.

The fact that Fungwa had way too many priors, and was generally regarded as a delinquent; this latest transgression was viewed under a very serious light. We are talking about a guy who somehow got his hands on concentrated sulphuric acid, and with a syringe and needle used that to inject the chemical into some mice he had caught.

That incident almost had deadly repercussions. What Fungwa did after catching the mice was invite everyone to the laundry room, and filled the syringe with the acid, and then injected the mice. I heard many years later that that acid had been stolen from the Agriculture laboratory. One of the mice was cooked right before our eyes and burst open, and the acid sprayed on some of the onlookers in the immediate vicinity. Fungwa was very fortunate in that the acid just missed his eyes, and landed beneath his eyelids instead. Sebei caught some on the chest, but to their credit everyone sprayed reacted with lightening quickness, and most importantly the huge laundry sinks were filled with water and clothes as someone had them soaking, so they washed it off before any serious damage was done. Sebei says the scars on his chest are still visible to this day. I shudder to think what would have happened had the acid not missed their eyes.

Then on Sunday during lunch time since it was his turn to serve, and that was the day we had chicken, he distributed the chicken by holding his plate next to the bowl, and as he put a piece in someone's plate he subsequently did the same on his.

"One for you, one for me, one for you, one for me …" in the end there was more chicken in his plate like you never know what.

Incidents like this, and numerous others crowned by the window breaking episode in the end led to his downfall. All the other eccentricities I am sure could have been overlooked if not forgiven, but when he attacked the BM's house there I personally think he had gone too far, and nothing could have saved him from the wrath of the administration. Thus soon after the *'one for you, one for me'* fiasco, Fungwa was suspended from school indefinitely pending the Ministry of Education's final decision on the matter, and soon the verdict was handed down, which was expulsion! And what was worse, he also lost two sisters in a horrible car crash later that year.

This I regarded as a tragedy, because despite his shenanigans, Fungwa was deep down a very wonderful human being, and a brilliant one at that. In retrospect, I realize this was a stage we all go through as adolescents even though his was more pronounced. Years later I was to be totally amazed at the transformation I saw in him, and he went on to make a great life for himself.

***

One day a spat started between us and the girls who sat next to us in the dining hall. We called these girls 'the models' not because we thought they were, but this remark was made out of sarcasm. They were pretty yes, but not the knockouts they truly thought they were. They all like us lived in the same dormitory, and by the look of it this had been pre-arranged by all the parties involved.

This started when someone from our dormitory went a little earlier than usual to the dining hall to set our table, and was just in time to catch one of the 'models' at our table trying to exchange our bowl of bread with theirs, and even pilfer some of our slices. This was a big coup catching them in the act, because it turned out that these girls did this all the time. Sebei later remarked that they had 'invaded our bread'.

With people like Big Joe and Lekobe being the big talkers and the unofficial dorm 12 spokespersons they were; there was no way these girls were going to be let off the hook simply because they were beautiful. The guys let them know about it at every given opportunity. For instance, someone would say loudly enough for them to hear something like, "Hey Sebei, I did not get my share, and the kitchen people swear that there was enough bread to go around, what do you make of all this?" It was all a fabrication of course, and meant mainly to get a rise out of the girls.

"Are you saying our bread was invaded yet again by some unknown forces?"

"I don't know about unknown forces, because eye witness accounts bear testimony to the fact that the invaders were dressed in blue." Someone would remark, a clear jibe at the girls as part of the Lotsane girls' uniform was a blue tunic.

This later escalated to a point of open hostility between the two tables, which became really uncomfortable for people like me who wanted no part of this silly conflict. All I wanted was to eat and leave, and not be a party to anything that in most likelihood would ruin my appetite. However, in high school, one thing everyone is susceptible to is peer pressure, and Lotsane was no exception.

One major change that second term was that at lunch we did not eat at the same time as the girls. This I think was because of a massive shortage of utensils, and the fact that the kitchen staff was now tasked with the job of washing the dishes that we ate from; as opposed to the previous term when we did the dishes. The girls would eat first, and then soon after it would be our turn.

So one day Big Joe rounded us all up and said, "Guys I have come up with a plan in which we can humiliate these girls and this will require everyone's participation." I did not quite like where this was going, and I just knew that I wanted no part of whatever scheme Big Joe had hatched. "Here's what we are going to do, we will sit on one of the benches facing the dining hall, and once any member of the 'models incorporated' steps outside, we will all applaud." Wow! That was it. That was Big Joe's brilliant plan! The question I ought to have asked, but did not, was how on earth was that supposed to humiliate them?

"Eh guys … I'm not going," I said, anxious not to be put in an unnecessarily uncomfortable situation.

"Hey Sebati … you are going," Big Joe informed me.

I tried very hard to wriggle myself out of this one but in the end I caved, and reluctantly went along with the rest of the guys. Not present among us that day of course was Mmabaledi, Pema, Max, and Katu. I suppose they had better things to do than be pressured into participating in so shallow a thing. My reluctance was mainly due to the fact that I had a girlfriend now, and I did not want to put myself in situations that would make me look like a punk or worse still a trouble maker, such things were known to destroy relationships; that and general bashfulness on my part played a big role, but then again on the flip side I did not want to be looked at as a wuss by my dorm mates.

We got to the dining hall, and as planned took up position at the benches facing the main entrance where we knew the girls we targeted would use. The rest of the area was devoid of any activity and we did stick out, which made me even more uncomfortable, and right at that instant the one thing that I dreaded the most almost happened. Alice, of all people, suddenly appeared from the back entrance of the hall, and was rushing toward the main doorway. I was just in time to duck behind Mathabathi, but for some miraculous reason she did not even glance in our direction nor was she even aware of our presence.

To be quite honest I never really understood the purpose of this whole sham, because whenever one of the girls even as much as peeked from the entrance we would applaud, and she would dart back inside the dining hall smiling like we were playing some kind of game. To me it seemed we were just giving them unnecessary attention, and attention is what these girls sort at all times from the opposite sex.

Thankfully all this nonsense was put to an end when their prefect went to lodge a complaint to the matron (a matron is to the girls what the boarding master was to us), who contacted BM who in turn summoned Big Joe since he was identified as the ringleader, and was warned in the strongest possible terms to stop instigating us to tease the girls. Big Joe wisely took heed of this warning, and the quarrel ended just as abruptly as it had started.

The open hostility ceased yes; so whatever was left was very subtle. Like one Saturday night after lights off we were talking about what had happened during record night when Tonkana said, "Man I saw the models together (they did almost everything together even dance together on record night) I passed by them, and then I sprayed them with a silent fart like a skunk." We all burst out laughing, and our imagination ran wild as to the torture he had subjected his victims, because by his own admission his gas was 'toxic'. "Man, I then saw them scatter in different directions, and then later when they regrouped and I passed by to gauge the situation, I saw them looking at this one guy like he was worse than dirt." Naturally, we felt bad for the innocent victim, but then again this was hilarious, and only Tonkana could dream up something as mischievous as this.

That second term after Alice agreed to be my girlfriend felt like a breeze. I was happy, and it must have been evident, because one day she said to me, "You know Sebati, Balisi says whenever he sees you these days you are always full of smiles." We looked at one another, and she smiled knowing that she was responsible for that. If I could sing I would have performed KC and the Sunshine Band's 1970's hit *'Keep it comin' love.'*

I must admit that for a teenager's first huge crush seeing her every day, and mostly from a distance, always brought joy to my heart knowing that I was not wishing anymore - the lass was actually mine. What was even more amazing was that I was falling in love with her all over again, and that love seemed to be growing every day. She also did confide in me that she was impressed by my brief breakdance performance (just as I had desperately hoped) when the Tutume students came, and admitted that she had no idea that I was a breakdancer.

A lot of my friends including a certain Tlholego, whom we called 'Tlholeza', a fast talker from Ramotswa, even said to me one day, "Man you really are patient to pursue a girl that long, for me a week is too long, but I suppose she was worth all the trouble." Which is why when she left one weekend, shortly after we became an item, to participate in the National Science Fair, I missed her terribly. And much later I was to curse the day that she went to that Fair.

***

I was rapidly establishing a wide circle of friends at Lotsane, among them was a gentleman I met through Olefhile Thelo named Lepholetha Gofhamodimo 'City' Senne. City always came to our class at evening prep to study with his friend. He was member of our soccer team, and he is hands down one of the best players I have ever met, and the most athletic. We were to become even closer as time went on.

Also, that second term, one would think that Jewawa would have eased up on Robot, especially after the two had a sit down just a day or two before the first term ended; this was done at Robot's initiation. What had happened was that since schools were about to close, everything was laid back, as there was no teacher around during regular class periods. On one of those days Jewawa happened to pass by Robot's desk, and the latter called him.

"Jewawa, can I have a word with you?"

"What is it man?" Jewawa wanted to know.

"Trust me it won't take long, come on have a seat."

Jewawa sat down on a chair that had been set previously in anticipation of this meeting.

"You know man," Robot began. "This whole term you have said things to me or about me, and I have had to endure and many times swallow everything however hard and humiliating, but then it just dawned on me and you know what that is?"

"What?" Jewawa must have wondered where all this was heading.

"It just dawned on me that everything, and I mean everything that you've said, were going to say, have dreamt or even thought of saying to me that was disparaging, all that and much more you were saying that not to me but to your father. Is that clear?"

"What?!?"

"You heard me."

Jewawa was stunned as he stood up shaking his head and came up to me. "Can you believe this guy?" he asked.

"Who?"

"Him," he pointed at Robot who immediately dipped his head. A habit he had learned whenever he sensed that Jewawa was about to make fun of him.

"What happened?" I asked.

"He says that everything I've ever said about him I was not saying that to him but to my father. Can you believe that?"

"Robot actually said that?" I feigned surprise, when the truth really was that the poor fellow had been teased often enough and his reaction was only natural.

"Yes," Jewawa responded. "But you know what's funny?" at this point he raised his voice for the whole class to hear. "We all know that everything I said I meant Robot not my father. My dad was not here so it is Robot I was talking to wouldn't you agree class?" This of course never stopped Jewawa, and the ragging continued unabated.

The one thing that had us concerned though that second term were the whispers going around that one of our classmates was pregnant; her name was Nancy Lekalake. As the term progressed this fact started to become more and more apparent to all of us, but then as it was always the case we did not expect her to return the next term.

The field trips continued and one that I remember clearly those early days of the second term, 'the term of love', when I had a new found girlfriend, some club in the school had a fundraising event to be staged at the Morupule Power Station in Palapye where a lot of Korean and Polish expatriates worked. This club invited two break dancers, Maulter and I, to help them with their cause. The Morupule Power Station supplies the whole country with its electricity, and is one of the very distinct landmarks of Palapye, and the reason why this village, as of this writing, is fast turning into a town. As this trip was on a Friday evening, me and Maulter were more than willing to be a part of the group.

The club did their traditional dance routine, singing, and poetry, but I must say the highlight of the night was when Maulter and I took the floor. By this time my skills had improved immensely, but Maulter was just outstanding and the two of us were told later on that inviting us to come with the club proved to be a very good move. I remember that night very well, and I also recall the stench of the nicotine in my throat since many in the audience were chain smokers. I must declare that I pushed myself far more than I would normally, because I was cognizant of the fact that one of Alice's dorm mates was present, and I knew she was going to give a full report of what had transpired, and blissfully she gave a good account I was to find out later.

***

Drinking was still a bit of a problem at Lotsane, and I would not be surprised if that held true for the majority of secondary schools in Botswana, and as I earlier mentioned; this was a very serious offence that was almost always dealt with accordingly. The school came down hard on drunks, and the punishment dished out was also meant as a deterrent to those who harbored similar intentions of hitting the bottle when the opportunity came. In short, the administration showed no mercy when it came to this transgression.

Looking back, I see drinking in boarding school not as something that was done for recreational purposes, but rather gave one some kind of street power or credibility; something Americans call 'Juice'. If you drank you were looked upon as a grown man, someone with power in a weird kind of way, which is what made it all the more tempting for many students. That, curiosity, and the ever present behemoth called peer pressure played a great role no doubt.

This brings us to an incident that occurred between Katu Phori and Alfred 'Tonkana Ya Lebowa' Ntseane, 'the little donkey from Lebowa'. One Saturday evening I came into the dormitory to find everyone tense. I soon noticed that Tonkana's left eye was swollen, and Katu was speaking in a fierce tone to a fellow named Jackie, who like him was from the deep south of Botswana - the Kalahari district. I realized that Katu was speaking in his native dialect, something he very rarely did when among us. Whatever he was saying was about Tonkana. He was visibly upset. It was the first time I had seen him like that.

I was soon to find out what had happened. Apparently that early Saturday evening, Tonkana had snuck out of campus to go to Palapye, and had gotten himself drunk. So when he got to the dormitory he was unnecessarily rowdy, perhaps showing off. He was being a complete nuisance, I heard, to a point of joshing Katu and invading his space at every given opportunity. Katu after a while got really angry, and kept pushing Tonkana away saying, *'get off me man'* each time, but the latter would not let up. Now, because his protests were obviously falling on deaf ears, Katu felt he had no choice but to punch Tonkana in the eye - thereafter in sheer anger - he went to report the matter to the boarding master.

Normally, this kind of thing was uncommon, because reporting Tonkana on so serious an offense could mean immediate suspension, or worse expulsion, and what was bad was that Tonkana was one of us. So, upon hearing that Katu had gone to report him to the BM, Tonkana miraculously became sober in no time, but it was too late. He was summoned to Mr. Mahole's house. Legoro was entertaining some guests, a heavy drinker himself, I would think he was in a cheerful mood that evening.

"Stand on one leg you naughty boy," Legoro said immediately to Tonkana when he entered his living room. "Spread your hands in the air and stay that way until I say otherwise. You fall and I will know for certain that you've been drinking."

Tonkana did as he was told, and stood at a corner of the living room while Legoro concentrated on his guests, and basically forgot all about Tonkana, who later was to tell us what a great ordeal it had been to stand on one leg. The alcohol was still flowing through his veins making it a huge struggle to maintain his balance. At some point he said he realized that the floor seemed much closer than it had been, and caught himself just in time as he was about to fall. I would think the terror about the possible ramifications kept his adrenaline pumping. After what seemed like an eternity; Legoro suddenly remembered him.

"Go back to your dormitory, but just know that you'll have to appear before the disciplinary committee on Monday. You know you're in serious trouble don't you?" I am positive Tonkana agreed wholeheartedly with him; even though he had passed the sobriety test albeit with great struggle.

Consequently when I entered the dormitory that night, it was shortly after Tonkana had arrived from the headmaster's house. Soon thereafter, Max filled me in on everything that had happened. We knew that all Tonkana could pray for was at least a lengthy suspension. There was no possible way he was going to escape a stiff punishment. This we all agreed to. So it is fair to say the state that night, in the usually jovial dorm 12, was really desolate.

Somehow Katu softened up; tempers and bad feelings were soon abated, especially after a now very sober Tonkana begged Katu for forgiveness. The next morning after church service the two were seen together for lengthy periods at a time speaking in low tones, obviously planning on how to diffuse the potentially explosive meeting set for the next day. I would think that had to have been one of the worst weekends in Tonkana's life at Lotsane.

They were presented before the disciplinary committee at the staff room after lunch, as arranged. The committee was led by the formidable Felix Mhuriro. The group comprised of the boarding master, the matron, and a few teachers. Any student knew that a meeting of this stature meant serious trouble.

The case was presented, and both Tonkana and Katu were asked to tell what happened. There were so many inconsistencies in Tonkana's version of events, which I would attribute to anxiety and nervousness; that Katu had to bail him out on more than several occasions.

For instance, when Katu was asked; "Did you or did you not say that Alfred was drunk?"

"W-well, I may have said that you see, but then I could have been mistaken."

"Mistaken?" BM asked incredulously.

"Yes sir, you see, earlier I thought I saw Tonkana, I mean Alfred, drinking a generous portion of cough syrup. I know when I drink that I get a little buzzed which I would assume is the same for Alfred, right Alfred?"

"Huh? ... Oh y-yes sir ... it's true. I have been having a severe headache lately, I mean... a cough." I think this had not been part of the game plan, but in stressful situations one is expected to adapt on a whim. I would presume Tonkana did not realize that quick enough, which is why he did not sound quite as convincing as he otherwise should have.

"Now what of the swollen eye, didn't you say you punched Alfred in the eye after he kept bothering you?" One of the teachers asked. All this was documented, because they were consulting the written report they had in their hands.

"Well sir, it just so happened that when Alfred was standing right next to me I was reaching for a comb on top of my locker and in so doing, I elbowed him in the eye by accident."

Mr. Mhuriro, like everyone else in that room that day, I am sure, could not believe his ears. "This obviously had been pre-planned," he said.

Finally, the disciplinary committee had no choice but to give Tonkana the lightest punishment under the circumstances, because their star witness Katu Phori had recanted his earlier statement to the authorities. Without his true testimony there was nothing to warrant a stiffer punishment for Tonkana. He was ordered instead to fill a wheelbarrow with two loads of dirt, which he afterward did, very gladly, and in record time I was to hear.

Later, a very relieved Tonkana, and Katu were back in dorm 12. We had been eagerly waiting to know what had transpired, and that is how from Katu we got to hear everything that had taken place, including Tonkana's goofs. In the end, we were all pleased that all had been forgiven and that Tonkana was saved. It had been a close call, and to the best of my knowledge, Tonkana never misbehaved or indulged in Babylonian waters after that. As a matter of fact, Tonkana went a step further much later in his life at Lotsane, and decided to seek penance with God, and started attending Scripture Union (SU) meetings, but was discouraged by the behavior of some of the members who turned out to be hypocrites. And what was worse was that they were in the majority.

Chapter 10

Sometimes a club would be lucky to secure one of the 'casual' Fridays for fundraising purposes, and present some kind of show at the dining hall; there was always a nominal cover charge. This type of thing became very common in 1985, until much later, when the administration put an end to this practice; stating that it was a clever excuse by students to extend the weekend, and they were right. Friday evenings, if there was to be a performance at the hall at all that would interrupt evening prep; it would have to be educational.

One Friday evening the sub team Santos organized a fundraiser, and the event was a dance competition among the Pantsulas. The way it worked those days was that if you were not interested in attending whatever fundraising event at the hall; you were expected to be in class as evening prep was still on as scheduled, and for many of us the choice was easy.

The way the competition was set up was that the dancers would boogie individually and from them pick the best 8, and from there the elimination would go on until there was one man left standing, and that would be the champion. The favorite to win it all was none other than a certain Alfred Moloi, who was known to everyone as 'Ali'. A form 4 who had attended Gaborone Secondary School for his Junior Certificate, his moves were breathtaking, and whenever he took the floor to dance the din was always deafening wherever we went.

So when we heard that there was going to be a Pantsula dance competition that Friday night, for us it was not a question of who was going to win, because the victor had already been declared. The question in everyone's mind was who was going to claim second place. What always happened whenever there was a contest of any kind the committee members of that particular club staging the event, which was Santos in this case, would ask two teachers to be judges for reasons of impartiality and candor, because this was an assignment you could never assign to students for obvious reasons.

The two judges in this case were Mrs. Palalo, a Home Economics teacher, and the redoubtable Mr. Emmanuel Mudidi. He was a tall gentleman from Rwanda who later, and to the astonishment of his former students, became the first Minister of Education after the 1994 genocide that shook the whole world. Mr. Mudidi, a math teacher, is one of the most proper and disciplined by the book educator I had ever met. A man who encouraged us to be proud of our African roots, and who taught us to break the myths that stereotyped Africans in the eyes of Westerners, students called him '*Letsopa*' which literally means 'rich clay', but in this context it meant a true son of the African soil.

Among the dancers that night was a chap from Francistown named Chad 'Choiza' Banda. Like Da Quanch, not many people knew his real name because he went by either 'Choice' or 'Choiza'. The strange thing was that Choiza was not a Pantsula by any stretch. I think his participation was due to the fact that he was a member of the Santos sub team nothing more. Everyone was dressed accordingly, but Choiza wore his khaki school uniform of all things. He was a very likeable fellow nonetheless and very brilliant. It turned out that I had known Choiza since we were kids.

The competition started in impressive fashion with the first dancer, a form 4 named Joseph, also known to his close friends as 'Megarty', who performed very well. He was followed by a few other dancers including a well-known form 5 Pantsula named Charles, but known to everyone as 'Charlie', but pandemonium reigned supreme when 'the king' took the dance floor.

Ali mesmerized us with his moves as usual, at some point doing movements with his head that thrilled the girls. Charlie also did his thing, and when went down on his knees to do his trademark dance, I remember Mr. Mudidi taking particular notice. However, everyone who was there that night remembers Choiza.

To begin with his dancing was way off beat, and in his khakis he looked really out of place, but Choiza is one of those people who care less about what people say or think about him. That was not all though, because as he danced he would occasionally grab his crouch and look straight at the girls and even at Mrs. Palalo, with no pun intended though, but the nightmare was just beginning. In the next instant none of us could believe what we saw, because Choiza right there and then went flat on his belly, elbows locked, and started simulating the missionary sex style and was actually humping. Later, I tried to relate the whole episode to Alice as that happened to be the weekend that she had gone to Gaborone for the National Science Fair, but I could not find the right words to clearly describe the whole scenario without sounding vulgar or uncouth - especially saying it in Setswana.

In the end after the competition was done and the points were tallied, it was time to announce the winner. Mr. Mudidi being the professional and thorough judge that he was had to go over the list, critiquing each dancer pointing out his strengths and where he could use some improvement. One of the things I remember him saying was something to the effect that dancing is an art to be enjoyed, a coordination of spirit, mind, and body, and how it was also important for a dancer to love the song. The man was simply way ahead of the times.

On the strength of this he said, "Surely you cannot call shaking your head like this dancing now can you?" As he said that he started to demonstrate albeit comically a dance Ali had performed that had thrilled the girls. Knowing Mr. Mudidi, as he was also my teacher, when I heard him say that the first streaks of doubt began creeping in – maybe, just maybe Ali was not going to be the shoe-in we all believed he would be. Mr. Mudidi went down the list, and when he got to dancer number 7 he took a brief pause and sighed. That dancer happened to be Choiza.

"Now this dancer ladies and gentlemen, dancer number 7 ... very, very, embarrassing. I mean how could a grown man display himself like that in public ..." the rest of his words were drowned by the laughter that followed.

This incident was to dog Choiza for a very long time, and if you wanted to see the angry side of this otherwise gentle individual just mention that night. I remember one day not too long afterwards Choiza was in our dormitory, so was David Makuni, and the latter suddenly hit the floor like he was going to do pushups, but instead imitated Choiza during the now infamous simulation scene.

On seeing that Choiza turned around, looked at us and calmly said, "Guys, just watch the action I'm going to take." And he immediately grabbed the nearest broomstick intent on causing serious bodily harm to his tormentor. David quickly apologized and all was forgiven.

Back to the competition, when it came to announcing the winners the way it was done was that the third place contestant was announced first, followed by the second, and then of course the champion. Third place went to a form 4 named Sparks, second place was a shocker, and that was Ali. The winner was Charlie. Everyone was stunned and disappointed and that included Ali, but with Mr. Mudidi in charge I was not really surprised, he took everything into account exploring every move and possibility – he was that thorough a man. In the final analyses I think even Ali took it for granted like everyone else that he was going to win, and thus did not give his very best performance.

That would prove to be the very last time Ali would end up being second best to anyone, and he was to later redeem himself in ways that have made his name etched in Lotsane lore along such people as Blackie Kealotswe, Balisi Bonyongo, Albert Ditlhakeng, Roukes Nokane, Andries 'Hotstix' Ryan, John 'Max' Moreti, Mojasegoro Kgosinkwe, Diirilwe 'D-One' Matoto, Bathusi Dinkie 'Two Six' Seretse, Gilbert Kabelo Sebei Gaboutloeloe, Lepholeta Gofhamodimo Senne, Mojadi Kwerepe, Kgotso Monamoledi, Elijah Legwaila, Kabelo Lebotse, Polite Mabalane, Mbumbi Manyothwane, Bame Krug, Godfrey 'Mafia' Morgan, Dineo Motsamai, Lillian Setlalekgosi Tlholwe, Rinah Phoko Makgosa, Matlhogonolo 'Matt' Temane Motsoela, Betty Bolaane Mathiba, Ruth Botlhole, Netty Nkala, and Adam Masebola to mention but a few for the list goes on and on that pages would be required simply to mention them all.

That was also the weekend when my kid brother Rama paid me a surprise visit. It was Saturday early evening and the guy just showed up. I was stunned when I saw him, but immediately disappointed because his lips were slightly dark, and that there and there told me he was a smoker even though he was barely 15 years old at the time. He had been sent by my father to deliver a few items that included, most importantly, money, and a nice brand new sweater to help me cope with the bitter Palapye winter. Since he was to spend the night, Max and I had a hard time convincing BM to let him stay as non-students were not allowed to sleep in the dormitories. In the end BM made an exception, but told us that he would not be as understanding next time.

I was also presently surprised to find out that Ali and Rama knew each other very well. That Saturday night happened to be 'record night' and I saw them talking like long lost brothers reunited.

"Where do you know Ali from?" I asked.

"Well he's a Pantsula from Gabs, and I'm one too," he replied, what a small world I thought to myself. "He also says" Rama continued, "that he had been cheated from winning the Pantsula dance competition last night. He says one of the judges was a foreigner who knew nothing about our Pantsula dance culture." It was the first I was to hear about Ali's disappointment.

"Oh, I see." We were heading to the dining hall for the dance. I remember wishing he came a week earlier or later, because in that case he would have met Alice in person.

"Who is Charlie?" the question caught me and Max off guard. My brother was not a Lotsane student, and he had barely been on campus for over an hour and already he was acting as if he belonged even asking about people we were certain he knew nothing about.

"Why do you want to know?" I asked.

"I just want to see how good he is. I want to battle him."

Max was dumbfounded, but that was classic Rama. In the end even though he wanted to, a battle never happened, and however many times he tried to bait Charlie the latter would not fall for it. After all he was the champion, and petty battles were beneath him. Other than that the weekend went well, and it was a pleasure having my brother around. He was well received, liked, and treated well by the rest of my dorm mates, and when it was time for him to leave that Sunday Max, Sebei, and I escorted him to the gate, and remained there and waited until he got a ride back to Gaborone.

***

Muhammad Ali I hear was once asked why he called himself 'the greatest', he answered by saying he just said it, stepped into it, and then it took a life of its own. Napoleon Hill, the great motivational and self-help author; mentions in one of his books that we have the conscious and sub conscious part of our brain. The conscious mind he says processes everything that we allow to enter. The sub conscious part of our brain processes whatever thought process is fed to it be it negative or positive, in very much the same way. One thing Mr. Hill emphasizes is that this part of our brain cannot tell the difference between the negative or positive energy that it is fed, making it the most important of our psyche. I am of course paraphrasing Mr. Hill.

Big Joe is one person who like the great Ali declared something as a joke, and it later took a life of its own. Almost every day after taking a bath and combing his hair, he would come to the dormitory and pronounce very seriously: "Guys ... you know, I was just looking at myself in the mirror and as I was combing my hair, I could not believe what I saw."

"What?" Someone asked.

"Guys, no false modesty or jealousy ... I am a strikingly handsome guy." It was true though.

We would laugh, because such a thing was almost unheard of in our generation. We were taught that if we said anything good about ourselves, we would be perceived as arrogant, and that people would not like us. Big Joe is one of the few people I know who destroyed this myth. And I also believe that his colossal success in life today can be traced back to that one single attribute he developed as a joke during our time at Lotsane. He was never afraid to talk highly of himself. Muhammad Ali, I would imagine, when he first started saying he was the greatest people scoffed until his words came true. Big Joe is as closest to meeting a younger Muhammad Ali in person as I have ever been. This was never done in arrogance, but this was a man who knew his self-worth, and dared the world to tell him otherwise.

Big Joe was always the life of the dorm and everything he did always got your attention, because he had a way of making it funny. For instance, he and Tonkana shared an unusual camaraderie when it came to laundry time. Laundry was a chore we hated but had to do, much like cleaning and inspection. We did not have washing or drying machines so everything was hand washed – even blankets, even though this (the washing of blankets that is) was usually reserved for the end of the term. Now if hand washing was a nightmare try ironing. This was hated of all the chores, not because it took time and had to be precise, but not every student owned an iron. So even after the clothes were dried; you had to wait in line for that single iron that someone was kind enough to let you borrow, but even then there were only three power outlets in the laundry room for over sixty students.

The trick was to do your laundry on Saturday if you could, since Sundays were crowded, but doing laundry on Saturday took too much on a day we held sacred, so for the most part we would bite the bullet and do it on Sunday, and somehow we always managed to get it done. There were some lucky ones who had their girlfriends do their laundry for them.

Now if there is one thing Tonkana hated with a passion that was ironing clothes, with Big Joe it was washing, so the two had an agreement which was always fun to watch when it was time for washing.

"Big Joe, give me your clothes to wash, and please no messing around this time, because I want this over and done with." Tonkana would say because it was always drama whenever Big Joe was involved; even with something as simple and straight forward as washing clothes.

"Okay, let me see what I have for you," and as he said this, a load of dirty clothes would appear miraculously. "That's not all you know how about this?" And then Big Joe would get his sneakers and say, "Look I don't want you to wash the whole shoe. I just want only the bottom washed."

"*Monna* Big Joe, come on man I don't have all day."

"Sorry man I just can't help it. How about this" and then he would pretend as if he was going to rip the cloth that covered the mattress. "You know I can make you wash this too."

"Hey man stop playing," Tonkana would protest vehemently. In the end though the clothes would be washed and Big Joe would iron them all at once, and when he did he was very thorough. Also one time he had people in stitches over one incident. Being near a village it was not rare to see goats roaming around our school, and one time a few passed by our dormitory and then Big Joe said casually; "I can bet you Sebati is one of the few people who have never seen a goat before, and only has seen it for the first time here at school. He is a city boy." Everybody including me laughed. That was Big Joe for you.

***

One of the last trips we took that term was to Serowe when we visited Swaneng Hill Secondary School, and the moment the Pantsula dancers took the floor, Ali put on an electrifying performance like never before. The fact that he had come second best in the competition only a few weeks prior, Ali was taking no prisoners this time around, that even the champion Charlie kept a safe distance. It was as if Ali was the only dancer on the floor that night; this judging by the way the audience cheered for him.

Max doubled for the break dancers and the Karatekas, not to be outdone the Swaneng martial artists joined in, and instantly a tournament was in the works. One of their best fighters I would presume, because when he stood up to take on one of our combatants, the Swaneng crowd roared its approval. Something they did not do with their previous fighters.

This fighter faced our own Cowden Sechoni, who was also head of our club's disciplinary committee, very tough and an able fighter as one would expect being the head of our disciplinary unit. At first the fight looked even, but as seconds ticked on, the Swaneng fighter began to tire just as Cowden got stronger, and in the end our fighter won easily.

Max impressed as a break dancer, and when he and Khudzani did their exhibition sparring they got a very long ovation afterwards. Also that day, Max was to deliver a message to a girl Big Joe had met on our earlier trip to Swaneng the previous term. I think the lady in question had forgotten all about Big Joe during the intervening months, because when Max approached her she was instantly swept off her feet, and any minuscule memory of Big Joe was quickly eroded. Being strikingly handsome and having had the audience buzzing not too long before could have had a great first impression on any girl.

"Hi," Max said to her.

"Oh hi, I understand you have a message for me. Is the message from you or someone else?" I can still to this day see that pretty girl's smile, and that was when I left the two of them alone. I knew I was going to get a full report later.

"Man every time I would mention Big Joe's name she would get upset, and instead ask personal questions like if I had a girlfriend and all that. In the end I could not deliver the intended message because the girl claimed to have no recollection as to who Big Joe was." I still think it would have helped if Big Joe had come with us, because he would have brought the same broom that he had used to sweep her off her feet the first time.

Also that term, our soccer team was making strides in the regional interschool league that in the end we qualified for the national finals in Gaborone. This is when the champions from all the four regions of the country met to slug it out. Besides Lotsane, the schools participating, and representing their respective regions were: Lobatse Secondary School (Lobsec), Mater Spei College, and Gaborone Secondary School (GSS). The way the tournament was set up was that the team with the most points (after all playing each other) would be crowned national champions.

Of the schools we were facing, the most feared and also the heavily favored was Lobsec, because at the time they boasted two of arguably the best attacking midfielders in Isaac 'Brenda' Ncenga and Samuel 'Tornado' Bokole. I knew both players from my days at Itireleng Secondary School; mainly Brenda who was an Itireleng alumnus, and star player during my time there. He completed his J.C. a year before me, and then transferred to Lobsec for his Cambridge where he met up with Tornado.

The school was tense with anticipation; especially after the news reached us that we had easily disposed of GSS in our very first game. Our next game was with Lobsec. That afternoon right after lunch we all crowded the laundry room listening to the 1 O' clock news. At the time Radio Botswana rarely announced sports results, let alone secondary school soccer scores, but we figured that since this was a huge tournament they would make an exception. We knew it was a long shot, but we huddled around the radio nonetheless, hoping and praying really hard. The news seemed to go on and on for some reason, and this did not help in reducing the tension that was already at its utmost.

"...*and now sports*," Andrew Sesinyi's distinct voice over the radio was suddenly the most important thing in the world at that moment. "*In the Secondary School Coca Cola tournament, Lotsane Senior Secondary School beat Lobatse Secondary School by two goals to one and ...*" mayhem reverberated like never before in the entire 'Block C'.

"*Da zett … da zett …*" "That's it … that's it …" everyone screamed including an otherwise calm gentleman who was a form 5, named Peace Katse. Dakune, a former Lobsec student himself, walked out of the laundry room saying to himself, "Yes that serves them right for not accepting me to do my form 4 at their school … good riddance."

We were very relieved, because with Lobsec beat we naturally assumed that the trophy was ours, but it turned out that things were not as easy as we had thought, we were to hear the rest from our players themselves including the great Lepholetha 'City' Senne. That weekend though, our school was also shocked by some unexpected and yet again dreadful news.

***

Dixie Ndlovu was a form 5 student from Zimbabwe who had come to Botswana originally as a refugee. He was much older than us, and was well liked by the students and kitchen staff. The rules about selling cream donuts and buns were clear, only clubs were permitted to do that as part of their fund raising efforts, but Dixie openly flouted this regulation, and when he was hauled before the school's administration Dixie is said to have answered in his defense: "Hey look, I have no parents who send me money nor do I have any relatives, I am just a poor refugee. When everyone goes back home I go back to the refugee camp in Dukwi."

No one with a clear conscience could argue with this line of reasoning. Dixie was told to continue with his enterprise but on a low scale. They might as well should have said *'Man, go ahead and sell your buns and cream donuts'* because he did it now with impunity. His prices were always higher than normal, and he always appeared to have a constant supply even when no one had any. I think it helped that he was also friends with the people who delivered the bread and the donuts. In retrospect, I think this gave Dixie the advantage over many, because we always wondered why sometimes clubs could go for a couple of weeks without fresh supplies, and yet Dixie never seemed to have that problem. I personally thought he controlled the market in a way, but I kept those thoughts private.

Besides that Dixie also had special privileges like no one I have ever known. For instance, during tea break, we had two slices of bread and tea (starch water for me) through the winter months and juice when it was hot. In addition to his share, it was very regular to see Dixie with a bowl of mouthwatering chicken broth mixed with hefty chunks of meat courtesy of his friends at the kitchen.

The Friday of the weekend of the Coca Cola tournament was an extremely hot day. It was early August and thus the cold winter months were behind us – thankfully. I was with Allim near the administration office. Dixie was there too holding a bottle filled with very cold water thanks to his friends at the kitchen. The water was so cold that the sides of the bottle were dripping wet. Everyone was looking at the bottle until someone, and I believe that was Lali, was brave enough to go up to him and ask if he could get a drink of the cold water. I say this because even though Dixie was well liked, he was also feared. We all had seen what he had done to a fellow student who dared to fight him, and ended up getting Dixie a three school day suspension.

"Sure," Dixie said as he nonchalantly handed the bottle to Lali. "You can have it all." No sooner had Lali had the bottle in his hands did everyone else in the vicinity jump all over him like a pack of ravenous wild dogs; anxious to have a drink of the icy cold water on that hot day that even Dixie had to say, "Guys, please no need to scramble there's enough water for everyone to go around."

"Yeah ..." Allim agreed. "No need for that really."

As it turned out, those were the last words I would hear from Dixie; as that was the last time I would ever see him again.

That night I was hanging out with Alice, in an area that was considered out of bounds, and we were talking about the future, about how I wished one day she could be my wife and mother of my kids, and how she promised me that she would, and thereafter how I almost leaped with joy upon hearing her assert that. I still cannot help but laugh aloud at the things I used to say, because I really meant it at the time. Earlier as we were talking, she had mentioned that a Lotsane student had been hit by a car that afternoon on the main Francistown Gaborone road while jogging.

"I know he will be fine," I said and thought no further about the matter, but focused my attention, being, and energy on the angel standing in front of me, and I could only guess her on me, so much such that we did not notice a teacher walking towards us in the dark until it was too late.

"Oh my God ... Sebati," she said softly.

"What?" I asked equally softly expecting her to say something earth shattering about her eternal love for me.

When I took a closer look at her I noticed that she was terrified, I turned around and saw none other than the man himself Mr. Felix Mhuriro. Now, if you were going to get caught by any teacher as a student; you had to pray that that teacher would not be Mr. Mhuriro – anybody but that man! So as he approached us I was under no illusion as to what awaited us.

He merely looked at me, pulled Alice closer so he could get a good look at her face, which he did, and then turned around and left without a word to either one of us, which made things even worse. I was terrified, but tried very hard to put up a very brave face for the sake of Alice. I don't know if she bought it, but that was not the primary concern at the moment. We each went to our respective dormitories right after I assured and reassured her that everything would be fine, and for her not to be afraid; she must have been thinking *very funny*. I got back to the dormitory with a heavy heart. A movie was playing at the hall, but I was too distraught to make an appearance.

No sooner had I arrived at the dormitories did prefects appear; instructing everyone to be at the dining hall. It was a command, because we were not being asked but told. Among the prefects telling everyone to get out of the dorms that night was Albert 'Alibaba' Ditlhakeng, who like Balisi, our paths were to cross much later in life. I was filled now with renewed dread. Could all this have anything to do with Alice and I being caught? I wondered.

Max was also among the prefects who were telling the students to go to the hall, and as me and him were headed there the school siren sounded, which was extremely rare under the circumstances - something was terribly wrong. I then felt it prudent to confide in my brother about what had happened before he heard it from someone else.

"Max, I don't know how to say this man ..."

"What is it?" he obviously did not like where this was going.

"I ... I've been caught." There was no need to explain what I meant by that. By saying you were caught in boarding school only meant one thing.

"No man, please don't say that." I hated to tell him that, but I had no choice, because by telling him I was caught also indicated that I was facing possible suspension. And this likelihood gravely troubled him I could tell. As for me I was now completely numbed by the fear. "Is that why we are being called?"

"I don't know," I answered as if the thought had never crossed my mind.

We got to the hall, and as Max and I sat down there was an unusual buzzing going on among the students in our vicinity. Max turned to me, I could see the shock on his face.

"They say Dixie is dead Sebati!"

"What? ... I just saw the guy not too long ago ... please say it isn't so." I could not believe all this was going on. In addition to my personal problems; someone I knew very well, who I had just seen a few hours ago extend a kind gesture was no more. This was hard to digest all at once, and I must say that had to be one of the worst days in my first few months at Lotsane.

"They say he was hit by a car."

At that moment, the headmaster Mr. Mahole, and a few teachers including Mr. Mhuriro entered the hall from the southern entrance. He did not have to call for order because the hall was immediately silent.

"Ladies and gentlemen," Legoro said in his booming voice, "tragedy has once again struck our school ..."

There was an audible gasp mostly from the girls. By saying that Mr. Mahole was echoing the painful memory of the previous year, when three Lotsane students died after coming back from some sports event; this after the truck transporting them overturned. Among the deceased was a great soccer player named Phenyo 'Tornado' Selebogo.

"I'm sorry to say this, but Dixie Ndlovu was struck by a car and killed while jogging ..." the rest of his words were drowned by the instant wailing and sobbing from the girls mostly the form 5's, and the ladies who were his classmates. It was a sight I wished never to see again, especially after some of the girls actually collapsed and fainted with grief, and had to be carried to their dorms. As for the boys, we listened in stunned silence, and when it was all done we headed back to the hostel. The only thing we could hear were the sounds of our footsteps.

The next day we had a memorial service for our fallen colleague, who just less than 24 hours earlier was telling the guys not to scramble over the water he had given to Lali. Festus even said every time when in his dormitory he would expect to see Dixie enter the dorm like he always did; selling his cream donuts and buns. None of us could accept that our beloved Dixie was gone forever.

Alice and I made eye contact during the service. Our problem seemed impervious in light of this great tragedy, but again I was under no fantasy that our case was over. I was expecting to be summoned to the administration office anytime; however I was too troubled by Dixie's death to worry too much about my situation. The only problem, regarding Dixie's funeral; was that the burial was going to happen after school closed as we were just a few days away from the end of term.

I also decided to confide in my other closest friend Allim, about the possible danger I was in; this after briefing Two-Two who was sympathetic. Telling Allim though was something I would very soon regret.

"Allim," I began, "I was caught last night."

"Good gracious Sebati no ... this is terrible ... terrible!"

"Yes, I know man, no need to rub it in."

"Where did this happen?"

"By the fence."

"By the fence?!" he echoed. "My God this is even worse than I thought. It would have been better if it was in the academic area not out there. Sebati, do you realize the seriousness of this whole thing?" I could not believe my ears.

"Who caught you anyway?" the anguish continued unabated.

"Mr. Mhuriro."

At this revelation, Allim my friend looked at me for a while, and then whistled long and hard, shaking his head in sympathy, as if he was looking at a man headed to the gallows. He had to for Mr. Mhuriro was his English teacher, and was thus very familiar with his methods of punishment.

"I don't think these will be the fun holidays we thought they would be I'm afraid."

"Thanks for all your support and words of wisdom man," I said as I got up and left. I was now terrified beyond reason.

In the end all the worrying proved to be unfounded as nothing happened, but I was very careful from that time on, and never was I caught again. There were some very close calls though. Later, Allim was to tell me that he had deliberately amplified the possible danger I was in; this so that if and when the time came I would be more than ready to handle whatever it was that was thrown at me. I have yet to get back at him for putting me through that anguish though.

***

That was a bittersweet weekend, because on Sunday the minibus that transported the soccer team arrived early that evening blowing its horn continuously, unaware of the tragedy that had just occurred, and raced to the soccer field where it did a few spin moves much to everyone's delight. This could only mean one thing – we were the National Champions!

A while later City, still dressed in the brand new red and white kit supplied by the tournament sponsors Kalahari Breweries, as they had the Coca Cola emblem in the front of the jersey was later to tell Sebei in glowing detail how it went down.

After we beat GSS by five goals to one, we played Lobsec in our second game. They were the first to draw blood as they from the very onset were set to destabilize us, and for the better part of the first half we were on our back heels, but somehow we got back into the game and scored; tying the game one all. The second half was much similar to the first with the 'terrible twins' Brenda and Tornado wrecking untold havoc, but could not score. Then against all odds, our diminutive player with the heart of a lion, Diirilwe 'D-One' Matoto, scored the killer goal, and our defense led by the great and evergreen Lepholeta Gofhamodimo 'City' Senne closed shop, and Lobsec's waves after waves of attack were easily thwarted, and at some point D-One almost sealed their doom with a goal bound ball that somehow missed its target by a whisker. Our goal keeper Bathusi Dinkie 'Two Six' Seretse made certain that Lobsec did not score any more goals, and our victory was secure. I mention these players individually; even though the game of soccer prides itself as a truly collective team sport, but there are just times even when everyone rises to the occasion; like that gallant Lotsane team of 1985, but even then there are just those players like D-One, Bathusi, and City who rise a bit higher.

After Lobsec our next opponent was Mater Spei. By then we only needed a tie with this school to be the National Champions. Mater Spei were a familiar foe who we had easily disposed in a friendly game earlier that year. So naturally, we took it for granted that this match was going to be easier than our previous one. Mater Spei had other ideas of their own apparently, and came out guns blazing because they stunned us with an early goal, and we found ourselves chasing the game.

We were confident we would equalize sooner or later, but Mater Spei, the supposed minnows of the tournament were hanging tough. The game of soccer, or football, as it is widely known the world over (except the United States); can be very strange at times let alone entertaining or even heartbreaking. People have been known to collapse and die at the end of games, because results are never guaranteed, and a David always kills a Goliath on a very regular basis, which makes it such a unique game, and we were seeing the makings of such a scenario unfolding in that game.

A loss to Mater Spei would put us at a huge disadvantage, because that would mean we would be level on points with our nemeses — Lobsec. Meaning we would have to face that monster again. We knew that if we played Lobsec again we would be in deep trouble. They were not going to repeat the same mistakes. And, it was little wonder as the game progressed that the entire Lobsec fan base rallied behind Mater Spei; when an upset seemed to be in the making.

The Lotsane heroes on the other hand bared their teeth in search of that elusive equalizer, and as the clock ticked a replay with Lobsec loomed large, until two minutes from time when our speedy striker Gabriel 'Muller' Matlakele scored just as Lobsec were starting to celebrate. Muller's goal sent our supporters into a frenzy, and whatever hope Lobsec had went up in smoke, and that was how we became the National Champions that year.

The players later said that ironically Dixie Ndlovu was the constant subject of their conversation on their way back to school that day. It was a premonition I know, and they were just as saddened and shocked to learn of his death like everyone else. Later I was to see the pictures of our victorious school lifting the trophy in Gaborone. Among the people who were there to witness this historic occasion was none other than Andries 'Hotstix' Ryan. He was not a player, nor was he in any way connected with the team other than being a Lotsane student, but how Hotstix managed to be there is still to this day a mystery to me.

Chapter 11

Second term, 'the term of love' finally came to an end. We left for Palapye earlier than usual that day. Alice and I said our goodbyes and promised to write each other over the holidays. I walked her to the bus that day. Alice and I lived seemingly poles apart so she did not catch the train with us. I missed her terribly, but I was much happier than the last time we were getting ready to catch the train back home.

Since the train was not due until about 10 pm that night, and we were dropped off at the station around 12:30 pm in the afternoon; we had a lot of time to burn. Our breakdance crew had some new members including a muscular gentleman from Letlhakane Secondary School, a school at the then mining boom town, named Caesar 'Stellafunk' Mooketsi; a very likeable fellow, warm, and kind, but with a quick temper that was at times amusing to watch.

Caesar like me not too long before, had no breakdance experience, and with the same zeal and determination got to be a very good dancer. He had a wicked back spin that was to become even better. There was however, an unsubstantiated rumor that Caesar had remarked that ever since he became a breakdancer; girls had started flocking to him like bees to honey. Whether he said that or not is really of no consequence, because such a thing was very common in those days. There were however many guys, who took offense to the comment Caesar allegedly made. The general consensus was that Caesar had grown a big head overnight.

That afternoon we hung out at the Palapye station, playing different new songs and sharing ideas. I also recall running into Tonkana that afternoon and the first thing he said to me was, "Hey man did you see it?"

"See what?"

"The car that killed Dixie."

"No." And I did not think I wanted to.

"Man, it is badly dented like it had hit a cow" he said, and I was instantly glad that I never got to see that accursed automobile.

This time around, there were no extracurricular activities like going to the nearest liquor store to get a couple bottles of *Autumn Harvest* like the previous term. That day we were kept busy and entertained by each other's company, and being the true breakdancers that were highly regarded, it was silently agreed upon by those who indulged in that practice that that was now unnecessary. We called ourselves '*The Electrons*', and earlier that term we took a group picture with all of us posing in our favorite moves that soon vanished, and was to reappear at the girls' dormitory, where it was passed from one eager hand to another. How it got there I have absolutely no clue.

When the mixed south bound train finally arrived at around 10:30 p.m. we ran into our old buddies B-Coll and Double-G. Like Two-Two and I they were headed to Gaborone. It was great seeing them again, and I could not help but be caught up in a nest of 'what ifs'. What if the Tutume McConnell College students had not come that night? Better yet what if B-Coll and Double G were not part of their program, and subsequently had not got the chance to participate in the breakdance show; would things have changed between me and Alice? I would never know the true answer to these questions, and truth is I did not want to.

The journey was uneventful all the way, and when we arrived in Gaborone the next morning the sun was up and bright. As I was heading to one of the taxis that was to take me home I saw Pema Dibotelo, my dorm mate, waiting for a connecting bus to Moshupa. I looked at him and smiled. I had not seen him on the mixed train just like before.

"*Pema, a o tlile ka special?*" "Pema, did you come on the special train?" I asked.

"*Nkabo ke ithaya ke rialo.*"

"That's what I ought to be telling myself." There was a big grin on his face as we were both expecting that answer. I on the other hand laughed outright. I then wished him well, and he did the same as we looked forward to the next term; the last for him and every other form 5 including Max and Alice.

One thing I noticed that did not seem quite right that second term break occurred to me when I was on my way back home a week or so later; this after visiting my friends in Lobatse. When I got to our house a reflection on the kitchen window revealed something that was shining around my neck. I realized that I was wearing the necklace I had given to Alice, but then why was I wearing it?

Shortly after Alice and I became an item I recall being very excited that I scrapped every penny I could find, and on our next trip to Palapye for shopping when we were allowed by the school, being the romantic I thought I was, I bought her a necklace hoping that she would love it. I wrapped it up as best as I could, and gave it to her a few days later asking her to open the present when she was alone.

I was anxious to hear her reaction. She was wearing it on our next date. I was pleased, but the whole thing was ruined when she said, "I really don't like wearing this kind of stuff. I am just doing it for your sake." That stung, but when you are blinded by love you can endure anything.

Later that term we took some pictures together, and she asked me to hold the necklace for her, and never asked for it back. A vague feeling just within comprehension at the back of my mind told me something was amiss, and of course that was quickly dispelled when I received a letter from her a few days later declaring her undying love. I had already written one to her, and had asked my very asinine brother Rama to mail it for me; a thing I ought never have done it turned out.

Not much happened that break that was earth shattering, except missing Alice terribly, but I did meet regularly with Two-Two, and we would hang out at the mall quite a bit talking about the world we left behind, and which we could not wait to get back to. We also ran into a cocky breakdancer who was known all over the country in the dance world. He was also a member of one of the elite crews, JBC, and that was William 'Mawila Chill Will' Fergusson.

We talked about the possibility of perhaps JBC coming to Lotsane not for a battle, but to watch them perform. Trying to battle these guys would have been folly, unless of course if we did not mind being embarrassed in front of our own crowd. In the end nothing ever materialized, but 'Mawila' did invite me that summer to one of the JBC practice sessions.

***

The third and final term of the year began in mid September and ended early December – the first week to be more exact. It felt great to be back. I had bought a cap on which I had printed my street name. I was to keep that cap for many years until someone lost it. I think sometimes the things we hold dear should not be shared with anyone.

To our amazement Nancy Lekalake came back to school that term when all of us were expecting her not to. This was so shocking that Jewawa of all people felt he had no choice but to confront her about this issue, much to my amazement, because such a thing was unheard of coming from a boy, but then again with Jewawa anything was possible. This happened right after she came out of the administration office after paying her school fees.

"Nancy, what do you think you are doing?" he asked her.

"What are you talking about?"

"I'm talking about you paying school fees in your condition."

"My condition?" She feigned surprise.

"Come on Nancy, you're fooling no one, yes your condition, you are pregnant. This is just a waste of your parents' hard earned money because we both know that sooner or later you are going to drop out of school."

To this she smiled and walked away, and that would be her reaction from that time on whenever the subject of her pregnancy was raised. It became a closely guarded classroom secret, but not for long, and when the cat was let out of the basket it did so in a way that would shake the whole school to its knees.

Most importantly it was great to see everyone else again. We talked about the latest moves; our meeting with Mawila Fergusson and the possibility of having JBC perform at our school. I remember everyone being a little guarded in as far as how much we had learned over the break. I for one knew I had not practiced as hard as I did the last break; even though I felt I was good enough I was not as great as I should have been.

The downside of this focus on break dancing is that it made me neglect another art that I held sacred since I was 11 years old – Karate. As time went on I was spending less and less time at the *dojo,* much to the disappointment of Roukes because I was being groomed to be the next instructor. But being the great teacher that he was, he never took me to task over that or said anything that would make me feel guilty, instead he concentrated on the students that were actually attending class regularly.

The mantle of instructor had somehow been placed on my head the very first term it turns out. Two form fours were scrutinized every day at training, and that was me and a fellow from Moshupa Secondary School named Kelibile Kelibile. There was a silent rivalry between us, because at the time we stood out as the best among the form 4's and even some seniors, although I must admit each of us thought was the better fighter. And thus we avoided each other like the plague until one day.

It had happened the previous term, second term, *'the term of love'*, but this was before it became known as such. What always happened was that after each regular routine of exercises and forms; it would be time to put what we learned into practice and that being sparring.

The way it worked was that after training we would seat in a circle around the common room (our *dojo*), we did the same at the cement when we were at the outdoor place of practice. What would happen was that whoever was conducting class that day, whether it was Max or Roukes, whoever it was would look around the room and would pair two fighters by saying *'ous* up'; *'ous'* being a Japanese term for a student of Karate, but literally means friend, and is considered a very old word and thus rarely used in everyday talk. Then the instructor would pick another student by saying the same thing to him. Thereafter, the two would then stand at an arm's length in between the instructor who would say 'fight'. In an actual tournament the referee would say in Japanese *'aka shiro shobu sun bon hajime'*. One fighter would be red and the other white so what the referee was saying was 'red white let the three point tournament begin'.

After saying that the fight would begin even though at practice it would not be as formal, we did not have protective gear so any blow in the torso area no matter how hard was legal. Once in a while someone would get you in the face if you were not careful, or on the groin. That is why after a large class at the beginning of the year the size dwindled considerably. However, as our bodies grew stronger absorbing the blows and the inevitable pain that followed became easier.

That day Max was conducting the class, and it was sparring time. These were always tense moments because the thought of hitting each other is something you can never get used to. Max looked around the room and picked one guy, and was just about to choose his opponent; when all of a sudden he changed his mind and said as an afterthought, "No ... no ... I have a better idea. Sebati up, Kelibile up; they say you two are next year's instructors so let's see you spar."

I was not very surprised that Max would pull something like that, he could be that mischievous at times, and there was a smile on his face as he said that. We both stood up to face each other – the moment I think everyone was waiting for had arrived. My mind starting working fast, Kelibile was a tough opponent no doubt, probably the toughest one yet, and I knew right there and then that to win I would have to fight smart, and thus adjust my technique a little.

My fighting style has always been comprised mainly of kicks. I guess my height has a lot to do with that. This has always held true even when I was a kid. Roukes, and even Max, as my instructors, had on numerous occasions told me not to always rely on my kicks – good as they were, because that would not always be to my advantage; especially when facing a fighter like Kelibile who was very good with his hands.

When the sparring began, Kelibile, and everyone else in the room that day immediately expected an assortment of front and side snap kicks. I normally did this kind of thing to subvert my opponent. Instead I relied more on my hands, and used my kicks whenever I saw an opening, I also took my time to conserve my energy. We went back and forth; attack and counter attacks were the order of the day. I won the contest, but not as clear cut as I would have liked, but it was really close and could have easily gone the other way. Later Max was to tell me in confidence that he was extremely happy with my performance, and had to keep himself from smiling out-and-out during the sparring. The rigorous training with Manqoba during the break had paid rich dividends. Hence I was well on my way on being the next instructor; until breakdance curtailed these carefully laid plans.

***

Seeing Alice again after the break of course was the highlight of the first day of that third term, the first thing I asked her was if she got my letter, and I was very shocked to learn that she did not even though she had mailed her's after mine. I was to find out much later that my brother never mailed it. Instead he opened, read it, and with the 7 Thebe I gave him to buy a stamp he bought a cigarette. Again that saying of why a Rock rabbit has not tail came to mind, but I never expected such chicanery from my own flesh and blood.

Alice did not seem too concerned or upset that she never got a letter from me. She seemed a little distant and tired albeit for a moment, and then she said to me, "There's something I need to tell you."

The last time she said that to me was the previous term, shortly after we were an item, when she said that back then I felt a cold chill at the back of my spine. I tried to pry it out of her of course telling her that postponing it would only make me all the more anxious, but she would not let up. In a way, I think she was in some twisted manner enjoying watching me squirm, or she was conflicted in what she wanted to tell me. I discussed my concerns with Max, and he just brushed off the whole thing as no big deal really.

"She'll probably tell you about her boyfriend from last year."

Max's prediction turned out to be dead bolt accurate. She also went on to tell me that that was the reason it took a while for her to agree to be my girlfriend; even though the feelings were there. In the end the letters between them stopped, and with it the relationship, which to me was not a bad idea at all.

So when she said she wanted to talk to me that evening about something I was forced to wonder what it was this time. Why was it so important that she could not tell me right there and then? Not being one too pushy I decided to let it be for a while. I had learned that from past experience.

When she did talk about it, I found it rather strange that a boy she claimed to have rejected his advances at the Science Fair would still be pursuing her, and even talking about coming to visit her at school in a desperate attempt (according to her) to try and finish what he had started. The chap in question went to school at St. Josephs College. In retrospect, I think I was too young, innocent, and naïve to comprehend that there was more to it than what Alice was had led me to believe – it was much worse, and more than I could have ever imagined.

***

As the term progressed, my classmates and I were becoming more and more alarmed at Nancy's growing condition. It was now clear to everyone that she was indeed pregnant, and it was a now a question of when she will finally pack her bags and withdrawn from school by her parents. Many times when a girl got pregnant, and it started to show; she would be gone before anyone noticed – particularly the guys.

One evening I remember as I looked at her; I thought she was in pain since was almost bent over as she was seated at her desk. She had a belt around her belly that made her look like she had two stomachs. Something was definitely wrong with this picture.

The following day she was noticeably absent from class, and we were assured that she had gone to the local clinic in Palapye. We naturally assumed once there, they would advise her to go back home, and notify the school on her behalf about her situation. I remember feeling slightly relieved that the poor girl had finally confronted the reality that she could not go on like this, and do the right thing under the circumstances – sad as that was. The truth it turned out was horrible.

Nancy went to the administration office and asked for an exit permit so she could visit the local clinic in Palapye. The permit was granted, but instead of going to the clinic like she said she would, she went back to her dormitory, which was empty at that time of the day as everyone was in class, and gave birth to a baby girl. She then threw the baby through the bathroom window! A little later the tiny body was discovered by the ground working crew. There were boys nearby, among them Cross and Batisani, who were the first to witness this terrible scene, everyone shuddered as the headmaster was alerted.

In no time the news spread around the school faster than the speed of light. The irony about all this was that we were the last to hear of what had happened. I was stunned, and so were the rest of my classmates. That evening our class teacher Miss Demetrio came to our class to tell us that had we reported this to someone this tragedy would have probably been averted. She did not in any way dump the blame on our laps, but she did mention that this ought to be a painful lesson that next time to speak up if we saw something wrong. We all agreed with her.

Nancy was arrested later that day, and I never really knew what became of her afterwards. Some said she was sentenced to serve two years in prison. This rumor was never authenticated though considering that she was a minor at the time. Big Joe called what she did 'first degree murder'; a phrase I was hearing for the very first time. The news was so sensational that it was picked up by one of Botswana's foremost newspapers at the time *'The Botswana Guardian'*. Legoro warned us to be careful of what we said when questioned by the press. Lotsane was self-contained, and away from everything and everyone back in those days, which is why it was surprising that there would be reporters snooping around. When I first heard that the story had made it to the papers, I could not help but think to myself that *'Radio Lotsane'* had outdone itself this time.

Chapter 12

It did not take a long while for things to get back to normal. And after they did, we planned a crew competition among ourselves, which we dubbed 'the greatest ever'; meaning that it was the greatest breakdance show ever staged at Lotsane. It was to happen on a Friday night and we expected a huge turnout, and it would be the first time that Alice would see me perform full force in public. It was exciting. One of our dancers, Caesar 'Stelafunk' Mooketsi was having girl problems, and I think was planning on using the competition as a means to win her back. The plan backfired dismally, because I think Stelafunk kept trying way too hard, and ended up getting some boos for over performing.

Taking a page from our friends B-Coll and Double G, Two-Two and I wore matching outfits and were on the same crew. We had divided ourselves into two. Our crew comprised of me, Two-Two, Breke, Maulter and Tso. The other was Dakune, David, Noble, Stellafunk, Kgopolelo (who Dakune called 'Dodgers', because of his habit of willfully skipping practice), Cracker, and Benjamin 'Body Roc' Thupe. The months and hours we had put into practice had paid off because everyone loved our performance that night.

A few weeks later Festus came up to me with a big grin on his face.

"Man, I was at the tuck shop this afternoon and had a long chat with Alice."

The school used the storeroom in Room One as a mini grocery store that opened on Wednesdays. Room one also happened to be my base classroom where we were when engaged in afternoon and evening prep. Kgomotso, my co-monitor, always placed her desk in front of the locked door that led to the storeroom whenever she studied that she earned the nickname 'Tuck Shop'.

The tuck shop opened right after afternoon prep, and the class would be immediately crowded as students would line up to purchase whatever it was they needed. Mr. Irvine ran the tuck shop with the efficiency of a machine and much more. He did not require a calculator let alone a cash register; he did all the calculations mentally. He would tell you the exact amount of all the items you purchased right to the last penny, and even the change would be exact as he executed these figures in record time. It was amazing to watch, and that is a feat I have yet to see from someone else up close and personal.

Thus it was common for students to hang out in the classroom during tuck shop days, and on this day Festus happened to speak to Alice, and before I could find out what they were talking about Festus babbled on.

"Man that girl truly, truly, loves you Sebati. She was telling me how much of a sweetheart you are, and how she'll never leave you for another man. It was the first time I had spoken to her at length; the very first time in my life." We were in my dormitory and Allim was seated on one of the top beds silently observing us.

"Oh man! ... She really said that?" I was ecstatic.

"I swear to you man. That's what she said; we were at the tuck shop when she was telling me all this. She was raving about you nonstop." This was ecstasy. I remember even giving him a long bear hug, and all this time Allim, who had been watching this scene unfold, was shaking his head. After Festus left I went up to him. Obviously he had something on his chest.

"Okay what is it?"

"Just what do you think you are doing?" Allim asked instead.

"What are you talking about?"

"Didn't this guy just a few months ago go behind your back and try to get the girl for himself instead?"

"Yeah, but that was a long time ago man."

"Oho, so what you are saying is that you trust him now, because now I see you guys all hugging and all that."

I kind of began to see things from Allim's point of view. Festus could not really be trusted, at least not just yet. Allim must have been reading my thoughts because he immediately said a bit exultantly, "Oh, you got it now." That Allim Milazi I tell you.

Not too long afterwards something exciting started brewing that term. We were told that a long trip could be in the making. The whispers were rife that we would be taking a trip first to Moshupa, and then Kagiso Secondary School. These were very long trips and definitely sounded like fun. The question was could such a historic trip be pulled off though? We all wondered.

Also that was the term when I had to re write my form 3 math paper. I got help, and lots of it from math demons like Lekobe, Cromwell, and Sebei. Everyone close to me knew of my intentions to repeat my form 4, and study Science so that one day I could be an Engineer; something that was instilled in me before I could walk.

I had to take the exams at a school in Palapye, and I had to make a classmate who I had befriended named Ditlalelo, promise me that Alice would be kept in the dark about all these developments. Ditlalelo and I had become good friends and she had with Alice as well, and the two always confided in each other and I would get a full report the next day.

After spending the whole day in Palapye I thought no one would notice. I took the exams, and then much later as I was at the Palapye mall treating myself to a packet of chips (French fries), fat cakes, and Coca Cola, a gentleman came up to me.

"Don't you attend school at Senior or was that not you I saw?" he asked. Palapye residents always referred to Lotsane as 'senior'.

"Saw?"

"Yes, at the exam place writing a JC paper."

"Oh yes that was me."

He was very affable I could tell, but a little confused and needed clarification.

"But why do you have to take a JC exam when you are already at senior secondary school?" It was a good question and I took the time to explain. I think in the end he understood what my plans were.

The highlight of that moment of brief absence from campus was when I spoke to Ditlalelo the next day. She was as usual giving me the daily report.

"Oh Sebati," she said. "I spent almost the entire night with Alice after lights off. She was telling me how much she loves you. She said it felt strange, because she had not seen you all day, and that had left an emptiness in her heart that she could not come to grips with." Once again I was happy to hear that. Our pre-arranged dates were on Tuesday, Friday, and Saturday. I was flattered that she missed me that much.

I felt great about the exam, and was certain 1986 was going to be an interesting year, how interesting I had absolutely no idea. The prospect looked bright and a bit chilling. Then again I could not in all honesty say I looked forward to 1986. Yes, 1986 held promise, but 1986 meant there would be no Alice Mukokomani and John Max Moreti. Allim and I had spoken about life without Max, and the thought was too hard to even contemplate let alone bear.

***

As break dancing teens we were cognizant of the latest outfits, especially the hottest styles. Even something as simple as a cap with your street name written on it could be a huge fashion statement. During the second term break this belief held true. I had seen B-Coll and his MBR cap with his street name screen printed on it. I knew I had to have one like it.

I met Max and Body-Roc in Gaborone at some point during the break. It was a wonderful reunion yet again, and we even ran into the great man Mr. Mudidi. I told them of my desire to get a blank cap on which I could have my street name printed. We were at the mall and went to a clothing store named *Chicco's*. This store was owned by the Bhamjee family who were successful business people of Indian origin.

While in the store, as we were looking at an assortment of caps, a female employee who had been following us as we were in the store (an annoying practice at these kind of places) finally came up to us.

"Can I assist you gentlemen in finding something?"

"Yes" I said. "We are looking for caps that are blank and have nothing printed on them." As I was saying this I kept using my hand to twist my brow into a frown, something I had seen Big Joe do, and was always funny to watch.

"Okay, but now why are you doing that to your forehead?"

We all laughed and the slight tension was immediately broken, and then right at that moment we heard the store owner shout something. She was seated behind the counter at a very elevated position where she could have a hawk eye view of every corner of the store. In an instant one of the store workers ran to the other end; we heard a slight fracas, followed immediately thereafter by the clapping of hands in rapid succession, and saw a woman, old enough to be our mother; her eyes were wide open with fear and was pleading with the store employees. She had been shoplifting. All this happened before we could blink twice.

"*Intshwareleng tlhe bathong ...*" "Please forgive me good people ..." she said as she clapped both hands in the typical African fashion when someone is pleading to a point of beseeching.

The store owner, who could speak fluent Setswana; as most Indian business people did, would hear none of it.

"*Wa utswa?!*" "You're stealing?!" she fumed. "Call the police!" These hardworking business people hated thieves with a passion, and would show no mercy whatsoever. And it was really hard to blame them.

Upon hearing that most dreaded word 'police' the woman was now in desperate earnest.

"*Ke motsetsi tlhe bathong intshwareleng ...*" "I just had a baby people please have mercy on me ..."

"*O motsetsi, o motsetsi wa utswa?*" "You just had a baby and yet you're are stealing?" the Indian store owner was not going to let up; new born baby or not. "Call the police."

At that point Body-Roc, Max, and I had seen and heard enough. We walked out of the store with our heads hung in shame. We were silent for a while as we strolled through the mall; each of us captivated in deep thought about what we had just witnessed. Max and I never spoke of the incident until many years later, when the softening vista of time had blunted the blows somewhat.

I did get the cap eventually, and later that term after schools reopened, we were soon aware that a retail store in Palapye had stocked the latest breakdance pants called 'balloon trousers'. We all coveted them, but we did not have the 19.99 to buy a pair. Max was the only one to acquire a cream white pair, and I believe that was the first and only time I was ever jealous of my friend.

He was wearing those same pants one Saturday evening when he walked into the dormitory and into a little tiff between Lekobe and Roukes.

"No, no, no I'm not going to keep quiet," Lekobe said.

"What's going on here?" Max asked. He was calm as usual.

Roukes immediately turned around with a big smile on his face that was meant to placate Max it turns out. On seeing Max, Lekobe immediately said, "Oh good Max you're here let me tell you what happened your …"

"Be quiet," Roukes interrupted him. "I would like to tell him myself if you don't mind. Thank you very much."

"Tell me what?" Max wanted to know. His calmness was disarming to say the least.

"Max …" Roukes said, "there's been a slight accident my man …"

"You call what happened a slight accident?" Lekobe interjected, and at that moment Big Joe entered the fray. This kind of thing was just too juicy to pass up.

"I wouldn't call it a slight accident either - more like major," he said with comical calmness.

"Hey I said be quiet," Roukes said.

"Alright, could someone please tell me what's going on?"

At that moment Roukes picked up Max's beloved radio tape that he had borrowed earlier that afternoon. There was only one problem though - it was missing the handle.

"Sorry Max … this is the accident I was trying to tell you happened."

Max just lifted his arms at about chest level, still maintaining his calm.

"This is not my radio."

"Atta boy Max, that's what I've been trying to tell Roukes that this is *not* your radio," Lekobe said triumphantly.

"Sorry Max, it fell and the handle broke."

"Like I said this is not my radio."

"I have got to agree with Max. I don't recognize this radio either," Big Joe said.

All this instigating was not helping matters, and Max was visibly getting upset just as the two had intended, and for the first time Roukes was getting angry himself; something I was seeing for the very first time.

"Hey, I said shut up, and that goes for the both of you." Big Joe was about to say something more, and Roukes realized this quick enough. "Not a word or I swear to God I'll make you snack on your teeth."

Big Joe understood immediately that he was treading on dangerous ground and wisely backed off. Lekobe on the other hand just would not shut up.

"Man you can do what you want, beat me up or whatever, but that does not absolve the fact that the falling of the radio that broke the handle was not violating any physical laws. Force of gravity was definitely at play." It was a typical Form Five Zero science student speaking.

In the end a compromise was reached, Lekobe finally shut up – thankfully. Max and Roukes talked it over in private, and then all was forgiven and peace was restored; after all the two were like brothers not because they are distantly related, but they just naturally get along even to this day.

***

The on again off again great field trip finally came to fruition, and we were all ecstatic. We were scheduled to leave Saturday very early in the morning. The night before we performed at the Palapye Community Center to add more money to our growing coffers, and I even borrowed a bag from Alice in which I could carry my belongings for the duration of the trip. I had a bag I could have used, but I just wanted to have something of her's with me. In my mind it looked to me that she was coming with me at least in spirit. We left school at around four in the morning that Saturday.

The journey was long and pleasant. We took in familiar sights, and when we drove through Gaborone later that morning I was able to point out my home, which you can see from the main Francistown Gaborone road, (known now as the Nelson Mandela drive) to some of my friends. Our home was not complete back in 1985, and I could tell that some of my friends were surprised that I lived in a house which at the time had no running water. I did not care for I was not ashamed of where I came from. Nor did I ever give the impression that I came from a filthy rich family, and that my dad owned the only palace in Botswana.

We arrived in Moshupa at around 10:00 am. There was a prize giving ceremony going on when we got there so the Moshupa students were all packed in the hall. The campus was very similar to ours, even their dormitories, and thus we immediately felt as if we belonged.

With us that day was a tall light skinned gentleman, who was also part of the Pantsula dancers and a Moshupa alumnus, a form 4 named

Keamogetse 'Ngamula Mzeetho ka Daa' Moilwa, but known to everyone as Mzeetho. The moment he peeked inside the hall as the ceremony was going on there were immediate screams of 'Mzeetho, Mzeetho ...' and it took a while for order to be restored. That in itself told us that Mzeetho had been a very popular student during his tenure there.

We were fed thereafter by the wonderful Mrs. Kgaodi the matron, as we were extremely hungry, and got our much needed rest. Our performance was scheduled for 2:00 pm that afternoon. After resting we hit the showers, which again were just like ours, but with one distinct advantage – these juniors had access to hot water. The shower was extremely refreshing especially after so long a journey. As we were bathing whenever one of the Moshupa students would as much as come inside the showers to even wash his hands; he was immediately chased away like a dog.

"Hey, hey, hey, can't you see we are taking a bath here ... get out!" all of us would say. There were some big and intimidating guys among us (like Molefi Sanoto for instance), mainly from the Pantsulas and Karatekas that the poor Moshupa students would have no choice, but to silently walk out of their own showers.

At this school it turned out that there was a young teacher who was a martial artist, and was feared by his students. Word was that he practiced at a local *dojo* in the village. During our Karate demonstration he decided to partake in our sparring exhibition. He was dressed in his *gi* and decided to take on Roukes 'Leruga' Nokane, our instructor, and a natural fighter to begin with. Looking back, I think this gentleman was mainly trying to show off his martial arts prowess to his students – a grave mistake it turned out, because Roukes not only won, but humiliated him right in front of his students.

You would think that he would have learned from that, but then he decided to engage another fighter we had brought with us named Alexander. He belonged to another martial arts club at Lotsane - the Kung Fu beat. Apart from Alexander they had other great fighters; guys like About Tekane, Isaac 'Jones' Masedame, and Metric Rathebe. The latter was known for being the only martial artist at our school who could do splits very easily, and high leg suspensions many a martial artists could only dream of.

When this young teacher faced Alexander he had no idea of the type of opponent he was dealing with, and I think he even underestimated him. The fight began, and after landing a couple of punches and a few kicking combinations, Alexander's confidence grew into showboating, and he began performing the fancy Kung Fu moves of which he was known for; much to the delight of the audience, because many of the moves Alexander was executing where the type you saw only in the movies. I could not help but feel sorry for the teacher, because one thing I realized was that he was good, but had not been training regularly. If he had, the degradation would not have happened, and who knows he maybe would have been a much worthier opponent.

Now when it was time for the Pantsula dancers to do their act, we could hardly hear the music because the chants of 'Mzeetho, Mzeetho, Mzeetho ...' were deafening as the Moshupa students cheered their long lost hero on. What was amazing was that Mzeetho was doing nothing spectacular.

This all came to an end when the *'Cheek to Cheek'* song *'Show me right'*, which was a hit at the time, reached its climax. This was when Ali and Shadrack Olopeng immediately went into their dance sequence, and when Ali let loose the Moshupa students suddenly had a new idol to cheer for. Ali then went wild, showing why he was the best Pantsula dancer there was, with moves that, even we had never seen, that made the audience literally stand up, and shout their approval, and just like that the 'Mzeetho, Mzeetho ...' chants were suddenly forgotten.

The breakdance show belonged to Benjamin 'Body-Roc' Thupe. It was not surprising because he was like Mzeetho a Moshupa alumnus. All in all it was a very successful show, and on our way to Kagiso where we were scheduled to perform that evening it was time for Roukes to give us a break down of our gate takings. Our goal like every club at school was to raise at least 300 Pula for the end of year party.

So when Roukes announced: "Ladies and gentlemen," and as he was saying this he was clapping his hands in anticipation. "We made SEVENTY EIGHT PULA!!!" he shouted, and we followed suit. "Give all yourselves a round of applause!"

I personally thought the amount of money did not justify the attendance I saw, I kept my thoughts private though. I was to learn some years later that my intuition had been spot on from Roukes himself. The actual amount was closer to three or four times the number we were given. In any case, none of us were too concerned about that as long as we had a great party at the end of the year, and taking into consideration the number of shows we performed during the course of the year; no one could bet against that.

When we arrived at Kagiso later that day, we were met with the bad news that we could not perform as scheduled. There was some mix up somewhere and miscommunication, because that night when we were supposed to perform; there was a beauty contest going on staged by the school. The news was of course met with disappointment.

Some people like Charlie even said, "Honestly I am not really surprised, this trip did not want to materialize, and it was forced."

All was not lost though. The former Kagiso students like Max, Phillip 'Star' Kaloute, and Roukes were back home and reunited with old friends. Max had told me so many stories about Kagiso and events that had happened. He told me of a fight that happened between two of his friends, one of whom was Samuel Sebobi, and how the other friend ended up with his foot stuck in a bucket as he was backing away from Sam's barrage of attacks. Max was glad to show me the exact spots where these historic events took place.

When it came to girls, especially with Alice in my life, I had always thought of myself as an oak. I could be swayed by no other woman. That conviction was about to be put to serious test at Kagiso that weekend - there were so many beautiful girls. I found myself looking with interest; that even Alice's image that had always succeeded in thwarting off such temptation was useless in face of this adversity.

When the beauty contest recessed so that the judges would tally the scores, the Kagiso school break dancers provided the entertainment. They were amateurs compared to us, and that is not meant to be disrespectful. I was later on a bit surprised when Caesar and Body-Roc appeared with the Kagiso dancers, later Dakune joined in, and there was an interesting duel between him and Kagiso's best dancer whose name happened to be Toy.

It did not take long for Two-Two and I to crash the party. When I walked onto the dance floor wearing my outfit, and my now famous cap, the cheers from the ladies made me feel like a rock star. I spotted

Max in the audience surrounded by a throng of female admirers. I was instantly caught up in the moment, and without really thinking about it I took off my cap and tossed it in Max's direction with style like I was some kind of icon. I had never seen so many eager hands try to reach out for a cap like it was some kind of elixir that gave eternal youth.

Among the contestants that day was a girl I had never met, but somehow looked familiar, like I had known her for many years. I did not know why until a few years later when I ran into Sebei who at the time was a Bachelor of Science student at the University of Botswana. The young lady in question turned out to be Sebei's younger sister. I saw her picture in his room and promptly told him I had seen her before, and Sebei told me when and where, and that was when I found out that they were family, which was why she looked so familiar.

We left the following day, which was Sunday morning, and headed back home. We arrived at school just before lunch. A few serious stomachs were disappointed, because by us arriving at the time that we did meant there was no extra chicken to go around. It was great to see Alice again, and the numerous temptations of the previous evening became a thing of the past, and whatever thoughts I had were locked secretly away in some place in my mind never to be opened again.

***

I could not quiet discern what it was, but as days went by that third term it seemed to me that Alice was somewhat becoming a little distant. It was too small for the eye to catch so to speak, but it was there nonetheless, and as always I was blinded by love to catch the bread crumb clues.

For instance, pictures were something that high school lovers exchanged on a regular basis and without question. Alice always took great pictures because she was very photogenic. I recall one time she had taken a bunch of photos, but would not part with even one. I was to hear later on that a good number of those turned up in someone's shrine.

The distance became a little more apparent when the break dance crew accompanied the ballroom dancers to Swaneng Hill School yet again. It was the third time that year that we had been to that campus, and the very first time ever that I had been on a field trip with her.

On our way back as we were cuddled at the back of the truck like lovers always did, I could sense an emptiness that was never there before. The form 5's whose course emphasis were science subjects like Alice, Max, Lekobe, Katu, Balisi, and Sebei had recently taken the Pre Entry Science Examination Course also known as PESC. This was a program offered by the university where students took a special test, and if successful underwent a seven month course, which when well completed gave the student an opportunity to pursue a Bachelor of Science degree, and later specialize in such disciplines as Engineering and Medicine.

Alice had taken the exam, and on our way back she told me that someone had written to her, telling her that she had in fact passed. The results had not been announced yet. The question that bothered me was who did she know who would be purveyed to that kind of information? Also this person had to be living in Gaborone. At the time Alice was merely a country girl (again no disrespect intended), she did not know much about Gaborone, judging from the conversations we had or a lot of people from the city for that matter. So who was this supposed fairy that kept her informed on things even the school had at the time no knowledge of?

A few days later she was to tell me that the guy who had been hitting on her all this time had said he was coming to visit soon. What on earth was all this about? I would ask myself time and again as the subject of this fellow came up, and who was slowly but surely becoming a regular in our conversations.

I think the answer to that question was due to my misplaced love, trust, and to some extent arrogance. Since it had taken me such a long time to win Alice's affection I had thought, and wrongly so, that our affair would go on until thy kingdom come. It was inconceivable to me that she could fall in love with someone else, and this is where I was blinded by my arrogance and vanity. I had a lot to learn about life's hard lessons, and I was about to have a very rude awakening - one that I was to remember for a long time. One thing I was certain of at the time is this: I would have given that girl the world had she stayed true to me.

That was also the term of the sub team tournament that started on Thursday and ended on Monday. Of the four sub teams ours, Callies, also known as 'The Romans', were the perennial whipping boys of the tournament over the years, and the strongest was Chiefs also known as the 'Lotsane Bombshell,' and had the largest following.

That year we were still considered weak even though on our team we had players like Sebei, Montshiwa 'Wagga' Montshiwa, and the great Diirilwe 'D-One' Matoto. Also that year we recruited a player from Chiefs, who was also a form 4 at the time, and small in stature called Tshwenyego 'Carlos' Tawana. He was so skilled a player that he like Lepholetha would become legendary at Lotsane.

Each team contributed 45 Pula, and in the end after playing each other the team with the most points won the 75 Pula first prize, second place got 55 Pula, third place 45 Pula, and 35 Pula went to the last placed team, a position I was told had been entrusted onto Callies from time immemorial. No one would dare bet against that happening again.

When the tournament took place there was always a festive mood around the school, which turned out to be tradition at that time of the year. Everyone wore colors that were associated with their team. Callies wore blue, Executive Cosmos white, Santos orange, and Chiefs red. In these tournaments even players who were not part of the school team, but had rudimentary skills of the game played. So you would see a player like say Choiza go up against a player of City's caliber. The fun part about this tournament was that many times it reminded us that these great players were mortal after all.

The first game that Thursday afternoon was between Santos and Chiefs. Robot was a staunch Santos supporter and was on the sidelines cheering his team on, but he and every Santos supporter that day and for the duration of the tournament were heart broken. This time it was Santos who were the whipping boys of the tournament that year. What was worse was that they did not score a single goal the entire contest.

Callies on the other hand were just unlucky, we could have ended second or who knows even first place on the final log. Our very first game we tied with Executive Cosmos, and we would have won that game had the great Diirilwe Matoto not miraculously missed a goal that seemed much easier to score. Had D-One not missed that goal, we would have earned maximum points that would have put us at least at second place, instead we were third place, and not rock bottom as everyone expected. Chiefs won the tournament that year as expected and Executive Cosmos got second place by the skin of their teeth.

At our end of year party D-One talked about that miss. The one Saturday we worked toward and waited for had finally arrived. That was the day set aside for many clubs to throw a party and celebrate. This was also when a new committee was elected for the next year. I was elected team manager; not to be confused with coach, but business affairs. Our Callies party was a success, and even made more entertaining by our guest of honor, a fellow student and a form 5 who was highly respected, and was also the deputy head boy named Baatlhudi Molatlhegi. He had a terrific sense of humor, and made it worth our while to wait for the delicious food we could not linger to get our hands on. The genius of Baatlhudi was that he was aware of our anxiety and thus did not over extend himself.

We talked about our accomplishments that year, and our relative success in the just ended tournament. This was when D-One got to talk about the goal he missed that would have at the very least given us second place.

"Man that ball," he said, "if only I had kicked it differently." We did not mind at all. Diirilwe was still our hero; after all he had scored that all important goal against Lobsec that put us in pole position to be national champions. We could take the miss against Executive Cosmos any day. The rest of the celebrations went on without a glitch, and there were only a handful of people at the dining hall that day for supper, because the rest of us were stuffed to a point that just the thought of food was enough to make us regurgitate.

Third term was also the time when the administration with the help of the prefects picked from the form 4's the prefects for the next year. I suppose my chances were as good as anyone especially since I was a class monitor. Many, myself included, considered me to be a shoe-in, as well as Alice. We all wanted to be prefects for the simple reason that it would look good on our permanent records.

One Sunday evening as Max and I were getting ready for evening prep Lekobe looked at me and said, "Sebati, I can see you are campaigning to be a prefect. Don't raise your hopes too high son, because you may just lose." It was a taunt and I fell for it, which is all Lekobe needed.

This was to go on and on until one day I simply snapped and said, "Man, okay yes I'm campaigning. I want to be a prefect when was that such a bad thing? Just because you failed last year does not mean I will. Heck if not prefect why not head boy?" We were in bed after lights off and everyone laughed.

"Sebati a head boy that would be a sight wouldn't it?" Pema said.

"I tell you what as a head boy Sebati would say once angered," Max said and then started to mimic the sound of my voice, which invited more laughter. My chances of being a head boy that year were just as good as those of Al Capone elected Pope; so it was flattering to hear them talk about me in that regard. The prefects were chosen and I missed out. Festus was picked and so was Mzeetho, and it was agreed upon that he (Mzeetho) would be our prefect the following year.

As we were approaching mid November another crew competition was in the works. It was dubbed *'the greatest ever 2'*. A date for the battle was set, which was Friday November 15th. The final exam for the form 5's was set to begin on Tuesday November 19th. I would think Max was aware that this would be his final battle, and I believe he prepared himself mind, body, and spirit for this occasion.

The crews were set up differently this time. Tso, Maulter, and I were on the same side like before only that this time we had Caesar and another muscular fellow named Ballman Kealotswe, a Kung Fu practitioner, who had just recently taken a liking to break dance.

Ballman and I were in the same class, and had a brother named Blackie. When English teachers needed to explain to students the difference between 'introvert' and 'extrovert' they always used to say *'a typical example of that are the Kealotswe brothers, Davis and Ballman'*. Teachers referred to Blackie as Davis, because that was the name he gave himself. Now of the two brothers he was the extrovert. Ballman on the other hand rarely raised his voice. The only time when I heard him do was when he and Nancy got into a verbal altercation.

In the heat of the moment Ballman said to her, "Thank God Almighty you're from a poor family. I hate to even imagine what we'd be going through if your parents' cash flow was not challenged." This was delivered with incisive accuracy; every word was like a dagger. Blackie I imagine would have gone for the kill.

Our rivals were led by Dakune and Max, my dance partner Two-Two was on the other side which was odd. Although Max and Caesar maintain that this second battle was the greatest ever I still strongly disagree. For me it was a disaster.

In the first competition Two-Two and I wore matching break dance outfits. Maulter, Tso, and Breke's were basic; grey sweatpants and a grey sweater that was part of our school uniform. We all agreed that we would all wear the basic outfits that Tso and the rest had. I welcomed a different look this time as I was already tired of my regular outfit.

However before our performance, I was surprised to see Maulter and Tso dressed in completely different and much nicer looking attire despite our agreement. Max and Dakune's crew performed first. As we waited our turn in a nearby classroom we could hear the screams from the audience. That right there told me that things were going to be much different this time around.

When our turn came we did not impress at all, but I had my own personal concern. Alice was not in the audience. This to me was unacceptable. She was supposedly my life, light, and inspiration why could she not be there? It got from bad to worse. Besides our performance being a disaster, we lacked imagination and basically did the same moves we performed the last time. The only highlight of our performance was Caesar's wicked backspin that was unmatched that he even got a long ovation. Our opponents on the other hand were outstanding. We were dancing to 'Lisa Lisa and the Cult Jam's' *'I wonder If I Take You Home.'*

Also on that day Lekobe, Katu, and the usually reserved Pema were at the fore front of the crowd when it came to heckling.

"Alright Sebati those eyes are a little too big, make them a little smaller," Lekobe shouted.

These were my dorm mates, I had lived with them for the past year and I knew their remarks were not meant to humiliate me – crude as they were.

"S.B., S.B." Katu shouted, "man I tell you, you are a superstar my boy, you got fans. The ladies are ready to throw their panties at you with their phone numbers written on them. Oh, I forgot ... we're in boarding school, and none of them have a phone number to give ... tough luck son it's not going to happen tonight ... sorry." Everyone was in stitches by this time. S.B is short for Sebati.

Katu was saying this because 1985 was the year when the Michael Jackson mania was starting to wane a little (at least in Botswana) as 1983 and 1984 was when the craze was at its peak, and the stories of beautiful girls tossing panties at the mega star when on stage was always a hot topic among teenage boys.

When the critics felt someone was spending a little more time on the dance floor than they felt necessary, one of them, Lekobe in particular world say, "Alright ... alright ...you can take a seat now – next."

There was a young handsome teacher that night named Mr. Kgotla, who was taking pictures, and later when I saw the photos; I could clearly see the hecklers in the background led of course by none other than Lekobe.

It only got worse when we faced off with Max and Dakune's crew. To this day I do not know where Max got all that energy and inspiration from. That he was a great dancer was beyond dispute, but that night this fellow was simply possessed. Each move he made was followed by one ovation after another. As for us we were made fun of and even mocked.

"Bale ba imelwa ke di jesi." "Now for those the jerseys are just too heavy on them." Some people in the crowd would say amid the laughter. That was just the beginning, Maulter and Tso decided to do an acrobatic move where one would lift the other and the legs would spread in the air like a helicopter, and then upon landing the one who had been lifted would perform the same act on his partner. Maulter and Tso had done this move before at the last crew competition, and even in practice, but on this night they seemed to be rushing it, and while in the air with his head facing the hard cement floor Maulter slipped through Tso's hands, and fell head first with a loud thud to the floor. I immediately looked away.

Miraculously Maulter did not suffer a concussion, but he lay on the floor without moving for over a minute. One of the most important things in a teenager's life is not getting embarrassed especially in front of a multitude of his peers; that I think ranks just above food and shelter. This was a very humiliating experience for my friend I would assume, and I really felt bad for him. Even Cromwell of all people later made an underhanded comment as far as Maulter's accident was concerned.

"Man those break dancers' heads are made of rock."

The other crew even had an 'ace' up their sleeve, because just when we thought the nightmare was over; they surprised us by introducing a female dancer whom they had kept hidden. Her name was Victoria, a form 4 and one of the most desirable girls at the time, and equally beautiful. What happened was that Dakune, sly as ever, was holding secret sessions with this girl teaching her basic moves. She turned out to be a very quick learner and a natural, and when she was unleashed we were stunned.

We lost and lost badly. Big Joe was extremely disappointed at me. He was also one of the judges. This time around students were given that rare opportunity to do the honors.

"Sebati what was that all about? I know you can dance far better than what I saw today what happened man?" I had no answer.

Allim added, "also all those sequences like the clapping of hands and the back glides is stuff you already did last time, we as the audience were expecting much more from you."

The night was a disaster no doubt, but disaster or not, I still could not comprehend as to why Alice had not attended, maybe it was for the best under the circumstances, but it would have been great to have a shoulder to lean on afterwards, added to that this in all likelihood was the last performance of the year. Later on Jugi was to tell me that the sweatpants I was wearing were way too tight and revealed everything, which is why I could hear furtive gasps from the women hard by. I saw the pictures later and Jugi was right.

The next day, Saturday was like any other, but for some strange reason that to this day still eludes me, and it had nothing to do with the previous night's disaster; I stayed in the dormitory studying, something I never did that year. At around 3:00 pm or so I took a short break and stood in front of the dormitory, from here I had a clear view of the academic area, and then caught a glimpse of Alice walking northward toward the Chemistry Lab, she had on a brown mini skirt that I really liked. I smiled at this coincidence, and was going to tell her about it when we met later that evening. As it turned out I never got the chance.

That evening another strange thing happened – no one knew where Alice was. I waited for an hour or so and sent someone again to call her. The girl came back with the same debilitating news; she was nowhere to be found. This was unusual to say the least. I went back to the dormitory and again stayed there and did not go to entertainment night. I was not unduly worried, but that now familiar uneasy feeling that was just within comprehension came to me, but I still could not grasp its meaning. Little did I know that calamity like I would never envision was about to strike.

Later that evening just before lights off, my new dormitory mate, who had replaced Fungwa named Potso Piet came up to me, and in a somber voice said, "Sebati, I need to talk to you …"

I had bought some candy from him a few days earlier on credit, and naturally assumed that he was attempting to collect a debt.

"Potso, I'll have it for you on Monday man relax," I said.

"No, I'm not talking about that."

"Okay man, but can't it wait until tomorrow?"

"Well … I suppose so." It seemed whatever it was he wanted to tell me, he had reached that decision with great difficulty.

I finally got a chance to meet Alice the next day, which was Sunday afternoon just after lunch. To me she looked quite different from the person I knew. Perhaps it was because she had trimmed her hair, and her beauty had miraculously diminished, and this time her distance was even more perceptible.

"Alice, where were you last night?"

"I was at the dormitory."

"That's not true Alice, I sent more than three people to call you and no one knew where you were."

"Well, I don't know who could have been telling you that, but I was at my dormitory." She was lying I could tell, and being defiant at the same time, it seemed to me that she was turning into that person I had encountered in the beginning, who not only thwarted my advances, but humiliated me. Things were different now, and I was getting angry by the minute.

"Alice, I can be the nicest guy in the world, but if you keep lying to me we're definitely going to have a problem. Now, I'll ask you one more time; *where* were you last night? Because we both know that you were not at your dormitory." I think she could tell now that I meant business.

"I was with Ramasia." *Ramasia?* Now why on God's green earth did that name sound so familiar? In a blink of an eye I realized who she was talking about, the supposed stalker, the fellow who had been hitting on her (or so she claimed) whom she had met at the Science Fair. I just felt my whole world crumble in an instant. This only could mean one thing, and one thing only – my beloved Alice was in love with another guy! I could not believe it, but the nightmare had not even begun.

"Ramasia, who the *hell* is Ramasia?"

"The guy I've been telling you about."

This was incredible. This bold confession had caught me off guard, and succeeded in sapping all the strength out of me.

"What?! ... Alice, did you just hear what you just said to me?"

"Yes." It was the typical defiance of someone caught, but trying to hide the shame with the only tool available. I suppose she thought I knew more about what had happened; when the truth was that I was in complete darkness all this time.

"You were with him all night;" my teeth were gritted, "is that why nobody knew where you were?"

"Yes."

"Where were you?"

"At the parking area." Another bold face lie. It has always been in my nature to be very gentle with the opposite sex, and not even raise my hand no matter how badly provoked. This was a virtue also instilled into me by my father to never be violent toward women, but this girl stretched me to the limit. It was just miraculous that I did not slap her as I very much wanted to - something I am not proud to admit.

At this point Dakune came to us, and asked me if I could let Alice go and call his girlfriend for him. I flatly refused and later felt bad about it. After he left I heaved a very heavy sigh. I had no choice but to ask her the one question I dreaded to ask, because the answer was obvious.

"Alice, are you in love with this guy?"

"Yes," she answered softly. I was floored. Not my Alice of all people!

"Alice," I remember saying, "what if I were to do the same thing and tell you right to your face that I was in love with another woman how would you feel?"

"I'd be hurt." Goodness gracious! If only she could tell little white lies perhaps the pain would not have been so bad. She was leaving me no choice.

"Well, I suppose this is the end of the road for us."

"What do you mean?" For the first time I could see that I had gotten the two timing lass's full attention.

"I mean it's over."

"No."

"What do you mean no? Do you expect me to share you with someone else?"

"No, but I still love you." The thing that surprises me, even to this day, is that she was delusional enough to think that she could carry on a relationship with me and the other guy at the same time, and have me pretend like nothing happened.

"We're beyond that." I must say I was getting no pleasure in all this, every word I was saying was causing me great pain like I never imagined. There was nothing I wanted more at that moment than to squeeze the life out of this guy's scrawny neck – the guy who had succeeded in putting a wedge between us - with her total and willing participation of course. Perhaps it was best that I never met the guy then.

In the end I was forced to end the relationship. It was going to happen sooner or later, because I believe, looking back, I was perhaps way too serious for both of us. That and really, let the truth be told: the girl never really loved me as a person; she was only in love with the idea of dating a 'cool cat', who had suddenly become popular among the ladies. So it is hard not to say that breakdance played a major role in her agreeing to be my girlfriend to begin with; even though she always denied that to the end - plus we were both young, and had not really experienced life in general.

Later I was to find out that she flaunted this guy in public at the academic area, and around campus while I was at the dormitory. Everybody was shocked. This right there and then told me that the girl had absolutely no regard for our relationship, that is if there ever was one to begin with, because she obviously took me for granted. What hurt the most was that she even got to have sex with him. And all this happened right under my nose, and I was the last to know. She had played me for a fool - played me like an old piano.

Potso, it turns out has seen them together at the river that night on his way from Palapye so did a lot other people including Dakune, a guy named Fish Dingalo, Ballman, and a chap named Lamech Mamuze. That was what Potso had wanted to tell me the night before. Most of the damning facts I was to get from Dakune when I went to him to apologize for my behavior earlier on. What I did not understand was why any of my friends did not come to tell me what was going on; that is not including my brother Max (and Two-Two) as he was just in the dark as I was. On the other hand, the news of this betrayal, and Alice's indiscretion, hit the boarding house like a typhoon. This was because she was well respected and admired; for everyone thought the girl was too classy for such kind of behavior and angelic. Well, I would say she was *maybe* an angel but definitely *not* a saint.

"Man Sebati," Tonkana said. "How can you let some s.o.b. dip and wet his you know what into your girl's you know what, and let him get away with it?" That's how graphic things could get in a room full of boys.

"I wouldn't if I had known." I tried to sound valiant but it was useless.

"You see, the disadvantages of having a beautiful girl, because yours are not the only pair of eyes lusting over her." When was this nightmare going to end? I wondered to myself.

Strange as it may sound, Tonkana was speaking from a place of love, but in a very twisted way undeniably. Everyone, including me, could tell that he was feeling my pain. At that moment Two-Two dragged me away sparing me more misery. Besides Max and Allim, and to some extent Sebei, Two-Two was a constant companion who helped, and was with me throughout this whole ordeal. Believe it or not even Festus of all people was there for me. This no doubt had to have been one of the most traumatic moments of my teenage years, and for the very first time in my life that night I cried myself to sleep over a girl. I cried for the love I had worked so hard to earn, and lost it in an instant. I cried for what could have been, but *never* to be. This was made worse by my very vivid imagination of what took place when the two were alone, and intimate, in some dark corner.

I tried to find solace in whoever would listen, even from my classmate Thuto Tomeletso, who to this day can recall those moments as if they happened ten minutes ago. In the end I realized that it would be up to me to face my demons head on, and slay them one by one. I was not looking forward to the summer break like I normally would. It looked like it was going to be a long and painful endless summer; as I wondered how I was going to shake this 'love Jones' with no friends around. But one never knows what he is capable of until tested to the brink of beyond human endurance.

Chapter 13

Incredible as it may sound, Alice and I attempted to reconcile. In spite of all that had happened it was hard to let go that easily and let the other guy win, and the person who made this reconciliation possible was none other than Jewawa Febion Khembo, my partner in crime. But alas, the magic we had before was lost and gone forever. Max my brother shared my pain, and told me to just go with the flow and see how far that took me.

I did go with the flow, but in my eyes Alice was tainted and filthy. She was no longer that smooth and silky fabric I had known. The hard cold fact was that she was in love with someone else - no matter how hard she tried to hide it. Especially since this was the beginning stages of a new love when the excitement was at its utmost, the honeymoon period, and sadly I could relate, because I had been there not too long ago. She was smitten by the guy I could tell, and that was even more painful to bear.

The form 5's took their exams and gradually the size of our dormitory was getting smaller until the very last day, which happened to be the first week of December. I took the train with the last group of students including Dakune and Alice. When we reached Gaborone as she was headed to Molepolole for the National Service orientation (*Tirelo Sechaba* better known as TS) we said our goodbyes, and just like that the tumultuous and bitter sweet academic year that was 1985 had come to an end.

That summer break proved to be harder than I had first imagined. Alone now, and away from the familiar surroundings of Lotsane, I was able to ponder my situation. Why had Alice betrayed me in a way that I could have never imagined? Why didn't I see this coming in spite of all the warning signs? Was I paying a price for what I had done to Joyce Sebolao, the one and only girl who truly loved me? Why did I even pursue this girl so hard? When I could have just given up, and looked elsewhere or better yet stayed true to Joyce; by so doing had I brought this sorrow upon myself? For a long time I was wallowed in anger and self-pity, and was grateful that during these times, Terrence Jacobs, a friend from Lotsane, who also happened to be Festus's dorm mate was with me all this time, and let me burden him with my sorrows. Terrence turned out to be a friend indeed as he was in need during that time. I have never forgotten his kindness to this day.

    I also got my results of the math exam I rewrote. I had passed, but not exactly with the grade that I had anticipated, but good enough to put me in the science classes next year when I repeated my form 4. I also recall writing a long and angry letter to Alice as the impact of the breakup had finally hit me like a tidal wave. I said things in the heat of the moment that I later regretted. I did much later apologize to her, and then that chapter of our lives was finally closed forever.

    That summer break I had the pleasure of meeting the great *Sensei* Vusumuzi Mwalimu Ndlovu (late), the founder of Tsosamotse Karate Club, the club where I was first introduced to the art at age 11. *Sensei* Vusi as he was known, had gone to America to study TV production and film, which was why I never got to meet him until that December in 1985 shortly after his return, but I had heard all about him, he was a legend and to some extent still is in the martial arts world. Meeting him could not have happened at a better time, because I now trained at my childhood *dojo* with great zeal that in no time I was to forget my pain.

    I looked forward now more than ever to 1986. That year was to prove to be my greatest redemption in ways that I never imagined. I still smile whenever I look back at that blissful year. God bless Lotsane for all eternity! I sometimes shudder at the thought I once had of wishing to be accepted at Lobsec for my form 4. And that is said not to put down that great school, but to thank the high heavens that I had ended up at Lotsane after all.

Book Two 1986

Chapter 14

The night leading to the countdown to 1986 was a hot one. The full moon seemed brighter than usual. My parents were out of town, and Rama was with some friends somewhere partying the night away. I was alone at home, and my thoughts kept me company – perhaps too much company, as I was still hurting inside though not that much anymore.

The moment the clock struck midnight the celebrations suddenly erupted, and I could not help but wonder what Alice was doing right at that moment. I could see her celebrating in her brown mini skirt, and having a great time under the summer moonlight, and when that particular thought hit me, I felt that she and everything that happened were part of history now. It was a miraculous feeling that took me by surprise. I looked forward to 1986 with renewed hope.

I arrived a few weeks later with the form 4's as I was a form 4 myself. The form 5's always arrived at least two weeks before. It was great to see my old dorm 12 buddies like Mathabathi and Tonkana. Mzeetho was our new prefect, but then I missed Max terribly. The same issue of moving just like last year reared its ugly head again. Dorm 12 was still the most coveted dorm in the boarding house, and now as form 5's some of my dorm mates from last year would be required to move. I had no such concerns since I was still a form 4.

I immediately occupied Max's bed as I was still holding on to my absent brother. One of my new dorm mates, was a gentleman I knew very well from our temporary classes way back in February of 1985 named Steven Sekute, who was very brilliant, and also strong willed and argumentative.

It was also great to see Allim, Two-Two, and the rest of the gang. Allim even mentioned that there was a girl they had seen whom they believed would be right for me. I could not wait to see who she was, and possibly meet her as I had not seen all the *manyewane*, but word was that she was stunningly beautiful.

Allim and company were right, the girl was very pretty, her name was Anthea Toni Williams, she was of mixed blood origin from Cape Town, and I soon found out that she had a brother who was also a form 4 named Ferdinand Ivor Williams whom we later nicknamed 'Harare' or 'Mr. short story long' as he seemed to say more than was really necessary. Her family lived in Palapye, but then very soon, and to my utter disappointment, I found out that she had a steady boyfriend, who was not a student, but a local from Palapye just like her, and thus I decided not to pursue her any further. I was not about to wreck a happy home, but Anthea and I were to become very good friends.

As the form 4's kept coming this meant that the situation of the form 5's in our dormitory was becoming precarious by the day; no one except the form 4's and prefects were guaranteed a bed in dorm 12, not with the form 4's arriving on a daily basis and the common rooms filling up.

Some like Thuso Godson Ramodimoosi, whom to this day I am still surprised, was never chosen to be a prefect, actually moved out on his own. Things came to a head when a form 4 named Bonang Mosupi had to move to dorm 12. He had spent the night before in one of the form 5's dormitory, and now with him moving to dorm 12 as he was entitled meant some people were going to have to relocate.

Relocating was a prospect no one was looking forward to, because the destination would either be Block A or Block B. To further complicate matters, since the Block C common room was filling up the assigned prefect, a fellow by the name of Boipuso better known as 'BP' or 'Ace' had moved into dorm 12, which meant the dreaded axe was going to fall on a few. Those in imminent danger were Steven, Moeti, Mathabathi, Lucky 'Melba' More, and Tonkana.

Now, since nobody was willing to go the boarding master did the onus of enforcing the move. He came to dorm 12 one night accompanied by the new head boy Kgotso Monamoledi, who was very big and muscular, and looked fierce. Kgotso was in fact a very gentle and kind individual I was to find out much later.

Kgotso had tried on many occasions to persuade either of the guys to move voluntarily, but his pleas fell on deaf ears, which is why he came with the BM that night. They arrived just before lights off, and we had no idea what a long night it was going to be.

BM began by saying, "Alright boys it seems we have a problem in dorm 12, but I am here to tell you that this problem is about to be resolved. So before I go any further I am asking for three volunteers since three people will need to move."

There was complete silence. This was dorm 12 and no one was prepared to move. Sensing the danger coming Steven Sekute cleared his throat.

"Mr. BM, and really I say this respectfully, I don't see why anyone should move," he said.

"Really and how so?"

"We are all happy here and I don't see the need to break up a happy home sir."

"Well that's your way," BM said "not mine."

"With all due respect BM that's dictatorship," Steve protested vehemently.

"Be that as it may but tonight three people are going to move."

The argument went back and forth for a good hour it seemed. To me the whole scenario was entertaining, and ours was the only dormitory whose lights were on at that time, because Steve was relentless in his argument as to why form 5's had just the same rights as the form 4's to live in dorm 12.

In the midst of this heated debate, Moeti divulged a very crucial piece of evidence that I thought would have, and so did everyone else in dorm 12 that night, swung the tide in Steven Sekute's favor.

"Kgotso lived with the form 5's last year when he was a form 4 why can't form 4's do the same?" he asked.

It was true. A few months after Dixie Ndlovu's tragic death, Kgotso moved from dorm 20 to dorm 2 to take Dixie's place. It made sense to us, because he was obviously being groomed to be the next head boy, and since he was a bit older than the rest of us form 4's it was only befitting that he be among the older students.

To this day I still find it a bit puzzling as to why Steve never pounced at that loop hole like a hungry cat on a mouse. Was it because someone else other than him thought about it first? I am saying this because his response to that was astounding to say the least from someone like him.

"Yes, what business did he have living with those guys anyway?" It was a weak argument, and with that Steve blew a golden opportunity.

At this point I think BM had had enough, because as Steve continued pleading his case BM was busy jotting down something on his miniature notebook - a list of names it turns out. A wise move also, because Steven Sekute was still grinding his axe.

"Okay," he said at last. "I have come up with the names of people who are going to move to the dormitories they've been assigned here henceforth." The atmosphere was tense once again.

"Steven Sekute dorm 2, Moeti Matlhabaphiri dorm 2, and Alfred Ntseane dorm 5." BM had laid down the law, and was not prepared to brook any further argument.

As he and Kgotso were leaving BM looked at me and said to Kgotso, "What about him isn't he a form 5?"

"No BM ... he is a special kind of form 4."

"I see," BM said. He could be a man of very few words when he chose to. He was well known for never forgetting names and faces. I had only spoken to him once, and that was in early 1985, which is why I probably looked familiar to him.

The trio were given less than 48 hours to move to their new dormitories. Moeti seemed to be the only one resigned to his fate, and actually moved the next day. His only complaint was where he was going to get more glue to paste the numerous magazine posters he had on his locker, but in the end he moved without a hitch. Tonkana was defiant only in rhetoric, because a few days later he and Ace came up to Mathabathi, and begged him to move to dorm 5 instead. Tonkana even stated some none existent ailment as one of the reasons why he needed to remain in dorm 12, and that in an emergency Ace would be there and know what to do. All this was a ruse of course.

And Mathabathi agreed to move not because he bought Tonkana's cock and bull story, but his best friend and class mate Kepaletswe 'KP CK' Madeluka lived in dorm 5. That alone I think made Mathabathi agree; otherwise he would have told Tonkana to get lost. Steven Sekute would prove to be problematic though. He kept coming up with one excuse after another as to why he could not move.

In the meantime the bed in dorm 2 needed to be filled. And then the unthinkable happened. One morning Kgotso came up to me and said, "Hey Sebati would you mind moving to dorm 2?" A sweat broke at the back of my neck and under my armpits. Yes, I *did* mind, because I did not want to move to dorm 2, but then with Kgotso's imposing figure hovering around me I was too afraid to refuse. Later Kgotso said he felt bad asking me, because he could tell I did not want to move and I did it only out of fear. Needless to say I am very glad that he did. Dorm 2 was to become my home away from home for the remainder of my stay at Lotsane.

Besides Kgotso the head boy who was also our prefect, I became good friends with Moses Galeboe, who like Cromwell was a gifted artist, other members of dorm 2 were George Mackenzie a colored from Werda who we later nicknamed 'the Wiseman', Motseothata 'Dizzy' Keabetswe from Moshupa, Thomas 'Starks Cocksheba' Mosenki from Moshupa, Isaac Mafokate who like Cross was from Bobonong, Ernest 'MaEnzo' Gosalamang from Moshupa, Patrick Fani and his best friend Pheneas Kgari also from Bobonong, Mothusi Mompati who like Moses, Hex, and Caesar was from Letlhakane, Ontumetsi 'Reverend' Marokane from Moshupa, Gaolatlhe Modibedi from Lobatse, and of course Moeti Matlhabaphiri who had attended Naledi Secondary School in Gaborone.

This was my newest family after my dorm 12 days. They were all form 5's; meaning that I knew all of them very well. I was a form 4 again, but technically in their eyes I was a form 5 meaning that I adapted very quickly.

One of the main reasons why these dorms in Block A were unpopular was because everyone thought that since this block was the closest to the BM's house, it meant he paid more attention to these dorms than he would others, but I soon found out that it made no difference whether you lived in dorm 1 or 20, because BM could only be at one place at a time and had to rely on his prefects. If anything dorm 2 was a much better place than the 1986 dorm 12 could have ever been. The 1985 dorm 12 aura was gone and a new one waited in dorm 2. I later thanked Kgotso repeatedly for thinking of me.

Very quickly I was getting to know the new student body quiet well. I was known to quite a few of them, mainly those from Moshupa and Kagiso. The two schools where we had gone to perform the previous year. I was placed in form 4 Three, a class that had a few of the Kagiso and Moshupa alumni. I made friends quickly among my new classmates, both male and female, and it was simply great.

Among the friends I made was a gentleman named Joseph Makabe who we later nicknamed 'Strong,' because he liked to use the word as emphasis. For instance, if he had the hots for a girl or found her attractive he would say she was 'strong'. It was him and another Kagiso alumnus named Victor Tsebe whom we nicknamed 'Honey', because of the way he wrote his name it looked like the word 'Nectar'. These two gentlemen were to become my lab partners and I learned a lot from them.

I also became very good buddies with a lady by the name of Ruth Tseleng Botlhole. We were in the same class. She was originally from Ramotswa, but attended Naledi Secondary School for her junior certificate. We became so close that she later told me that there was a rumor going around the girls' hostel that me and her were an item; that is how close we were.

All this time Steve was still holding out at dorm 12, and the situation was getting even more complicated. He even suggested that he could as a compromise sleep in the common room right next door, but still keep his locker in dorm 12. This certainly was unacceptable, and the longer he was holding out; the longer he was delaying the settling of a new student. In the end this state of affairs got so out of hand that it was escalated to the deputy headmaster.

Mr. Kabelo Mosimanegape Keakile (no relation to Cisky as far as I know) was the new deputy headmaster who had replaced Mr. Maganu. I later found out that he held a Master's degree (Honors) in English from one of the elite Universities in Canada. He had an excellent command of the English language, and was well liked because of his simplicity.

When Steve arrived at his office one afternoon upon being summoned, Mr. Keakile was intent on ending this tomfoolery once and for all. So when Steve presented himself, Mr. Keakile, being the formidable man that he was, immediately went on the offensive.

"Don't even open your mouth to offer a greeting young man, because I will be the only one doing the talking. I don't want to hear a word, not even a sound, or a grunt, and not even hear you clear your throat. What you are going to do is listen and thereafter do as instructed."

Steve I can imagine knew right there and then that he had met more than his match in Mr. Keakile.

"When I am done talking," Mr. Keakile continued, "you Steven Sekute will turn around head to dorm 12 pack your belongings and then move to dorm 1 right this instant. I am not even going to ask you if you understand because by answering you will be making a sound."

Steve swallowed hard and just as he was about to turn around and carryout to the letter what he was instructed, Mr. Keakile very much as an afterthought said, "Oh, and just to make sure that what I said will actually register through that thick skull of yours just bend over for a little." And just to show that he meant business, Mr. Keakile went on to give Steve five of the best with his cane. I ran into Steve just after his encounter with Mr. Keakile. He was by one of the numerous taps around campus washing his hands.

"I am only moving because Mr. Keakile ordered me to. If it was BM I would have refused outright." And then that's when he went on to tell me what had transpired.

To me it was just unbelievable that a simple issue of moving from one dorm to another could escalate to the administration office, and specifically to the second most powerful man in school. I was in a way impressed by Steve's resiliency, and many years later as a friend said when I told him this story - hard headedness.

Since I already understood the importance of having a good foundation, I hit the books hard. I studied at every opportunity even waking up early in the morning, which is something I enjoy very much even to this day. I had a young Math teacher named Ms. Sara Pearson whom I still hold in high regard. This Welsh woman made math fun and easy, and for the first time in my life I started getting excellent grades on a consistent basis. I was also determined to win the best student prize at the annual prize giving ceremony held in November, just before the form 5's wrote their finals. The previous year I had to watch others get theirs, and I was eager to be among the winners this year. I chased this goal with single minded determination.

During math, I sat in front of the class as I did in most other subjects, next to a lady with whom I had also become fast friends with named Mabulili 'Lilist' Pelaelo. She was a Macha Secondary School alumnus, and we were able to talk with nostalgic joy about the people we both knew who had also attended her former school; people like Katu Phori and Diirilwe 'D-One' Matoto. One thing Lilist had was a very beautiful smile that was hard to ignore let alone forget.

Since this was the beginning of the new academic year with new students that meant that the 'Beginners Concert' issue again raised its ugly head. Hotstix was the new chairman of the entertainment committee, a committee of which I was a member (I was elected by my classmates toward the end of last year), and thus the only form 4 in this elite group. Hotstix, with Legoro's blessings, was eager to get this show on the road that some *manyewane* even started calling him *'Beginners Concert'*. He went from one form 4 class to another demanding participation.

"Listen up people," he said, and what was worse was that he was attempting to deliver his message in Setswana, and when he did it sounded something like this: "The headmaster has given me bones, you will partake in this concert and I am not even going to kneel down and pray for you." Everyone laughed. What he really meant to say was "the headmaster has put me in charge so you are going to participate whether you like it or not so I am not even going to beg you."

Many of my classmates looked at me and I could see the questions on their faces.

"I never participated last year. It was more like volunteering."

At that moment as I was saying this to some of my classmates within hearing range, Tso came up to me, he was also a member of the committee, and spoke to me in confidence.

"Sebati please, by saying stuff like that you are encouraging them not to participate," he said.

"You're right," I agreed, but after Hotstix and his entourage left I announced to the whole class "people, this whole 'Beginners Concert' is a ruse, you don't have to be forced into participating. The same Hotstix did not even partake in the concert last year."

"Oho!" was the universal chorus.

In the end that 'Beginner's Concert' never happened, if anything it was done away with forever. Instead a break dance show took place where the school was introduced to the new dancers namely, Ipha Gumbalume, who reminded everyone of Dakune that night, because he was small in stature and a great dancer, Steven Moepi, and Henry 'Hex'

Sejoe. Dakune had not returned in 1986 and was sadly soon forgotten.

Soon thereafter on one of those early Fridays of the term Santos staged a beauty contest that was to be remembered for a very long time. The contestants were mainly form 4's and we got to see the cream of the crop, but we all remembered the winner, who was subsequently crowned Miss Santos, and was to carry that mantle for the remainder of her tenure at Lotsane.

Her name was Bame Krug. I had heard of the name in the past and was finally able to put a face to it. I am saying this because Bame was to me like some kind of enigma. Back in 1980 when I was but a little boy living in Bontleng (a ghetto in at the south part of Gaborone), a playmate of mine who attended Bontleng Primary School named Maniki, used to talk about a classmate of his who was very pretty – her name was Bame. So when I finally got the pleasure to meet her, I was able to determine that she, and the girl Maniki talked about way back then; was one and the same person. Maniki was right, even though she was even more beautiful than I had imagined.

Her screaming beauty, and elegance, made her one of the most sort after and desirable girls at Lotsane, and winning the beauty contest further added to her magic. There was a rumor soon thereafter that she was seeing Joseph, the gentle Pantsula, who had been one of the contestants at the Choiza Pantsula debacle the previous year. This particular rumor proved to be false, and I had no idea how it started.

She did however date a guy from Moshupa who was now a form 5 named Edward. The relationship lasted for a short while, because of prince charming's perpetual swanking to the rest of the boys in his block (Block B); about how he had the affection of one of the hottest girls in the school. Somehow, Bame found out through some leak in the boys hostel, and promptly ended the affair. She was not a novelty to be displayed she was to say later. Thus for a long time she remained single, making her the most eligible 'bachelorette' at the time; until one day in the future when all that changed.

Chapter 15

The first term also meant track and field season. The inter house competition of 1986 is remembered mainly for the first event that took place that day, which was the 5000 meter race, or the 12 lap race that Devil had lost by a whisker last year.

That year one person stole the show in a way that is still talked about to this day, and was one of the first of many incidents that was to establish his legacy at Lotsane, and this was none other than Blackie 'Onketsang Davis' Kealotswe. Tall, dark, loud, and very handsome, Blackie like 'Big Joe' was always the life of the party, but on a much, much, bigger scale. This guy craved and got attention in a way that was to become legendary.

Since the 12 lap race was open to everyone, Blackie decided to participate. He for some reason was among the fore front runners, and at first everyone dismissed him as a rabbit (one of those who start the race in front and not finish), however after about six laps we began to take notice. On seeing this Blackie took off his t-shirt, and as his dark skin on his torso shone due to the perspiration, Blackie suddenly had everyone's undivided attention. Soon it looked as if Blackie was going to do the impossible like winning the race or at least ending up among the top three. *Is this really happening?* I remember thinking to myself, and just as everyone began cheering Blackie on, he walked out of the track with a big smile on his face, and the school was stunned. Why would Blackie quit on a race that seemed easier to win?

I found out later that he did that just so that he could be remembered as the first and only Lotsane student to walk away from this type of race at that juncture. And you know what? It worked. To this day I can recall a lot of things, but I cannot recall who won that race, and that stands true for a lot of people who were there that day, but we all remember Blackie; just as he had intended, and this was just the beginning we would soon find out. A legend was born.

***

Mr. Monty Fanikiso Moswela was my English teacher, and a great one at that I might add, but that term he was to unwittingly change my life forever. He formed the drama club, because later that year rumor had it that there was going to be a drama festival, where all the schools in the region where going to compete, and word around school was that this epic event, the very first of its kind, was going to be hosted by our school.

I have always loved acting from as far back as I can remember. At Itireleng I even wrote and produced a play with the help of a Peace Corps volunteer, who was my math teacher named Miss Nanette Ebersol. The play was a comedy called 'The Greedy Man,' which was a surprise hit among the students at the time. In 1985 another English teacher, Mr. John Geary tried to form a drama club, but that died before it even began.

That year 1986, things were different, because we had a purpose, and with Mr. Moswela at the helm we hit the ground running. The play that we were going to perform was Zulu Sofala's *'Wedlock Of The Gods'*. I was excited; as a matter of fact we were all excited. I was also studying hard and training hard at the *dojo* where I met Cornelius 'Cornmaster' Msipha, a very handsome young man from Kagiso and his friend Victor Ditlhong, but known to his friends as 'Sukulu'.

Tonkana was the new *'sensei'* for the simple reason that his sparring was good, and that in a tournament, as always the case, he would face the instructor of the other team. Since I had taken more of a liking to break dance than the art I missed out, and did not complain – how on earth could I? I had the chance and blew it. Kelibile's prowess as a martial artist, on the other hand, had surprisingly diminished considerably. Bashima, another member of our club was great as an instructor, but not a great fighter; so him and Kelibile ran the day to day training and the role created for them by Roukes was that of 'general trainer'.

The only problem was that Tonkana became like a solar eclipse at the gym - we rarely saw him. And slowly but surely our club started deteriorating to a point that it was a pale shadow compared to the well-oiled machine that we saw in 1985. The club would have sunk, especially after a mini tournament in Palapye when we faced our Kung Fu rivals, had it not been for Bonang Mapolanka. In that clash one of their best fighters named William Rammoni made Tonkana look worse than a beginner.

Bonang Mapolanka was a form 4 from Francistown Secondary School. He had started his martial arts when he was a kid to a point that he lived and breathed Karate. I found out about him when we heard that there was a form 4 martial artist, who was being pursued by the Kung Fu guys with single minded resolve. Bonang was a Karate practitioner, but the Kung Fu guys overlooked this fact, and I never blamed them because Bonang was that good, and having someone like him in your club was crucial. In the end nature followed its course. Bonang was advanced, and is pound for pound one of the best martial artists I have ever met.

Bonang was amazing. I have never met someone so dedicated to his art as he was at the time in 1986 – the great Roukes notwithstanding. I still think the two were the best Lotsane ever had those years when I was there. In as far as the fundraising for the end of year party that was nonexistent, actually the club never took a single trip, but things were to change under Bonang and in a very, very, big way.

***

Those early days of 1986 a word was to become a constant part of our vocabulary because of its romantic connotation, and how it came up to be. The word was '*jola*'. Jola is a colloquial word that means falling in love or having a relationship.

How this came about was that a week or so before our arrival, BM called all the boys for a meeting at the public benches in front of block A. From what I heard was that he started talking about the imminent arrival of the form 4's, and how it was very important to welcome the new ones with open arms and make them feel at home.

Now when BM spoke everyone listened, but at that very moment as he talked about welcoming the new arrivals 'with open arms' right there and then a voice in front of the crowd blurted out: "Jola!" and this sent everyone into a chaotic laughter.

There was no need for those in the back to wonder who it was who had said that. The distinct voice came from none other than Andries 'Hotstix' Ryan. By saying the word 'jola' what he implied was that the new ones were coming and among them new girls, and with their arrival the new possibilities of finding new love, and thus the word 'jola'.

It was delivered with such accurate timing that that was to be the catch word of 1986. Whenever one saw a girl he liked, or was encouraging one to go after his heartthrob, the one word someone said was 'jola'. At the time when Hotstix said that he was wearing a pair of sunglasses that seemed to befit the moment. I heard that BM just looked at him as he would a sick puppy, and continued with his speech as if nothing had happened.

There was a lady with whom I had become good friends with named Motlalepula Magina. This happened because at some point she was Tonkana's longtime girlfriend from Kagiso, and they had continued their relationship at Lotsane until it died a natural death. One day just before evening prep as I was talking to Motlalepula, who also was now the new head girl, I immediately took notice of a very beautiful and gorgeous girl coming out of the class next door to mine. My heart skipped a beat, for the first time in a very long while, and I think Motlalepula must have noticed my gaze.

"Oh that's my cousin by the way," she said with a smile on her face. My jaw must have been laying somewhere on the ground because I was at a loss for words.

"She is beautiful," I managed to gasp.

"Her name is Olivia." Motlalepula answered the one question that suddenly seemed elusive at the moment.

After last year's debacle I had sworn to myself that I was not going to cast my pearls at swine again. I would be very careful in choosing a girlfriend and not be the village idiot I was the previous year. That is why I think I did not go, as the Americans say, *'goo goo gaa gaa'*, that very first day, but she was to leave an ineffaceable mark in my mind that was almost impossible to ignore.

Over the next couple of weeks I could not help but to take note of her; but then again, she seemed to be hanging out with a guy I knew very well named Fredrick Molelekeng or 'Congo', as he was better known among the student body. He was a form 5 and a very gentle guy.

One day, during record night, I saw him seated with her. After she left I came up to him and said, "Man Congo, you hit the jackpot ... not only is she beautiful, she's gorgeous." There was a rumor going around that the two were seeing each other.

"Sebati, I don't know why people keep saying that. She is *not* my girlfriend."

"No man, stop playing around."

"I'm not kidding, we're just friends."

"Oho." For some reason that was reassuring news.

It turned out that Congo was right after all. She was not his girl. Aside from Bame, Olivia was also one of the most beautiful and desirable girls at Lotsane, and that year there were many to pick from. Blackie immediately took advantage. He knew that by befriending Olivia it would look as if the way to her would be through him, which would inevitably enhance his popularity, and again this maneuver worked.

As time went on I started wanting to know more about her. I talked to Blackie and arranged that we meet later that evening after lights off. It was going to be easy because he lived in dorm 1, and thus was a neighbor.

"So Blackie, where do you know this girl from?" I asked him that night when we met as arranged. We were in his dorm and I was lying on his bed next to him. This kind of thing was very common during our time at Lotsane. This conversation was supposed to be in confidence, but with Blackie no such protocol existed.

"Okay S.B. let me tell you something, just know that I've known Olivia long enough to know all her likes and dislikes," he said.

"So do you think I stand a chance?"

To this Blackie took a deep sigh, deliberately building the suspense.

"Your chances are as good as anyone's Sebati. You like the girl that's no secret." At this point I winced, because everyone could hear him, just as he intended, on the other hand I was trying to keep the knowledge about my interest in this girl minimal. The less people knew about my intentions the better, but try telling that to Blackie.

"So what of Congo, why didn't he make a move?"

"Oh, he asked her out and I told her to say no, and she did."

At this point I realized that really I did not need Blackie's help. He was a front, more like a smoke screen; an illusion he had created to fool everyone in school into thinking that he called the shots in as far as who Olivia dated. I was to find out later that my instincts were correct.

Meanwhile, our drama club was gaining momentum, it showed at the meetings and the enthusiasm was contagious. Most of those early meetings were conducted by Ferdinand Ivor 'Harare' Williams, with whom I had also become very good pals. I was making more friends faster than I could count. Ferdinand took to calling me 'Mr. Jones'.

At one of these meetings he had people brainstorm ideas for a play that we could improvise, and possibly write. At this time, a lady who was a classmate of mine, named Mmathebe Kalane came up with a brilliant idea for a play. It was after lunch when we held this meeting, and I was seated next to Mmathebe as she was pitching her story. Her voice was so smooth and so soothing, making me develop goose bumps that in the next instant, it seemed, all I heard was a sound similar to that of buzzing bees - it was laughter.

What happened was that after she pitched her idea Ferdinand nodded in agreement and said, "Nice concept. What do you think Mr. Jones?"

No answer.

"Mr. Jones!" he raised his voice, but still there was no answer.

"Mr. Jones!"

I had placed my head on the table and fallen asleep. This I could attribute to the fact that I had developed a habit of waking up very early in the morning, sometimes as early as 3:30 AM to study, and that happened to be one of the days. I usually would take a nap after lunch, but not even a broken back was going to keep me from a drama club meeting. That is why Mmathebe's soothing voice put me to sleep. I was startled awake by Ferdinand's voice, and the laughter that followed after everyone realized that I was asleep, among those laughing was my friend and classmate 'Lilist'.

Afterwards, when I was now fully awake, it was agreed upon that we would meet after church service on Sunday. The concept of the play was simple; it talked about an impossible father who had a beautiful daughter, who would not let her marry her suitor unless the parents parted with an exorbitant amount of money for *lobola* or bride price.

I was to be the father, and when Sunday came I was prepared. It was all improv, but I had had a lot of practice the year before with

Jewawa, and mostly at Robot's expense. Olivia was also a member of the club, and I always made certain that my jokes and participation were funny. Many times I would catch her in my peripheral vision, and I could see her smiling whenever I had the entire meeting in laughter. The truth of the matter was that I was like a peacock spreading its colorful feathers to attract the female; just as I had done with my break dancing. However, I was never under the illusion that I had swept her off her feet – even though I always hoped I did each time.

The improv was a success, even Blackie was there and somehow played the role of the uncle, though a natural actor I would think, but he could not give his best performance because he could not help but laugh when the situation called for his character to be serious. I was pleased to rediscover my number one and long lost passion, and how comfortable I felt. That improv turned out to be an audition for a much greater role I would soon find out, and it was just as well that I gave a good account of myself.

On Monday Mr. Moswela called a meeting. The moment had finally come. The play *'Wedlock Of The Gods'* needed to be cast. It was now official that there was going to be a drama festival in June that year, and we were going to be the hosts. The play was kind of an African version of Romeo and Juliet. The story took place in a Nigerian village, and thus the characters had Nigerian names.

The male lead character was an emotional love struck Romeo named Uloko, and his love interest was a woman named Ogwoma. Mr. Moswela stated that we needed a strong actor for the role of Uloko as it was pivotal to the success of the play. What was great was that I could totally relate to the character.

"Who should that person be?"

"Sebati!" was the immediate response from all and sundry.

I don't think this decision sat well with my good friend Hex, who incidentally was also a member of the drama club, and was too vying for the lead role. He was chosen as a shadow, a backup, if in case I got sick or was not able to perform for some reason.

"Man why did you take the role when you already have a lead in the other play?" Hex asked me later that day.

"Why shouldn't I?"

"You're just being selfish man." Hex was known to never be afraid of speaking his mind no matter what. I just scoffed, because as far as I was concerned Mmathebe's play was dead and buried. Besides why would I pass up a once in a lifetime opportunity to please someone else?

Lillian Setlalekgosi (now Mrs. Tlholwe) was cast as my character's love interest, and Tefo Manga was cast as the wicked mother in law Odibei. There was also Bonang Mapolanka, and the other Bonang, Bonang 'Stoner' Mosupi who were part of the council of elders. From that moment on, I lived and breathed drama, my studies, and whenever I could Karate, but drama was in my blood now.

Chapter 16

Life in dorm 2 was such that every day I just looked forward to being among the guys at every given opportunity. It was that much fun. There was George McKenzie, who almost every night entertained us by mimicking a certain teacher named Charles Molilo from Zimbabwe. From what I heard was that when Mr. Molilo was much younger he had been involved in an accident that left him with a slight speech impediment, and a head that was almost always tilted to the side. He always liked to say that students should be matured, which earned him the nickname 'Mature'. He was George, Kgotso, and Dizzy's substitute Chemistry teacher, and George would always have us in stitches whenever he imitated him.

At Lotsane there were students who sold cigarettes surreptitiously to other students who were smokers. These students were called 'spotters', and they always had loyal customers, and never refused anyone credit for the simple reason that if anyone got cigarettes in this manner, and refused to pay the 'spotter' the latter never took him to task over the debt. This was because there was always going to be that day when the smoker was desperate for a cigarette, and there would be no other 'spotter' selling them except the one he owed. And 'spotters' like any other good businessman never forgot a debt, and the defaulter would not be allowed to buy a cigarette until he settled his outstanding debt. That right there would be a painful lesson learned by the smoker that 'spotters' were not to be messed with. Cromwell was at some point a 'spotter,' and for the most part they were nonsmokers. We had such a person in our dormitory, and those early days of the first term Hex was a constant visitor as he was at the time an occasional smoker until he quit sometime later.

"Hey form 4 don't keep coming here," Patrick Fani said to Hex one morning. The latter just ignored him and went about his business. The next morning at the same time, which happened to be after breakfast and before school started, Hex came to our dormitory and again received the same reception from Patrick.

"Form 4, I told you that your presence is not needed in this dormitory."

"Man why don't you just back off," Hex said "you know yesterday you said the same thing and I let it fly, and now here you go again. I mean what's the matter with you? Does the fact that you are a form 5 make you think you are better than all of us form 4's? No, we are all the same no matter how many times you have showered in the Lotsane waters, I know you have your head up in the clouds, come down to mother earth brother, I know it's difficult but as you keep on trying you'll find out that it's not as difficult as you made it out to be come ..."

"Hey man enough already," Ontumetsi the reverend interrupted, which was totally out of character.

"Hey, no one's talking to you so shut up," Hex snapped "what are you, a comedian? Newsflash, you're not funny stick to the bible or something reverend," he said, and then soon after turned to Patrick and continued where he had left off as if nothing had happened. "As I was saying, just give it a try and don't give up if the going seems tough, that's part of life," and with that Hex turned around and left. For a while everyone in the dormitory was captivated least of all Patrick.

"Man the form 4 was really giving Patrick a dose of life's lessons," Moses said at last and we immediately all laughed, breaking the ice, except Patrick who was pondering, with awe, over the whipping he had just taken.

The phrase *'I know it's difficult but try'* was to be part of the dorm 2 vernacular, and very much so between me and Mothusi. It always seemed like there was always never a dry moment in dorm 2 especially when it came to George McKenzie's timely wit. For instance, one day at supper a student who was making an announcement on behalf of his prefect said, "... These clubs are to meet immediately after *saphara*" meaning really *'immediately after supper'*.

"What on earth was that?" George said.

"What?" someone asked.

"I mean" George replied, "if one is going to speak English speak English, if you are going to speak Setswana speak Setswana. 'Immediately after *saphara*,' what is that?"

We all understood his logic and immediately gave him a round of applause, which attracted the attention of other tables. Also, when it came to setting the table when your turn came it was normal to miscount, but during these times it was becoming increasingly obvious that whoever was on duty would encounter no such problem, because Dizzy was always quick to remind the person on duty about who was present and who was not. This was to become such a trend that without even realizing it Dizzy would become animated as food was being dished out - even to an extent of breathing heavily.

"By the way Moeti is not here today, I heard that he will be in Palapye, and thus miss lunch, Kgotso too, he said he was having a prefect's meeting with the staff therefore they'll be served lunch." He would say and very fast mind you. If someone was missing that meant more food for us, and thus Dizzy's enthusiasm was understandable.

At times if we felt that the salt was not enough in the food, we would go to the kitchen and ask for raw salt. After a while, this became a habit so much such that we would get the salt even before tasting the food; to which Dizzy would be the first to take note.

"Guys why not taste the food first and then determine whether you need salt or not?"

Suggestions such as these, and Dizzy's apparent enthusiasm during lunch time became somewhat of a comic relief.

"Guys, have you noticed how keyed up Dizzy becomes when at table during lunch time?" Patrick asked one day when we were in the dormitory during Dizzy's absence. For an answer we all cackled.

Not too long afterwards George was ostensibly in a sour mood as we were headed to the dining hall, which was unusual because he was always a very jolly individual. I later find out that there had been a quarrel between him and Dizzy in class earlier that day. At the table as lunch was being set, Dizzy immediately went into his regular routine, and George said softly, "You know some people when they see food their excitement just goes sky high like they've never seen chow before."

All that pent up laughter from over the past few months was suddenly let loose by everyone. My goodness! It was long, it was hard, and it felt really, really, good. And right away Dizzy knew he had been the target.

"Go and say that to your father man. Your father is the one who gets excited when he sees food," Dizzy said, which really was unlike him, because he never would say such things to anybody, and that was the first and last time I would hear him talk like that to anyone.

"I don't think so, because my father is the one who actually puts food on the table," George fired back.

Later I was to tell Ruth about it, and that was when she nicknamed him 'the Wiseman'. In the end Dizzy was much more conscious of his behavior at the table. A few days later, when I reminded George about that episode, he simply said, "Man S.B. you didn't know it at the time but I was really, really, angry at Dizzy for what he had said to me in class earlier that day, and I decided to get even at the lunch table," and even he did get.

***

As I was getting more and more into character I just enjoyed drama even more. It got to a point where I thought I could introduce that aspect into our Karate club as well. I came up with a three act play in which I wrote what only happened in the three acts with no dialogue. It was a classic tale of an unlikely romance between a street urchin and a very beautiful rich young woman. In the midst of this romantic tale the girl gets kidnapped by a bunch of street thugs, and in the process beat up the boyfriend to a pulp.

To get back the girl, the boy then seeks the help of a recluse martial arts master and learns the required skill to not only destroy the gang, and get back his girl but to bring about peace in the whole neighborhood that had been terrorized by these ruffians. There was no script to follow, all I told the actors (all members of the club and volunteers) to do was just improvise, and in doing so I unearthed unpolished gems, because the guys were simply amazing.

The role of the street gang leader was played by Mathabathi, and his deep imposing voice added more credibility to the character. That and throw in people like Cuspido who were naughty by nature, and everyone was instantly in character. I was more amazed by Cornelius 'Cornmaster' Msipha who played a store owner victimized by these hoodlums. Cornmaster was a natural, I have repeatedly asked him why he never joined the drama club, and I have yet to get a straight answer from this great friend of mine.

I played the street urchin turned Romeo, and the role of my character's love interest was revived by the beautiful lady Mable Maphane, who could also sing very well, and was also a member of our drama club – the Setswana version of it. Just as we had a play to present, our Setswana group had a play of their own entitled *'Letlhokwa'* which means a tiny stick in Setswana, and the lead was Thuso Godson Ramodimoosi. In our little play to be staged by our Karate club Bonang Mapolanka played the recluse master.

A date was set when we could perform our play, and we rehearsed whenever opportunity allowed. Considering that I had the real drama to attend, as now rehearsals for *'Wedlock of the Gods'* were gaining momentum, Karate, our play, studies, and lately Cross Kgosidiile, and I, had teamed up to present a science project at the National Science Fair coming up next term, I still to this day wonder where I got the time and energy to balance all these things, because I did so successfully.

At rehearsal Bonang was impressive in playing the venerable Karate master. For instance when my character said to his teacher, "Master, when do I get my black belt so that I can go and get my beloved Maggie back?" His answer would be something along the lines of, "Son, there are certain virtues in life that can never be rushed. Just like no man can control when the sun rises and sets, and the moon also."

To this everyone in the common room that day would shout their approval followed by a round of applause.

"Man, listen to that philosophy," someone would say "we're definitely going to thrill the audience."

And thrill them we did when the day came, but for some reason, and I don't know if the fact that this time there was a real audience, but the change from that venerable recluse Karate master to something totally opposite was instant. Whether it was stage fright or what I have no idea, but all of a sudden Bonang was completely out of character.

To begin with he started doing somersaults and screaming instructions in his high pitched voice at his student, and now even resorted to speaking Setswana, meaning that the philosophy we were accustomed to was now a thing of the past. The audience thought this was all part of the act and roared their approval. The play was a huge success, and we succeeded in attracting new members, but our number one fans were the cooks in the kitchen who always reminded me and

Mable of the great performance we put up – especially my costar who was just so believable. Perhaps had I pushed this fan base more I would have received the privileges the late Dixie Ndlovu had enjoyed last year, when he befriended all the kitchen staff.

***

There must have been something about the month of March those first two years at Lotsane, because that was when I decided to make my move. Even the previous year in March is when I got to ask a girl out face to face. I felt the time was right to make a move on Olivia . After all I was starting afresh. We met behind our base class that we used for drama as this was a late overcast afternoon right after our drama meeting. I told her how I found her attractive, and how I just felt it fitting that she and I be boyfriend and girlfriend.

"You know it's just going to be hard for me," was her immediate answer after my sales pitch.

"Why?"

"Well, I don't want to be in a relationship at the moment." Now why did this sound familiar?

In the end I decided not to be pushy, but instead paced myself. I had lots of fish to fry to worry too much about falling in love all over again. Meanwhile, my breakdance skills had hardly diminished all this time despite my increased load of extracurricular activities, and my total focus on my studies. For the first time in my life I was actually enjoying every single day of my schooling life.

Consequently, when I was invited to perform with Hex, and some of the guys at the intermission of some fund raising show by some club I readily agreed. Two-Two and I for some reason were beginning to drift apart. It turns out that the performance we both featured in at the very beginning of the term was the last one with my 1985 dance partner. None of this was ever planned, I would think my new found passion in other activities like drama and studying had a lot to do with it. We remained friends, perhaps not the friends we were in 1985, but a friendship that has lasted to this day.

Around this time when Ferdinand heard that I was asking Olivia out, he started calling her 'Mrs. Jones'. At first he was indiscreet, but with time he got even bolder, and started calling her that to her face, until she approached me, and told me to tell Ferdinand to refrain from referring to her as such. I must say that when I heard that she wanted to see me, I was flattered into thinking that this was my coronation, but I was wrong.

Ferdinand did stop, but in a way he still played cupid in making certain that Olivia and I became an item. He was a number nine in this instance, and a very good one at that. Like one time during church service Olivia and I were seated at opposite sides of the hall. During church service we always sat facing east. I was at the south side of the hall; Olivia was at the north end, and Ferdinand in the middle. What he would do was casually look at Olivia, and after making sure that he had silently gotten her attention, he would then turn and look at me, and I would look at him, and then he would in turn look at her, which would inevitably have our eyes locked on one other – just as he had intended. This would go on throughout the service, and sleek as ever he would have that innocent look like all this was not his doing.

Again she came to me and asked me to tell Ferdinand to refrain from calling her 'Mrs. Jones.' When I talked to Ferdinand about it he denied any wrong doing.

"Sebati, it's funny that she should say that to you again when the truth of the matter is I stopped calling her that the very first time when I heard that she did not like it," Ferdinand said, and I believed him. Why then would Olivia say that? I wondered.

Later that day, I consulted two of my classmates turned friends in Joseph 'Strong' Makabe and the ever smiling Justice Boemo also from Kagiso about the matter.

"What do you make of this guys?"

"Jones," Strong answered "I don't think the girl minds being called Mrs. Jones – if anything she likes it."

"Yeah," Justice agreed "give the girl what she wants man."

Buoyed by my two friends I again the next Sunday evening asked her out, and coincidentally we were wearing matching sweatshirts with the 'street dance' insignia on the front. Olivia's was purple and mine from my breakdance days in 1985 was light blue, and that was the day I was privileged to be her boyfriend, it was my coronation, and the ghost of the year past was further exorcised forever.

Instantly we were the 'it' couple. I did not know it at the time, but by the look of things I had pulled a major coup that shook the whole boarding house. No one but a few knew that I had been asking the girl out. It really was not a popularity contest as far as I was concerned for I really liked the girl, and I was lucky to have her. I had no idea how much she was sort after until a friend of mine, also a martial artist, but of the Kung Fu beat, named Fish Dingalo came up to me one day as we were walking back to the dormitories after tea break.

"Man Sebati, how did you do it?" Fish asked.

"Do what?"

"How did you get the most beautiful and the most desirable girl in school? Man I'm scared of you." His smile was wide and I could tell he was genuinely happy for me.

I blushed as Fish went on and on. In the end I succeeded in changing the subject. The Friday before was when we faced our Kung Fu rivals at the community hall in Palapye. Fish had sparred with someone who was overly aggressive with his punches and kicks, and when he dropped Fish with what looked like an illegal hit; the latter retaliated with a high flying vicious flying kick to the head, and his rival instantly backed off.

"Tell me something Fish, the way I saw you react when that guy roughed you up and got your own back with that flying kick to the head; that told me one thing – you were mad weren't you?" It was part of our creed as martial artists to never lose our cool. So Fish, the gentle and honest friend I had gotten to know simply smiled and nodded in agreement.

Chapter 17

The science project Cross and I were planning was starting to gain momentum. It had to do with an aircraft and an airport, and coincidentally, some years later Cross himself was to become Head of Finance at Air Botswana, a position he held for eight years. We had the help of our physics teacher Mr. Ruf from Germany. He even suggested certain equipment we could use for our project, which would enhance the effects even more. Mr. Ruf was God sent and thus Cross and I were charged up. However, things slowed down a bit when our benefactor went back home suddenly for a brief vacation for reasons we never knew, and our project suffered a series of setbacks.

Not only was Cross my friend and partner in my science project, he was also my math tutor. It has always been in my nature to ask for help whenever I had difficulty in my academics; even if that help came from a fellow student. Despite being a very gifted scholar, Cross was also a natural teacher. He explained problems so clear and concise that he would do it only once and I would get it. There was also a certain Batisani German, who was a classmate of Cross, who would tutor me in physics whenever Cross was not around. My great success that year was a result of help from a lot of people, but Miss Sarah Pearson, Cross Kgosidiile, Batisani German, and Uncle Oupa Kwape are unsurpassed.

Also through Cross I was introduced to two individuals who would later become acquaintances I would always remember. One day I went looking for Cross at his dormitory, and was told he was elsewhere at dorm 8, where a few of his classmates and friends from Bobonong, like Adam Masebola, and McKenzie Gopolang had taken up residence. I found him there.

"Cross, Mogzen-Flagzen and I have been looking for you, where have you been?" I asked him.

Mmueledi Ramasiya was a form 5, and also Cross's classmate, and was given the nickname 'Mogzen-Flagzen'. There was a lady who lived close to our school near the river named Mma Amogelang. She made a living by selling fat cakes, cigarettes, *chibuku* (a traditional beer packed in a paper carton made from sorghum), and there was also a rumor that she sold dagga (weed) as well. Her primary customers were students. Since she sold fat cakes, and her property was out of bounds, the only way to get the goods was by sneaking in and out of campus undetected, because if you were caught out of bounds without permission, you could end up in serious trouble. That morning Cross, Mogzen-Flagzen, and I had planned to buy some fat cakes from Mma Amogelang, but at the agreed time Cross was nowhere to be found.

When I finally found him in dorm 8 he immediately went on to tell us what had caused him to miss our appointment. He had just witnessed a fight of epic proportions between two very big form 4's. The two titans were namely Godfrey 'Mafia' Morgan and Kakambi 'KK' Bahiti. They were both from Francistown secondary school. What had happened was that when Cross was in 'Block C' he and a few people were attracted by a fracas in the laundry room, when they arrived they found the two Godfrey and Kakambi engaged in a heated argument, and as more people piled into the laundry room their movement sparked an altercation.

The fight according to Cross was evenly matched as the two giants went at each other. Even though they were both strong, as the fight went on, Godfrey would prove to be a little stronger than his opponent as their muscles took the strain. No one stepped in to separate them. After evading what looked like a killer blow from Kakambi, Godfrey sidestepped and somehow managed to knock Kakambi off balance, and when the latter fell Godfrey was on him in an instant. After a series of hard punches to the face Kakambi weakened, and Godfrey had a field day.

"Gentlemen," he said as he sat astride over Kakambi's torso "you are all witnesses, this boy started it all," he would say before turning around and hitting Kakambi in the face yet again. The beat down continued until at last a few people stepped in to end the torture.

We listened to Cross as he described the event with picture perfect accuracy. At the time I did not quite know who the two pugilists were.

Mogzen-Flagzen then said, "Cross, take me and Sebati to meet these two guys."

"Let's go." Cross readily agreed, witnessing a fight in high school was always a treat for a lot of the students who were not involved. That is why me and Mogzen-Flagzen were kicking ourselves for not having been there to see for ourselves what had happened.

We went first to the laundry room; the site of the battle. Mafia was still there, silent and leaning against the wall, we then speculated among ourselves as to what was going on in his mind.

Cross said, "I bet this guy is saying to himself … I won, I'm the champion of the titans no one will dare mess with me."

We then left to look for the vanquished – Kakambi. He lived in the 'Block C' common room and his bed was beside the window. He slept on the top part which meant we could see him clearly from where we were, which was on the public benches in front of 'Block C'. He was lying face up on his bed, and seemingly in deep thought.

"He is probably saying to himself," Mogzen-Flagzen said, "how man, how did I let this fight slip out of my hands? Why couldn't I connect with that punch that could have ended it?"

At that moment Kakambi stretched his leg and Mogzen-Flagzen said, "Man, I should have kicked him like this when he had me pinned down."

We all laughed as we ran off. The timing of Mogzen-Flagzen's last remark was just too fantastic. I would much later feel bad about this after Kakambi and I became pals since we took a history class together. I did however enjoy the company of my friends a lot, and we had each other's back. For instance someone I don't quiet remember who it was, threatened to beat up Cross over some issue I don't quite recall, but when Mogzen-Flagzen heard about this he just brushed the whole issue aside.

"Don't lose a blink of sleep over this Cross no one will even think of laying a finger on you. Not with me and Sebati around." It was true. I felt blessed to have a wide circle of friends that included the likes of Cross and Mogzen-Flagzen.

This brotherly bond extended to members of our dormitory as well. For instance, one day when Ernest was in class joking around with a girl named Shelly, and when she playfully hit him with a book he grabbed it from her, and suddenly assumed a serious demeanor upon taking a closer look at it.

"Shelly, where did you get this book?"

"Why? Someone let me borrow it."

"Are you sure about that?" Ernest's demeanor had not changed.

The school library was a haven for many students. We did not have a very wide range of books at the time, and novels from the Macmillan Pacesetter series were always in high demand. It was therefore not uncommon to reserve a novel or any book for that matter and wait weeks if not months for it to become available. The library was run by a staff member. In 1985 it had been Miss Esplin who had since returned to England, and in 1986 the teacher in charge was Mrs. Geary. The 'Librarians' were students, and Ernest just happened to be one of them. It turns out that there were some books that were locked in the storeroom. They were brand new and had not yet been made available to the students; not even the 'Librarians'. These books had a special code on them. Why then did Shelly end up with one?

Ernest then took the book to Mrs. Geary, as he was expected to in such situations. Mrs. Geary then accompanied Ernest back to his class to question Shelly as to why, and how she ended up with a book that had obviously been liberated from the school library's vault; so to speak. After holding out for about 5 seconds, she then revealed that she had borrowed the book from a fellow named Brian who was also a 'Librarian'.

Upon hearing this George McKenzie, 'the Wiseman' said, "let me get this straight, this guy was a librarian and he stole a book from the library, books he had unlimited access to? What's to say he does not have his own little library at home as a result? I'm telling you he has finished them, he has finished them."

Brian was subsequently removed from his position as 'Librarian' and was suspended from school for a few days, and he came back I'm told with the intention of getting even with Ernest. On hearing of the rumor that was circling about Brian's planned vengeance Patrick said, "The guy is just blowing hot air Ma Enzo, he messes with you, and he messes with all of us. Isn't that right fellas?"

"Oh yeah," we all agreed.

To this Ernest simply smiled.

"Thanks for the support guys but I can take care of myself." I did not disagree with him. Ernest was a Karateka, and in 1986 as fighters like

Kelibile declined people like Ernest rose steadily and took their place. In the end nothing happened.

***

Living with Kgotso the head boy turned out not to be the scary experience I imagined it would be. If anything Kgotso was patient, gentle, and kind; something I would attribute to his Christian background. However, Kgotso was not someone to be taken for granted. I realized this immediately about him and thus earned his respect just as he had mine. He became like a big brother I never had, just like a certain Peter Maphumulo was some years earlier at Itireleng.

One Saturday early morning a few members of our dormitory including George and Dizzy woke up and were making so much noise while the rest of us were asleep, ignoring Kgotso's pleas for calm but they did not let up, and Kgotso accused them of 'howling'.

He then wrote all the names of the perpetrators and gave them to the boarding master. Things were fast beginning to get out of hand in dorm 2 and Kgotso felt it proper to stamp his authority once and for all. This was a shocker to everyone for we were all used to Kgotso's gentle disposition, but everyman has his limits - Christian or atheist. The resentment that followed was unavoidable.

"This is a travesty, I was not making noise let alone howling as Kgotso says," Dizzy protested.

"I agree. I don't see why something as trivial as this could have been reported to the boarding master. Kgotso is overreacting," said Moeti, a perpetual Kgotso critic.

"But guys be honest you were making noise weren't you?" Ontumetsi said.

"There's a difference because howling is not necessarily making noise, so you can't say they were noisy." That was me being the smart mouth. To this Kgotso suddenly turned around in anger and looked me straight in the eye. I think he saw this as betrayal on my part.

"Aha! Sebati" he said, "you must keep on supporting them okay, just keep on supporting them!"

"N-no no Kgotso," I said, anxious not to offend my very formidable ally. "T-that's not what I meant you totally misunderstood me." I then continued to senselessly prattle on, some people who were there later said my eyes were unusually big, which they attributed to panic, and they were correct.

Later when the dreaded moment came for Kgotso to present the culprits to the boarding master that morning George went off, for he was a bit nervous.

"Things have gone bad, bad, bad …" he said as he, Dizzy, and others left to meet BM at the dining hall, which was empty at that time of the day, and a setting BM always chose to deal with the boarding school problems. George was to later say Dizzy out of sheer panic lost his cool. He said it happened immediately after they were ordered to sit down.

"Kgotso hates me BM; he does h-he hates me," Dizzy said even before anyone was asked to speak.

"Okay," BM said "would you kindly elaborate what you mean by that."

"W-well he just hates me. I just know it. That is why I was howling."

"Oh, so you do admit that you were howling."

"He just hates me that is why we were howling." By his own words Dizzy almost hung everyone.

"Oh, now it's 'we'." This I'm sure BM thought was going to be a very easy case to preside over. Sensing the serious damage Dizzy was bound to wreck George McKenzie intervened.

"BM, what really Dizzy and the rest of us are saying, or rather should be saying is that we are really sorry for having caused that ruckus this morning. Kgotso has done nothing other than being a great prefect and head boy, and we're truly sorry that things had to escalate. I'm not speaking for all of us, but I believe that is the sentiment we all share." This I later heard was delivered with calculated ease and calm by 'the Wiseman' that immediately tensions subsided, and BM felt that the apology was genuine, and then after careful consideration warned them not to do that again.

"Dizzy almost messed things up for us you know," George was to tell the rest of us a little later after the quarrel was settled.

However from that time on taking a page from Kgotso I would make light of the situation. For instance, he had a kid sister whom he loved dearly and spoke of her affectionately whenever opportunity allowed.

"My little sister knows that I'm there for her at all times."

"So you keep supporting her?"

"Oh yes I keep supporting her." He would say and not realize the full import of his words until much later when we were to laugh about the 'howling' incident.

That night was when Mothusi recounted Kgotso's conversation with me verbatim.

"Oh yes, and Kgotso said 'aha Sebati you must keep on supporting them okay, just keep supporting them." Then everyone recalled the experience like it happened five minutes ago.

Amidst all this Kgotso laughed softly for a while and said, "Oho, Sebati so all this time you've been mimicking me that's what it was." We then all laughed. Just like there was never a dull moment in dorm 12 last year the same held true in dorm 2.

***

It took a while and a lot of perseverance and persistence, but in the end our play was slowly but surely making strides. At this time we were able to separate the wheat from the chaff in a manner of speaking, because we lost a lot of members. The enthusiasm that was evident at the very beginning was gone, even Ferdinand of all people had dropped out of the club, but we were so caught up in this creative endeavor that whoever left for whatever reason was not causing any major ripples. We were determined to not only put up a great performance but to win the drama festival.

Toward the end of the term when we were getting quite comfortable with our lines Mr. Moswela invited two teachers, whom I knew very well, namely Mr. Mudidi and Mr. Mhuriro. They watched our play from beginning to the end and were really impressed – especially Mr. Mudidi. He was seeing another side of me that he had not seen before. He hated breakdance, not breakdancers, because he thought it took away from our studies, and last year he seemed a bit disappointed that I put too much into the dance when I could be concentrating more on my schoolwork. He had even told my father that as they had become acquaintances.

This year all was forgiven, and the great man was impressed to a point that he started coming to our rehearsals regularly, and I think tapped into one of his many hidden talents one of which was directing. He was to become at first the unofficial co-director with Mr. Moswela until much later his role was more defined and thus official.

Also at this time I also thought I found solace in Christianity by joining the school's Scripture Union (SU); a move that surprised many. I was determined to lead a Christian life with the encouragement coming mainly from Mothusi and Kgotso, I did not feel comfortable with the other members some of who were fakes just as Tonkana had discovered, but it was worth a try nonetheless.

In early March we got the news that the Cambridge examination results that the 1985 form 5's had taken were released. I was anxious to know how Max and Sebei fared, but that news was not readily available as we were getting the news in bits and pieces. We did hear that one of Lotsane's brilliant minds Mojasegoro Kgosinkwe had aced the exam. This came as no surprise because this chap was a genius. It was the same Mojasegoro in 1985 that put our school on the map by winning the national Math contest; in the process beating every math whiz in the land. We expected even greater things from him in the future.

Finally, Tonkana came up to me with the news that our two friends Max and Gilbert had both gotten first division passes. I was floored. Balisi and Lekobe Albert Mochotlhi were among the top performers, and almost everyone I knew had passed and passed well – even Alice. Although I felt she could have fared far much better than she did. I was particularly pleased also with Big Joe. When taking the exam he had predicted that if he at least got a 5 (equivalent to a 'C') in math he would get a division 1 (or First as we called it), and not only did he get a better grade in math he passed with a solid First.

"Fungwa would have gotten a First too." Everyone was saying, and we were all unanimous in our agreement. I wrote a long congratulatory letter to both Max and Sebei. The latter was already serving his national service duty in the north part of the country; since he was part of the first intake because of the Pre Entry Science Course (PESC) program. I too felt I would never let my friends down and vowed that I would get nothing but a First.

In the meantime Moses and I were becoming real close friends, not the friendship that I had forged with Max, because that would never be reached, but a great one nonetheless. What I think brought us together at first was the fact that we were both early risers. Those moments when all was quiet as everyone was asleep we would talk about girl issues – his mostly. There was a girl he had been chasing who was a form 5 just like him, but the deal had not been closed yet.

Amazingly that first term was fast coming to an end, and before we knew it, it was Easter. This time I went home for the long weekend. It was four days long, but by then I was on such a roll that even at home I was studying as hard as ever. When schools finally closed I could not help but count the days until it was time to go back.

The future looked bright. It was April and the great drama festival was just a few months away. I remember running into Tefo Manga at the mall in Gaborone. We were thrilled to see one another, and all we could talk about was what awaited us this second term coming.

"You know we're going to win that drama festival don't you?"`

"Is there any doubt?" Tefo said, equally confident as I was and we went our separate ways wishing each other a great vacation until we met again.

Those holidays I also visited friends of the family whom I knew from Zambia. They were from South Africa like my father. They were Oupa Kwape and his wife Seipati. Rama and I called them uncle and aunty as we were taught from childhood when addressing an elder. They lived in Otse, which is a village about 37 miles south east of Gaborone, where aunty Seipati was a nurse at the local clinic and was given a house close by. Uncle Oupa was a math whizz and thus tutored Rama and me, and also taught us chess. I also enjoyed that stay with the Kwapes because they had a television set. The last time I had access to one was when I was a kid in back in Zambia. Thus I would stay up late every night when everyone was in bed and watch shows like *Benson, The Cosby Show, MacGyver*, etc ...

Chapter 18

The Second term came at last. We were all fired up for the festival was now around the corner. The winter of the second term was just as bitter, but I did not seem to feel it that year. The activities were keeping me warm I would think. Also, I was so far ahead in my academics, particularly in math, and thus I was amazingly having more and more time to burn during study time. In those days I was always the first in class at evening prep and the last to leave, and all that it seemed was beginning to pay dividends.

One evening prep as a joke I got a blank piece of paper and started writing a story. In no time I had completed three pages, and thereafter handed the pages to Mabulili (Lilist) to read. She was intrigued. I then gave them to Ruth whose reaction was just the same as Mabulili's, and even said it had what in Setswana we called 'pull' like you wanted to know what happened next.

I then rewrote what I had written on fresh paper; this time putting more emphasis into character development that in no time the story started to take a life of its own. My three other classmates namely; Omponye Moruimang, Rinah Phoko, and Margaret Ponatshego joined in reading the script every moment when I finished a page. Their input and enthusiasm was priceless, something I still carry with me to this day whenever I engage in a writing project.

As a writer, budding or professional, I found out that we all are for the most part sensitive as to how others will perceive our work. Objectivity is bliss, but if your work is not up to par and someone is frank with you, it is hard not to get discouraged, which I think is why many promising writers give up on projects before completed.

I was blessed to have those five women; Ruth, Mabulili, Omponye, Rinah, and Margaret in my life at that time. They were my pillars of strength those early days. They were objective just as they were constructive in their criticism especially Ruth. I gained immense confidence as a writer those days. With them on my side the story was quickly taking shape, and before I knew it the story turned into my very first novel.

'The Act of Brutality' was never published, it is still lying somewhere in an old suitcase at my parents' home, but writing and completing it is one of the best things I have ever done. That one feeling of euphoria was for the ages. Although the story was fiction, I wrote about things I knew and imagined, I wrote about my first crush, about love, conflict, heartbreak, and about Karate.

Writing the novel was always a pleasant form of relaxation from my studies. It was another activity added to the numerous I already had, but it was a welcome addition nonetheless. However something had to give for even Aladdin had only three wishes. During Mr. Ruf's absence our science project collapsed, but the fact that we had put a gallant effort in making it work, Cross and I were invited to attend the National Science Fair held at the University as it always has. It was a pleasant trip, and we enjoyed it immensely, especially the lunch.

I also received a sad letter from Max. He was at his national service orientation at the Botswana Agricultural College at Sebele in northern Gaborone, when he bumped his head opening a big gash, and had to be rushed to the hospital. On his return a little later he was told of his brother's passing, which had occurred right at the time when he sustained his head injury. I felt my brother's pain and grief, because I too felt as though I had also lost a brother.

Meanwhile, rehearsals were getting more and more intense as the days were going by because the great drama festival of 1986, the first of its kind was looming large, and so was the excitement. And then something happened that almost curtailed those carefully crafted plans.

One overcast Monday morning, I woke up with a feeling that something bad was going to happen that day. The premonition I had was that I was going to fall down in front of the whole school. I am saying this because that day marked the first day of my week setting the table. What used to happen was that because of the shortage of teapots, after assembly; setters would run to the dining hall, and be among the first, so that they would not have to wait for a dorm to serve their tea or juice and then use their teapot. As a result setters would be at the back of the line during assembly, and when the teacher on duty said 'assembly is over,' setters like me would be off to the races.

My dorm mates liked me when it was my turn, because during tea break I always out ran everyone and got our tea and bread early, and thus giving my dorm mates more than enough time to eat, relax a bit, and get ready for the second and last phase of classes. This was a very welcome trait especially on days when assembly was long as it turned to be at times.

That morning was just like any other before. I waited at the end of the line. I had been winning the races to the kitchen whenever it was my turn, but that Monday I could tell that there were eager setters that day who were anxious to beat me, among them my good friend Cornmaster, who I would soon find out that he was like me a very good sprinter.

"Assembly is over …" the teacher said and we were off and running.

Cornmaster, a fellow named Kingston 'Setlhaku' Kedumele, and Meshack 'Lani' Mauco got off to a very good start. I took off right after them, and passed Setlhaku with relative ease, Cornmaster and Meshack were a little faster, but I soon gained on them. The whole school was behind us watching, and as we were approaching the hall I thought I had gained enough ground to pass Cornmaster, but I did not see the storm trench in front of me and lost my footing and fell hard into the trench.

I got up quickly and disappeared around the corner and into the dining hall. Amazingly I was not seen by a lot of people when I fell, and those who did were not sure if it was me who had fallen or a fellow named Kabelo Lebotse, because we were both tall and had similar type of jerseys, and I was wearing mine that day. This was the same jersey Rama had brought for me last year.

Initially I did not feel the pain until after a few minutes. My knee and hip were badly bruised, and with the throbbing pain it was hard for me to enjoy my bread and tea. The next day the swelling on my knee started to get worse, and I walked with a painful gimp. A few people tried to come up with a nickname for me, and that being 'Tea Break', but backed off after threats of physical violence, and a public mention about their parents intimate parts – again, this was something I was not too proud of I must say, but under such circumstances it was hard to take ridicule when I was in so much pain. I now fully understood how Robot, I mean Tshimologo felt.

That afternoon right after school as we were heading to the dormitories just before lunch the pain became unbearable, and the swelling a great deal bigger. Every step I took seemed to make the pain all the more worse. Half way to the dormitories I could not bear it any longer so I stopped and sat on the ground. I just could not move my leg.

Kgotso heard about my plight and promptly notified the administration, and the school's small truck was deployed to take me to the hospital in Palapye. The ever caring Kgotso even carried me to the car. Later on it was determined that I had a bruised knee cap and would have to walk on crutches for the next four weeks, and the drama festival was barely five weeks away. Panic reigned supreme within the drama club. Hex had since dropped out of the club and I had no shadow, so if I was not healed by the time the festival came who was going to replace me?

The most hurt by this accident was Olivia . She came to my class that evening red eyed, and I was told later that she had been crying all afternoon after she saw me in crutches. I reassured her that I was okay and would be back on my feet in no time. I was and still to this day touched by this act of kindness and devotion that she so openly displayed. I still rehearsed nonstop with my crutches, and one thing that was clear to me and everyone was that I, and my costar Lillian Setlalekgosi, had great chemistry between us as the two lovers who were at the center piece of the story.

A little over a week before the festival, Mr. Moswela notified us that there was going to be a workshop at Madiba Secondary School; on the Saturday exactly one week before the festival, and that one representative from the English, and one from the Setswana play would have to attend.

"So who would you like to represent your play at Madiba? Mr. Moswela wanted to know one day right after rehearsal. Since it was winter we did our rehearsals outside for the most part; we were outside that day as the classrooms were forbiddingly cold.

"Sebati," a girl called Bokani who was also Lillian's shadow said.

"Thapelo," another girl, Abigail said.

Thapelo Obusitse played one of the main elders in the play, and was an experienced stage actor who had done his JC at Madiba, for some reason he was not present that day. Since the decision could not be reached unanimously to be fair Mr. Moswela came up with a solution.

"Okay, write the two names on separate pieces of paper and put them in a hat." That was done and Bokani picked my name. I was thrilled so was she.

The person chosen to represent the Setswana play was a lady I had known only by sight, but as time went on we would become real good buddies as we shared the same interests. Her name was Albertina Mokgware, an intelligent and energetic actress. We left for Madiba that Saturday morning and arrived less than two hours later. There were students like us who represented their respective schools. It was then now that I realized that this festival was actually going to be a reality. It was a very exciting moment.

The work shop was a breeze, Mr. Mhuriro was also present that day, and we were hosted by the grand MS. Kgomotso Motlotle who at the time was a teacher at Madiba Secondary School. Yet, what I remember vividly about that day was the food we were served after the workshop. The food was prepared by the Home Economics students and as such they more than outdid themselves. I had never before seen so many dishes like I did on that day. It was like we were at a very high profile banquet; the type you saw on TV and magazines served at Palaces and State houses. Albertina and I were to talk about those dishes for a long time, which is why I understood Thapelo's resentment when he heard that he had been passed over when it came to representing the drama club. His notion was that his experience in previous plays would have given us more insight.

We were back at school about half an hour before supper, but the very idea of the inferior food at the dining hall made me sick, but I did not want to be alone at the dormitory so I just went along with the guys and watched them eat.

Ernest was in an exceptional mood that day. I was later told that he and a few friends had paid Ma Amogelang a visit. This visit coincided with the fact that she had just so recently replenished her *chibuku* supply which would explain his mood; plus *chibuku* was very affordable. As he was eating he suddenly burst out laughing and stood up with two slices in one hand.

"Look fellas, Patrick thinks these are the best pair of slices in the world hahaha!"

We were taken aback but joined in the laughter nonetheless. Shortly after he brusquely sat down, and in so doing he hit an empty chair that came directly into the path of a girl who like the 'models' last year had her nose in the sky.

Her name was Kelebogile, a form 5. One could argue and say that Kelebogile was fairly beautiful, but the downside was that she was too proud of whatever little the Good Lord had blessed her with. Every day she always timed her entrance in the dining hall after we all sat down; so that we could all see her latest hairstyle as she was very particular about her looks, and went out of her way to make sure that we noticed her. That day her entrance coincided with the moment when Ernest was sitting down, and the chair that he pushed was inadvertently in her way and almost tripped her. Instead she stumbled, which was bad enough, as she was instantly embarrassed.

"Hey dunce head … what do you think you are doing?" she said as she hurriedly walked away mainly to spare herself further blushes.

It took a few seconds to sink in, and then Ernest said, "Wait a minute, did that broad just call me a dunce head, is that what she just said to me?"

"Yep," someone confirmed.

I was seated right next to Ernest so he looked at me and once again assumed that serious demeanor that had become well known.

"Sebati, I'll beat up Kelebogile you know, I swear to God I'll beat her up and badly too." I had no doubt that if pushed any further; Ma Enzo would definitely fulfill his promise so no one egged him on as would have been the case normally. From where I was I could see Kelebogile at her table grumbling. Later she was to confront Ontumetsi as he was headed to the trash bins behind the hall to throw away what he had collected after cleaning the table.

"What was Ernest saying?" she demanded. And Ontumetsi, who was not really comfortable around the opposite sex, unless they were fellow Christians, stuttered a bit.

"W-well you s-see ma'am I ... I know nothing," he is said to have responded, and we made fun of Ontumetsi regarding that scenario for the rest of the year.

A little later Ernest strode over to Motlalepula the head girl's table.

"Magina," Ernest said, calling her by her last name as most students did, "please warn Kelebogile not to display her rude manners because I'll beat her up, please warn her ..."

Motlalepula's demeanor was cool and calm and went far in diffusing the highly volatile situation.

"Okay Ernest, what really is the matter?"

"I'm asking you to talk to Kelebogile, I'll beat her up and very badly too." Ernest went on and on until Motlalepula was able to at last calm him down. We were all to reenact these episodes whenever we were bored.

***

I was set to debrief the club about the workshop, so after church service the SU student in charge Mbanga Maurice Mbanga, announced that I wanted to meet all the drama club members at our base classroom; in order to give my report concerning the workshop I was privileged to attend the day before. The turnout for the meeting was incredible. I was gratified to see so many faces, many of which I had not seen since our first few meetings at the beginning of the year. The atmosphere was electrifying, and this we could all attribute to the upcoming festival, thus something of the enthusiasm we saw at the beginning had returned. I gave my report and everyone listened attentively, and just as I was about to dismiss the meeting following the usual questions and answers Tefo intervened.

"Excuse me Sebati, I'd like to say something before you end this." Then the impressive woman paused before she continued in a voice loud enough for everyone to hear. "People field trips are starting and that time soon. So for all you who have not been coming, and you know yourselves, and are just now gracing us with your beautiful faces please forgive us – don't come." Her message was clear and inimitable. Another staunch member of the club, a lady named Dineo Motsamai echoed Tefo's suggestion, and would have chased the opportunists outright if she had her way. Dineo was a no nonsense woman, who was known to take no prisoners when it came to situations such as these.

No one including me could argue with that reasoning. We had all worked hard to be where we were at, and even though I did not mind at first at seeing all the people jumping on the bandwagon, I did now see things from Tefo's point of view and I totally agreed with her, and we continued growing from strength to strength.

The great drama festival was scheduled to begin on Saturday at 10:00 am and was to go on until Sunday around 4:00 pm. Mr. Moswela talked about having what he called a 'dress rehearsal' a term I was hearing for the very first time. It meant on Thursday night we were going to perform for the very first time in front of a live audience – fellow students and teachers in this case.

My knee was feeling much better, as a matter of fact I had not used the crutches since the workshop at Madiba, but still it had a tendency of 'giving in' once in a while as it was still weak, which was a concern for many in the play, because I had to carry Lillian when her character announces to mine that she is with child (his), even though she is barely widowed (her husband had died under suspicious circumstances), and her mother in law Odibei (Tefo) is eager to see justice served in her own way. The consensus was that with a weak knee I might not be able to carry Lillian, and if I did I would fall and her on top of me, which would be disastrous. All these fears were soon allayed.

The costumes for the rest of the cast were measured and skillfully tailored by one of the teachers; the ideal MS. Ntwaagae. I was lucky to have Mr. Moswela let me borrow his dashiki, which added more realism to my character and to the play. Thursday came and the dining hall was packed. The stage that was designed by the Technical Drawing teacher Mr. Porter was magnificent. The labor was provided by the drama club boys and we had a blast that week, and that is when I became really close to others like Goabamodimo Mhaladi, an actor from the Setswana play which made the work all the more fun.

We made a tactical blunder that day. The Setswana play performed first, and with Thuso Ramodimoosi as the love struck Metsimantsi the audience were thoroughly entertained; so much such that when it came our turn the audience were burned out if there ever was such a thing. Our performance was below par and the audience quickly grew tired, and it did not help matters that as we performed we could see some people in the audience leaving.

The dress rehearsal was a blessing, because we immediately identified our weaknesses and areas we needed to work on, we spent the whole Friday evening working on these. There was even a suggestion that we switch around two of the actors who played the elders. Elijah Monamelo Legwaila played Ogwoma's uncle Ike, but had fewer lines than Oaitse Madume who played the elder Okoli, which was a pivotal role for that matter, but he seemed to struggle with his role quite a bit.

We decided to gamble and have Elijah and Oaitse switch roles. The elders had rehearsed long enough to know each other's lines, but it was a little confusing as they were not comfortable with their new characters, and at this point Bonang Mapolanka brought us back to reality.

"Guys, do you realize what's at stake here?" Bonang asked softly as we were in the midst of rehearsal. We were holding our preparation at the girls' common room.

"What?" Tefo asked.

"Is it wise to switch roles now when the festival starts tomorrow? Besides, are you guys aware that the government has set aside more than fifty million Pula for celebrations alone, and that if we win we will head to Gaborone where we will be part of the celebrations, and thus part of that fifty million?"

September 30th 1986 marked Botswana's twentieth year of independence, and as a result, the Twentieth Anniversary Independence Celebrations Unit (TAICU) was set up to make sure that this was a celebration to be remembered by a generation. That is what Bonang was talking about, and we all agreed that it was too late and folly to change the cast, but we were worried about Oaitse though.

A scene from 'Wedlock Of The Gods' with Tefo Manga as the wicked Odibei. 1986

Flanked by Matlhogonolo Temane (left) and Mr. Appadoo, at the Prefects party. 1987

My 1987 dorm mates. Standing from left to right, Isreal, Keebonye, Sebati, Ferdinand, Itumeleng, and Gerald. Seated from left to right, Phatsimo, Moemedi, Archie, and KK

Me and John Max Moreti at the Lotsane River 1985.

Part of our breakdance crew. From left to right standing, Maulter, Ballman, Sebati, and Benjamin 'Body Roc' Thupe, middle row 'Two-Two' Dakune & Noble front Tso and Ceasar. 1985.

Supper time in the dinning hall with my dorm 2 mates. 1986.

Some of my dorm 2 mates. 1986

> Lotsane Secondary School students raised P500-57 for Kabo Matlho. The students brought the money all the way from Palapye to Gaborone on Wednesday. Picture shows Sebati Mafate (holding Kabo) whilst his fellow students presents the money. *Pic:— By Josiel Nare).*

The day we presented the money to Kabo Matlho. 1987

With Allim Milazi and Moemedi 'Two-Two' Raperekisi. Note the R5 on the chairs, that was in room 5 we were watching the Ballroom Dancers. 1985.

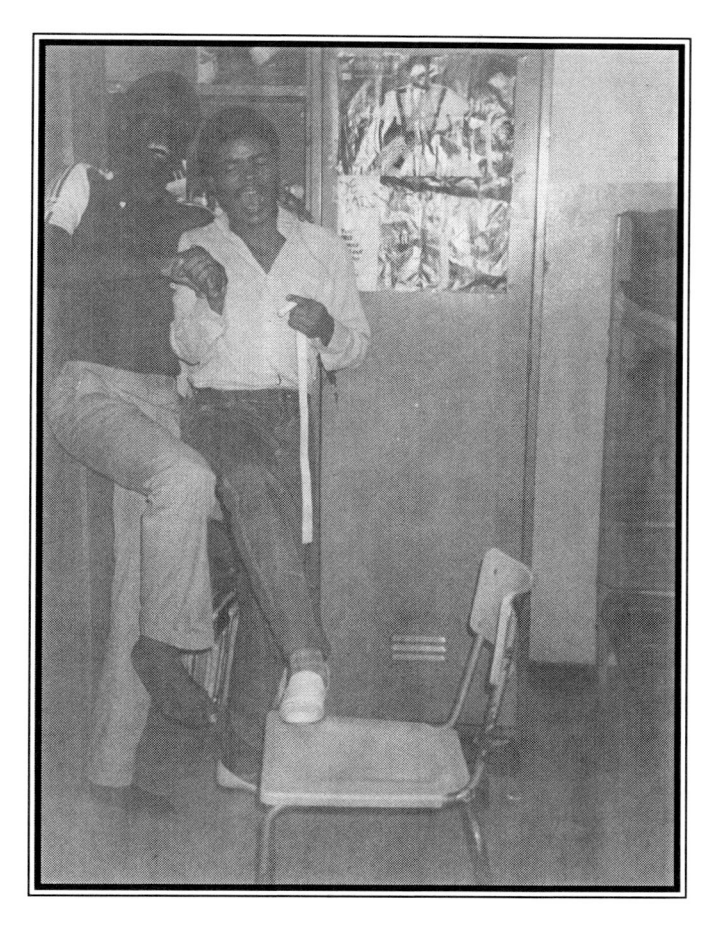

With Andries 'Hotstix' Ryan. 1986

With Osupile 'Osu' Kgabi, the day after the GSS tournament. 1986.

Chapter 19

The big day, the day that up until now existed only in our imagination finally came. As if to signify the moment; that Saturday morning was bright and shiny, and all of a sudden our great school was buzzing with activity as students from all over the north central region of the country arrived. We were scheduled to perform our play *'Wedlock of the Gods'* at 8:00 pm that evening. Our Setswana play *'Letlhokwa'* was scheduled for 10:00 am the next morning.

There were a total of four adjudicators among them Mr. John Geary the English teacher at Lotsane, and the great Dr. Victor Mtubani, a professor of English at the University of Botswana who was also head of its travelling theater. The first play was presented by Selibe Phikwe Secondary School, and just like that the great drama festival of 1986 was on. We watched the different schools as they performed their plays throughout the early part of the morning, there didn't seem to be much of a competition as far as we were concerned, and our confidence was growing by the hour.

Hosting an event like this one meant many schools came, and with them many new faces and prospects of the female persuasion; that within a short period of time Lotsane Senior Secondary School was a favorite hunting ground. Since the tables where staked up high at the sides of the hall, guys like Pheneas, Stoner, Patrick, and a few others sat at the very top and were perched a little over six feet high. They were in their territory and wanted everyone to know – particularly the girls.

As the event went on, one of the tables at the very bottom slipped and in plain view of all those watching Pheneas, Patrick, Stoner, and company fell backs first from their vantage position. I remember the thud as their backs hit the cement floor simultaneously, and momentarily attention was drawn from the stage and on them. Luckily no one was hurt, if anything they were more embarrassed than hurt, because this happened mainly in front of the girls they were trying to impress.

After the fiasco the plays continued unabated, and our confidence kept growing until after lunch when the Madiba students took the stage. They performed a Setswana play called *'Ditiragalo'* loosely translated means 'Happenings', and from the get go they had the entire audience spellbound for the very first time since the festival began. These students were outstanding to a point that they received an ovation during the play – something usually reserved for the end. And we right away knew that we now were faced with a formidable opponent.

The other Bonang nicknamed 'Stoner' who played an important elder in our play was seated next to me that afternoon. I looked at him.

"Nothing to worry about 'B' we're going to beat them," I said, trying to put on a brave face. Bonang smiled, and his smile told me otherwise.

"I don't know man; these guys are good, and I mean *very* good."

He was right, and worse still they were getting better as the play went on and the audience was feeding off their hands. To beat Madiba we would have to put on more than a stellar performance. There was no doubt that there and then they were the school to beat hands down.

Taking into consideration that our performance at the dress rehearsal tanked, and some of our actors like Oaitse seemed to be struggling, for the very first time since the formation of our club, I began to have doubts. I started to think that we were over confident and that could very well be our undoing. These were the thoughts that were going through my mind as I walked out of the hall. We were recessed after the Madiba play, and we all needed to catch our breaths, because the Madiba actors had taken it away. When I got to the lawn near the administration office where I had last seen Dixie, I did a rapid somersault, just to get my bearings in order as I was now a bit worried.

"Sebati, just what do you think you are doing by hurting yourself like that?" I turned around to see that Motlalepula had been watching me all this time.

"Oh, nothing really."

"That did not look like nothing to me, are you alright?"

"I'm fine," I fibbed and Motlalepula could see right through me.

"Come on Sebati this is me you are talking to."

I relented, and soon I was pouring my heart out to her mainly about my fears as far as Madiba was concerned.

"Don't even worry about that Sebati. Just stick to the game plan, and forget about Madiba, you guys will be just fine." Her words went far in as far as allying my new found fears.

I was not the only one apparently who was feeling the heat, because just before supper I happened to pass by one of the classrooms and saw the 'elders' at work in fine tuning the crucial scene when the counsel meets. They were in a 'zone' and I did not disturb them. Finally, our moment came. While we were in the classroom preparing to take the stage Mr. Mudidi came to give us words of encouragement.

"Okay ladies and gentlemen this is it. Just go out there and have fun like I know you will. Don't even worry about Madiba." He was brief and to the point, and then he left knowing that we were going to meet him backstage. The hour we had envisioned had finally come.

Once on stage I just knew that we were hitting on all cylinders. Shortly after my character entered the stage and declared his never-ending love for Lillian's, and after carrying her we received an ovation. One of the fellows back stage who was a member of our club even though he did not have a role was impressed; his name was Gerald Usher.

"Guys, you keep up this performance and I swear to God we will be picked up by bus the next time we go to perform."

Most of all we were amazed and impressed by Oaitse Madume's performance. Our supposed weak link somehow reached deep down within him and gave a performance of the decade. This time *we* had the audience awestruck. There was laughter, tears, and finally a long standing ovation - there was no stopping us.

Among the audience that night was Mr. Kgotla, a young and handsome Agriculture teacher, who was later to tell my father when he ran into him in Gaborone to have me consider acting for a living, and there was also MS. Kgomotso Motlotle who came to congratulate me backstage. I was thrilled, because MS. Motlotle had every reason to be bias since our schools were bitter rivals. In all we were extremely pleased with our performance, because we outdid ourselves.

That evening, before lights off, I had a chat with my great friend Terrence Jacobs who was just as astounded as everyone else; in fact the whole school seemed to be buzzing about our performance. Terrence was a prefect now and lived in dorm 1. I asked him about the judges' reaction.

"Man, they were smiling and nodding, and all I could say was they are throwing all the points at you guys," he said with a wide smile on his face. I went to bed feeling greatly reassured.

The festival continued the next morning with the play *'Letlhokwa'* kicking off the event. That Sunday was an overcast day, which helped, because in the play there was a ghost and the girl Bagomotsi, who played the ghoul, scared a lot of people into believing that she was the real thing. Ronald Molosiwa and Grace Manake also gave a performance that was to be remembered for years. At the end of the day it was time to announce the winners. The chief adjudicator Dr. Victor Mtubani gave his report regarding the festival. As an English professor at the University of Botswana, he had an impeccable command of the Queen's language, and a booming voice to back it up. He talked about the performances, and the importance of realism in a play, and called out two incidents in particular.

"For instance," he said. "If a play is a period piece set convincingly in the past like the Shaka Zulu play it takes away the realism if you have actors wearing watches. In addition to that was a scene where a gentleman went to relieve himself after receiving the news that his daughter was bitten by a snake - such things are not real." The scene Dr. Mtubani was referring to was from our Setswana play; where Julian Mokgatle's character relieves himself after hearing about his daughter's death.

The scene was meant to be funny as it was not scripted, but part of Julian's improvisation and one of our members, a lady by the name of Patricia Diwanga (now Mrs. Ntshole), went on to say that Julian at times overacted, which was true, but that was part of Julian's humor, and later in life the actor, Jim Carrey, reminded me of him. Dr. Mtubani continued by saying, "One thing about me is that I call a spade a spade, if you're weak you're weak, and if you're great, well ... you are, which brings us to the results. We divided the plays according to language, meaning that English plays were judged separately from the Setswana plays, and in each winning play we picked the best actor and actress. In some cases the acting was so great that we had to award that to the whole cast. Just like we did with the Madiba play *'Ditiragalo'* and the

Lotsane play *'Wedlock of the Gods'.*" At that point we were squirming in our chairs as this last sentence took us by surprise.

"Now in the English category second place went to Sefhare Junior Community Secondary school with their play *'Shaka Zulu,'* and in first place by a margin of ten points was the play *'Wedlock of the Gods'* ..." We all jumped up and screamed! I looked at Mr. Mudidi, and he looked at me maintaining his great calm and dignity with a look that said *'I expected nothing less'*. "We awarded the best actor and actress to the whole cast, but even then as in life we can be all equal, however there are those who are more equal, and in the best actor category *Sebati Edward Mafate* and Bonang Mosupi were outstanding, and in the female category that was Tefo Manga and Lillian Setlalekgosi." Although I had expected the recognition, but hearing it was a whole different thing, and I felt pats on my back and cheers, and then came the announcement of the Setswana play winner and like before we held our breaths.

"In the Setswana category we had joint winners and those two being *'Letlhokwa'* and *'Ditiragalo'*..." pandemonium like never before erupted – *both* our plays had won. In the midst of this Dr. Mtubani went on to say, "The best actor was of course Thuso Ramodimoosi, and Bagomotsi Ramatopo, who played the ghost better than the ghost itself in Shakespeare's Hamlet, was the best actress." It was a well-deserved honor he had bestowed on Bagomotsi. I later heard from Mr. Keakile that Madiba had been winning, and Bagomotsi's portrayal of the ghost in the play tipped the scale. At the end of his speech Dr. Mtubani introduced us to the TAICU representative in our region, a certain Mr. Malikongwa.

"First of all," Mr. Malikongwa began. "I would like to congratulate the winning plays and those others that participated in this festival. The winners are therefore first invited to the President's Day celebrations, and thereafter will be part of the twentieth anniversary celebrations in Gaborone. For all participants, transportation, room and board, as well as new costumes will be provided all at TAICU's expense ..." I do not quite recall what he said next, because his words were drowned by yet another wave of bedlam, which was by now in the midst of a frenzy – we were totally jazzed.

It took a while, but finally when the dust settled we were able to look back with pride at what we had just accomplished. We recalled our first meetings, the castings, the losing of key members like Ferdinand 'Harare' Williams and Henry 'Hex' Sejoe, and patted ourselves on the back for soldiering on. The President's Day celebrations were in a few weeks, and we had time to recuperate and bask in our glory. Life on the other end was moving on, and second term was football season, our team under the leadership of the great Lepholetha 'City' Senne, and one Odiretsimang 'Jomo' Molao was making strides of its own in a way that was to be remembered for years to come. And Blackie continued making waves.

Chapter 20

Blackie had always been a loyal member of our Callies sub team. The previous year he was our number one goalkeeper. Not the very best, but our keeper nonetheless, and Blackie would always turn whatever he was doing into a memorable event. In 1986 he switched his allegiance to Santos.

The move was a surprise at least to me, and I heard many years later that the reason for this switch was that when Cornmaster joined the team, and became the number one goalkeeper, and the best Callies had in a while, Blackie was relegated to second fiddle, and this was a position he could not accept thus his decision.

It was a wise move it turns out, because at Santos he was the only keeper at the time and as a result indispensable - a situation that suited Blackie just fine. I would not be surprised if this had been a calculated move all along. One day there was a friendly match between Santos and Executive Cosmos. Back then the back pass rule was still in effect. That means a player could pass the ball back to his goalkeeper, who was allowed to catch the ball, and hold on to it before kicking or throwing it back into play.

This rule was later abolished by the international governing body known the world over as FIFA (Federation Internationale de Football Association); to discourage delaying tactics by a winning team and encourage the spirit of fair play. At some point during the game, one of Blackie's teammates, named Kaiser Osenyeng, had the ball inside his own 18 area, and thus closer to the goalposts.

"Pass the ball to me," Blackie said to him since he was sandwiched by two opposing players and if dispossessed that would likely spell disaster.

"No way, I don't trust you man," Kaiser said much to Blackie's fury.

I think Kaiser's response was due mainly to the fact that Blackie was known to commit juvenile mistakes as a goalkeeper. One instance many recalled was during a game last year when he could have easily caught the ball and left it at that, but with Blackie nothing was that simple. He caught the ball, and then decided to dive to make the whole thing look fancy, in doing so the ball slipped out of his hands, and slowly bounced beyond the goal line and into the net, and subsequently gifted the opposing team with a goal. Normally, a goalkeeper dove to catch the ball not catch the ball and then dive.

"What? ... You don't trust me ... why the hell am I the goalkeeper then?" Blackie fumed, and then proceeded to do the unthinkable - he actually walked out of the game. "Let us see who you trust to be your goalkeeper now." Blackie was tall, sinewy, and handsome, but in his orange jersey and shorts he looked taller and almost majestic, as he slowly, and with deliverance; walked out of the football field.

Upon realizing that he had the entire teams' attention and that of the spectators - the stage was set. "Don't you know who I am? ... I have a famous father for Christ's sake," he said loud enough for even people in Palapye to hear. His father was the renowned Radio Reporter Bright Kealotswe. "And to make matters worse you guys are embarrassing me in front of my girlfriend Mapholwana who came all the way from the girls' hostel to watch me play. How dare you!"

At that moment we looked around the field, and sure enough spotted Mapholwana with several of her friends talking as if nothing was happening. She was used to her boyfriend's sudden eccentricities. He then did something that to this day still makes me shake my head in awe. Blackie actually began to declare his undying love as he walked out of the field; almost stopping the game as even the opposing players took notice.

"I love you babe ... it's just you and me ... you and me only babe!" he shouted as he blew her kisses. By this time I was beginning to question Blackie's sanity while the rest of the people cackled to a point of almost falling to the ground. I heard that many girls came up to Mapholwana afterward; telling her how lucky she was to have a man who was not shy to display his emotions in public. They thought Blackie's affirmation was truly romantic.

The Santos players, among them Steven Sekute, out of desperation, crowded the goalposts as now the opposing team, realizing that there was no goalkeeper to worry about, was firing shots from all angles. After much pleading from the team, including the very Kaiser who had sparked this fiasco, Blackie gladly returned to the posts, and sanity was restored. Blackie had done it again, because none of us ever forgot that incident.

***

A few weeks later, the first two official games were played on the same day. We took on Madiba in the first game and hammered them by six goals to nothing, all six goals were scored in the first half. We were the defending champions and thus the school to beat. Besides City we had other players from last year's victorious team. Players like Montshiwa 'Wagga' Montshiwa, Odiretsimang 'Jomo' Molao, and John 'Stop Nonsense Buddha John' Monyai the South African, tall and imposing and after City one of the best defenders Lotsane had at that time. Other players who were now form 5's blossomed in 1986. Players like Eric Kelemogile 'Chippa' Mokgwa, Motseothata 'Dizzy' Keabetswe, Tshwenyego 'Carlos' Tawana, Kgosietsile 'The Horse' Sanka, Ishmael 'Ten Ten Machibichibi' Tebelelo Mphela, Gabriel 'Muller' Matlakele, and Terence Jacobs to mention but a few.

This was to become one of the best teams ever assembled in all of high school football. The boys were simply amazing, and no one could dare bet against Lotsane repeating that year. Our second game was against Moeng College, also our opponents in the recently ended drama festival, whom we beat by three goals to one. Moeng would prove to be a tough cookie, but there was one school in particular that strongly believed could derail our quest for a second straight championship, and that was none other than the school by the hillside from Serowe - Swaneng Hill Secondary.

Swaneng like any other school had aspirations of becoming national champions, but that road went through Lotsane and they knew it. They had to beat Lotsane no matter what it took. At the Swaneng helm was a teacher we knew simply by his nickname 'Find the ball', who was a tall man with glasses and always screaming on the side lines. Our first game against Swaneng was an away game, meaning that we had to travel to their back yard to play them. I was not there that day, but from what I heard the reception from the school was blatantly hostile. This was done of course to take us off our game. What's worse is that the refereeing that day left a lot to be desired, and not surprisingly we lost by two goals to one courtesy of some dubious calls. We later found out that the referee was actually an ex Swaneng student who had also been a head boy during his tenure there.

Our team came back to school in a very somber mood, but this soon changed to an anger that was quickly harnessed. A return match was due in three weeks, and this time it would be Swaneng coming to our school, and we could not wait to exact vengeance. The following weeks we quickly disposed of Madiba this time by six goals to one, followed by Moeng College who we beat by two goals to one.

Upon his return after the match Dizzy was asked by Patrick, "Dizzy, how come the score against Moeng was low?"

Dizzy's answer was, "Hey man, make no mistake about it Moeng is tough."

Meanwhile Swaneng was not doing badly either, and the week before the showdown they were trailing us by a point, meaning that to get to the playoffs they had to beat us. We on the other hand needed a tie to return to the final round and defend our title. However a tie with Swaneng was inconceivable nor was it an option. We wanted to beat them, and beat them into submission. For this reason the stage was set for a battle of epic proportions that was to be remembered for a very long time.

I could sense, and I am sure the whole school could that week that our team meant business when BM, who was also the coach, went to practice wearing shorts - something none of us had ever seen. The guys were so determined that every day of that week when we were taking a shower before supper Terrence would say to us, "Guys, I can tell you this, come Saturday when the first whistle goes off Swaneng will be picking the ball from the back of their net in less than five minutes – mark my words." No one doubted him.

The school was tense with anticipation as the days dragged on. We were even told that on game day Swaneng had required that, we the spectators, stand at least two meters away from the sidelines. We grumbled of course as this was unprecedented. However our sports master, an Aussie named Mr. Pearce, was philosophical about the whole issue.

"Listen up guys, I understand your frustrations," he said to us at assembly two days before the derby. "Swaneng is scared and thus looking for an excuse to protest, so we will hurt them where it matters most, and that's on the scoreboard." We agreed, and subsequently applauded the wise words.

Finally Saturday came. Immediately after breakfast for some reason I headed to the football field. It turns out that I was not alone in this quest for there were quite a few guys headed in that direction. Most of them were colleagues from Bobonong who I had not in the past hung out with, but that day was different. These were guys like Fredrick Molelekeng, Kago Nkageng, Ditshupo Motlhatlhubi, Adam Masebola, Jacob Pitso, and Sedumedi 'Seduction' Pule. There were many more of course, and we all shared one common wish – we wanted to witness Swaneng brought down to their knees. And we were definite it was going to happen that day.

The sporting events kicked off with much fanfare later that morning since the first events were softball, volley ball, and netball. The majority of the students were not too concerned about the outcome of these games, because the main event kicked off at 3:00pm. The Swaneng students seemed over confident and cocky, and as if that was not enough; the truck that had dropped off the early participants went back to Serowe, and picked up more fans. We were advised to be on our best behavior that day, and just watched as they appeared to take over our school.

Finally the moment arrived. Apparently the news of this showdown had reached Palapye as the locals came in droves in their vans and trucks to cheer their heroes on. That day before the game, I went to the 'Block A' common room where the team was making its final preparations, and BM and a certain Mr. Onneetse who was BM's assistant, and my Setswana teacher, were giving the team game time instructions. This was something I very rarely did since I was not a player, but it turns out that there were others like me who were there, and were just as anxious. Once in the common room the atmosphere felt like that of troops preparing for war.

"Boys," BM said. "Play this game like your life depends on it, that's all I can say to you right now. We've worked on the basics all week and you know what your duties are. The moment you lose possession don't wait for the defense to bail you out, do what you can to get the ball back this is a team effort." He went on to say more and Mr. Onneetse added his two cents then it was time.

People like Pius Malikongwa blew their homemade trumpets as they led the gallant Lotsane team to the field. The din rose to a frenzy when the team, dressed in all red, the same kit they wore last year during our moment of great triumph, took the field. Soon after the Swaneng team entered the field, and their fans cheered them on; some of them creating a ruckus as they jumped up and down at the back of the 5 ton truck that had brought them.

The game started at lightning speed. We did not get the quick goal that Terrence had boldly predicted nor did we hold it against him, but all the players were shining. In defense, whenever City cleared the ball those first few times, he did it in classic acrobatic style. He had one wicked scissors kick (also known as the bicycle kick) that he did facing the ball, as opposed to the conventional one; where the back of the player was to the ball when implemented. His was magnificent and all the more to watch. This would be followed by a resounding cheer of 'Cityyyyy!' from all of us.

The third time when he executed that same kick he did not get up, but instead stayed down with his head almost between his knees. We immediately held our breaths. Was City hurt? Without him to guide the ship our chances of winning would be greatly diminished.

"City ... get up please!" one concerned spectator yelled from the sideline, he was visibly worried like the rest of us. "City ... a-are you okay ... man get up ... please." Still there was no answer to his pleas. "Come on City, talk to us," another pleaded. Finally City looked up and shook his head; there were tears in his eyes.

"*Majita Swaneng re tla e bolaya!*" "Guys we are going to kill Swaneng!" he shouted. And we roared our approval in response.

Shortly thereafter I did not quite see what happened, but there was a penalty kick against Lotsane. For some reason none of us were alarmed at the prospect of Swaneng going up by a goal, but when their player took the penalty kick, our goal keeper, a form 4 who had replaced Bathusi 'Two-Six' Seretse named Patrick 'Jomo' Rammidi, caught it as though he was in practice. Now, in soccer, whenever a goalkeeper catches a ball that was bound for a sure goal this inspires the team, in many instances, to feats hitherto unheard of, and we were just about to witness that.

The moment Rammidi threw the ball back into play, and got it to the speedy Gabriel 'Muller' Matlakele; the latter outran the entire Swaneng defense and scored. We were literally still celebrating the goal when play resumed, and Tshwenyego 'Carlos' Tawana, diminutive as he was, ran the entire Swaneng backline ragged and scored. We were up two goals in a matter of seconds, and from that moment on, it was a one way street as the Lotsane heroes took the game to the now shell shocked Swaneng that by half time; we were up by three goals to none.

Swaneng had pinned their hopes on their star player nicknamed 'Strong man', but the impressive John 'Stop Nonsense Buddha John' Monyai had him shackled the entire game that he became a mere spectator. There was a saying at Lotsane that two things happened when you faced John with the ball. One, either the ball stays and the man passes, or the man stays and the ball passes – never both. And we were witnessing a classic example of that.

After half time, the team took off where it left with players like Eric Kelemogile 'Chippa' Mokgwa and Odiretsimang 'Jomo' Molao marshaling the midfield with strength, and doing untold damage. Being the dead ball specialist that he was, City scored two more goals from near the center line, and toward the end of the game we were up six goals to one. And in the closing minutes of the game, Tshwenyego 'Carlos' Tawana struck the final nail in Swaneng's coffin by scoring the seventh and final goal. As a late second half substitute, Terrence Jacobs almost scored, but as he sped toward the Swaneng goalposts he was inadvertently impeded by his own teammate, Patrick 'Ace' Rakwadi, much to our disappointment, and I would think mostly Terrence, because he almost mugged him right there and then. It was our turn now to taunt the stunned Swaneng students, who left soon afterwards, and the silence from them reminded us all of a funeral procession for their season was dead and buried. Our revenge was complete and it was sweet.

It is worth noting that when Lotsane was in cruise control during the game, and the outcome was pretty much obvious, Blackie somehow secured a loud boom box I have no idea from whom, and then convinced a bunch of some of the most beautiful girls on campus (there were a lot to pick from) and had them surround him, and played one of the most popular songs at the time by a South African artist named Rex Rabanye. The song was called '*Onketsang*' and he walked around the field several times surrounded by the gorgeous girls, like a celebrity, and everyone including the Swaneng students took note. That is how he earned the nickname '*Onketsang*', which means literally 'what are you doing to me,' because Blackie liked playing that song and Blackie 'did it to us' all the time. There was no way on earth he was going to let an opportunity to shine slip through his fingers.

Chapter 21

President's day marked our very first drama club trip. I was so excited the previous Friday evening that I could hardly sleep, because finally, a club that I had been a part of its inception and growth; was now on the verge of making its very first trip. We were scheduled to perform at the Tsholofelo Community Center in Broadhurst Gaborone that Saturday evening. The night before I kept wondering if the trip would materialize, because we were supposedly going to need two trucks to get to our destination the other truck was to be provided by TAICU, but it had yet to arrive.

My concerns were soon laid to rest when early in the morning Gaolatlhe told me that the truck had indeed arrived. We waited for a long time before we finally departed. The school truck since it was open was to carry our baggage, and the other, the TAICU truck, was covered and we were in it. However a few members rode in the baggage truck and among them Elijah Legwaila, I wondered, like everyone else, why he was seated at the very back of the truck among the baggage, and at the mercy of the wind, but it turns out that right next to him there was a bag of oranges, and Elijah enjoyed a hefty feast all the way to Gaborone.

A few days before we had one final rehearsal, in the scene of the counsel of elders, Elijah's character, Ike, says: '... *it is to a friendly concubine that a woman hops in times of need ...*' and then he went on to hop providing some comic relief to the scene, and we all laughed except Mr. Mudidi and Mr. Moswela, who did not find the whole thing amusing.

"This is a serious matter ladies and gentlemen, and no old man can actually stand up and hop," Mr. Mudidi said as he demonstrated even though humorously.

"But sir that would be great for the audience to see," we argued, but Mr. Mudidi would not be swayed, and looking back he was absolutely right. We did tell Elijah to do it anyway once on stage thus defying Mr. Mudidi and he agreed.

When we arrived in Gaborone, we were based at a Primary School in Gaborone West (G-West), which in 1986 was a still brand new suburb. Here we rested and were fed with so much meat and mealie pap than we could handle. Later after lunch, I even had the opportunity to go home, and let my parents know that we were going to perform at the Tsholofelo Community Center. We lived in Broadhurst and thus this venue was not very far from our house.

That evening, I performed for the very first time in front of my parents, and it was a great experience. The funny thing was that during the performance I looked around the audience, but could not find them, and only did when I was in a scene with the other Bonang – Stoner, who reprised the role of one of the foremost elders. Stoner is one of those people who I know had he been in the right place at the right time; he would have perhaps been a very strong Academy or Tony Award contender and maybe winner hands down. In this particular scene his character was having a heart to heart talk with mine, and one of the things he said was, *'your father and I were very good friends'*, and right at that moment I looked at the audience and spotted my father, step mother, and aunty Musa Malepa for the first time. I almost smiled at the irony of Stoner's line, and with my father in the audience I tried to give my best.

Also one thing I recall about that night was that when it came to the scene of the elders and tempers flared up, and it was time for Elijah's character to say *'it is to a friendly concubine that a woman hops in times of need ...'* he stood up, and right there and then was about to hop on one leg like we had told him to do, but came face to face instead with Mr. Mudidi and promptly abandoned the idea.

"Man I was going to do as you guys asked," Elijah was to tell us later on, "but then I came face to face with Mr. Mudidi just as I stood up." Mr. Mudidi as the co-director was standing back stage behind the curtains with Mr. Moswela watching the proceedings.

The performance, by both our plays, was a success nevertheless and we completely overshadowed Madiba who were there with us, but for some reason seemed to have lost that touch that had made them crowd favorites at the great drama festival a little over a month earlier.

I had never seen my father as proud as he was that day. He was really thrilled by my performance, and told me that I was a natural actor and jokingly said that I ought to pack my bags and head to Hollywood. It was a successful trip by every account, and this was validated by a definite invitation to the 20th anniversary independence celebrations in September. I am emphasizing this, because for some reason Madiba was not invited back. We looked forward to the TAICU celebrations, but there was an immediate concern in our minds as we headed back to Palapye the next morning – midterm examinations.

***

The midterm exams were the ones I knew I had to excel in if I were to win the Best Student prize, which is why I woke up very early in the morning, even on Saturdays, to stay on top of my academics. The very first paper we wrote was Setswana. I did not feel very good about it at first. The thing is that Setswana, like Mathematics before, had been one of my weak subjects, but that term I knew that to get that first position in class I would have to get good grades in every subject. I could not afford to lose ground on any subject, and hope that points from another test will make up for the deficit.

This is because I had a very tough opponent in one of my classmates, and after Ruth my very best female friend as well named Rinah Phoko (now Dr. Rinah Makgosa). This lady was very smart, and I owe part of my overall academic success at Lotsane to her. I knew that Rinah's strength was virtually in all the subjects, perhaps she did not score as high in English, but she was well balanced, and I knew I had my work cut out. Rinah was the reason why I studied extra hard. At the end we both did not know which one of us had gotten to be first in class. We would have to wait until the holidays (which were fast approaching) to find out. It was so much fun nonetheless for the competition was healthy, and as we got our papers back I was surprised to find out that I did much better than I thought I did – even in Setswana of all subjects. The early morning studies had paid off, but still for the overall results I had to wait until the report was sent to my parents.

Shortly after our examinations our team headed to the playoffs to defend our trophy. This time the finals were held in Selibe Phikwe. I remember that morning Terrence Jacobs was in a buoyant mood; as he said to me and others in 'Block A' that they were just going to display the trophy and bring it back. We were all confident that we were going to repeat as champions. After all this team was even better than the one that won it all last year. Another school had other ideas though, and that was Moeding College.

News reached us that our first game against the hosts, Selibe Phikwe secondary, we won by five goals to one. We then faced Moeding College the next day which was on a Saturday. I was in our dormitory around five o' clock when I heard a fellow student, Phinda Khame the wag, announce outside our dormitories: "Guys, this just in, Moeding beat Lotsane by two goals to one." I was stunned and soon felt sick to the stomach as I rushed outside.

"What?!?" I exclaimed, not for a moment believing Phinda, who like me was also repeating his form 4 due to the fact that he had fallen very ill the previous year, and had missed a lot of school days.

"Yes, Mr. Pearce just arrived and told us." This was unbelievable.

"M-maybe Mr. Pearce left before the game was over, and is not informed of the latest results." I was desperate now for the chances of that happening were as good as those of the moon being made out of green cheese.

We still had one more game to play, but having lost to Moeding would prove to be costly, because Moeding, just like Lobsec last year, were the only school that posed a serious threat to our school repeating as champions. They had to, because many of their players were ex Itireleng students who were the Junior National Champions in 1985. That triumph had been bittersweet for me, because it happened after I left and this after we lost the previous year in heartbreaking fashion to Kagiso Secondary School.

Having disposed of Lotsane there was no way Moeding was going to drop points against either Selibe Phikwe Secondary School or Molefi Secondary School from Mochudi. Plus, they were hungry. We thrashed Molefi by eight goals to zilch, meaning that had we at least tied with Moeding, we would have repeated as champions since we had a superior goal difference, but in the end we had to watch as Moeding hoisted our trophy up high. When the team returned the first thing I did was ask a now solemn Terrence what had happened. How on earth could we have lost to Moeding?

"Sebati," Terrence said. "We were tied one all, City had the ball, and then he passed it to Wagga who then passed it to Rammidi who caught it. However, just as Wagga passed the ball, the Moeding guy who tried to disposes him kicked him in frustration, Wagga in anger turned around and kicked him in retaliation, but unfortunately the referee saw his foul and not that committed by the Moeding player, and ordered a free kick against us just out of the 18 area. Their guy kicked that ball so hard that there was no way our keeper could have caught it, and that is how we lost."

Montshiwa 'Wagga' Montshiwa was a very wonderful guy, unassuming, gentle, kind, and this is God's honest truth. It was just unfortunate that his temporary misjudgment of the situation cost us the game, and subsequently the championship. I would say he was caught up in the heat of the moment, especially after being deliberately fouled, and the perpetrator getting away with it.

Years later, when I was in the United States, and had the pleasure of reuniting with the Cornmaster himself; he introduced me to a couple of friends also from Botswana one of them being Motse Mokgosi also from Ramotswa, but had attended Moeding College, and was now enrolled at Kansas State University studying Chemical Engineering.

"So Motse who was that guy who scored that killer goal against us?" I asked.

"Oho, that was Maxiba."

"Man I heard that he unleashed a powerful shot no human could have caught."

"Yes," Motse agreed, "we did hear about Maxiba's shot. As a matter of fact that guy was so athletic and gifted too in other sports like softball. Actually, there was a tug of war going on between the softball and football teams, both needed his services badly as they were both in the playoffs at the same time, but in the end football prevailed." I personally wished softball had succeeded, and I know many from Lotsane would agree with me.

The one good thing about those playoffs is that our team got another brand new kit. I saw it when Dizzy arrived at our dormitory as he was still wearing it. Sadly, that would turn out to be the very last time during my stay at Lotsane that we would come close to being national champions again. We should have repeated in 1986, but such is sports – there are many great tragedies.

∗∗∗

As the term drew to a close we planned a class party that did not materialize for the simple reason that money was slow coming. We had asked that everyone contribute two Pula, but the number of those who did not in fact contribute far outweighed those who did so the idea was dropped. I felt very good about my exams but I was not certain if I had enough points to secure first place, and thus be eligible for a prize at the ceremony the following term. My social life could not have been any better; Olivia and I were getting along just fine. We did have our disagreements here and then but nothing earth shattering. In all, 1986 was turning out to be an amazing year, and I was enjoying every minute of it.

On the very last day of school the campus was almost empty as many had already left. I like many others like me were going to catch the train that evening. So with nothing much to do I wandered around campus and from dorm to dorm until I ended up in dorm one. Here I found a few of my friends including Cornmaster, Strong, Julian, and Thuso in a heated discussion, suggestions were being thrown left right and center.

"I say we head to Palapye right now and talk to father Brown I'm sure he'll understand and then we can catch the next bus …" someone said.

"Is this really going to work?" Thuso asked.

The debate and the endless flow of suggestions and alternatives went on and on. I did not quite understand what was going on, but from what I gathered somehow I had a feeling that these guys were headed for some kind of trip that was in danger of being called off. They were all Catholics from Ramotswa, and had strong ties with the local Church in Palapye. Strong was to tell me later that a camping trip had been organized where they had to head to some place up north, but at the last minute plans changed.

"Man I saw you guys giving out suggestions."

"Jones, we really wanted to go man, we just did not want to head back home to Ramotswa just like that without a fight," he said.

"Did you end up going though?"

"Yeah man, we did. You know what's worse? Julian was saying we drop the whole idea and just head back home; that of course was not an option. We had to go."

Years later, I was to ask Cornmaster what really was the motivating factor for this camping trip that these guys had to wreck their intellects for a solution.

"Jones," Cornmaster said to me, "you must understand that at these camps we met girls from other regions which made it all the more fun. Girls were what we were looking for, that and nothing else." To me that made perfect sense.

I went back to my dormitory where a few people were left. I looked around and spotted Ditshupo. Not too long ago him and Blackie had gotten into a fight right after tea break. Fish was the only witness and according to him the clash was brutal. I only arrived just as Blackie, who had been dragged away, went back to the scene of the fight looking for his foe. Hotstix stood at the door of dorm 6 where the fight had taken place, the whole area was crowded.

"Hotstix make way please …" Blackie said teary eyed.

"Blackie please don't fight man it's not worth it man let it go," Hotstix pleaded.

"No man Hotstix please, you don't understand this guy insulted my father man, my father I ought to teach him a lesson."

"Blackie, fighting solves nothing just go back to your dorm, relax and take a deep breath."

I think Blackie realized that pleading with Hotstix would get him nowhere so his demeanor immediately changed.

"Hotstix!" he shouted, "now it's a command. Get out of my way!" Hotstix duly stepped aside and let Blackie through.

Once inside Blackie was prevented from getting any closer to Ditshupo and the latter from him. This continued on and on. Whenever the two saw one another they were ready to rip each other's heads off, and then people would step in to stop them, and was at times a bit funny to watch as they would be both crying, and it seemed to me really that they were enjoying to the fullest the attention there were garnering. This would have continued had Blackie's big brother Ballman not intervened.

"Hey leave those guys alone," he seethed when a few colleagues were separating them for the umpteenth time. "If they want to fight let them. Are you going to keep separating them all day long? Be realistic man let them be, if they want to rip each other's eyeballs out let them. Just leave them alone." That solved the problem, because we did not see them anywhere near each other after that, and they were buddies again not too long after.

Chapter 22

Later that day we were transported to the train station where we had a lot of fun as usual. Just like last year we waited for the south bound mixed train, and Olivia was headed to Francistown and had to wait for the north bound train. I hung out with Ruth for a little while as Olivia was busy with a relative who attended Moeng College, and was brought by school truck just like us to the train station same as the Swaneng students. We talked at length about the great term that just ended, and the characters like Ediretse Nthobatsang and Kebagaisitse 'Triple K' Mapena, who we were going to miss during the break.

Ediretse who was later nicknamed 'Mogzen-Flagzen' in remembering Mmueledi, was the official class clown who never took offence nor offended anyone, and always had a smile on his face. Not only that he was also very brilliant especially at mathematics. Me and him were the tallest in the class. This was made obvious when Miss Pearson and a young good looking visiting teacher from the States named Mr. Munroe, did a fun activity with all of us by taking measurements of every single student in class, and then created a bar chart. The average height of our class was one meter and fifty two centimeters (about 5 feet.) So at one meter and eighty six centimeters (six feet one and half inches) I stood alone followed closely by Ediretse, and I was the only one in my group height and thus had a single bar that represented just me. This chart was displayed in our classroom for the public to see, and soon there were tiny comments written in pen on my bar that read: 'this has got to be Sebati' another one read, 'Sebati I reckon – Uloko'.

Kebagaisitse, whose name means 'I've beaten them', was also a very interesting individual. I recall Ruth always saying to him, "Kebagaisitse, the day I have a baby I want you to take care of it from time to time." I never really understood what she meant by that until later. You see Kebagaisitse was soft spoken and his voice was soothing, Ruth said it sounded more like a lullaby, and that a baby would most definitely fall asleep in his arms if he just as much as spoke to it. Strong remarked that sometimes when he spoke it's like he really did not want to or he was too tired or lazy to talk; that is how his voice sounded like when he spoke according to Strong.

We talked about these individuals and events that had happened during the term, and when it was time to leave we promised to stay in touch through writing, and the same with Olivia. The journey back home that night was very fascinating because I got to meet an old friend I had last seen in Lobatse about two years earlier, which for a teenager feels like ten years, his name was Sello. He attended Lobsec back then, and had transferred to Tutume McConnell College. I mention Sello because it was through him that I met Joyce Sebolao my very first girlfriend back in Lobatse in 1982. It was a wonderful meeting, and I in turn introduced him to a few friends from my school including a dynamic lady I had known since we were kids called Matlhogonolo 'Matt' Temane (now Mrs. Motsoela).

When I first saw Matt at Lotsane, I knew that I was not seeing her for the first time, and what was worse was that I was a bit standoffish at first, which I hated until finally we had a chance to talk. She had attended Naledi Secondary School, and while at Naledi was my best friend Osupile 'Osu' Kgabi's girlfriend. We will come to 'Osu' later. Matt then told me that she had attended Lesedi Primary School at the same time that I was there, and that she and Rama had been in the same class. That was when it suddenly made sense why she looked very familiar. Matt also went on to say that she and Rama always got into fights. Not surprising, because Matt is the type of person who never backs down from anyone, and I truly admired her for that. Not only was she very brilliant, she was very beautiful too and our friendship continues as of this writing.

***

Upon my arrival at home, I was ecstatic to find out that we had a portable black and white television set of our own that was powered by a car battery. Also that was the time when my uncle Vincent 'Rizzah' Malepa and his beautiful wife aunty Musa (who sadly succumbed to leukemia in 1995) were living with us. When I met uncle Rizzah back in

1981 he was a math teacher at GSS. This is after he got his Bachelor of Science degree in Economics at the University of Liberia. He taught for a while, and even had a brief stint at Swaneng Hill Secondary School, and then went to the University of Delaware were he read for his Masters in Economics, and had just returned in 1986 when they were living with us before they got their own place. Besides being distantly related, and the obvious age gap between them, my father and Rizzah have maintained a friendship that has stood the test of time, and it was through my uncle's influence years later that I was to come to the United States on a full Engineering scholarship.

Uncle Rizzah was very intelligent, and had a terrific sense of humor, and just like 'Big Joe' there was never a dull moment with him around. I was able to catch up on a lot of current events and shows on TV, I watched anything from educational programs (which I enjoyed immensely) to shows like *MacGyver*, and *Miami Vice*. The latter was to strike a chord in me years later. I was watching one episode where an actor of Japanese origin Cary-Hiroyuki Tagawa guest starred, and I was to remember his face from that day forward and so was the whole world, because he has a look you never forget. What I did not know that day, nor would I have ever dreamt; was that one day I would have the honor of working with Mr. Tagawa on a movie I wrote and produced, and he played a character I created from my second novel entitled *'When The Cobra Strikes'*. I also watched a popular show called *'Santa Barbara'*, and the leading man, Mark Arnold, who went on to star in such movies as *'Teen Wolf'* and *'Threesome'* among many; worked with me in a feature film I wrote, produced, and directed called *'Geraldine'*. Life can be very interested if not amazing at times. Finally my report came. I was constantly making trips to the post office at the mall whenever I had the opportunity, but when I finally saw the official brown government envelope I froze. Many thoughts were flashing through my mind as I looked at the envelope. The report of course was addressed to my father, but I just had to open it. I could not bear the thought of taking the long journey back home speculating what the results were. I slowly opened it. My head was now spinning with eagerness and my hands were trembling.

Slowly and carefully I opened the envelope. I did not completely unfold the report, but instead peeked at the potion that said *'Class*

Position' and it was followed by the number 1. I was crossing the main road at the southern side of the mall, and while in mid traffic, I think I must have jumped at least five feet high if not more. I did it! And I could not wait to break the news to my father. Even though I was not surprised by the result for I had really worked my tail off, I was nonetheless excited beyond words. I was going to get the prize I coveted most, and hopefully, in front of my father sometime in early November. Needless to say I was relieved and the rest of the holidays were a breeze. I still have that report.

I did run into Hotstix on one of those days when I went to the mall. The movie *'Indiana Jones And The Temple Of Doom'* was just released, so we bought tickets for the matinee show. Since the movie did not begin until 3:30 p.m., and it was only around 11:00 a.m., Hotstix felt that it was not necessary for me to make that long journey home, and to just meet up again later that day. He lived close by, therefore, he invited me to have lunch at his place (even though he was from Bokspits, his family owned a house in Gaborone), and then from there we would go to watch the film. In the meantime, since we had time to kill we decided to take a walk to the park not too far off in the affluent neighborhood north of the mall. A place locals called *'Tshaba Ntsa'* or 'Beware of the dog', because of the numerous signs bearing that warning.

As we walked in this quiet neighborhood talking about Lotsane, and the highlights of the last term, we noticed two old white ladies ahead of us carrying grocery bags walking home and chatting cheerfully, one of them had her purse tucked underneath one of her armpits. Then out of nowhere from ahead of them, a chap who obviously looked like he was not from the neighborhood came trotting toward them. Our natural inclination was that he was headed somewhere in a hurry, but when he got to the two ladies he casually grabbed the purse from underneath the old woman's armpit, and trotted backwards on his heels as if nothing had happened. He was even whistling a tune to himself. On reaching a safe distance he turned around and ran like the wind.

At first the two ladies were too stunned to react immediately, and when they did they screamed as they dropped their grocery bags and attempted to go after the thief. However, each time they covered little ground away from their bags they would scream, run back to the bags, because they left them unprotected, and then try running after the thief, who was now almost out of sight, and then remember their groceries, and head back to them and once there try to run after him again, and the same routine would repeat itself. They were obviously in shock, and even when we tried to help they chased us away like we were the criminals. So Hotstix and I let them be. Although this was a very unfortunate incident, it was hilarious to watch and thus we found it very difficult not to laugh.

Sometime later we went back to Hotstix's home, and all this time his eyes were red from the tears that came as a result of continuous and prolonged laughter. We enjoyed the movie nonetheless, and as members of the entertainment committee, we agreed that this was a type of movie that would be great if it were to be shown at our school. Since Broadhurst was far from the mall, I had to catch a taxi and Hotstix graciously walked me to the station, and we looked forward to meeting up again at school. The third term was around the corner which meant that for people like Hotstix, Blackie, City, and my dormitory mates this was to be their last term. Their final exams were coming. I was amazed at how fast time flew.

Chapter 23

Third term came, and once again it was just so much fun to be back at school. The term began at the beginning of September, but that year was special because of the impeding celebrations to mark the country's 20th anniversary, which were just around the corner. Batswana are a fun loving and peaceful people, which is why everyone looked forward to these celebrations, because we knew there would be no holds barred. We resumed with our rehearsals like nothing happened.

Mr. Geary came to one of our rehearsals to give us pointers concerning observations he had made at the drama festival. For instance with my character and Lillian's he had something specific to say.

"Sebati," Mr. Geary said, "when you are embracing Lillian try not to leave any space in between the two of you. Remember she is the love of your life and you want the audience to believe that." He then asked one of the girls to stand in front of him. "Don't worry I'm not going to kiss you," Mr. Geary could be humorous like that, and went on to tell me that when she was standing in front of me to look her in the eye, and my look should tell her everything that I felt. He did mention that the scene with me and Stoner was magnificent except for one thing. Stoner's character reprimanded mine by hitting him with his walking stick, now his character was supposed to be very advanced in years, but the way he hit me with the stick was like a young man, he went on to demonstrate, and this was followed by laughter from all. Mr. Geary's tips were priceless and we were glad to implement them.

We were scheduled to perform our play at 2:30pm on the 28th of September, and our other play was to perform the same day but at 8:00pm that night, which worked perfectly because of the ghoul in the play. I on the other hand was a bit disappointed that our performance was not at night, but we gave it our best shot nonetheless, and the audience was thrilled. We performed at the renowned *Capitol Cinema*, which was at the mall, and at the time the one and only state of the art Movie Theater in the country. I only just got word out to my parents about our performance that afternoon; that my father barely made it to the end of the performance, but was there nonetheless.

Everyone's performance that day was on point that when our scene came; Lillian and I were so much in character that we actually kissed for real on stage this time, a bit more than what Mr. Geary had suggested, and this show of affection led many to suggest that Lillian and I continue our love affair in the real world. After all, some suggested, we were both passionate people, tall, and made a great couple on stage so why not let art imitate life and vice versa? Although it was tempting I must say, but it was not that simple – we both belonged to people who loved us dearly.

That evening just before our Setswana play took to the stage, we were honored to watch a fine performance by students from the University of Botswana, and members of its travelling theater as they performed a play about the great Tshekedi Khama, who ranks in Botswana's history as one of her foremost people. One of the cast in that play was a lady I had seen perform when I was 12 years old in a play called *'The Chief's Bride'*. Her performance was stellar and I was totally impressed by her portrayal of the bride named Tamara, and vowed that one day I would be on stage just like her for I assumed at the time (and still do) that I would never find anything else in life that would have made me happier. At the time she attended St. Joseph's College, and her name was Potlako Jankie. I made sure to meet her back stage, and tell her how much I loved her performance, and how she had been an inspiration to me. Mr. Moswela earlier in the beginning had said, 'give a great performance and people will *never* forget you.' I was seeing a classic example of that.

The great thing about those independence celebrations that year was that they were a week long. We had to have permission from our parents if we were to be away from school; I was granted mine and thus stayed behind when the rest went back to school. Olivia too stayed with her relatives in Gaborone, and later we met at the annual Trade Fair. I had not been there in five years, but coming back this time around was a great treat. We then met at the mall the next day, and it was refreshing to meet in a different environment far from the surrounding *mophane* forest or *lephaneng* as it was known by the students.

However, the highlight of that week and that year was meeting my long lost brother John Max Moreti in Gaborone. He was still serving his national service in the northern part of the country near the diamond mining town of Orapa. And was given time off to visit friends and family during that week of bliss and plenty. It was an exciting reunion once again more so that we were joined by Caesar 'Stelafunk' Mooketsi, whom I had resorted to calling 'the hunk of the year' and Moemedi Patrick 'Two-Two' Raperekisi. We met at the revamped national stadium to watch the celebrations, which were to be crowned later that evening by a football match between Botswana ('the Zebras') and Malawi ('the Flames'). We eagerly anticipated this clash, and knowing that if we went to our respective homes for lunch, chances were good that we would miss out on the great seats we had secured, and worse still miss one another. So, we decided that the best thing would be to go to one of the 'Take Away' (Fast Food) restaurants and lunch there.

We agreed that the best place to go to would be a place called '*Middle Star*', which was north of where we were. It turned out to be a poor choice because when we got there, there was not a single place in the shopping complex that sold any kind of fast food; so we were forced to settle on a loaf of bread and four pints of milk. The bread was not sliced so we had to break it with our hands to divide it among ourselves. For teenagers a sight like this one can be a bit embarrassing, which is why whenever girls would pass by 'Two Two' would pretend as if he was just drinking milk only, and had nothing to do with the bread, which was funny to us because we told him it was folly to deprive his stomach of food simply because he was shy, but then I could relate as such a thing made me really self-conscious only last year. On our way back to the stadium we started filling Max in about life at Lotsane since he left.

"Did you know that Sebati is a very good actor?" one of the guys asked him.

"Oh yes, without a doubt. I saw that quite a bit last year when he used to perform his skit with that girl Daisy Alexander," Max responded. Incidentally, Daisy had dropped out after that first term at Lotsane when we were form 4s, and later moved to Germany after she got a scholarship. I was to run into her several times over the next few years. As we were walking back to the stadium a thought suddenly occurred to me.

"Guys, what do you think of setting up Max and Bame?" I could think of no one else suitable to go out with the enigma.

"Yes," Caesar agreed. "I really think that would be a good idea."

"I think so too, she's beautiful Max is handsome I'm sure they would make a great couple," said Two-Two.

There was a smirk on my brother's face when he said, "Yeah, I would like to meet her."

When we arrived at the stadium we were able to occupy the best seats on the northern side. We patted ourselves on the back as we waited for the game to begin. A multitude of people was pouring in, and among the people I spotted an old friend from Itireleng, Tlhaloso Semausu, who also saw me and immediately came to seat by us. Tlhaloso was a year behind me at Itireleng, and had transferred to Moeding College for his form four. The fact that they had deprived us of a second straight national championship was not lost to me.

"So you guys beat us eh?!" I said to him soon after everyone was settled down and properly introduced.

He smiled widely and said, "Oh man you should not have reminded me. We killed you guys' man." Following a brief pause he continued, "But man that guy from your school what's his name again … City? Man I'm scared of that guy, he's very good and I would say he was the best on the field of play that day."

The game started at last and we were at the edge of our seats. We had every reason to, because at the time Botswana had the dire reputation of being known as *'the whipping boys of Africa'*. Facing a team of Malawi's caliber meant that we were in danger of seeing that dubious trend of being *'the whipping boys'* continue. The game started at a frantic pace with Malawi's Ian Banda causing havoc in the Botswana defense led by the great Walker Rathedi, but as the game wore on Banda was somewhat contained but only just. Cheered on by the vociferous crowd Botswana's goal keeper Mooketsi 'China' Mading was just incredible, and then toward the end of the first half with the game still at a goalless draw, there was corner kick against Malawi, which was taken by the corner kick specialist Rio Maswabi. Rio is still to this day ranked as one of the best dead ball specialists the country has ever seen. He was so good that he could score directly from a corner kick.

Rio took the corner with the grand Terrence Mophuting playing the decoy. Somehow, Malawi could not quite clear the ball out of danger and conceded yet another corner kick, and again Rio was called upon to do the honors. And again Terrence did his part. These mind you were not the best corners Rio had ever taken, but were effective nonetheless. This time the ball bounced around inside the 18 area, and I did not quite see what happened, but the referee blew his whistle and pointed at the penalty spot. It was a penalty against Malawi. The partisan crowd went wild at the prospect of Botswana going up by a goal. We on the other hand were tense, Malawi's towering goalkeeper, Thomas Zimbili, seemed confident enough judging by his body language, but was instead sent the wrong way as the ball hit the net for Botswana's first goal – the crowd went berserk.

The second half proved to be a battle of nerves as we constantly looked at our watches willing time to move quicker as Botswana clung desperately to a 1 nothing lead. There were obvious delaying tactics from the ball boys, who were assigned to get the ball as quickly as possible when it went out of bounds; that the Malawi players felt obligated to do the honors themselves whenever the ball went out of bounds, and belonged to the host nation. Tlhaloso even began praying loudly to God Almighty to grant us this improbable victory. Toward the dying minutes of the game Malawi threw everything into attack, and on the counter Botswana's speedy and volatile striker Cornelius Mudzingwa, known to everyone as 'Matoni', breached the Malawian defense and sprinted toward the goal posts, and buried the ball in the net beyond Zimbili's long reach. Botswana was up 2 goals to none, and this goal proved to be the knockout punch 'the Zebras' needed, and 'the Flames' were doused. Matoni out of sheer joy sprinted the length of the entire field on the running track mind you, and when he passed by the dignitaries he punched his fist in the air. Botswana had won, and instantly Matoni and the Zebras of 1986 became folk heroes.

It was a befitting victory to a great celebration that had gripped the country. And for many of us that memory was to be etched in our minds forever. Following the game we all went our separate ways, but Max and I knew we would stay in touch now more than ever, as a visit from him sometime during the third term was imminent. I returned to school a few days later, and was told about a big celebration that had taken place during our absence. A cow had been slaughtered I was told, and that there was merrymaking among the teachers and students alike. All in all it was a wonderful week for everyone, just as it was meant to be, because 20 years of independence in Africa is a momentous achievement, and with her system of government Botswana was a shining example to the entire continent.

***

The interesting thing I found out about that third term was that Rinah and I were both number ones in our class. Although this had been befitting, because the competition was fierce, and we were best of friends; deep down I was worried that perhaps the prize for best student might just go to Rinah and her only. Especially when I heard 'Reverend' Marokane say he had seen a thing similar to that happen to someone at his previous school.

"The two were dead even on points," he said. "But then they gave the prize to the other girl." This kind of talk had me worried.

Ernest on the other hand was more comforting as were many others. "They will give the prize to both of you," he said matter of factly, because he did not see any reason why they would not. Even when I mentioned my concerns to my father, he told me not to worry, because whether I got the prize or not I should be proud of the fact that I had done very well. I agreed, and thus played the waiting game. My friend Moses on the other hand was certain the Art prize had his name written all over it. He had every reason to feel confident. The previous term he had won the first prize in the national Art competition, and was presented the cash prize at the national museum in Gaborone a few weeks later. I was very happy for him.

Since it was the third term, and the end of year parties were just around the corner; clubs intensified their fund raising efforts. One such club was of course Santos. They organized a disco competition this time to be staged in Palapye at the local community center. The competitors as usual were members of the club, interestingly but not surprisingly, Blackie was one of the contestants, and Hotstix was the master of ceremonies and wore his khaki uniform which made it look like the true Lotsane event that it was, because he looked good in it.

To give himself a better shot at winning, Blackie mobilized as much support as he could. Besides his dorm mates, led by Terrence Jacobs, he invited nonmembers from school including girls. This was easy to do, because the event was held on a Friday and transportation was provided by the school. Knowing that it was either study that evening, or go to Palapye to cheer for Blackie, the latter knew he had all the advantage in the world, and thus he had so many willing volunteers that in the end he had to turn down many. There simply was no room to accommodate everyone even though he would have gladly taken the whole school if could.

This canvassing for support by Blackie worked wonders, because when the competition started all of his supporters crowded themselves at one end of the room, and screamed when Blackie appeared on the dance floor. He was dressed for the part, and like a true disco king he danced away. The decibel level from his supporters hardly let up; if anything it rose even higher that we could hardly hear Silver Pozzoli's song *"Step by Step"*. This swayed the judges most certainly, because Blackie was declared the winner in the end. The judges mind you, were people of great standing from Palapye, and had never met or seen Blackie or any of the competitors for that matter before that evening; so no one could accuse them of being bias. Even though it must be said that Blackie was dazzling that night. In second place was Caesar, and in third place was Blackie's older brother Ballman. Yet again Blackie had rocked Lotsane.

Shortly thereafter there was a disturbing rumor that a bunch of form 5's, among them Pius Malikongwa, would go about at night before evening studies, a time when lovers spent time together around campus, and harassed the couples. They meant no malice, but this was a very annoying practice especially among the form fours who felt their privacy violated. Unfortunately for these fellows they came across Bonang and his girlfriend on one of their silly quests.

When they realized that it was Bonang they had harassed they quickly apologized, and later on Pius, on his own volition, decided to go to Bonang's dormitory after evening studies to placate him even further, but Bonang wanted no part of it.

"Man just get out of here," Bonang said.

"Come on, I came to tell you that really it was not you we were after; why can't you understand that?"

"Pius, I'm not going to tell you again." Bonang I heard was fuming, but Pius was one of those hard learners, who knew not when to quit; especially when a guy like Bonang was getting vexed.

"Hey, I came to apologize why can't you just …" he did not get to finish what he was about to say, because in an instant Bonang grabbed him by the arm, with both hands, and threw Pius out of the dormitory like he was tossing out a sack of potatoes. And in Pius, we are talking about a guy who was over six feet tall and weighed at least 200 pounds compared to Bonang's 5 foot 7 inch 150 pound frame. The ease with which he threw the much bigger guy was to become a thing of legend in the boys dormitory; that almost the entire form 4 boys decided to enroll in Karate, and Bonang chose to break away from the main club that consisted of the form 5's and was going nowhere really, and formed a new club that was to make even the 1985 group seem like amateurs in as far as running the club and raising funds. And we all had Pius to thank.

A week or so later, we got word that Gaborone Secondary School (GSS) was coming to our school for a tournament in both Karate and Kung Fu. In addition to that they would be bringing their modern dancers to perform as well. This was great news. GSS was one of the elite government schools in the country for the mere fact that they were based in the capital city. Had they made the same trip last year, I am sure we would have been privileged to watch JBC perform in person, but by 1986 the hip hop craze had slowly fizzled. We were thrilled nonetheless at the prospect of having them come to our school. As Karatekas, we knew that we were going to be facing formidable opponents, because their students for the most part trained at local clubs, and were supposedly more advanced. My best friend, Osupile 'Osu' Kgabi for instance, trained at our club Tsosamotse Karate Club daily, and as for me I only had that opportunity when schools closed.

We were excited nevertheless and trained hard. With less than two weeks to go our training, headed by Bonang Mapolanka, included now roadwork by running around the football field no less than 12 laps (jogging off campus was banned after Dixie Ndlovu's tragic death). Surprisingly we were joined in these rigorous workout sessions by none other than Blackie Kealotswe. He was not a martial artist, but somehow he had secured a complete *gi* when he took to running with us. The fact that he was there with us partaking in the painstaking activities motivated us. Here was someone who was not even a member of the club right there in the trenches with us, and even dressed the part. But then again everyone on campus knew what our objective was, and our outdoor training drew quite a bit of attention, and it was no coincidence that Blackie was there training with us.

I do think we over trained a bit, because even though I felt in shape, my muscles were fatigued as we awaited GSS anxiously. I was also excited at the prospect of seeing my friend Osu again. I had even arranged that he spend the night with us in dorm 2, and not in the common room like all the other visitors. That time when we trained for GSS also showed me how good Bonang really was, if anything he was better than anyone of us had imagined. He was simply light years away, and with him on our side many of us were silently confident that we were going to win the tournament after all. That Saturday afternoon, I took a long nap and was woken around 4:30pm by some activity in front of our block.

"What's going on?" I asked as I got up from my bed.

"GSS is here," someone said excitedly. My heart skipped a beat as I rushed outside. And sure enough I could see the new faces all over the place hanging around the public benches in front of our dormitories. I looked around with a smile on my face hoping to spot my friend. I then heard a familiar voice.

"Look at him ... hey are you blind?"

I turned around and saw my friend Osu with a big smile on his face. It was yet another happy reunion as we talked at length as he filled me with the latest events at the club. We also agreed that at the tournament we would face one another and we also promised that even though we would try very hard to compete to win for our respective schools; we would try very hard not to hurt one another.

Chapter 24

Since it was Saturday evening; the performance by the GSS students was to be the entertainment that night, and no one was disappointed. The ladies did their acrobatics and modern dance which was fun to watch, and another batch performed another type of dance that was equally impressive. I must say that there were some very beautiful girls from this school and it was very hard to look away.

The GSS students it seemed had come to show us that they could entertain us with their dance and that they were advanced, but we had dancers at our school who were not going to sit back and watch while the others took over their school. When the GSS girls recessed Henry 'Hex' Sejoe, Steve Moepi, and Ipha Gumbalume took the dance floor. They were all dressed to kill, and danced to Romano Bais's *'Dial My Number'*. These three guys were out to prove that our school had dancers who were just as good, if not better, regardless of where we were located, which in this case was in the middle of the boondocks; some 150 miles away from the city.

Hex was unleashed. He was simply incredible that night. Hex was a natural dancer; that is what he lived for and loved to do. To this day he cannot stop dancing - it is just in his blood. That day the song seemed to emanate from his very pores when he jumped high in the air and while up there, spun around, pulled the flaps of his white jacket and spread them out like he was flying, and then landed on one knee and started to bounce backwards. This was something that none of us had ever seen, and the 'city girls' were screaming in spite of themselves. One of our own, the other beauty queen Nametsegang, now a form 5, was brought to tears.

"Ijooo! Hex wa bina tlhe bathong ijooo," "Oh my God Hex can dance," she kept saying repeatedly.

She was right, and we were all impressed. Not to be outdone Ipha and Steve also surpassed even themselves, but really that night Hex felt challenged on his own turf and he answered the call. Not surprising really, because during the second term holidays Hex had won a dance competition that was staged at Lotsane, which qualified him to participate at the national dance competition held at the National Trade Fair. He won this competition as well and in addition to that he was rewarded with 15 albums of his choice. Being the very smart guy that he is, Hex knew that if he got cassettes (Compact Discs were unknown to us at the time), he would be tempted to take them to school with him where they would either get lost or stolen. So he chose instead to get vinyl records. Winning the national competition qualified him for the international championships. He was the only high school student to partake in such an event, which then inevitably coincided with school days, but Hex had gone so deep into the competition to quit now that he went missing from school for a very long time. At last when the whole thing ended, he did not win but ended up among the top 15. A momentous effort considering that he was going up against dance professionals from all over. When he finally returned to school it seemed as if he had not missed a day as far as his academics were concerned. Hex was just simply amazing.

At last it was time for the much awaited tournament. Moeti, Ernest, and a fellow named Elias Moasi were our first three fighters. Of the three Ma Enzo won most convincingly and so did Olefhile 'Chamzen' Thelo. Mompati from our school faced off with Misani from GSS, who was one of their best fighters, and a great martial artist as well. Misani won by half a point, which is how close the fight was because Mompati was also good. Osu and I were the last to face off, and the moment we stood up the audience was in raptures. This I think was mainly due to the fact that we were both dressed in our *gis* and thus looked more professional; not because we were better than the other fighters – if anything our sparring was a disaster.

Perhaps it was because we were both very familiar with each other's style or my muscles were just too stiff from overtraining, but whatever the case was we were not impressive at all. We relied too much on kicks and what was worse was that when I kicked he kicked, and our legs would meet in the air time and time again that Bonang and Moss, the instructor from GSS, pulled us aside with Moss fuming.

"Guys come on spar; stop fighting like chickens!"

After promising them that we would improve we would resort to the same thing again much to the two referees' (Bonang and Moss) frustration. As I was getting tired, Osu accidentally hit my right hand, and I subsequently punched myself in the eye. The pain was excruciating that the fight had to be stopped for a brief moment, while Bonang and Moss attended to me. Osu, as required by martial arts tournament tradition sat on his hind legs, and faced the other direction. I looked up outside and saw Mr. Mudidi, who gestured at me to come to him and I did.

"Are you alright?" he asked. I could tell he was really concerned in a very fatherly way. At that moment Moss and Bonang followed suit. "Did you people get permission from the police to stage this tournament?" It was just like Mr. Mudidi to go by the book.

"Sir, this is just a sport like any other sport," Moss said respectfully.

"How are you feeling Sebati?" he asked again.

"I'm fine sir."

"Okay, just be careful."

I walked back into the hall thinking that the fight was over, but I was mistaken. We were ordered to get back into the ring and take our positions, much to my surprise and the crowd's dismay. Instead of kicking this time I delivered a straight punch aimed at Osu's chest, but Osu executed an upward block that diverted the punch to his mouth making it an illegal hit. There was a bit of blood. I felt bad for that was not intentional. In the end, Moss I think had enough of all this claptrap, because he stopped the fight and thereafter disqualified us both.

"Sebati," Blackie was to ask me later, "were you intent on getting revenge, is that what happened?" there was a big smile on his face.

"No man, I wouldn't do that."

"Why not?"

"Believe it or not Blackie, Osu is my best friend, and not only that we belong to the same club in Gaborone."

"Oho, no wonder. Ballman suspected the same thing judging by the way you guys fought."

The whole scenario was a nightmare for Olivia though, and I am told that she could not watch the fight at all and kept her face averted at all times. I later introduced her to 'the villain' Osu. Many people around school were surprised to find out that we were indeed very good friends. This was confirmed by the fact that we shared the same bed that night. The GSS students left the next morning after breakfast. Osu and I promised to hook up again when the summer break came, which was drawing all the more closer.

***

That third term I devised a strategy to benefit Max as far as Bame was concerned. I knew she had no idea who Max was, so to plant a seed I came up to her one day and said, "Bame, a friend of mine said to say hi to you. His name is John Moreti, but known to his entire friends as Max?"

"Who?"

"John ... Max ... come on don't tell me that you don't know him."

"Sorry Sebati, but I have absolutely no idea who you are talking about." One could have been able to tell this by looking at her pretty face.

The next time I saw her I made sure I had a picture of Max with me. She was in the dining hall cleaning with some of her dormitory mates, who included the energetic Josie, who was the female version of Blackie, but to a much less extent. Ironically, the picture I had of Max had been taken in the very same dining hall in 1984, and Bame and I were standing close to the exact spot when I showed her the photograph.

"You're certain you don't know this guy?" I asked her again, and like before she shook her head just as I had expected, but now she had a mental image of Max in her head – I hoped.

It is worth noting that a few months before I had a conversation with 'the Wiseman' George Mackenzie regarding Bame.

"S.B." George said to me one day, "why don't you ask Bame out?"

"I already have a girlfriend George ... remember?"

"I know but you two would make a cute couple."

It was a charming idea at the time, and I would be lying if I say I was not tempted to make a move, but that would have complicated matters though, because asking Bame out would mean I would first have to break it off with Olivia, and there was no guarantee that Bame was going to agree to my advances. Even though I could be persistent in chasing a girl I wanted, I was not prepared to do that again. I did talk to my good friend Ruth about this possibility since she knew her better, and I did not get a ringing endorsement from her thus the idea was discarded. I was somewhat relieved and glad that I did not break Olivia's heart, and really there was absolutely no reason to because we were both happy.

I arranged with Max to visit the day when we had a record night so that he could have ample time to speak to her. And when the day came, Max arrived as planned and soon thereafter I had someone call Bame, and she met us at the academic area. I introduced the two, and just to put Bame at ease I sat there with them the entire time as we made small talk. By the way they were looking at each other I could tell that the two hit it off just as I had hoped. If I could I would have patted myself on the back.

Before I go any further, it is worth pointing out that the previous year Max had a girlfriend whom I will call Joy. She was a form 4 at the time, and the unspoken rule was that I would be around in 1986 to look after her, and make sure that she stayed true to Max. That was not the case I'm afraid, because a few months into 1986 she fell in love with another guy who was also a form 5, and in the process severed ties with me. For some reason I was suddenly the enemy in her eyes and she stopped talking to me. And that marked the end of her relationship with Max.

Now when Max came that day and it was clear to everyone, especially Joy, that there were fireworks between him and Bame, Joy wanted everyone to believe that she and Max still had a thing going on. Although Max was very gentlemanly about it; his body language told her to get lost and that time soon. Joy got the message loud and clear. Now unimpeded, I left the two alone this time, and at record night seeing them together dancing and chatting like long lost lovers brought sheer joy to my heart. The next day after lunch Bame, myself, and a few friends escorted Max to the Palapye/Serowe junction where he was to catch a ride back to his Tirelo Sechaba post. The rest of us walked ahead as he and the enigma walked hand in hand talking softly and giggling. Later when I told my friend Ruth about what had transpired, and the fact that Bame had a new man in her life (I had never seen Bame that happy) Ruth smiled.

"Why didn't you ask 'the Wiseman' to give them words of wisdom about their blissful future right after Bame crowned him?" Ruth asked with a wide grin on her face, and we both laughed.

A few days later Bame sent for me and we met in the academic area. Bame always had a sweet disposition about her that really made one feel very comfortable around her. She was smiling as usual and we sat on one of the public benches.

"I think your friend is cute," she said. "I just wrote to him telling him how crazy I am about him."

There was no need for her to elaborate any further, because what she was telling me was that she and my brother were now officially boyfriend and girlfriend. I was thrilled to hear that, and I remember walking around with a grin on my face that day. The two went on to carry that relationship for a long time, and I was always proud of the fact that I played a part in bringing them together. Truly, because I felt they were both wonderful people who deserved one other at the time.

***

One day at supper we found out that part of our table was missing. The type of tables we used were long and thin, and had to be joined to a similar partition that made it complete. The missing partition was taken by our neighbors from dormitory one. Having one partition of the table was very inconvenient, and really cramped our way of eating.

"Hey, bring back our table," we demanded.

The dorm one fellows just ate their food in silence and dared not look at us as our anger mounted.

"Are you guys' deaf? We said bring our table now." Our orders started to become all the more threatening until Kgotso told us to leave them alone, which we reluctantly did.

Shortly thereafter, I think someone accidentally tipped the table a little hard, because in the next instant a whole bowl of hot tea spilled on Gaolatlhe's lap. He jumped, and that again tilted the table, but luckily we were in time to avert further disaster by quickly shifting away from the flimsy partition. By this time we had attracted the attention of the entire dining hall, and when Gaolatlhe walked out awkwardly because of the burning tea and wet pants he was laughed at. It was indeed an embarrassing scenario for him.

Another row with dorm one happened not too long after and this involved none other than Blackie. It was again at suppertime when Isaac said something unflattering to Blackie, and then the latter responded in kind. Blackie could be playful yes, but that did not mean that he would let everyone walk all over him like what Isaac was attempting to do.

"*Ke tla ntsha ditedunyana tseo ka setlhaku,*" "I'll kick that little goatee off your chin," Blackie fumed. Isaac was growing a goatee that he was extremely proud of.

At that moment Moses added his two cents directed at Blackie that was just as disparaging as Isaac's remark had been. In his mind Blackie was probably thinking *'oh not Moses of all people'*, because he immediately stood up and looked around to make sure that everyone was listening, especially the girls, and cupped both hands on his mouth to amplify his voice, and shouted:

"*Moses, o marete*!" "Moses, your coconuts!" In Setswana the insult was more pronounce, and Blackie said it in such a way that made Moses feel naked – just as he had intended. Soon thereafter order was restored and the victims knew that Blackie was not one to be trifled with.

Third term also marked the sub team tournament season. My team's strength, Callies, it seemed had declined a notch from the previous year. The first game of the tournament was between Santos and Executive Cosmos. That year Santos had assembled a fine team that included the likes of Eric 'Chippa ' Mokgwa, Motseothata 'Dizzy' Keabetswe, John 'Stop Nonsense Buddha John' Monyai, Tebogo 'Why give me Korobela' Maruping, David Khunwane, and also a new goal keeper who they got from Chiefs named Gaofenngwe 'Ngui' Ngwato - better known to the whole school by his epithet. I suppose that they took a very close look at their goalkeeping department, and realized after the last incident with Blackie that it would be folly to have only one man as keeper. Especially if that one man was Blackie. To Santos' advantage, Ngui was good, and proved to be a viable addition to the team because he had the reflexes of a cat. Something I would definitely attribute to his martial arts prowess (he belonged to the Kung Fu club, and was their instructor).

Also, Santos had been humiliated at the last tournament. Not only were they rock bottom, but they had not scored a single goal the entire competition. This was more than extra motivation for them to come out guns blazing in their first match against Executive Cosmos. The play of Chippa was particularly impressive, and when they scored some twenty minutes into the game they celebrated that goal like never before. Judging by their performance that day, it was clear to everyone that the defending champions, Chiefs, were not going to have things that easy this time around. A team had risen from the ashes like the Phoenix that day to challenge them. As the game wore on Santos got stronger, but unfortunately it started to rain just before half time and the game was called off, and was set to be replayed on Monday.

The next day the game was between Callies and Chiefs. At our meeting that day before the game I insisted, against my better judgment, that Hotstix be included in the lineup. Not because Hotstix was my friend, but even though he was not a footballer by any stretch, I liked his aggressive way of play which was totally unorthodox, and hoped it would throw the opposition off balance. But the only drawback, besides lacking natural soccer skills, was that Hotstix yelled a lot, especially at his teammates, and would at times use expletives, which would discourage a fellow teammate; particularly those who were not used to his at times abhorrent ways.

Something similar to that happened a few months earlier when during the game he insulted his own teammate, the ever smiling Justice Boemo, for not passing him the ball. That he did it in his broken Setswana, and in the process inviting laughter did not help at all. To make matters worse is that he almost brought the game in disrepute by refusing to be substituted, and I had to use all my negotiation skills to have him continue playing.

That is why I took a lot of heat after we lost that game to Chiefs after holding a one nothing lead deep into the second half, only to have Chiefs, led by the evergreen Lepholetha, come back and score three goals in rapid succession. During that game Hotstix was marked out of the game, by Ediretse 'Flagzen' Nthobatsang my tall classmate, to a point that it seemed as if Chiefs were playing with eleven players against ten. The only thing that stood out in as far as Hotstix was concerned was his jersey and shorts; he looked real good in them like a professional in the English Premier League – nothing more. It was so bad that even Terrence Jacobs voiced his dissatisfaction.

"Jones, to be honest you guys took a huge gamble by putting Hotstix in the game. Who came up with that bonehead idea anyway?" he asked.

I looked at him and pointed to my chest. He softened up a bit but his criticism was not dampened.

"Sorry Jones, but you shouldn't have done that. That was a huge blunder."

I wanted to tell him that there was no use closing the stable after the horse had already bolted, but I wanted to do it in such a way that he would feel as though he was poking his nose into affairs that were really none of his concern. After all, it was not his team that had lost, but mine. If anything, I had seen him cheer all of Chiefs' goals on the sidelines even though he was an Executive Cosmos member, and all of us saw Chiefs as the enemy. I could have told him that I suppose, but Terrence was a friend and a great one at that, who had been there for me through tough times, so I forever held my peace. Nevertheless things got worse that in the end even Hotstix came to me to apologize.

"S.B. sorry man, I know I let you down. It just hurts me that you are the one who is bearing the brunt for my dismal performance on the field today."

"No don't worry about it Hotstix, none of this is your fault, after all we cannot place the blame on a single individual's shoulders," I said. It was easy to place the blame on someone like Hotstix, when the truth really was that we were no match to the likes of Lepholetha 'City' Senne and company, and everyone seemed to overlook that fact.

"Don't worry I will make it up to you."

"How?" I asked, and silently wondered if he was high on grass or something, because the only way would be for him to be put back in the lineup for our next game, and for him to score goals that would win us the game, and after that afternoon's debacle who in their right mind would *ever* let Hotstix play again?

"One way or another I will make Chiefs lose a game that they will feel it to the bones." I had no idea what Hotstix had in mind. In truth I just scoffed at the thought as simply hot air coming out of his mouth. His words though would prove to be prophetic.

The next day, which happened to be a Saturday morning, Chiefs faced off with Santos. The sidelines were colorful with the orange and red from the fans of the respective teams that even Bame, as the reigning Miss Santos and dressed in her ceremonial robe, was serenaded when she went to pick up a ball that went out of bounds to give back to a player of her team. The game itself was a very tense affair that even City, of all people, missed a penalty and the game ended in a stale mate - one goal each. And with the current standings there was no telling who the champions were going to be. It was a tossup among the three other teams namely: Executive Cosmos, Santos, and Chiefs. That scenario changed the next day in a way that was never to be forgotten, and the person responsible was that man again - Andries 'Hotstix' Ryan.

When Chiefs faced Executive Cosmos the next day late in the afternoon; the atmosphere was just as electric as the day before. The whole school it seemed was behind Cosmos to pull off the upset. They were led by Hotstix who was dressed in white short pants, and an unbuttoned shirt with no shoes, and many ladies were looking at his hairy legs that needed a tan. I know this may sound redundant, but even dressed as he was he still looked good, and stood out. That was not all; he had with him an empty vessel, which he filled with stones that he continually shook to create more noise. I had never seen Hotstix that animated so did a lot of people that day I am sure. Whenever a Chiefs player was in possession of the ball he would yell, shake the vessel, scream obscenities at that player; all done in his broken Setswana that it proved to be a very effective form of distraction. For ninety minutes straight all that was heard from the sidelines was Hotstix's voice, the shaking of the vessel, followed by laughter thanks to his Setswana. Even the Cosmos girls, dressed in white, who were grouped at the western end of the field, and screamed bloody murder whenever City was in possession of the ball, and the other loud chap Cuspido; were no match to the din created by the man from Bokspits.

What was worse, is that he even became personal in his attacks; leveling insults at the players individually and collectively about their intimate body parts, this done in front of girls mind you, and the fact that no one in school liked them because they were so stuck up and thought there was an aura of invincibility about them. Taken off their game play mentally by Hotstix's utterances, the Chiefs players resorted now to rough play, which ended up in one of the Cosmos star players, the speedy Gabriel Matlakele, seriously injured that Mr. Mudidi had to rush him to the hospital the moment he was taken out of the game. However, when Cosmos scored what proved to be the killer goal from the boot of Thuto Tomeletso; the whole school it seemed went wild. Hotstix, vessel in hand, ran their entire length of the field screaming like never before. The mighty Chiefs had been brought down to their knees at last. I must say too that on that day players like Emmanuel Thekiso rose to the occasion, and had a hand in the mighty Chiefs' demise.

After the game a few of the Chiefs players who did not take kindly to Hotstix's theatrics, namely Ditshupo and Ishmael, decided to attack him. From my dormitory I saw Ditshupo grab Hotstix from behind and punch him on the head, a little later Ishmael came with a high flying kick aimed at Hotstix's chest, and before they could get at him again a Chiefs supporter, a big and fierce looking fellow also from Bobonong, who was a martial artist named Gaetshwane Matsiara, also known as 'Stax', immediately came to the rescue, and warned any one of the guys, and those harboring similar intentions that should they as much as lay a finger on Hotstix; they would have to deal with him first. Tempers cooled down a bit after this declaration, because vexed as these guys were none of them wanted to cross Gaetshwane. And I did not blame them.

This attack on Hotstix did not win Chiefs any friends either. They were seen now as spoiled brats who could not take defeat like true sportsmen, and sort to vent their frustration on a fan. After all, didn't such a thing happen in sports where opposing fans routinely abused players who were rivals? They were seen as sore losers who had been so mentally weak that they had been destabilized by only one person. Hotstix was seen mainly as the hero for single handedly bringing down a team of eleven individuals. The Chiefs guys felt this loss to the bones just as Hotstix had promised, and this was to further enhance his mystique at Lotsane in 1986; just as Blackie had done.

Now with Executive Cosmos severely weakened due to injuries and the emotionally draining victory over Chiefs the previous day; it was a walk in the park for Santos the next day when the two teams faced off for the replay that had been rained out. And finally a team other than Chiefs that year was crowned champions of the sub teams in 1986. It had been a great year for Santos in many respects. They had raised funds successfully during the year, which included the beauty contest everyone still talked about, and yes Blackie's disco competition in Palapye. As expected their end of year party was a hit. I was invited and so was Hotstix, but we had eaten at our own party and our stomachs were full, but the kind gesture of the hosts, and in particular Loruo Bruce Rakanye was touching. At that end of year party I was elected president of the Callies sub team for the upcoming year, and with players like Tshwenyego Carlos Tawana and Wagga Montshiwa leaving, who had been the stalwarts of the team for the past two years, I dreaded to think what the state of affairs our team would be the next year.

1986 was also the year of Halley's Comet. We were told about this comet and the fact that it appears once every 75 to 76 years. We stayed up at night, way past bedtime and lights off searching the bright stars for this spectacular heavenly body. I never saw it. One night though Blackie gathered a bunch of guys together and claimed to have spotted the comet. He had everyone awed as he pointed at a constellation and picked it out. However, as everyone was headed to bed someone asked the guys:

"So did you see the comet?"

"Yes," a fellow named Dikatso answered. "We saw a comet alright."

"You guys *actually* saw Halley's Comet?"

"No, I said we saw a comet, as in *Blackie's Comet*."

Everyone was in raptures upon hearing this. Of course, we all knew that somehow Blackie had to be a part of this historic occasion that happened once in a lifetime; or twice if one is blessed with longevity.

Chapter 25

The weekend I was looking forward to with some trepidation had finally come. This was the weekend that marked the 1986 prize giving day. It was not a great deal to a lot of people, but it was to me for the simple reason that I had not, up until then, won anything of real value in my life. And like I mentioned, I had seen students get theirs last year and this year I wanted desperately to be one of them. As of yet I was not certain how this was going to happen. The question I could never get a straight answer to was: who was going to get the prize, was it going to be Rinah or me? I was going to get that answer on Saturday November 8th 1986. It was a day I would never forget.

The final exams for the form 5's was fast approaching, as a matter of fact the exams were set to begin on Tuesday November 18th, and the Friday before the ceremony was the 'Completer's Ball', also known as the prom. On that day everyone was very well dressed. It was also tradition at Lotsane that in the days leading to the Ball, or prom, the guys had their parents purchase them brand new suits, and with the girls that would be a beautiful evening dress, and keep it hidden until the big night. Cross Kgosidiile was the only person I know that year who deliberately broke that rule, and wore his school uniform instead. The Ball was held in the dining hall and the area became out of bounds for the form 4's. None of us were allowed anywhere near the hall.

Since this was to be a memorable occasion for all involved, it was common to have students, particularly girls, go to hair salons in Palapye and have they hair treated to the latest styles. This led to an incident that I am certain Kelebogile will never forget. Although the rules were a bit slack at this time of the year, especially when it applied to the form 5's, because they were soon to leave Lotsane; that did not however mean that certain regulations like leaving campus without permission could be flouted, which is what happened in this instance.

What Kelebogile did was that since she was so into her looks; was go to a hair salon that was at the Palapye/Serowe junction, the same place where I, Bame, and a few other friends had escorted Max to. This time Kelebogile and a friend went there without permission. Unfortunately for them, and Kelebogile in particular, is that the administration found out, and upon their return they were ordered to go home and call their parents. The other girl had relatives in Palapye (some say she had older friends in fact; one of who posed as her father and brought him to school), and was off the hook immediately; following a stern warning from the headmaster not to repeat that again. Kelebogile on the other hand was not so lucky because her family was in Gaborone, and in heading back home that late Friday afternoon meant that she was not going to attend the prom that evening – just as the administration had intended as punishment.

Kelebogile was not well liked among the boys because of her holier than thou attitude, and when she passed by the guys, who were now relaxed on the lawn in front of the dining hall after cleaning it in preparation for the prom, as she was being escorted to the gate to hitch a ride to Gaborone; the guys let her have it.

"Oh, I heard that you decided to miss the party, and a great party at that what a shame," one of the guys I believe that was Mompati Keabereka said.

"Really?" another feigned surprise. "Did I hear you correctly or did you just say Kelebogile is going to miss out on this once in a lifetime event, an event that we live for and will cherish forever. What kind of person puts a lousy hairstyle ahead of that?"

"Yeah, a hairstyle indeed." The taunts continued unabated and Kelebogile was brought to tears in an instant, and that made the fellows go for the kill. Many believed it was a fitting punishment for a girl who thought she was God's only gift to this world, and it was really hard to disagree with them.

In any case, I was fortunate to be at the prom for the simple reason that the school hired Ferdinand William's disco equipment, and he was the designated deejay, and since he was a very good friend of mine, and we had agreed that we were going to be dorm mates the following year, all I had to do was sit next to him and I was at the prom even as a form 4. A little later his sister Anthea joined us and we had a blast. The previous year it had been Hotstix who had enjoyed this rare privilege.

As the form 5's arrived, and then later the invited guests and parents, I was shocked to see my father among the invitees. It would be a while before I would have a chance to talk to him but I was thrilled. That meant he was going to be there at the prize giving ceremony to watch me get my prize – I frantically hoped.

Motlalepula Magina gave a moving speech that night that received rave reviews, and I was happy for her. When it was time to eat I made certain that Bame served my father well, which she gladly did. Form 4's were the servers, and just like me, Bame was one of the few who were at that prom. We were able to eat the good food with a great appetite. When I finally got to my dad I told him how happy I was that he had made it, I told him of my fear that I might not get the prize I so desperately wanted, again he told me that I had done my best, and that is all he could ask for. He was going to spend the night at Legoro's house; so everything as far as his stay at Lotsane was well taken care of. After the Ball, the parents and teachers were entertained at the Domestic Science laboratory, and from the sounds coming from there we could tell that they were having a great time.

***

The guest of honor for our prize giving ceremony was none other than the great Dr. David James Rubadiri, a poet, playwright, novelist, university professor, diplomat, and one time permanent Ambassador of Malawi to the United Nations. Born in Liuli, Malawi in 1930, Dr. Rubadiri studied at the Makarere University College in Kampala Uganda between 1952 and 1956, and later studied Literature at King's College, Cambridge, and went on to receive a Diploma in Education from Bristol University England. At that time in 1986 he was a lecturer at the University of Botswana, and dean of the Language and Social Sciences Education department. He was also well known for a poem that was very popular among secondary school students called *'An African Thunderstorm'* and when Mr. Onneetse, who was the master of ceremonies that day, introduced the great man he did not hesitate to mention that milestone, and at that moment I could see a big smile from the man himself. I was a budding writer, and like all writers dreamt one day to be published, and seeing him that day, made me feel that one day it would be great to have that same smile on my face; when one of my works was mentioned in public.

We were seated in the academic area that day. I was seated next to my two dorm mates Mothusi Mompati and Moses Galeboe. All the teachers wore their graduation cap and gowns that made us all green with envy as it was meant to, for we wanted to see ourselves in those in a few years. Befitting tradition Legoro went on to state all the school year's highlights, achievements, and the inevitable disappointments like the dropping out of girls due to unwanted pregnancies, and also our hopes for the future. Finally it was time to award the prizes. It started with the form 5's. What would happen is that as the master of ceremony Mr. Onneetse would call out the name of the student who won the prize of a particular subject, and then Mr. Keakile gave that prize to the guest of honor Dr. Rubadiri, who would first shake hands with the student, and then hand him his or her prize. With the form 4's, prizes were awarded to the best students in each individual class.

Ironically, when the time to give prizes came, rain clouds started to gather and the dark clouds suggested that an African thunder storm was in the making.

"Due to the fact that it may start raining anytime, we ask that when your name gets called please run to get your prize," Mr. Onneetse said.

Adam Masebola, like Mojasegoro Kgosinkwe the year before; was the star of the show as he almost made a clean sweep of all the subjects he studied. He won the prize for Mathematics, Physics, Chemistry, Geography, and that of best student. The beauty queen, and former Miss Form 4, Nametsegang won the Biology and English prizes. It was a typical example of brains and beauty combined. I was a bit disappointed that my friend Mothusi Mompati had not won a prize, but he was much later to win an even bigger one when he had the highest aggregate (or grade point average) when the results of the international exams were released. He took it well, just as I had expected he would in a situation like this; with my other friend Moses though it was another story when it was time to give the prize for Art.

"Mmoloki Modise," Mr. Onneetse called.

A lot of people were wondering what prize he was being called for. I knew, and so did Moses, because that was his main competition.

"It is for Art," Moses said solemnly. He had been expecting it, and the disappointment on his face was obvious. I felt bad for him, but thought he would take solace in the fact that he had won the national prize, but to this day I don't know if he did, because he wanted it all especially the one at school because the stage was more spectacular, and I did not blame him.

Finally the moment came. It was time to give the form 4 prizes.

"In form 4 zero the prize," Mr. Onneetse said, "goes to Manyothwane Mbumbi." There was a big smile on his face when he said that, because Mbumbi was one of his best students and during the Setswana exam he had scored very high marks almost acing the test. Not surprising, because Mbumbi was one of the most brilliant minds Lotsane had ever seen at that time, much in the same clout as people like Mojasegoro Kgosinkwe, Balisi Bonyongo, Esau Mbanga, Gilbert Gaboutloeloe, Nametsegang Sennanyana, Mothusi Mompati, Elijah Legwaila, Bakani Bagwisanyi, Albert Ditlhakeng, Rinah Phoko, Benjamin Bolaane, and Adam Masebola who was also known as 'Mastermind' to those closest to him. The tension was mounting as he called out two other names; those being Baudubi 'Dubs' Baatshwana of form Four One and Kabelo Lebotse of form Four Two. I was a nervous wreck when it was time to announce the winner for our class. At that point I noticed that Mr. Keakile picked up two prizes from the pile, and this maneuver was not lost on me. I patted Mothusi on the back excitedly.

"Mothusi, is it just me or did you see him pick up two prizes?"

Mothusi simply gave me that trademark one million dollar smile of which he was well known for, and tapped me on the back in return, in essence telling me that everything was going to be alright. I said a silent prayer, and in that short entreaty I asked the Lord to bless Mothusi many times over for the rest of his life.

"And now ladies and gentlemen, in this class the competition was fierce and at its utmost because we had two students who were the best. May Sebati Mafate and Rinah Phoko come forward please?" Those were the best words I had ever heard. The fact that he had called my name first was not lost to me, and proved that all that worrying had been in vain. In the next instant I was racing toward the podium, but then I stopped turned around, and waited for Rinah, and grabbed her hand and both of us went to get our prize. The audience, including the teachers, were thrilled. I even overheard Mr. Mhuriro saying something very flattering about me to another teacher.

I then had the honor of shaking hands with the great Dr. Rubadiri. When I unwrapped my gift it was a novel (all the prizes were) by Elechi Amadi called *'The Concubine'*. I also went on to win the prize for Best Actor. Paul Newman had won the Academy award for best actor in 1986 for the movie *'The Color of Money,'* and I could not help but imagine that I and this great Hollywood icon shared something in common that year. We are all allowed to dream once in a while, and I was having my moment. The event was sealed with a live poem recitation praising our headmaster Mr. Victor Isaac Mahole, which was performed with moving and colorful simplicity by Albertina Mokgware, and had the audience shouting their approval. Even Legoro was flattered, and he later confided in my dad that Albertina praising him was one of the highlights of the day if not his life.

When the ceremony ended, we were instructed to stay seated as the staff and parents left the academic area, and headed to the Domestic Science laboratory where refreshments awaited. They were led by the school's scout marching band. At that moment Mr. Mhuriro went to the microphone.

"May Sebati Mafate come forward please … Sebati Mafate."

I heeded to the call of course which was another honor. I got to him and discussed the evening's entertainment. I was now the chairman of the entertainment committee and the school's official projectionist – yet another honor, and after briefing him of what the entertainment was to be for the night; I had the privilege of joining my father as he and the teachers led by the scouts walked toward the Domestic Science laboratory. I still get the chills whenever I recall that moment, because that was unprecedented, and my father was extremely proud.

"Look at how people are looking at me son," he said with a wide smile on his face. The fact that he had seen me get a prize for my academics is something he was to cherish for a very long time.

Later on Hotstix came up to me with a big smile on his face.

"Man Sebati, I bet your father was your number one fan today, when he saw you getting all those prizes," he said and I could also tell that he was equally happy for me.

I was later made Assistant Head Prefect; Kabelo Lebotse was the head prefect, and Mbumbi the deputy. This was yet another tradition at that time of the year since the form 5's were just about to take their exams. I could not help but smile when I thought of Lekobe's remarks only a year earlier; when he said I was campaigning to be a prefect. I was now in fact a senior prefect. Although we were still form 4's, we were required to carry out our duties with immediate effect. The next inspection was conducted by BM, the three head prefects or head boys as we were known accompanied him. When we got to dorm 11, which happened to be Mzeetho's dormitory, (there had been some reshuffling apparently) Ipha's bed was in a very bad state. Not surprising, because small as he was in stature, Ipha was known to be a trouble maker by the BM and staff alike even though his pranks were harmless really and mostly practical jokes, which made him liked by many; including the very teachers that Ipha was always giving a hard time. However, this Sunday BM was not amused at all.

"Hey what is this?" he asked Ipha, as he pointed at his bed.

"My bed," Ipha answered in somewhat of a defiant tone, and standing not as he was supposed to, which was upright and at attention, but stood instead in the Pantsula gangster way. On seeing this, BM felt that this was just the kind of behavior that could not be tolerated, especially from the likes of Ipha. He then went on to grab the flaps of his blazer, and pulled them together on the front.

"*Basimanyana ba tshwana le bo Ipha ba batla go otlhaiwa gone ho,*" "Small boys like Ipha need to be punished right away," he said. Somehow with his very sharp vision he saw a stick outside that none of us were aware of. "*Mphe thupa eo,*" "give me that stick," he continued. Mbumbi went outside and got it.

I had heard of BM's skill in as far as corporal punishment was concerned, especially last year, and mostly from Big Joe and others like Johane. When it came to using the cane BM was unmatched, which would explain why he was not a man to be messed with, and why a lot of us went out of our way to be in his good books. But even the best of amours get tarnished with time, and BM's stringency was to decline over the years, but that day with Ipha he ran the clock back in time. He gave Ipha one of the most precise canning on the butt; that we all felt every single stroke with him. And all that defiance, gangster stance, talk, and walk went out the window when BM was through with him. I later that day after inspection went back to dorm 11 looking for Ipha and found Mzeetho instead, and 'Ngamula Mzeetho ka Da' went on to recreate the scenario; even imitating BM's voice that seemed to come from his nostrils to a tee.

***

Meanwhile the breakaway karate club formed by Bonang was making remarkable strides. The splinter club consisted mainly of form 4's, which was fitting because we were going to be the core of the club next year. And in Bonang we had a very credible instructor. Instead of the common room we trained at one of the classrooms. Not only that we even had our rigorous trainings in the very early hours of the day. Bonang's teachings were very effective and easy to grasp that soon he had very able products in people like the grand Collet 'Ngamula the Big Man' Mosudisa, Motlotlegi Moameng, Elijah Legwaila, Meshack 'Lani The White Man' Mauco, Bose 'Ninja' Moremi, Moemedi 'Nthaps Moex' Nthapelelang, Meshack Seagiso Ramatshaba, Benjamin 'Computer Compral' Moube, Cornelius 'Cornmaster' Msipha , Israel 'Di Eyes' Mpugwa, Mmoloki David, and Calistas 'Courage' Tchienda the Namibian to mention just a few.

At the official handover, which was just a formality really, Bonang was elected Sensei and I was his deputy. Also at a handover, the old committee leaves whatever money is left for the new committee as seed money to build on when the fund raising campaign begins in earnest the following year. Normally, the amount passed on is what is left after the end of year party, and for the most part is enough to get things going for the next year. In our case though, our Karate club had not organized a single trip in 1986, had not even raised 50 Pula, and here I am being very liberal. What we got was perhaps 35 Thebe (pennies), and a brand new winter blanket that was passed on from the Max and Roukes era.

What had happened was that in 1985 our then committee had organized a raffle during that second term - the term of love. The first prize was a brand new mini radio tape boom box that was won by Jabulisani Butale, the same Jabulisani who had advised Robot not to heed to Mr. Irvine's call in what now seemed a lifetime ago. The second prize was also something of value that I don't readily recall, but the third prize was the beautiful winter blanket that no one claimed. We pulled the winning number when we made the draw, the person whoever it was, was not a student because we sold tickets to everyone even during the first term break. And when we sent that blanket to the winner, it was returned three times, as that person apparently did not exist. Most likely, that person decided to give a fake name and post office box number for some reason. In any case we inherited that brand new blanket, and immediately Bonang found a buyer for it, and we sold it for forty Pula, which we kept and were to build on next year with Cornelius as our new treasurer.

We were ready now for 1987, and I wondered if that year would be anything close to what 1986 had been, for that year had been a great one. It was a year where I truly found myself. 1986 was a year that I had dug down deep and taken a very meticulous inventory of my soul, and discovered hidden talents I never knew existed. I am still to this day grateful that I lived to see that year.

Soon thereafter the form 5's started writing their exams. It was always a tense and yet fun moment (when looking at it through the softening vista of time), mainly because the school was quiet at the time. The form 5's stayed up in the 'Block A' common room even after lights off. This was the ritual, and as a form four living with the form 5's I could have taken advantage of it, but instead I relaxed. I had achieved all my goals that year, and even far more than I could have ever imagined, but the truth is that I should have kept on as later events would dictate.

The lockers in the dormitories were turned around to make an even more intimate studying environment. A week prior to the exams classes ended, and it was known as the 'week of peace'. Now the students were on their own 24 hours a day, all they had to do was just study, and then go to the dining hall to eat. The Cambridge Ordinary Level exam was the ultimate exam for all of us, and we knew that fact fully well.

At that time also as form 4's we were taking our end of year exams, which were not as intense as the midyear exams, and during this time we got a new Accounts teacher named Mr. Appadoo from Mauritius, whom we adored very much because of the way he made Accounting fun. One day during the 'week of peace' I decided after tea break to not go to my next class, which was Biology, and opted instead to hang out with my dormitory mates. I figured that since we had written our Biology exam, my teacher Mrs. Lena Mbulawa would be busy grading the papers and not notice my absence. I was wrong.

We were talking among ourselves at the dormitory since the guys had taken a break from their studies, I was enjoying my last moments with them to the fullest; when to my utmost horror a classmate of mine named Julius 'Mennex' Maabong entered the dorm, and came up to me. There was no need for me to even speculate why he was there.

"Sebati, Mrs. Mbulawa asked me to come and get you," he said, and I felt sick to the stomach with fear, because not only was Mrs. Mbulawa strict, she and her husband Mr. Zwide Mbulawa knew my father very well, and if word of any mischief on my part reached my dad I knew I would be getting a mouthful from him, and with that man just like Mrs. Mbulawa, you would prefer a canning as opposed to being admonished, which in this case was going to be the most likely scenario, and worse still in front of the whole class.

"Mennex, are you sure she said for you to come and get me?"

"Yes." Mennex or anyone would not lie about something as grave as this.

"But I thought she would not notice that I was not in class, isn't she supposed to be grading papers?"

"She is, but she became aware that you and Mmathebe were not in class. Someone has been sent to call her as we speak."

This was serious. How on earth was I going to wriggle myself out of this one? I wondered as we headed back to class; this after I had stalled as much as I could and ran out of excuses.

"Is she mad?" I asked him, anxious to discern what kind of mood she was in.

"Hard to tell, you know how Ma Mbulawa is," he replied. Now my heart was pounding even more. A dozen more excuses sprang to my lips but they died just there, and before I knew it we had arrived. The entire class was silent in anticipation of what was just about to happen it seemed.

"Okay Sebati where have you been, and why didn't you come to class?" There was a frown on her very beautiful face.

"Madam, I was hanging out with my dorm mates, and the stories were so great that I decided not to come to class." It was a bold face confession that surprised even me. Mrs. Mbulawa on the other hand could not help but laugh for she had not expected that.

"Hahaha ... class just listen to this. What did you just say Sebati?"

"Well ma'am I'm just being honest." I was becoming bolder now as I saw the tension subside.

"Okay go and sit down, I will deal with you later, see me after class." I could tell that my confession had deflated her, and she was not as angry as she otherwise would have been.

At the end of class Mmathebe and I stayed behind as expected, but by this time Mrs. Mbulawa was all the more calm. She just told us both not to do that again. Having written the end of year exam did not mean that school was over, we were still expected to be in class even if there was nothing to do, but we could always bring a comic or novel to read. And just like that I was off the hook, and from that time on I followed her advice always. I could not rely on bold face confessions to save me each time.

At last, the third and final term came to an end. The form 5's were the first to leave, and I remember when I walked my friends to the truck I was assailed by a sudden wave of sadness. I had started my life at Lotsane with these people. I could not help but recall the day of our very first lunch together when we were jeered by the form 5's, and now they were leaving me behind. There was a lump in my throat as I wondered about what could have been had I not repeated my form 4. Lepholeta City Senne must have been reading my mind that early evening as the truck was getting ready to leave.

"Hey Sebati, there's still room for you go and get your things we will wait for you," he said with a wide grin on his face.

The truck began pulling away, and everyone bid me farewell as I watched them, the last group to leave took one final look at the school that had molded us into the men and women we were to become in life's long journey.

"So long Jones!" everyone said as the truck finally left, and I was alone in the parking lot. That painful lump was still stuck in my throat, and it did not leave until tears started to trickle down my cheeks. For the very first and only time in my life at Lotsane I questioned the logic of having had to voluntary repeat my Form 4, but that was only for half a second. I returned to my dormitory, and soon the new members were moving their stuff and choosing their beds. Ferdinand and I were very careful in handpicking our dormitory mates for the next year, and none of us regretted the choices we made. If anything we all become brothers in arms in a way that was never to be forgotten.

Besides Ferdinand, we had Archie Seemule from Francistown, Itumeleng 'Zero' Tabengwa, also from Francistown, Israel 'Di Eyes' Mpugwa nicknamed so because he wore nerdy looking spectacles, he was from Matshekge Hill School in Bobonong, Peter 'Bo Quiet' Mafokate who was Isaac Mafokate's nephew and a very quiet individual by nature, also from Bobonong, Phatsimo Ramahobo from Francistown Secondary School, Mosimanegape 'MC' Keagile from Francistown Secondary School, Keebonye 'Magompi' Morake from Letlhakane, Kgakgamatso 'KK' Moloi from Francistown, Gerald Usher from Francistown, Bonang 'Stoner' Mosupi also from Francistown, Moemedi 'Nthaps Moex' Nthapelelang, and of course where would I be without Bonang Mapolanka? Who I later realized was a bit disappointed that he had not been chosen as a prefect because he had great leadership qualities, a virtue I could readily attest to and so would many others.

This was a special group of people, more than I had ever imagined, and in a way that has bonded us together for life. Not even the camaraderie I experienced in the 1985 dorm 12 came near what we had in 1987, and to this day I am grateful that I was in a position where I got acquainted with people of such caliber. We all looked forward to the coming year and we all promised one another that 1987, our final year at Lotsane, was going to be that of bliss. The last day of the term we happily cleaned out our dormitories. I was calling the shots now because I was a prefect, and it felt good.

I decided to hitch a ride to Gaborone as opposed to catching the train as I would normally do. Perhaps this was because I did not feel the need as all my form 5 friends were now gone. Me, a guy named Losik Gulubane or 'Maloss' as he was known, and a form 4 fellow at the time whose name still eludes me; were at the main road just outside the main entrance late that afternoon hitchhiking. We were all headed to Gaborone. The first car stopped, and the driver informed us that he was going as far as Mahalapye, and Maloss decided to take the ride saying that he would spend the night with relatives in Mahalapye. We got our ride to Gaborone not too long afterwards, and I spent most of the time reading *'The Concubine'*; the novel I had won at the prize giving ceremony, and the journey was cut in half seemingly.

All my father could talk about when I arrived home was how happy he had been at the honor I had bestowed upon him at the ceremony, he was proud and it showed. It was a great summer holiday and it was great to hook up with old friends again. I did run into Terrence Jacobs just as I did exactly a year ago at the mall. The difference this time was that I was not burdening him with my 'love Jones' like I was last year, same place same time, and as fate had it as we were walking toward the other side of the mall, I saw none other than Alice Mukokomani with a friend, walking along. She did not see me nor was I sure if I really wanted her to. Not surprisingly, my heart did not skip a beat like it would way back then. I smiled and looked at Terrence who as of yet had not seen her.

"Terrence, look," I said. He followed my gaze and his face did not show any sign of shock or surprise. It was a poker face.

"Hmmm, I must say she still looks good," he said, and we spoke no further of the sighting. My thoughts were with Olivia. She had left a couple of days before I did when her parents came to pick her up, and I missed her terribly. What was bad was that when she was picked up it was done during our last record night of the year, right when a song called *'Love Break Down'* was playing that even Kebagaisitse 'Triple K' Mapena, my classmate had to comment on the irony of the song as she left.

"Sebati, it's really a love breakdown with your girl leaving," he said.

I also ran into Two-Two at the mall that day. It seemed there were a lot of Lotsane students at the mall that bright early December late morning. It was great to see my dance partner even though we had drifted apart over the past year.

"Did you see her?" he asked.

"Who?" I asked as if I knew not what he was talking about.

"Her ... Alice man," he said.

"Oh ... yeah I saw her."

"I spoke to her, and she told me that she was way out in the boondocks for her National Service, but she was already getting used to the whole idea just as her tenure was coming to an end."

"I see."

To be quite honest I was not really keen in hearing all about an ex's livelihood. Especially one who reminded me of the bad times, and I think Two-Two sensed that and immediately dropped the subject. He of all people knew only too well how sensitive of a matter that was at the time.

During those holidays Osupile and I were in constant touch. I even got a job at my uncle's (Cecil Gumede) pharmacy at the African Mall, because he had two female employees at the time who were constantly being harassed by loafers. He figured that since I was a martial artist and could take good care of myself, I would be a viable asset to the pharmacy in as far as security was concerned. I must say that when I was there we never experienced any trouble from whomever it was who was causing it. I also had constant visits from friends who lived nearby particularly Osupile, and there was never a dull moment.

That summer we also had a surprise visit from a blood cousin from South Africa, Ezrom 'Tikkie' Mafate. I had last seen him six years earlier, and it was great to see him again after all these years. With him around, Rama and I felt like we finally had a big brother in our midst and it was great. The only disturbing thing about those holidays is that I did not get to hear from Olivia at all, no letter nothing. This was unacceptable, and I told her that in a letter I wrote to her, which she never bothered to reply making things all the more worse.

I also accidentally ran into Tonkana during those festive holidays, which was a surprise, because I thought that all this time he was in Kanye. His upper lip was swollen, and had a big scab courtesy of a well-aimed stone that was thrown at him by some ruffians. I was glad to see him, because at school earlier he had told me that he had a 16mm film projector that he was not using, and one day as a joke I asked him if I could buy it from him, and he said he would think about it. A few weeks later he told me that he would indeed sell it to me for about 300 Pula, which was a steal at that price. I had no idea where on earth I was going to get my hands on that kind of money, but I agreed nonetheless. Even later he was to tell me that he could reduce the price to about 250 Pula if I could pay some debts he had accrued at school, and in particular to Mr. Mothei, which I later gladly did. However, when he finished writing his exams, he left before me and him could finalize anything, and I had no idea where he lived exactly, which is why I was pleased about that chance meeting in Gaborone.

He took me to his place in Bontleng, and then we agreed that we would both leave for Kanye the following Saturday in the morning. I was excited, but wondered if there really was a projector to begin with. The ancestors seemed to be smiling at me, because the next day I ran into Boipelo, Tonkana's beautiful girlfriend, who was a form 4 like me. I told her that I had seen her boyfriend the day before and she was over the moon, because she, just like me earlier, had absolutely no idea that he was in Gaborone. I promptly took her to his place after work, and my former dorm mate was just as thrilled to see her, and he later thanked me profusely after she spent the night.

We took the trip to Kanye, but on our way to the station that morning as we were crossing at a roundabout near the diamond sorting center, known as 'Orapa House', I saw a truck with about four people seated at the back (in those days things were different) it looked like three kids and an older girl. Something about the girl made me pay closer attention at them because she looked familiar, very familiar in fact, because it was Olivia! I had no time to reflect because I immediately called out at her. She was surprised as she at first dipped her head, and smiled before she waved, and kept waving until the car disappeared around a corner. Many thoughts were flashing through my mind.

"What do you make of this?" I asked Tonkana who was watching all this.

"Obviously, she did not want you to know that she was in town otherwise she would have told you," he said.

That type of answer coming from Tonkana did not surprise me at all; especially if that answer concerned women whose intentions were not exactly the kind a guy tolerated. On the other hand I did not think there was anything devious going on; perhaps she had come to Gaborone at the spare of the moment, and had no time to notify me. I temporarily shelved the other destructive thoughts that were coming into my head, and concentrated on the mission ahead.

We arrived in Kanye later that day, and I got the projector from Tonkana just as he had promised. I still owe him some of the money, because for a very long time that projector was the magic goose that laid the golden eggs for the family. I also through my cousin met Motelebane Motelebane *wa* Mohutsiwa, a brilliant young man who had grown up in South Africa, and had known Tikkie as they both lived in Soweto. Motelebane had since relocated to Botswana, and for the two it was a chance and emotional reunion. Motelebane, or Sheppard, as he was also known, was like me a budding writer at the time, but far more advanced than I was, and that was when our friendship begun. He was a little older than me, and even though we were friends I did look up to him like a big brother.

I also learned that he had been a teacher before in Thamaga, because when I met him then he was working for the Gaborone City Council, where he still works as of this writing. It was through him that I found out a little more about the fellow who had swept Alice off her feet, and I finally got the answer as to why all those times she was refusing to part with her best pictures, because they ended up in a shrine he had made in her honor. I could understand about being crazy over someone, after all I was bitten by the same bug, but literally worshiping a girl to me was just madness plain and simple. I know this may sound like sour grapes, but it isn't. And soon 1987 was within reach, and this was the year that was to define my future and many others. I could not wait to be back at Lotsane this time as a form 5 at last.

BOOK THREE: 1987

Chapter 26

When we arrived as form 5's, the campus looked a bit strange as it was just going to be us form 5's for at least two weeks until the newbies, *manyewane* arrived. I was among the first to arrive in my dormitory, and a while later guys started trickling in, among them MC and Phatsimo. They all looked a bit different as everyone always did when schools opened. By 9:00 pm or so our dormitory was bustling with activity, even some of the girls including Matt and others like Ipha were there; the rules were not in effect yet as school did not officially start until the next day.

As we were about to retire, and the girls ready to leave, Ipha said something to them that there and then gave me the impression that 1987 was indeed going to be an interesting year.

"Tell me something, do you people ever have wet dreams?" he asked the girls casually as if he was asking them where the nearest bus station was. And we all burst out laughing. "No I'm serious," Ipha continued with comical solemnest. That was vintage Ipha Gumbalume.

I wasted no time in confronting Olivia about why I had not heard from her all summer long, and worse still that she came to Gaborone without telling me, I do not quite recall what her excuse was at the time, but whatever it was it sounded pretty lame, but then I was to learn the ugly truth as usual much, much later. In the meantime it was a bit awkward around campus, because, there were few of us since the form 4's had yet to arrive, but as far as entertainment was concerned we were having twice as much fun, because for some reason we were getting films sent to us almost every week and we were watching two and at times three films in one night.

As the senior prefects Kabelo, Mbumbi, and I were given badges that identified our ranks so to speak, something that had never been done before in the history of the school – indeed times were changing. Legoro told us that since the newbies were going to be arriving very soon they would immediately have to know which people to go to for help. The sad part about 1987 was that my beloved Math teacher, Miss Sara Pearson, had gotten married, and transferred to Moeng College; the sad part was not about her marriage, but her transfer. This was a blow for me personally, because this is one educator whose teaching reached to me in a way no other Math teacher did, and I was at last to get very good grades in Mathematics under her tutelage. Her replacement was an old man named Mr. Betridge. He was from England as well, and had also been a teacher to people like Mr. Mbulawa when he was a student.

Mr. Betridge was also a great teacher whose teachings were unique so one could say that I still was under great guidance, but he was not Miss Pearson that much was clear. Mr. Betridge was known to be very liberal I heard, meaning that one could go in and out of class as you pleased as long as you were not a distraction. I was not quite sure about this particular rumor, but one day I decided to put it to a test. When his back was turned to the classroom I sneaked out of the room and rushed back to the dormitory to pick up something I had forgotten. My plan was to sneak back into the classroom just as quietly as I had when I left.

Upon my return, he was facing the classroom so I decided to crouch on one knee, and wait until he turned to the chalkboard again. With the help of a classmate named Chabaesele Nelson Kelibile, I would know by his signal when Mr. Betridge's back was turned, but every time I would think my moment had arrived, and just about to make my move, he would immediately turn and face the class again. This went on until I started to hear laughter coming from the Biology lab behind me, and I turned around when I realized that the laughter continued unabated, and saw a teacher walking toward me. His name was Mr. Adams, a Biology teacher, who had noticed me from his class as I was trying to slip back in.

I was horrified and immediately stood up. I had been caught red handed. He had a long ruler, which he used to direct me into the class. Mr. Betridge immediately took notice, and before he could ask what was going on Mr. Adams saved him the trouble.

"I just caught this young man crouched on one knee on the ground by the door. I don't know if he was trying to sneak back in or get someone's attention," he said.

Mr. Betridge it seemed was not listening to him, but was looking around as he scratched the top of his bald head (a habit he was very well known for), and then looked back at me and said, "You're in Five three right?"

"Yes sir."

"Okay, find a chair and have a seat."

Since there was nothing else he could do, Mr. Adams left. Apparently Mr. Betridge thought that I was lost and had been looking for his class so as far as he was concerned there was no harm, no foul. I never pulled that stunt again for the remainder of the year. The great news that first term was that the wonderful MS Kgomotso Motlotle had been transferred to Lotsane, and was now our new Deputy Head Teacher after replacing Mr. Keakile, who had been transferred to another school where he became the headmaster. And sadly, we also lost Mr. Felix Mhuriro to transfer as well, but many years later he was to return to Lotsane as the headmaster. Nevertheless, MS. Motlotle was indeed a blessing in a way that was to make the staff, and those associated with that school proud for many years, but we will get to that later.

***

The form 4's arrived at last. And many were to receive the kind of reception, particularly from the girls, which made the humiliation we endured, and in particular Tlhase Malope Tlhase, back in 1985 look like a walk in the park. The jeering of *'form 4,... form4,... form 4'* was of course tradition and the boys had to go through that initiation, but the girls led by a certain Josephine 'Josie' Bagopi (now Mrs. Baffoe), who was also Bame and Ruth's dorm mate, took it to an entirely new level. I heard that the main victim was a young lady who was the first to arrive, and was escorted by a jeering form 5 crowd of girls to her dormitory that she immediately broke down and wept bitterly. It got so out of hand that Josie and her accomplices were rounded up, and summoned to the staff room that Sunday morning, and were severely punished - the corporal way.

Things were so bad that Legoro found it necessary to admonish the entire student body at assembly the very next morning. Like I mentioned earlier this kind of jeering of the new arrivals was custom at Lotsane, but that year our group had taken it to a totally unfamiliar echelon, and for the first time in the school's history the administration found it necessary to address this childish behavior.

"What is bad," Mr. Mahole said in an angry voice, "is that some of this yelling was done in front of their parents." This mind you was done by the girls, Josie and company especially, and their actions had greatly embarrassed the school.

Nonetheless, it did not take long for things to get back to normal, and as an assistant head boy I was making a lot of announcements at the dining hall mainly for the form 4's as they slowly settled in. There was one form 4 in particular who took quite a liking to me, and we became buddies almost immediately; his name was States Ndzimumbi.

The first Saturday with the form 4's was a performance by us of the play '*Wedlock of The Gods.*' The last time we had performed the play at school was during the great drama festival of 1986. Our performance was not as great as it had been in the past, but the form 4's were impressed nonetheless especially States whom I spotted among the audience wearing his classic big smile. I also later learned that there was a very beautiful form 4 girl who was mesmerized by my performance that evening, and she was to tell me more about it about a year or so later. Her name was Faith. The irony of this first performance was not lost to me, as I recalled that in the past there was such thing a thing as 'Beginners Concert' where the form 4's provided the entertainment; how times had changed I thought to myself.

I don't quite know what it was about those first few weeks after the form 4's had arrived, perhaps it had a lot to do with the fact that I had waited two years to be a senior finally, but for some reason I started walking around with a frown on my face mainly to keep the form 4's at arm's length, and let them know who was boss. For instance, I would be on my way to class, and on several occasions I saw some form 4's waiting in front of say the Chemistry lab, now instead of walking around them, I would stroll right in between them as they frantically parted like the Red Sea in order for me to walk through. The moment I turned around the corner and out of sight I would burst out laughing. When I look back at incidents such as this one, tells me how much growing up I needed to do; even though at the time I thought I knew everything.

Life with my new dormitory mates was never merrier. We got along very well, and as a prefect I was not always given a reason to extend my authority. Bonang Mapolanka was still a little bitter about not being chosen prefect. I could tell from some of the comments he made at night after lights off regarding prefects, but this was to change in an instant, and in a way that was rather a bit comical.

It turns out that Patrick Rakwadi who had been chosen to be a prefect had no intentions of carrying that responsibility on his shoulders, and let the administration know about it in no uncertain terms. Soon after an emergency meeting of all the prefects was arranged, and we were asked to offer suggestions as to whom we thought should replace Patrick. It was unanimously agreed upon that Bonang Mapolanka was the man. Since I was his prefect, I had the pleasure of breaking the news to him. I had that opportunity that afternoon when I talked to him in private in the long 'Block A' corridor (hallway).

"Bonang, it has been agreed upon that you will be the person to replace Patrick as prefect, would you like that?" I was to give the answer yay or nay that very day; so Bonang had no time to ponder his decision otherwise they would have to offer the position to someone else. And believe me there were many waiting in line.

"Absolutely," Bonang answered with no false modesty. "It will be a great chance to learn more about leadership." He was thrilled and relieved I could tell, and he did a very good job of not showing it.

When it was officially announced that Bonang was to be the new prefect to replace Patrick, I now suddenly had an ally in my dormitory that helped me keep order. The others like Bonang 'Stoner' Mosupi (the other Bonang) were not too thrilled about this new development; especially since Bonang had been one of them in as far as their 'us against the system' mentality was concerned, and they let him know at any given opportunity, particularly after lights off.

"Guys be quiet now I mean it," I said one night, not too long afterward, when the noise level threatened to get out of control.

"Yeah," Bonang added, "you fellows need to be quiet right this instant."

"I only think I heard one voice, and I think that was Sebati's voice the other was just a blow of hot air," it was Stoner, and this jibe at the new prefect was followed by laughter.

"Hey, watch your step Stoner," Bonang warned.

"Why should I listen to you?" Stoner would not let up.

"I'm a prefect now in case you forgot."

"Yeah, yeah, Mr. Prefect ... just last night you were ready to lay arms and die for us saying how unfair it is that prefects have all the power, and now here you are being the same thing you claimed to despise. You're not a prefect man – you're Butale, 'specially elected' and with no merit whatsoever." More laughter followed, not surprising too because much as he was a brilliant stage actor Stoner had a way with words as well, and he was also the school's unofficial poet, rivaled only by Albertina Mokgware.

On the other hand the man Stoner was referring to, Mr. Chapson Butale, was a cabinet Minister who had lost his constituency to an opposing party candidate and subsequently lost his seat in Parliament, but the then President, Sir Ketumile Masire, made him a 'specially elected' member as he was a viable asset to the government, so by that comparison Stoner was saying that Bonang had not been officially elected prefect as was the norm, and thus his appointment was not recognized. Bonang had no immediate answer to that taunt, and Stoner sensed that he had him cornered.

"Your mother did not send you here to pick on other students, she sent you to learn." This time though Stoner overshot himself, and suddenly the room was quiet with nervous tension. In African culture, and I would not be surprised if it were the same with any other culture, parents – in particular mothers, were out of bounds when it came to clashes among youngsters; just as Festus had pointed out long ago in his fight with Fungwa. I too felt the sting of that goad and did my best, in spite of myself, to egg Bonang even further so that he could get even angrier and slap Stoner who I felt was now deliberately overstepping his boundary.

"Man, lay off speaking about my mother," Bonang's teeth were clenched, and everyone could tell that he was fighting really hard to contain the rage that was threatening to burst like a volcano.

"Hey man where do you get off insulting someone's mother like that?" That was me trying, as Big Joe had done in the past, to fan the flames by adding fuel.

From that point on Stoner sensibly kept his mouth shut and let Bonang vent whatever it was that was on his chest, and there was a lot to vent that went on for the better part of the night. Thankfully, that proved to be one of the very few moments when there was a clash among dorm 2 members. A few days later, Bonang moved to dorm 9 where he was to assume his duties as prefect, and was replaced by Mpho Rammusi, a quiet and affable guy who had attended Matshekge Hill School in Bobonong, and we could not have picked a better replacement. That was also the time when Ferdinand suggested to all dormitory members who could, to pop 20 Pula apiece, to buy food to supplement our diet. Many of us did including Bonang Mapolanka, but he contributed half of what he was supposed to but got the same shares as we did; something Harare was quick to point out when our supplies started running low at a very rapid rate.

Chapter 27

As we got to know each other better in dorm 2, I found out that many of my dorm mates were prolific story tellers, like Phatsimo for instance, and I think I also had in my two cents especially when I told stories about Blackie and in particular the fight with Ditshupo. Blackie of course needed no introduction, and even though he was gone we still talked about him very fondly - him and Hotstix. I swear the stuff those two pulled left not only me but the new form 5's shaking their heads.

I went on to tell them about Blackie's reaction after the fight when he still wanted to continue it and Hotstix tried to stop him, Blackie's exact words that day were evidently:

"This guy insulted my father ..." however, when I told the story I repeated the words but added, "my father the great Bright Kealotswe, the one who announces in *'Tatediso ya Dikgang'* ..." This was a program that came right after the six O' clock news, and this concerned the local news around the country that could not all be covered by the main bulletin. The stories were also interesting, and at times bizarre, and were reported by Blackie's father. He was instantly seen as the voice of the program since he was the reporter.

On hearing this everyone laughed that even Archie looked at me and pointed a finger.

"No, Sebati that can't be ... he didn't say that," he could barely talk because he was laughing so hard. Later he added, "I mean how many fathers would a guy have that he has to specifically say *'the one who announces in Tatediso ya Dikgang'*?" later I had to admit that I had embellished the story a bit, and all was forgiven amidst more laughter. The bond among us was to get even stronger as time went on.

That early first term a chap, who was also a member of the drama club, named Clio Hlanganiso Roy came up to Mr. Moswela one day - he had something in mind.

"Mr. Moswela, over the holidays I wrote a play about the struggle against apartheid centered around two characters. I've called it *'The Winding Wheel'* and I would like to show it to you," he said.

"Oh, that is wonderful Roy, I definitely would like to read it when I get the chance," Mr. Moswela said. As an English teacher, he was always impressed and supportive whenever a student engaged in something creative as this.

Roy's initiative was also a very welcome attribute that year, because schools were being encouraged to stage plays that were written by local authors, and since Southern Africa was considered barren at the time compared to the West Africans, there were not many plays to choose from. That is why it was a relief that a student had written a play, and not only that, but a play that dealt with a very hot and delicate issue of the time. Later Mr. Mudidi and another teacher, named Dan Bhusumane, who became part of the drama club heads, were brought into the loop regarding this play. It was just as well that we started on it early since the drama festival of 1987 was set to take place in about five months, and this time Madiba Secondary School would be the hosts. It was agreed upon that every other day during afternoon study Mr. Mudidi, Mr. Bhusumane, me, Lillian, and Tefo were to meet and sit with Roy as he read the play to us. Tefo quickly lost interest and the rest of us soldiered on helping in making changes and suggestions wherever needed. Roy's creative endeavor was to become the critically acclaimed play called *'The Breaking Of Chains'*.

Albertina had written a Setswana play as well entitled *'Boloi'*, which means 'witchcraft', and Mr. Moswela was to be the director and producer as well, just as Mr. Mudidi was with our play and Mr. Bhusumane the co- producer. It took a while for things to get going on our end, but when they did there was no looking back. Something else that term happened though; that was to help me in ways that I never thought possible in the future, when it came to applying for acceptance at Universities in the United States and around the world, and that was track.

***

I have always been a fast runner from as far back as I can remember. In Zambia, when I was in second grade, I remember there was a pee wee meet that I won, but the disappointing thing about that victory was that my parents were not there to watch me. My father did not make it as he seemingly was away on one business trip or another, and my mother had divorced him and was starting a new family of her own.

At Itireleng I did try to compete, but I could never make the team because I was younger, and always up against human horses, centaurs, it seemed. When I arrived at Lotsane I pretended that I could not run that fast because I was too self-conscious, but things changed in 1987, and this happened by accident. The house I had always belonged to was Buffalo, and that year it was no different. The way it was done to identify the fastest runners in the group was no different either. We were told to stand at the east side of the field, and divide ourselves into groups of 8 and run the 100 meter dash, and the first four runners would make the team. Joseph Makabe aka 'Strong' was very excited that day, I remember, telling me that he was fired up and ready to show the school that he could win any race.

As for me I tried to wriggle myself out and watch instead, but the teacher in charge Mr. Maurice Habangane, who was also a great history teacher noticed that about me, and told me that he expected me to run like everyone else. At last I took my mark, and when the gun went off I ran like never before; leaving a big gap between me and the closest fellow behind. Everyone who was there that day was stunned, and when I got to the finish line Mr. Habangane jotted down my name and smiled.

"See, I always knew you had it in you. You're built like an athlete, and run like a world class sprinter and yet you wanted to go back to the hostels and avoid this race." There was no turning back now. I had opened Pandora's Box.

Later we were tried out for the 200 meter race and I won again this time by surpassing a fast runner, a form 4 named Rudolf, right at the finish line. I was now going to officially be a part of the team that was to represent our house Buffalo at the inter house competitions in just a couple of weeks.

"Sebati, all this time you've had us believing that you cannot run at all and yet you run like the wind blows," a girl, who like Sepankinyana of the class of 1985, had a heart of gold named Messina Gofhamodimo said with a wide smile on her face.

"I knew," Anthea Williams said. "I just knew it," she continued triumphantly.

That was to be the buzz of the boys' hostel that day especially when we hit the showers and later on at dinner when I ran into Bonang Mapolanka.

"Man Sebati, you sure had us fooled man. I had no idea that you could run so fast ... goodness," he said.

Even Olivia came up to me in the dining hall, something she very rarely did and whispered in my ear.

"I wish I could have been there to witness the entire hullabaloo that everyone is making a big fuss about."

I simply smiled, as I wondered to myself why this had been such a big deal to a lot of people. I did not realize it then, but I was becoming very popular at Lotsane, if I wasn't already, thanks to my extracurricular activities crowned now by this latest venture, which was track and field.

A few days before the inter house competition, I decided to study all night literally, and took a little more 'Stay awake' pills than I should have. A very dumb and dangerous move it turned out because the next day while in class, which happened to be Mr. Betridge's, I started feeling extremely dizzy, and by the time class ended I collapsed and fainted. Strong, and a few guys including Ediretse 'Flagzen' Nthobatsang and Tobokani Ndaba promptly carried me to the dormitory and summoned BM, who immediately got his car and took me to the hospital in Palapye. I spent two nights in hospital, and I was warned never to touch those pills again, and discharged on a Thursday and brought back to school in the hospital car (not an ambulance), and still dressed in the pajamas they had provided, which was a sight for many students as this happened just as everyone was coming back from supper.

The next morning it was the track and field day, and one year to the day when Blackie shook the Lotsane world. It was a bright and sunny day as it always has been. This time there was no great drama like the last two years. I would think the only drama was when I won both the 100 and 200 meter races, and this time in front of a shell shocked school. I was then part of the team that was going to represent our school at the inter school competitions later that term - to be hosted again by Madiba. We had won it all in 1986, and thus in 1987 we were the defending champions. For me personally this had been a momentous achievement. I had never up until that point been a part of a special team like this one. At Itireleng I was not fast enough, in football I was never good enough to make the team; even though I did make the bench at the very end, and that only happened because many of the regular players were not available, but outside Karate, and maybe breakdance, this was the first time I had earned a place in a team I wanted so badly to be a part of.

Meanwhile, a trip was in the works that was to top it all in as far as fundraising for our club was concerned. It turns out that all this time since he took over the Karate club, Bonang with the help of Mbumbi; was working feverishly behind the scenes to facilitate a trip to the mining town of Orapa. This is because both of them were familiar with the whole process involved in as far as whom to contact, and what to say. It also helped matters because Mbumbi's father was also a geologist for De Beers and was based in Orapa.

Finally the trip came to fruition and we were all excited. Orapa is like no other town in Botswana, especially back in those days, because it is a mining town and to enter one needs special permission. We submitted our names, and had to wait for a couple of weeks before everyone was cleared by security as was the norm. A form 4 named Moaloso, better known as 'Kempes' in the football circuit, took exception when he was told that he could not go on the trip, and promptly tendered his resignation from the club and joined the Kung Fu beat.

Looking back I do think there was some biasness in as far as choosing people who were to go on this trip was concerned, friends took care of one another, and since only a certain number of people could go, I saw some faces that were not part of either the drama or Karate club that came along – even teachers. In all fairness, Kempes had every right to feel resentment, more especially since he was a form 4, and it was always important to take form 4's on trips like this one so as to groom them for the coming year, and Kempes was one of those people we thought could lead the club in 1988 after we were all gone.

Meanwhile, another tournament took place during that time before we left for Orapa. Bonang again had arranged with the Botswana Defense Force karate club based in Selibe Phikwe to come to our school one Saturday afternoon, which they did in their humongous army truck. Collet 'Ngamula' Mosudisa even got to ride in the truck as he met them at the school gate, and directed them where to go. We were envious of him, because civilians rarely get that privilege of riding in army trucks. The fact that the army itself had come to our school for the tournament was something none of us had ever seen, which went far in telling us what a great leader and organizer Bonang was. The BDF team by the way was led by an able martial artist named Chance Dichauto.

The difference this time compared to our tournament with GSS the previous year was that we did not train as hard, as for me I do not remember training at all, which is why that morning Bonang had me spar with three people in a row to at least get my conditioning to an acceptable level. That did not do me any good though, because I lost my first fight by a close margin, and the second I lost by disqualification, because I accidentally punched my opponent on the nose and he bled.

The other fighters like Cornmaster and Meshack 'Lani' Mauco did pretty well, but the day belonged to the big man Collet 'Ngamula' Mosudisa who was just magnificent. In the first fight, he faced an adversary who was almost as big as him, and a hard puncher apparently as all the army guys seemed to be, but instead of cowering, Ngamula took the fight to the better trained fighter and beat him by a wide margin. By the second fight, the big man had smelt blood, and now went for the kill as he paralyzed his opponent with two excruciating blows to the solar plexus, and as his opponent staggered backwards to catch his breath Collet finished him off with yet another well executed straight punch that knocked him out of the ring; by this time the audience were wild. Ngamula had made as proud. Even a fellow student, who was also a classmate of mine named Botsanang Latlhang summed up the whole scenario perfectly.

"*Di fene tsotlhe di tsamaile le Collet.*" "All the fans are now in Collet's corner." And he was right, even though Collet was not the kind of person, who like Blackie, would have instantly embraced the limelight - on the contrary. Ngamula was a very quiet and unassuming gentleman from Bobonong whom all of us had come to like and respect.

Not surprisingly, he was handpicked by Bonang to be the head of our disciplinary committee; just as Cowden Sechoni had been during the Leruga era. And Ngamula was to carry out his duties very efficiently; even Bonang and I were not immune to punishment if we flouted the rules.

In the end the tournament was a success. Speaking for myself, I learned a lot from this experience, and I was and use it to my advantage at many tournaments in the future after I left Lotsane. I would think Bonang learned a lot too in spite of himself, because in that particular tournament he faced off with an opponent just as good as him if not slightly better. He had at first underestimated him, but when the fight began he was in for a big surprise, and for the first and only time as far as I know lost the fight by a slim margin.

Later that night, after our visitors left, we had a fun time with a different form of entertainment called *'Pick a Box'*, where contestants bought tickets, and when the number on their ticket was called the contestant would come forward and answer a series of trick questions, and if successful would choose a box whose contents were unknown, and we would offer the contestant money or the box and he would take his pick. Bruce Kojane thrilled the audience when he came up to the podium after his number was called, and he went through the hoops. The grand prize to be won, which was Legoro's idea, was a dinner for two at the nearby Botsalo Hotel in Palapye all paid for by the school, which was why everyone who was lucky enough to be called would go for the box. I was conducting the interview with Bruce.

"So Bruce let's say I give you 5 Pula or the box, what would you want?" I asked

"The box," Bruce said to the mike. He was a bit nervous.

"How about 6 Pula or the box."

"I say the box man!" he insisted in a way that brought laughter.

"Are you sure? How about 7 Pula Bruce, you know there is a lot you can do with that at the Tuck shop."

"I say the box man!" Laughter.

In the end he ended up getting his wish and won a brand new digital watch, the type that was common in the 1980's. A fellow by the name of Philemon better known as 'Phil' won one of the dinner tickets. The other was won by a form 4 whose name eludes me, but I resorted to calling him *'Monna wa Saphara'* or 'the Supper man'. *'I say the box man!'* was to become the catch phrase of 1987. Just like word *'Jola'* had been in 1986.

Now, during this time, a group of girls all of whom were form 4's came together and formed a club known as 'Explo' short for 'Explosion', they were all beautiful, hip, and aware of the latest trendy fashions. Hex, being the genius that he was; incorporated them and the Pantsulas into a club, and arranged that a show be presented for the school in a way that many of us had never seen before. This was during a variety show at entertainment on a Saturday. I had never, up until then, seen a runway for models in person except on TV, but that day one was made out of the stage designed by Mr. Porter in 1986 for the great drama festival, and the club had everyone bring out their best clothes and model in front of the school, and they did that to a song by a group from Cape Town known as 'The Rockets'. The name of the song was *'Gimme a break'.* The show was fantastic and ingenious. My friend Ruth Tseleng Botlhole was one of the models and I was extremely impressed by her performance. She was a natural, and I had personal reasons for being proud that night because Ruth has always been like a sister.

Now the only problem as far as the 'Explo' was concerned was when the Pantsulas took the floor. Hex's instructions were that they were just going to do a brief presentation by merely dancing in single file, and then head outside and that would be it. A big mistake, because Hex of all people, since he was a performer himself, should have known that Pantsulas are dancers whose unique style cannot be constricted as he wanted. Thus, when the guys got on the floor to do their performance it became an instant free for all competition. This was motivated by the fact that there were new faces in the crowd, and that being comely form 4 girls. It was a known fact that the first few weeks as a form 5 if you had a girlfriend who was also a form 5 she loved you like never before, because there were new ones in the midst who now gave the senior girls serious competition. And if you did not have a girlfriend that was always the best chance to find one. This was true, because I found my eyes straying a bit those first few weeks; especially toward one girl in particular, who had a very uncanny resemblance with Alice to a point that was scary. It was like a ghost of my past that had come to haunt me. I never knew her name because she transferred to another school shortly thereafter. Even a few girls in my class including Laone Kesitilwe, who knew Alice very well, came up to me and reminded me of the likeness. I still wonder what would have happened had she stayed at Lotsane.

So it was no surprise why the Pantsulas went all out the moment they were on the dance floor. Led by Julius 'Mjulujulu' Tlholebe, as they danced to Chicco Twala's song *'Hitsikene,'* the Pantsulas went wild. This was made worse by the fact that the girls, especially the form 4's who were being targeted, were now cheering. On the strength of this Julius did something I had never seen before until then. He picked up a chair with his teeth, held it high in the air with his teeth mind you, and danced along to the other end of the hall. On seeing this, Otukile 'OT Legoro' Motukwa, not to be outdone, did a shuffling of his feet; dancing from the opposite end of the hall to the other side where Julius had started. This was electrifying. Julius, after putting down the chair, and still with one trick up his sleeve, pulled out a knife and in dramatic fashion through his dance reenacted a scene on the streets where someone is being attacked by a *tsotsi* (small time street hoodlum) many of whom were associated with Pantsulas; thus its origin as a 'ghetto dance'. The great Ali was gone, and a new king had to be crowned, but to this day I cannot say for certain who got the mantle because they were all good.

Apparently Hex, and a few members of the 'Explo' club, were not impressed by these antics, and at the meeting the next Monday (Hex had chosen me and Mbumbi to be the honorary chairmen of the club); he let them know that that was an 'illegal competition'. The guys took offense to that and walked out of the meeting. Later on they approached Bonang and I, and asked if they could be members of the Karate club as the dance unit just like Roukes had done in 1985, and we welcomed them with open arms.

Chapter 28

We left for Orapa after lunch a week or so later in two trucks. I felt the same excitement I felt in 1985 when we took that trip to Moshupa and Kagiso secondary school. It was a bright and sunny March afternoon and one of the school's cooks came along with us, and about an hour into the journey he suddenly clamped both hands to his head and looked down.

"What is the matter sir?" someone asked.

"I forgot the meat ... oh my God this is terrible," he said.

We carried our food supply with us, most of which had to be cooked, which is why he was brought along. We were stunned for a minute. We had gone too far to turn around and go back now to get it, and yet we would have to stop the truck and inform one of the teachers, Mr. Mudidi in this case, of what had happened. And just as we were wondering what our next move would be; we saw a Toyota Hilux headed toward us flashing its headlights signaling us to stop. It was the school's smaller truck, and the ever reliable Kabelo was at the wheel. They had also realized that we had forgotten the meat, and had sent for him to take it to us. We were relieved especially the cook, because he would have been severely reprimanded I would imagine.

The first stop we made was in Francistown. The last time I had been there was in 1979 so the city looked very different to me because I was disoriented. My uncle Peter 'Daddy' Nthite (to whom I dedicated my very first novel *Kahuru: The Making Of An African Legend*) lived at a place called Khaphamadi (the place of blood), and when at the town center I had absolutely no idea in which direction that place was. We were told that we could take a break for an hour before resuming the journey; however one of the trucks, which happened to be the one we were riding, had a problem with one of its rear tires and needed to be fixed so we ended up staying a little longer. Taking advantage of this delay, Meshack and a fellow by the name of Ambi decided to pay his sister (Meshack's) a visit who lived close by.

We were at least an hour or so away on the dusty road headed to Orapa when one of the girls, Abigail, noticed something terrible.

"Hey, people we left Meshack and Ambi behind," she said visibly shaken.

"Oh, my goodness she is right," someone confirmed.

We all realized the gravity of the situation our two colleagues were in. On such trips, it was an unspoken rule that no one was to leave the vicinity of the truck whenever we stopped that much was clear, however what was worse was that the two had not only left, but they did so without informing or asking for permission from one of the teachers. This kind of thing would have been looked at as absconding from school – a very serious offence.

Options were discussed as to what would be the best thing for the two guys to do in such a situation. Since no teacher was aware as to what had happened, and we were already over 100 miles away; the question of returning to Francistown in search of them was not even discussed.

"The best alternative for them would be to head back to school and be there before Mr. Mudidi reports this to the headmaster," someone said.

"Under the circumstances that would be the best thing to do," Cornmaster agreed.

We felt really bad for them and wondered what state of affairs they were in.

"Fine, but do they even have money to catch a bus, let alone hitch a ride back to Palapye?" I asked. Everyone was silent as that possibility was not talked about, and as high school students we all knew how hard money came by. It cost at least 7 Pula per person to catch a bus to Palapye from Francistown, and that was way too much money to expect a student to have readily.

These chaps from Ramotswa like Meshack, Ambi, Strong, Cornelius, Julius, and the like had a unique way of speaking among themselves. For instance they always referred to one another as 'lekgowa' which literally means a white person, but in this context meant 'pal', 'brother', or 'friend'. Whenever something went wrong they would say 'go go ntsho'. That literally meant 'it is dark' as in a dark cloud is hanging over us, or meant calamity in their colloquial.

That is why everyone laughed when someone said, "I bet you when the two arrived and found the truck gone they were saying to one another: "*lekgowa, go go ntsho.*" "Pal, calamity has befallen upon us."

In the end we figured that they would somehow find a way to get back to school, and did not converse about the matter any further, but we all silently wished that they would be safe. We arrived at Orapa at around 9 pm that evening and had to wait for at least another hour or so at the gate where they had to make sure that every name that was submitted was accounted for. Entering Orapa felt like you were crossing the border into another country. Not surprising because this is a diamond mining area and thus very restricted. Residents are not even allowed to keep live chickens, and killing an ostrich within the area is a very serious crime, because diamonds have been known to be found inside these birds' gizzards.

As we waited I kept everyone in our truck entertained with some tall tales, many of which I had heard from Roukes Nokane. Everyone was enthralled as I told some of these stories that Stoner, the other Bonang, had to say something from the other truck which he was in.

"Hey, hey, hey Sebati *letlhaku e be e le la eng*?" "Hey, hey, hey Sebati what is that entire tall tale about?"

I never quite could remember what I was talking about until many years later; when Olivia reminded me when I spoke to her on the phone one day. I do recall though telling her to be on my side no matter what, because it seemed as if she was on anyone's side who opposed me in the truck that night.

At last we were allowed into the town. There were brand new houses that were not as yet occupied, so we were divided into groups of about 10, and each assigned to an empty two bedroom house complete with a bathroom and shower with hot water. This was indeed paradise and we were all thrilled. Mr. Keakile our former deputy headmaster had been transferred to a junior secondary school in Orapa where he was the principal, and he hosted some of his former colleagues at his house. We were all exhausted and thus very soon asleep. Our first performance was scheduled for the next afternoon, which was going to be the Karate demonstration, and at night, the main event which was to be a performance of our award winning play '*Wedlock of the Gods*'.

The next morning around 10 am, we were shocked and amazed when we saw Meshack and Ambi arrive at our front door. Meshack was to later tell us about their ordeal, and how they managed to get to Orapa. When they found out that we had left, they were scared to go back to his sister's house, and chose instead to sleep at a local park on one of the benches and wait until morning. With nothing to eat and also cold I could only imagine what a terrible night it must have been for them.

"How did you guys get here?" I asked.

"Oh, by plane," he said nonchalantly.

"No man seriously," someone said. By this time quite a few people had gathered, listening to Meshack and Ambi's tale, even though it was Meshack who did most of the talking.

He went on to say, "Later that morning, as we were wondering what to do, someone was kind enough to let us know that if we headed to the Francistown airport we might hitch a ride from one of the DeBeers planes headed for Orapa, which is what we did after explaining our situation, and of course when we arrived they confirmed that our names were indeed on the list of people permitted to enter the town." The veracity of this story has been hotly debated, especially by people back at school, when they heard about it. Even Kabelo Lebotse the head boy questioned its authenticity.

"I mean fellows does one just come up to a pilot and say: hi we are also headed to Orapa can we ride with you?" This was after all Botswana in 1987; so such a thing as riding on a plane for free, and without prior arrangements, and into a restricted area was unheard of. I believed him, but many did not as they found his story to be a bit too fantastic.

At any rate the most important thing was that the two were safe and among us again, and Mr. Mudidi, being the understanding man that he was, did not hold the fact that they left without permission against them. Now officially off the hook and his troubles behind him, Meshack was invigorated.

"Man, I slept in the bush last night, and now when I hit that board this afternoon I will smash it to smithereens," he said as we prepared for our afternoon performance.

The first thing we did at a martial art exhibition, after the regular routine of kicks and punches, was perform synchronized moves in unison known as *katas*. I was not well versed or prepared on some of the *katas* and thus would embarrassingly make a wrong move and be out of sequence, which was unacceptable for someone who was supposed to be Bonang's right hand man that the latter had to whisper fiercely in my ear, but in a way that the other subordinates would not hear, and thus sparring me further humiliation.

"Sebati come on wake up man, *wake up*," he said.

I followed his advice by concentrating even harder and later redeemed myself by performing a solo *kata* that I had learned from Max and Roukes, and got an ovation. This was followed by the breaking of boards and then sparring. There is a technique to which bricks and boards are broken, a trick really, that makes it not as difficult or as painful as it looks. Bonang had taught us well, but that day I must have not hit the board the right way because my hand was throbbing for a long time. Since I could not spar, I was the referee and Bonang paired the fighters. There was drama as everyone seemed to avoid Collet like the plague until Meshack 'Lani' Mauco accepted the challenge.

I think that experience of sleeping in the park and surviving the possible repercussions had him psyched to a point of brilliance, because he was able to counter every move that Ngamula threw at him with a lightening side kick to the belly followed by a resounding *kiai* (a war cry very synonymous with the martial arts), the big man tried again, and this time attempted to destabilize his opponent with another of his trademark hard punches, but 'Lani the white man' would keep him at bay with his kicks that now seemed to find the target at will, that the fight ended with the great Ngamula scoring very few points. This was a shocking and unexpected result.

"*Hey, motho o ratile go bolaya Collet kana,*" "Man Collet had no answer to that barrage," some people said. They thought that Collet was invincible, but the big man will be the first to tell you that this is part of sports, you win some and lose some, and that day just happened to be one when he was caught off guard by another good fighter. It happens even to the best of us. The crowd was entertained nonetheless. This though was almost sullied by the sparring between Moloki David and

Elijah Legwaila, because during that encounter Moloki accidentally punched Elijah on the throat so hard that Elijah fell to the floor, and lay there face down, and when I knelt beside him to check if he was okay, I realized to my horror that he was crying – that is how much in pain he was that I feared the worst. What if his larynx was severely injured? I asked myself as he was carried from the floor, and rushed to the hospital. Luckily it turned out that the blow had not caused any damage, and except for some soreness Elijah was fine.

After the show I was pleasantly surprised to find out that we had made more money than I expected. 75 Pula would have been fantastic, but instead the figure was about 186 Pula and change! And we still had one more performance that night. At this rate we were going to reach our goal of raising at least 300 Pula by the end of the evening and on one trip, and the month was still March. We were thrilled. My hand did not stop throbbing though, and like Elijah I was taken to the hospital, and when I got there one of the nurses merely shook her head before attending to me.

"I bet you this is another of those karate kids I tell you," she said with some indignation. My hand was heavily bandaged and I was soon after cut loose. No X-ray was performed, because they must have thought that it was just a strain when in truth I had a fractured knuckle, and was not aware of that until many years later.

Throbbing hand or not the performance took place that evening, and before the main event, which was the play, we decided to entertain the audience a bit with the skit I had written a year ago about the street urchin who wins the affections of a beautiful rich girl. This time the role of the girl was reprised by Albertina Mokgware, because Mable Maphane had already graduated with the class of 1986. Although a great actor, I think Albertina kind of took this role a bit too seriously, because she was speaking of her undying love for my character in rich and poetic language often reserved for the 'real' plays. She was superb nonetheless, and the role of the leader of the thugs named 'Msomi' was played this time by Osborne Twenty, because Mathabathi, like Mable, was gone. Osborne was great, but he certainly was not Mathabathi.

We had to cut the play short, because Mr. Mudidi was anxious to get the real show on the road, which we did. Our audience liked our performance, but once in a while during recess, as we were preparing for the next scene; Mr. Mudidi was compelled to call out a few drunks in the audience who were becoming unruly, and they only took heed of his pleas for calm when he let them know that should that kind of behavior continue, after being given a polite warning, they would be thrown out without a refund. That definitely got their attention, and the ruckus at the back stopped. That was the thing about Orapa that we quickly noticed, and had been warned about in advance – law and order was maintained at all times.

There was a dance after the play which a lot of the guys and girls attended. An ex Lotsane student, Odiretsimang 'Jomo' Molao, of the fabled 1986 Lotsane football team, lived in Orapa at the time, and played for a local team there fraternized with his former colleagues at the dance. As for me I was too tired and my hand was still throbbing, and thus I could not make an appearance. I went to bed early instead and heard that the dance was a blast. Before we left the following morning, Bonang drew me aside just far enough from the rest to ensure utmost privacy.

"Sebati, do you know how much we made last night?"

"No." I figured from what I saw perhaps 300 Pula, 350 tops.

"858 Pula and 36 Thebe ..."

My jaw almost dropped to the floor, and I think my eyes were popped out of their sockets.

"Are you kidding me?"

"No man, we did it," he said.

This was unbelievable. On just this trip alone we had made over 1000 Pula; a feat not even the great Roukes's administration could have dreamt of. It took a while for it to sink in, and when it did I could not help but think what a great party we were going to have. With other trips in the horizon, and our other fundraising efforts at school that included cooking fat cakes at the Home Economics laboratory by our female members, which we sold to the student body; there was no telling how much money we would end up raising - the sky was indeed the limit.

We were in high spirits when we left later that morning. And to avoid eating the dust from the other truck, they were given a head start of about 20 minutes before we followed suit. We were well on our way, when for some reason I started to smell a familiar type of air that I should not have been smelling especially at that point in time. It was the smell of air from a tire. I looked at one of the back tires and quickly realized that it was flat. This was the same tire that had given us problems earlier during the first leg of our journey. The truck stopped and we all jumped out. The driver grabbed his head in frustration, and he had every reason to I was to soon find out. Government trucks did not carry spare wheels or jacks; that was the regulation. For it to be fixed word would have to be sent to the Central Transportation Organization (CTO), who would first get the report on the damage, approve it, and send someone out there wherever it was to fix the vehicle. That is how things worked in Botswana back then. And so we were stuck in the middle of nowhere.

"*Go fedile ka rona*," "It's over for us," Mbumbi said. In other words that chilling statement meant that we were doomed. And stranded in the middle of nowhere with no food and water and no help in sight, it was hard to disagree with him, even though that was a very poor choice of words at the moment. None of us wanted to hear the ugly truth.

We were with Mr. Mudidi, who started thinking fast, and came up with what could be a solution to our problem. Two people, Bonang and Mbumbi, were to go back to Orapa for help, and another two, Stoner the other Bonang, and Mpho Maposa were to head to Francistown with the hope that they would overtake the other truck, and inform them of the latest developments, and have them come back for us, it was a gamble but worth a try.

Bonang and Mbumbi were the first to get the ride back to Orapa as we were able to flag down an oncoming car, and shortly thereafter Stoner and Mpho were headed to Francistown, when a car going that way stopped to find out if we needed help. There was nothing to do but wait, and we had no idea how long that was going to be. We sat under a big shady tree trading stories among us. Tefo and I talked about people we knew from Gaborone before we met, but by the time we normally had lunch at school, which was around 1 PM, we started to feel the hunger pangs and the heat. Soon thereafter a man from a farm nearby came by us selling sour milk, which some of us bought and swallowed as if it were real food. The man was kind enough to inform us too that there was a well not too far off, and that he would bring us some water, which he did much later. That and the sour milk managed to keep true hunger at bay at least for a while.

Toward the late afternoon the other truck arrived from Francistown. Stoner and Mpho had made contact, and as of yet there was no sign of Mbumbi and Bonang, but we knew they would be fine. We were lucky that the duo were able to catch up with the other truck, because word was that they waited for us in Francistown, and when they did not see us they assumed that we had taken another route that went through Serowe, and were just about to resume their journey when Mpho and Stoner caught up with them. Had this not happened, we would have been in a very bad situation indeed.

We arrived in Francistown in the early evening, and resumed the rest of the journey to Palapye, which was very unpleasant, because now it was night time, and the wind blowing was cold; plus were we cramped like sardines since we had to all fit in with the other group. We got back to school way past midnight, and not surprisingly many of us overslept and missed some early classes, and we were punished for that. Mbumbi and Bonang arrived later that day visibly disappointed. They had sought and found help, and said that the DeBeers people even brought their mechanic complete with a new tire and tube that they were going to replace on the truck for free, only to find that we had left. After a few days we had all recuperated from this trip of many adventures and were able to reflect with pride over what we had accomplished. There was one more event that term that was rapidly coming to an end that I was looking forward to – the interschool track and field competitions.

Chapter 29

We did not fare well at all at the interschool competition at Madiba. Considering the fact that we were the defending champions in as far as the track and field events were concerned, and the way we lost was really deflating. Perhaps this had a lot to do with the fact that many of our top athletes like Ditshupo, Terry 'Harare' Richard (from whom Ferdinand Williams had inherited his moniker very much to his ire), Julian Mokgatle, Terrence Jacobs, and Gabriel Matlakele had left, which left us with very few genuine sprinters, and inexperienced athletes like myself had a lot to do with it. The only real highlights of the event was when we came second in the relay race, which we should have won had Motlotlegi not mistimed his run as the third man.

Lotsane was known to have never lost the 100 meter relay. This we were told by Ms. Molobe my History teacher, who was also a very big track and field fan. She let us know about that the moment we were ready to take the field. A form four named Moses was to start the race and hand the baton over to me, and I was to hand it to Motlotlegi who was to give it to our anchor man, who also happened to be the fastest in our school, and that was the great sprinter named Benjamin 'Computer' Moube. We had been well trained by Mr. Adams and thus upbeat about our chances in as far as maintaining Lotsane's great record in this event. The previous year, the relay team looked more like an Olympic dream team with, Terry Richard as the starting man, and then Terrence Jacobs who in turn handed the baton to Julian and then to our anchor man who happened to be Ditshupo. Now these chaps ran like the wind blows, and many wondered if the 1987 team would come close to what those guys had achieved in 1986 - they would soon found out.

When the gun went off, Moses like Richard before him, always knew how to have a great start off the starting blocks, which gave us an immediate advantage, and the hand off to me was magnificent, and I ran like never before urged on by a vociferous Lotsane crowd that jumped up and down the back of our truck; just like we had seen the Swaneng students do last year when they came to our school for that pivotal soccer game when we spanked them badly. Now, as I was approaching Motlotlegi I kept shouting at him.

"Go man go!" what I meant was for him to begin running as fast as he could, and since I was already at my maximum speed, I knew I would catch him before he left the area in which I could legally hand him the baton. I don't know if he heard or understood what I was saying, but he hesitated for a split second, and that was all Madiba needed, because after I handed it to him the closest runner from Madiba who I had left behind managed to close in, and when he handed his baton to his teammate he managed to outrun Motlotlegi, and thus our anchorman Computer was just a step behind his man, and we came second in a race that had looked much easier for us to win. We nonetheless qualified now for the national competitions that were to be held in Gaborone in a weeks' time. For me personally this was a momentous achievement. Ever since I was a boy at Primary School I had always wanted to run at the national stadium, but always came short because there were always a few who were a little faster than me that made the cut. I was finally over the hump.

Madiba on the other hand seemed unstoppable. They dominated every single event be it in the junior or senior ranks. Some people even went on to suggest that they had an unfair advantage, because on the Madiba campus there was some kind of vocational training school called 'The Brigades', and many of these students who attended this school came from all walks of life, and were mainly adults, who wanted to learn a skill like carpentry or auto mechanics that they could turn into a career. Whether that was true or not I have no idea, but Madiba's sudden surge in strength – especially in soccer later that year left many of us wondering. That year though was theirs; jealous aside.

In the high jump competition one big Madiba student was poised for an easy win, but then someone prevented him from doing just that, and that person was Michael Kaelo Gare. Kaelo who was also known as 'Moshene' among the boys was a brilliant young man from Moshupa. He had attended primary and secondary education in his home village, and passed his Junior Certificate with flying colors. Now a form five, and also a member of the drama club, he had a very deep voice and a great disposition about himself. That is why when he was seated at the top of the school truck screaming obscenities, and all kind of disparaging comments at the Madiba high jumper, much the same way as Hotstix had done, everyone felt it; none more than the intended target that in the end he ended up not winning, but was second best to our jumper who happened to be my form 4 friend States Ndzimumbi - all thanks to the man they christened Moshene.

"*Mmoneng ke o ka dipotongwane mo matsogong*," "There he goes with over grown calves on his arms and toes for fingers," Kaelo would say time and time again much to the fury of the Madiba students, and the contestant himself, but to the amusement of many.

The big Madiba athlete, who I later found out his name to be Bashi, naturally took offense to Kaelo's comments, and immediately after the event came after him followed by a throng of Madiba students eager to witness a beating. On seeing this Moshene realized the mortal danger he was in, and immediately climbed up to the roof top of the truck as the Madiba guy grabbed him by the foot. Thankfully, the school driver, a much bigger and powerfully built man himself intervened, and Kaelo was saved at least for the moment, because Bashi left only after promising Kaelo that their fight was not over – not by a long shot. So Kaelo for the most part spent the rest of the day locked up in the truck until we left.

We arrived at the school later that day to the news that there had been a fight that is still talked about to this day, mainly because of how it started. The fight was between Hex and Philemon, better known as 'Phil' to the rest of the guys. The two were classmates, but bitter enemies. According to eye witness accounts, specifically Bonang 'Stoner' Mosupi, and one Duncan Pholo, Phil had brought a female friend to school from Palapye, and when they were having an intimate moment in one of the classrooms, it just so happened that Hex and a few friends saw them and knowing Hex he had his chance to heckle his foe, and instantly a fight was on. Phil was fast developing the reputation of being a bully, especially when we were in form 5. He was feared by many and only a few people could stand up to him. Perhaps that is why he thought he could bring a girl from the village to school, and pleasure himself with her during the day even though the afternoon was an overcast one. For some strange reason though, me and him got along very well; one of the kind gestures he did for me, was bring me a delicious desert that he had saved for me when he had gone to eat at the Botsalo Hotel, after winning the *'Pick a Box'* ultimate prize. And in addition to that he was a very brilliant student.

The fight I heard was a very violent affair and a teacher was summoned to separate them. With a hearing pending before the disciplinary committee, similar to one that Tonkana and Katu had experienced in 1985, Hex swore to tell the whole truth and nothing but; come Monday when asked what had sparked this clash. Knowing Hex as we did, there was no doubting that he would definitely fulfill his promise. He was after all outspoken, and never really afraid to speak his mind, even toward authoritative figures like teachers; a characteristic that was rare in high school.

He promised that he was going to describe in vivid detail of what had transpired in the classroom - right down to the color and type of the young woman's underwear. And since there was no love lost between the two, and therefore no chance of reconciliation, we knew that if this was escalated; it was going to be a very serious issue that was most likely going to land Phil in hot soup. Yet, for some mysterious reason, the matter never reached the disciplinary committee, and Phil was saved, but he went on to tempt fate again a few months later and this time he was not so lucky.

The following weekend we competed at the national level and lost. Had we won we would have qualified for the international event, because we would have represented the country. This happened once a year when the Southern African countries, excluding South Africa at the time, got together and competed in all events. These countries were Botswana, Lesotho, Swaziland, and Zambia. This also happened at the football level, and in the past Lepholeta 'City' Senne had been the captain of the high school national team, and which was why Mr. Pearce had a year ago singled him out at assembly after he won the inter house high jump.

"City," he said, "you are the best footballer among all the secondary school students in the country, and not only that you are going to be the best high jumper in all of high school." We all felt the chills that day at assembly as the Aussie dished out the accolades. I always felt he deserved nothing less, and years later in 1994 not only was Lepholeta, now a full-fledged professional and teacher by trade, and the footballer of the year; he was also voted the sports person of the year. Meaning that he had beaten out all other athletes from other disciplines to win that coveted prize; none would have been more proud than Mr. Pearce that day for his words had come true. One of the prizes on winning that award was coming to Pasadena California in the summer of 1994, to witness the World Cup Final between Italy and Brazil, with the latter emerging victorious after a 24 year drought. I was also in Pasadena then, and I know Lepholetha would have given anything to be on that field that day in the Zebras' colors.

We took another trip before schools closed to the Teacher Training College in Serowe, and added yet more money to our growing coffers. By this time we were well within reaching 2000 Pula in funds raised, which was a staggering amount among us teenagers. How and what we were going to do with the money is something none of us ever thought about - until one day in the future. However, that term I noticed that my grades were starting to slip for the very first time. I was not waking up in the morning like I used to, and it seemed as if the drive I had had in 1986 had deserted me like an estranged lover. This year, 1987, was a year really when I should have cut down a bit on my extracurricular activities, and concentrate more on my studies. Instead it looked as if my load of responsibilities in as far as these activities were concerned had doubled. There was also Roy's play *'The Breaking of Chains'* that was looming large, and that was going to put more on the plate. But I was not complaining. I was enjoying myself, perhaps a little too much.

The first term finally came to an end and I welcomed the much needed break. The previous year this time I did a lot of studying as I was anxious to achieve my goal, which was to win a prize, but this year it seemed as if I was just riding with the motions, and had not set concrete goals except speculate what grades I was going to get after the ultimate exam which was in November, and November seemed at the time light years away. I did think with a little more hard work and dedication that saw me succeed last year; I would perhaps get the prize for English and History. I had special reasons for wanting and coveting the History prize, one of them being that it was and still is one of my most favorite subjects, and a person I admired a lot who was to later become a great friend, Balisi Bonyongo, had won the prize during his graduation year at Lotsane, and I desperately wanted to follow in his footsteps. However it is one thing to think with your heart and do nothing and entirely another to wish it, and actually put in the work to realize that dream; I chose the former, and still thought I could pull it off because I was so good at the subject.

Chapter 30

During the first term holidays, I met up with my friends like Motelebane, and exchanged ideas about writing and storytelling in general. I also got the opportunity to thank him for the 10 Pula he had enclosed in a letter he had written to me. That money was like manna from heaven, because I was seriously cash strapped at that point in time like every student was. My father and I discussed the possibility of me going to a university in the United States, a move I was wholeheartedly in support of. Although I had been conditioned into thinking that engineering was my forte, and with a father who was determined to pull all stops to make it happen, I was an artist at heart, and the only place I felt where this dream could be realized was in the land of opportunity. Time would prove me right.

Second term was crucial in that our midterm exams were used as a barometer to determine how we were going to fare in the final examinations come November. This was a time when every form 5 student, like me, was to really begin cramping down on his studies. People like Elijah Legwaila had quit the drama club to concentrate more on his studies. Many of us could have followed suit I suppose, but drama was just too good to pass up. It was my life, taking it away would be like asking me not to breathe again. Which is why when the time came we started preparing for the drama festival once again; over the holidays Roy had rewritten, polished, and fine-tuned his play what was left was casting.

The lead role of a country peasant turned freedom fighter named Uthando Nkululeko was given to me, which was once again a great honor, and I was truly humbled by the fact that Roy had written the role with me in mind. The main supporting role of his urban friend, also from the country side, named Amandla Ka Jobe was given to Meshack Mauco. The casting seemed haphazard on some roles like that of the father played by Ennocent Mmapadi, because while we were wondering who would play that role, Roy peeped through the window outside and saw Ennocent by the water tap behind the classroom washing his hands.

"Hey Ennocent, how would you like to read for a part in my play?"

"Sure, why not?" and just like that he was cast after reading the lines to perfection. He was instantly a member of the club, even though just twenty minutes prior to that, the thought of him being a member would have been far-fetched. The same thing happened when I asked two of my dormitory mates MC and Phatsimo to be a part of the play, which they readily agreed to, and were cast as the hated apartheid era policemen. Stoner, the other Bonang, was cast as the chief of police and really sounded like an Afrikaner. Mike Kaelo Gare was cast as the traitor Chombe.

Now these guys like Phatsimo, MC, and Ennocent had never performed in a dramatic play before, meaning really that they had no experience, but once they became comfortable with their roles they performed like the seasoned veterans we all were, and we were pleasantly amazed. Apparently all of us have some hidden talent we don't know of until it is given a chance to resurface, like it clearly did with these gentlemen, and we started rehearsing in earnest preparing for the festival at Madiba.

***

Life in the dormitory was all the more fun; we all got along and genuinely liked each other. Also as chairman of the entertainment committee, and the school still hiring Ferdinand Williams' disco set sound systems, we had very rare privileges never seen before. For instance whenever it was record night Saturday, Ferdinand would be driven from school to his home in Palapye, to pick up the equipment, either in the school van or some teacher's on the Friday prior to the dance, and have the equipment dropped off in our dormitory. Then at night after lights off we would bolt the doors with a broom, cover the doors and windows with blankets and Ferdinand would then play the system (at a very low volume), and even turn on the disco lights, and the guys would in their underwear, do the dance sequences to be performed at the record night the following evening – all this was done under the pretext of testing the system to see if it worked properly. The same thing was done with the movies.

There was a storeroom in Block C just by the common room where some of the entertainment items were kept. This room, I was told, had been converted into some type of office in 1984 by then entertainment committee chairman Dave Bagwasi, who was affectionately known to his peers as 'Gwebza'. The 1985 form 5's talked about him constantly. The key to this room was passed on from one entertainment committee chairman to the next, this year the office belonged to me, and I took full advantage.

This is where I was whenever I needed peace and quiet, and also where I studied after lights off. This is also where we watched the movies before anyone else in school did, as the film, when it arrived, and the projector were kept there. One night, we even made a brazen move by showing the film '48 Hrs' in our dormitory after lights off in the comfort of our beds. We did this by moving all the beds to one side, and projected the movie on the wall on the other end. This we did after we covered the windows and doors.

This kind of thing did not sit well with some students apparently, and one in particular. And that happened to be Bonang Mapolanka of all people. He let us know about it one night when he came to our dormitory after lights off. It was a Friday night, and I think earlier that day since it was one of those casual Fridays, he had paid ma Amogelang a visit, because he was a bit tipsy.

"Aha ... you dorm 2 guys," he said in his shrill voice. "You have this thing of showing the films among yourselves before the whole school does, which you know is not right, but you do it anyway. I tell you what; you guys pull a stunt like that again I will wake up the whole hostel, and expose you for the scum that you are."

We were stunned. Bonang was one of us supposedly, not to say that what he was saying was not true, but this is a guy who had lived with us before, and we shared everything together even food. Why on earth would he turn on us like that? Besides, if the issue was that we were watching the films before anyone else in school, and he wanted to be a part of it, all he had to do was ask, and we would have welcomed him with open arms like a long lost brother.

Perhaps Bonang's argument, and here I am just speculating, could be that months earlier when we got the movie *'Indiana Jones and the Temple of Doom'* we played it in my 'office' under the same pretext of testing the film, but the next day when we were to screen it for the whole school at the hall the sound was gone, apparently something had gone wrong since the projector needed a system maintenance. I could not help but feel guilty about the whole scenario, because had we not 'tested' the film, the projector would have held on for at least one more show, but then it is just as good that the problem was identified sooner rather than later. There was no way Bonang could have known about all this, but then again there could most likely have been a leak – thus his resentment. However knowing Bonang he would have definitely used that as leverage, which told me that he was most probably in the dark as far as that incident was concerned; or had forgotten about it due to his state. What hurt us the most though was his betrayal in our eyes, and this hurt soon turned to anger and resentment.

"Let's not take what he said to heart guys … it was the alcohol speaking not him," Gerald Usher said.

"No, there's no excuse for this kind of behavior. If he had the guts to say that then it is clear that those are his thoughts, and that is what he always says, and was using the *chibuku* as a carp out," Archie said and we all agreed with him.

A few days later Bonang, now calm and completely sober came to our dormitory, all smiles like nothing had happened, but the guys gave him the cold shoulder. Even Itumeleng 'Zero' Tabengwa of all people snubbed him. I am saying this because Zero was a fun loving individual who never took offence, and was loved by everyone in school. He always maintained his jovial mood even when some people made fun of his teeth, which was the first thing you always noticed about him.

"So how's it going guys," Bonang said as he entered the dormitory. The guys just turned their backs, and some even walked out of the dorm.

"*Eish*, guys I got to be somewhere where I don't feel suffocated," MC said as he walked out followed by a few more. Bonang then turned his attention to Israel 'Di Eyes' Mpugwa.

"How's it going Israel?"

'Di Eyes' merely looked at him and turned around like everyone else. It was sad to see. I on the other hand could not do that even if I had wanted to, Bonang was my friend, and also my partner, but I did let him know that he had jumped the gun. It took a while, but in the end all was forgiven, but no one ever trusted him again, and from that time he was treated like an outsider.

Apparently the guys had good cause for not trusting Bonang, because not too long afterwards we were in my office 'testing' a movie that had arrived. While inside I thought I heard a sound of a bed moving inside the common room (it was empty because this year's form 4 intake was the smallest seen in years, because many of the former JC only schools now provided senior secondary education), and I opened the door only to find that there were guys who were trying to bolt the door from outside so that we could not come out. Whoever they were ran away before I could identify them. I then shouted as they were fleeing that they better pray to God that I don't catch them. We were in the 'office' with Mpho Maposa, who a little later was involved in a heated argument with Meshack in the 'Block C' corridor.

"Man, don't you dare say that again," Meshack warned *"ever,"* he added for good measure. I then quickly went up to them to find out what was going on.

"Alright what's going on fellas," I demanded. As an Assistant Head Boy it was my duty to intervene in any conflict and they knew that, so did everyone else in school.

"This guy is accusing me of being one of the people who tried to lock you guys in the storeroom," Meshack said in exasperation. It seemed far-fetched and inconceivable that 'Lani' my friend would do such a thing. I then looked at Mpho.

"Sebati, I'm telling you I saw him, and this other guy whispering among themselves about what they were going to do next since their first attempt had failed." This was a stunning revelation - hard for me to swallow. It had to be someone else - not Meshack.

"Mpho, are you sure about that?" I asked.

"Sebati man I'm telling you ..."

"Man stop saying that," Meshack intervened. "You know that's not true."

I kind of had a slight inclination that Mpho was telling the truth, but I could not bring myself to believe it. In the end I dismissed the two guys before things got testy. I was to find out much later, after we left Lotsane, and from Meshack himself that Mpho was spot on. Meshack had been among the guys who were trying to lock us in the storeroom. He went on to say all this was orchestrated by none other than Bonang Mapolanka, who wanted to see to it that we be punished for watching movies before the whole school did - by locking us in there until morning. He said it was true Mpho had caught him it is just that he was not certain, and Meshack could tell thus his vehement denials.

I keep telling myself that had that happened, I would have found out who had done it one way or the other. And having spent the night in that small and cramped storeroom turned office, and discovered that it was Bonang who had made that possible; there definitely would have been a big fight between us. I never entertained such a thought but once in a while it would creep in and I would shudder, because it was like me thinking of fighting Max. I now knew why the guys in dorm 2 felt that he could not be trusted after the initial fiasco, but Bonang was right, what we were doing was wrong, nonetheless that was the thing with high school there were just those who had the privileges; you just had to be in the right place at the right time. Just like Dixie Ndlovu had been in 1985.

Chapter 31

The rehearsals soon gained momentum and in no time we were ready for the dress rehearsal. The festival at Madiba was to be on Saturday. This time we made it a point that the English play performed first and avoid last year's disaster. Our performance was great, but at the end we fumbled when singing the song *'Nkosi Sikelel' iAfrika'*, *'God Bless Afrika,'* a song originally composed as a hymn by a Methodist mission school teacher in Johannesburg named Enoch Sontonga in 1897. For decades during the apartheid regime it was considered the unofficial South African national anthem, and was declared official by President Nelson Mandela after the fall of apartheid in 1994.

We were lucky that this serious imperfection was caught at the dress rehearsal, because we did not know the lyrics to the song, and the next day with the help of Mr. Moswela we worked on it in earnest and by Saturday we were ready, and could have given either *'Lady Smith Black Mambazo'* or *'The Harlem Boys Choir'* a run for their money. Even one girl by the name of Peggy Selelo, who was a staunch member of our club, boldly predicted that our play was going to win at Madiba. The Setswana play was well performed, and during this time I was blown away by a stunningly beautiful form 4, whom I had a hard time keeping my eyes off ever since I knew her. And after one particular scene in which she and Bagomotsi's character faced off in a fight over a boy, I was so impressed that when their scene ended, and I met them back stage, I hugged them both and gave them a kiss on the lips – something I probably should not have done, because I immediately fell for her and she for me. This was something that was to complicate matters for me in a way I would never have imagined, because I was still with Olivia, and two timing was a practice I detested since it had been done to me, but I had succumbed to temptation! What was worse was that the girl, Faith, had a boyfriend as well, a form 4 named Godfrey.

The Setswana play *'Boloi'* even though well written and performed was met with mixed reviews, because a lot of people including me saw a lot of similarities between this play and last year's *'Letlhokwa'*. Even the names of some of the characters were very similar. For instance the witch doctor's name in last year's play was named *'Matlakadibe'*, loosely translated meant 'he who comes with sins', and in the play *'Boloi'* there was a witchdoctor played by Kaelo Gare, named *'Matlakadilelo'* or 'he who comes with tears or pain'. The form 4's of course enjoyed it, but for some form 5's it was a different story.

"Ahhh ... that play is just the same as the one last year," Keebonye Morake aka 'Magompi' said a bit dismissively.

No one could say that about *'The Breaking of Chains,'* because this was a play that went to the very heart of the struggle against apartheid, and Southern Africa in those days was a hot zone. I could also personally relate to the story, because my father was himself a freedom fighter, and I got the privilege of being one albeit on stage as I really got into character. We were ready for the festival at Madiba. That weekend also, was when our school team was to play a very crucial football game against the very same Madiba to determine who were going to represent our region in the finals.

***

The 1987 Lotsane football team was a pale shadow in comparison to the team that was led by Lepholetha in 1986, and after many of them left, among them Eric 'Chippa' Mokgwa, Gabriel Matlakele, Tshwenyego 'Carlos' Tawana, Odiretsimang 'Jomo' Molao, John 'Stop Nonsense Buddha John' Monyai, Ishmael 'Ten Ten Machibichibi' Mphela and Wagga Montshiwa, not even mentioning the great Lepholetha; the very heart and essence of our team was ripped right out of our rib cage. There were new form 4's like Moaloso 'Kempes', Motshereganyi 'Teenage', Michael 'Sporo', Herman 'Chapter 4' Molosi, Sidney 'Sunca' Kgwatalala and the like, but good as they were they could not fill the vacuum that was left by the class of 1986.

The problem is that the team of 1986 was so good that there was only one form 4 player who played regularly, and that being Kgosietsile 'The Horse' Sanka, besides him there was no one else who had the experience of last year save for maybe Patrick 'Ace' Rakwadi, but he hardly had any game time and thus the new team was built around

Horse. The games played when the league started, followed the same format as last year, except this time the first two games we played were against our good friends Swaneng and Moeng College. We beat Swaneng by four goals to two, and the game with Moeng college ended in a two all tie even though Moeng, always the tough cookie, should have won. That is when I realized deep down that we did not have what it took to be champions again – if ever.

To spare myself any further heartache, I did not engross myself into football as much as I had done the past two years. Things did not get any better than the two teams I had witnessed during my era at Lotsane. That did not mean that I did not care really, because I just wanted them to succeed just like the 1985 team had done, but we did not fare well at all and based on the bar that the previous teams had set, we came way short. That is why in our last game we were in the same position that Swaneng was in 1986, and this time the team to beat was Madiba, who, unlike last year, would prove to be our nemeses this time around.

The Saturday when the festival started at Madiba was when they faced off with Lotsane at our school. We needed to win in order to return to the final, and Madiba needed only a tie to get to the Promised Land. We left that Saturday very early in the morning for Mahalapye, and I knew later on, I would know the results of the game from the Madiba students themselves the moment their team arrived later that evening. In the meantime my mind was set for the festival ahead. We were scheduled to perform at 2:30PM that afternoon, and at 10:00AM the first play began, but most importantly the 1987 festival that was to be remembered for years to come had officially begun.

Like last year we were silently confident that we were going to succeed, but this year we were not as cocky. Sometime that morning during a short break we took a walk to one of the nearby stores, and I was surprised to find Kaelo hanging out with his good friend, the big Madiba high jumper whom he had verbally abused at the inter school competitions a few months earlier - Bashi. The two had become friends apparently, and how Moshene was able to do that is still an ambiguity to me, but it was great to see that the two had buried the hatchet. At the same store I happened to run into an old colleague of mine named Oabona Michael Kgengwenyane. We had both attended Lesedi Primary School and were in the same class, a very brilliant chap, who was doing his national service at nearby Pilikwe. It was a poignant reunion as we had not seen one another in years.

"Hey man, the drama students at our school say they are scared of you," Bashi said to me. "They say you are a great actor."

I smiled because I was truly flattered. The Madiba students I believe were referring to my performance at the President's Day celebrations last year, when both our plays including Madiba's 'Ditiragalo' was staged at the Tsholofelo Community Center in Broadhurst. I was hoping to instill the same fear in them during our afternoon performance. Needless to say it was good to know that our main rivals were worried, and this information coming from one of their students who had no reason to lie really. We knew we were ready to give a great performance, but how great we had absolutely no idea.

Dr. Mtubani and Mr. Geary had returned as adjudicators again this year, there were two other new adjudicators who I did not recognize, but one of them was South African from what I heard later. When it was time to perform our play the entire Madiba hall was packed to the bream, and when we began we were like last year hitting on all four cylinders, and got even better by the minute. By the time Kaelo Gare's character exposed his true colors of being a police informant, and the way he performed, left even Dr. Mtubani laughing as he shook his head in amazement. Phatsimo Ramahobo even made some people like our own Albertina Mokgware cry backstage; when he portrayed a South African policeman turned freedom fighter. All in all it was a telling performance by all. Meshack Mauco's energy was compelling and very hard to match, and on many occasions managed to steal the thunder away from me the main character, but I was not worried about that. If anything, it helped me up the tempo a bit, and I have been told time and again by those who were there that day over the years that that was the best performance on stage they had ever seen. Many of these people who have come up to me to give these accolades have been strangers mind you, people I hardly knew, but who were there at Madiba that day.

The scene that had almost everyone in tears, including the South African adjudicator, was when my character, Uthando Nkululeko, stands trial in an unjust court, chained and beaten like a dog. People back stage like Lillian Setlalekgosi, who herself gave a stellar performance portraying a domestic servant violated by her white boss, fixed my face with makeup that made it look bruised, beaten, and bleeding, for blood we used red Kool Aid, some of which I had under my tongue and would at times make me choke and spit in mid-sentence; adding more to the drama and suffering of a political prisoner who selflessly gives his life for the betterment of his fellow men. By the time we were done, and singing *'Nkosi Sikelel iAfrika'* there were very few dry eyes in the audience. I even had a hard time persuading Faith that I was okay as she had been among those crying backstage. That is how impactful that performance was on that day. Later on this play was recorded with a video camera at a different show, but if there ever was a time to have filmed a great performance; that act at Madiba would have been the most ideal to record, and anyone of us would have given anything to see that fulfilled.

Immediately after our play there was a short recess to have the audience catch their breath. I could not help feeling a sense of *déjà vu* when last year this time we felt the same effects after the Madiba play. What we soon found out was that the Madiba students had also produced a play that dealt with the apartheid struggle in South Africa, and after our performance they were so worried that they held an emergency meeting looking to counter our performance. What was worse, I heard later, was that we had sung the song in our play (*Nkosi Sikelel iAfrika*) that they were planning on singing. They were scheduled to perform at 8:00PM that evening, and had to make major adjustments in very little time which turned out to be a very bad decision.

Later that evening we saw the Madiba truck arrive from Lotsane. I was watching it like a hawk from where I was. The moment they climbed out of the truck I saw them jumping up and down, and that was when the terrible truth dawned on me. We had lost. There was not going to be a championship to celebrate that year, my last year at Lotsane. All I could do now was just dwell on the memories of the 1985 team, and the painful recollection of what would have been in 1986 had Wagga not lost his cool.

I soon found out that we had lost by three goals to two. I even overheard a bit of what had transpired from some of the Madiba students, who I could only presume were players, as they were now in the hall watching one of the plays on stage.

"Yeah, we won we're going to the finals," one of them said. "But man I tell you Lotsane was fighting with every breath, every fiber, and every being of their existence. Those guys had the heart of a champion."

I was instantly proud that the boys had gone down fighting and not sheepishly, but the season was over for us now, and it remained to be seen what Madiba would do once they got to Gaborone. However, after all said and done, Moeding College repeated as champions that year.

The Madiba English play, *'Come Freedom,'* which they performed and was also about the struggle against apartheid, kicked off with much fanfare. There was the beating of drums, the dimming of lights in the process, and a dramatic announcement of the play about to be performed that the Madiba students shouted in delight. Unfortunately that is as good as it got, because their performance was not impressive at all. They had great actors, but I think they had been rattled by our performance earlier that afternoon that many of them tended to overact, and instead of shouting in a controlled and dramatic fashion - they ended up screaming bloody murder. In some instances it was comical to watch that we even made fun of them when we got back to school; imitating how they were screaming out the freedom songs and slogans. In the end we knew that we had nothing to fear from our perennial rivals - *'The Breaking of Chains'* was in a class all by its own.

We left after the play that evening. Returning to school that night, I was at the back of the truck seated with Faith covered by a blanket as we talked more and more, getting to know each other even better. As hard as I tried not to, but I was finding myself irresistibly drawn to this girl, and I could tell her to me. I was a very popular high school student at the time, but did not think much about it. The price to pay was that being known by everyone in school did not necessarily mean that you knew everyone. There were embarrassing situations when during the holidays, like the one just past, where some girl greeted me cheerfully as she walked past our house. I had no idea who she was and she could tell which is why she went on to tell me that she was a Lotsane student and in form 4, which did not really help that much as I did not know many of the form 4's. I feigned recognition of course so that she would not think of me as aloof or one who thought too highly of himself. That was just one of many such instances.

When I arrived at school, I asked the guys what had happened, why did we lose to Madiba in our own backyard? Archie went on to lament missed opportunities.

"Kempes had a clear cut look at goal and fluffed the opportunity so did Sunca, many others went begging, and had we taken advantage we would be telling a different story right now S.B." he said. Missed opportunities are the order of the day in football, and many times if you do not take advantage those misses will come back to haunt you, which is clearly what happened that day, and with it that aura of invincibility, that swagger, that many of us had become so accustomed to was now a thing of the past.

I went to bed that evening pleased with our performance earlier that afternoon, and seeing at how panicked Madiba had been, and I was silently confident that we would be winners in 1987 just like we had been that blissful year that was 1986. We were scheduled to leave very early the next morning for Madiba, because our Setswana play 'Boloi' was set to perform at 10:00 AM. The great thing about that journey the next day was that we were for the first time since my time at Lotsane going to travel by bus.

Chapter 32

We arrived at Madiba just when their Setswana play was performing. It was called *'Molao wa Manong.'* The literal meaning of that is 'the law of the vultures' as in 'a child who does not listen to his parents will only listen to the vultures'. In other words, if a child does not heed to the wise counsel of his parents that child will be doomed.

Even though we did not see the beginning, we were on time to see enough that the performance of these students was fantastic. Now this was the Madiba we were accustomed to seeing, and in the end when the results were announced our play, *'The Breaking of Chains,'* got first place tied with Madiba's *'Molao wa Manong,'* and our Setswana play *'Boloi'* was in third place. We were pleased with the results, even though it would have been great to have both plays win like we did last year, but the outcome was great under the circumstances nonetheless. On our way back to school on the bus we were singing songs from our play from last year *'Letlhokwa,'* which made many of us nostalgic, wishing we could go back in time as we recalled the good old days.

A few days later, a rumor started to circulate around school that Faith and I were having an affair. I think what made this gossip all the more juicy was the fact that in some circles I was looked upon as a one woman guy, straight as an arrow, especially since Olivia and I had been dating for over a year, which in those days, and in boarding high school was almost unheard of. The truth really could not have been any more different at the time. Yes, it was true that I had the hots for the girl, but we were not having an illicit affair as people were suggesting. I think perhaps I could have been more discreet whenever I made contact with her; especially during that trip to Madiba. In any case, this did not of course sit well with Olivia, who immediately confronted me about the issue. I denied any wrong doing, and promised her to be more cognizant of our affair and not fraternize with the girl that much anymore, which made the whole thing difficult, because we were all members of the drama club, and thus it was impossible to avoid one another.

A few days later, word got to us that our play was invited to perform at the President's day celebrations in Gaborone yet again. Apparently, the play got such rave reviews that it was being talked about everywhere, even in the corridors of the Office of the President, because we were told that the president himself, Sir Ketumile Masire, had expressed a desire to watch the play whenever his schedule permitted. We were floored. Just the thought of having the most powerful man in the land watch our play was staggering.

On the other hand, preparations in another field were also taking place. It had always been my wish, to present a project at the annual Science Fair, held at the University of Botswana during the institution's long break; that took place during the months of June through August. Last year, my project with Cross died a natural death after Mr. Ruf took that vacation, now that Cross was gone, I found another partner, and that was my very good friend Ruth Tseleng Botlhole. The project this time, was one I had read about in a science book I had borrowed at the national library during the first term break, on how to make glue from milk. It was easy to put together and present, but in retrospect I think we should have given more thought to our visual displays, because they left a lot to be desired even though the project itself was fascinating – if I may say so myself.

A few days before we were to depart for Gaborone, Ruth had a family emergency that compelled her to go home on short notice. Apparently, a close relative in her home village of Ramotswa had fallen suddenly ill, and her presence was needed and that time soon. It was not easy finding a replacement, and when I did it was my dorm mate Kgakgamatso 'KK' Moloi. It did not take that long to bring him up to speed in as far as the project was concerned. There were also two other students who were going to make a presentation as well, and those were Betty Bolaane and Dorothy Sanoto. Dorothy was Molefi's baby sister, the same Molefi who had asked me if I wanted to join the Karate club when I first got to Lotsane. They were both in form 5 zero, and it was usually the norm that only students from this science emphasized class, who would take part in these events. That year though I was the first to break that tradition; just as I would have had the project with Cross been ready to be presented.

Also that year, there was a knock out quiz, which was introduced by the Science Fair organizers. The way it worked was that each senior secondary school that wished to participate, picked three of their best science and math students, and these students would compete with one another in a knockout quiz until a champion was crowned. Our school was represented by Mbumbi, Elijah, and Baudubi. We all left for Gaborone one late Friday afternoon in Mr. Mbulawa's canopied van, and arrived in Gaborone around 10 PM that night.

We presented our project the next morning to mixed reviews, and I think one of our main mistakes was that we could not quite answer one question one of the judges asked as to what causes the milk to actually turn into glue. We got the answer with the help of our Chemistry teacher from the Netherlands named Mr. Kerklaan, who was just more than a blessing for us. After the presentation, we recessed for lunch and while at lunch, I noticed several girls from another school staring at me for long periods at a time, and then I saw one of them speak to Kgakgamatso, who later on was to relate the whole conversation to me.

"What was that all about?" I asked.

"Oh, one of those girls came up, and asked me if you were the gentleman they had seen perform in that play about the struggle against apartheid and I told them that you were," he answered.

"Oh," I said, but inward I was truly amazed that the play, and in particular our performance, had had such a profound impact on a lot of people. I had no way of knowing that this was just the beginning.

"She went on to say that your performance was great, and that you guys were so realistic and that the play was fantastic, because it dealt with current issues affecting the people of South Africa," KK continued.

After lunch we attended the knockout quiz, and we kept our fingers crossed all throughout, and our guys reached the semifinals, where they eventually eliminated by Gaborone Secondary School, whose team was led by a fellow I knew very well since he, Osupile, and I went to the same *dojo* (Tsosamotse) in Gaborone, and that was Churchill Setloboko (now Dr. Setloboko). It was great to see him again and he had KK cracking up the whole time, because of his unique speech mannerisms. Churchill was a very brilliant chap, and one of the most proper, which had a lot to do with his upbringing. He chose every word carefully when he spoke, and was straight as an arrow. He showed a maturity that was way beyond his years, and for those who were not used to him, like KK for instance, were magnetically drawn to him just as I had been a few years earlier when we first met.

That afternoon, more students came for the day just like I had done last year, to attend the Science Fair they came in the school truck, and left shortly after lunch. Mbumbi and Elijah left with them, something we ought to have done as future events dictated. We stayed behind with the understanding that Mr. Mbulawa was going to pick us up. He did come as arranged, but for some reason he went to the wrong room (we were all staying in student housing), and assumed that we had left with the other students, and he left for Palapye without us. We did not realize what had happened until much, much later when the whole campus seemed devoid of any human activity. When we called the school we found out, to our utmost horror that Mr. Mbulawa was already at Lotsane. Word at school was that we had deliberately made ourselves scarce so that we could party on in the city, and many including my dorm mates thought we were going to be suspended.

We had no money among us, and thus no food, but luckily one of the girls and I think that was Betty, asked us to accompany her to the school's kitchen, where one of the cooks who was the mother of one of the girls at Lotsane under Betty's care (Betty was a prefect), and from her we got so much delicious chicken than we knew what to do with. After being fed we planned what our next strategy would be. It was obvious that we would have to find our way back to school. Luckily Betty and Dorothy had won second place in the Science Fair (our project had lost), and one of the prizes was cash that was enough for us to catch the train, and head on out to Palapye. We caught the train and arrived in Palapye at around midnight. There was no way we were going to walk that long distance to school; so we went to the police station who were kind enough to give us a ride back to school.

The next day during afternoon prep, we were summoned to the staff room to face the disciplinary committee, and explain why we were not in our room when Mr. Mbulawa came to pick us up, or why we did not ride with the rest on the school truck. We did nothing wrong as far as I was concerned and thus had nothing to hide, which is why we did not panic as we normally would have had we been up to no good, and subsequently faced by this dreaded group of people.

We told it like it is missing out nothing, and in the end it was all agreed upon that it was just a matter of miscommunication really and that no malice was intended, so we were let go, what was even great was that Betty and Dorothy were reimbursed the money that they had spent in getting us to school. I shuddered to think what would have happened had these girls lost just like us, because I am not sure where we would have gotten the money from. My father was out, because when I explored that possibility, I realized that he did not have any money to spare so it is just as good that these ladies came through.

***

Once in a while we had prefects' meetings, which were always held at the girls' common room. Ever present at these meetings was the headmaster Mr. Mahole, his new deputy Mr. Geary as, MS Motlotle's tenure at Lotsane was sadly but a few short months, as she had to go for further studies abroad, and when Mr. Geary moved up in rank his position of Assistant Headmaster was taken up by the overzealous Mr. Molilo; better known as 'Mature' to all the students.

At these meetings, we were always reminded of our duties, particularly by Mature, and also to air our grievances. Mr. Geary was more liberal, and sort to give us more privileges like automatic permission to go to Palapye, but then of course Mr. Molilo opposed such a move - much to our disdain. In these meetings, Mr. Molilo would always make it a point to remind us that if the students liked us that meant that we were not doing our duties. A prefect who was liked by students meant that he was just as bad as the students he was trying to oversee. 'You are the eyes and ears of the administration,' he would always say, but none of us ever took him serious, because many of us prefects believed in being firm but fair, a language that Mr. Molilo did not seem to grasp.

One day at one of these meetings, Mr. Molilo said something that caught us off guard, and made us remember it for years to come.

"Some students call me 'maturity' ... they call me maturity," he said softly. I was seated at the front and Mr. Mahole, naughty as he would choose to be at times, was smiling. Now the problem was that the teachers were always seated in front of us like a panel of judges, and since Legoro was seated at the other end, it would have been hard for Mr. Molilo to see him even if he wanted to. For me I was in physical pain from trying to suppress laughter, but when he repeated that statement Matt could not hold back any longer and laughed outright; much to Mr. Molilo's indignation.

"Ahhh!" he exclaimed. "That girl is laughing, and she is a prefect again ... perhaps she is one of those people who call me maturity."

To this day it I still wonder why Matt was the only person who truly expressed what she felt, because the whole episode was funny. She was to tell me years later that it was not fair that Mature had singled her out when even Mr. Mahole was also laughing. That, she has always told me, is the reason why she could not restrain herself. When finally order was restored, I suddenly remembered a very crucial piece of information that had been at the back of my mind. I then immediately raised my hand the moment the thought came to me.

"Okay Sebati what's on your mind?" Mr. Geary asked with a smile on his face.

"Thank you sir ... well here's the thing, last year's prefects had a party, and I only think it is befitting ..." I did not get to finish what I wanted to say, because I was interrupted by laughter from everyone. It was a very welcome suggestion that was popular with everybody, and with all this support there was no way I was going to let this proposal die. "It is really my contention that as diligent prefects we should also be rewarded with a party."

The teachers laughed and immediately spoke among themselves; even Olivia (she was a senior prefect as well and thus was present) looked over at me and smiled. After a bit of wrangling among the teachers it was agreed upon that a date in the very near future would be announced to us as to whether or not we would have the party. There were smiles when we walked out of that meeting.

"Man Jones you were really adamant about that party weren't you?" Cornmaster said with a big smile on his face.

"I had to man, because if I didn't do you think the administration was just going to say 'oh you guys are great you deserve a party' they are asking a lot from us especially that Mature, and that has got to come with some benefits wouldn't you agree?"

We did have the party the following weekend. It was on record night Saturday. We were expected to dress up a bit, since this was an occasion where prefects and teachers were going to socialize on a personal level. We all arrived at the girls' common room promptly at 7:00PM as arranged. The tables and food was already set by the Home Economics students as usual. There were all kinds of dishes that made us salivate, but the only complaint we had as we observed from outside, before being permitted to enter, was that the food seemed too little. We had some serious stomachs among us, chief of who was a tall gentleman from Moshupa named Boy Moalosi.

"No man I must protest this food is too little," he complained as we peeked through the glass.

"Yeah man I agree," I said, and it turns out that that was a concern that was shared by everyone, which is why when it was time to eat, we were among the first to rush inside, and in the process forgetting the gentlemanly code of letting the ladies in first, and try and gobble up whatever we could lay our hands on, but we had underestimated the amount of food, and overestimated our appetites, because in no time we were so full, and yet still there was a lot more food left even after we saved some for the next day. I had a lot of fun interacting with the teachers - especially my Principles of Accounts instructor Mr. Appadoo. He even insisted on taking a picture with me and Matt.

"I want you to show this picture in future and tell whoever sees it that this was your teacher who helped you get a 'one' in Accounts," he said. A 'one or two' in any subject was equivalent to an 'A' in the Cambridge Ordinary Level English examination grading system, and my teacher had boldly predicted on his first day of teaching us that I would be among the students that would get a 'one' in his class. He said the same thing about Rinah, Godfrey Morgan whom he called 'Mountain Man', a girl named Segomotso Nkwane, Hosea Gopalang, and Kobe 'Kobson' Motlhatlhedi among others. As it turned out Mr. Appadoo's predictions were spot on.

Chapter 33

We were scheduled to perform our play at a state of the art theater named *'Maitisong'* 'the place to hang out', which was located at the Maru A Pula school campus. A private international school known the world over, because of the diversity of students it attracts. Since it is privately run, the school fees are high, and for good reason too, because they routinely produce the best O Level results year in and year out, and are always in the 95 and up percentile. Perhaps this success can be attributed to the fact that from form one onwards, the students are prepared for the O Level exams, and the Junior Certificate system is bypassed.

Since the University was still on its long break; we were housed once again in the student lodging. An interesting thing happened during this trip. Roukes somehow found out that there was a performance by the Lotsane students, and that we were based at the University. It was great to see him again, and he had a surprise guest with him, and that being the big guy from Mmadinare - John Kagiso 'Bull' Obuseng. These two individuals were unknown to the form 4's and 5's as they had graduated in 1985, but very quickly Roukes was to introduce himself, and before long he became one of us again. The current crop of form 5's had heard of him as he was a constant topic among last year's group. Coincidentally, there was a form 5 from Moshupa who resembled Roukes, and was nicknamed such by the class of 1986. The gentleman in question was a very affable and gentle Christian, and one of the true members of the SU; his name was Olekae Thakadu. To this day, some of the fellows from the class of 1986 and 1987 still refer to him as Leruga or Roukes; even though many of these chaps from the class of 1987 had never seen or met the man himself.

That night I could tell that Roukes had had a few drinks, and thus was a bit louder than usual as he rode with us in the truck, keeping everybody entertained with his tall tales as usual, and then all of a sudden he paused and looked around. We were wondering what he was going to say next, and it did not take long before we found out.

"Fellows, did Sebati ever tell you that I once helped him get a girl he had difficulty convincing to be his girlfriend?" he asked. I on the other hand started squirming uncomfortably.

"Nooo!" It was a chorus from everyone as they anxiously waited to hear the juicy details from this natural born storyteller. There was nothing I could have done to stop him, I wanted to, but it was no use so I just had to swallow the embarrassment.

"Hahaha, there was this girl who was like the full moon and the sun in Sebati's life. For months he had been pursuing her, but to no avail until one day the master, that being me, intervened. All it took was a few minutes and I fixed everything." He paused to see if he had their attention, particularly the form 4's who always saw me as an oak, someone who always maintained his cool, and who got whatever he wanted and lived life on his own terms. They were spellbound. "This girl he had been chasing mind you wouldn't give him the light of day, but when she finally said yes … you should have seen my boy!" everyone laughed eager to hear more.

"What happened next?" a lot of eager questions came all at once.

"Man, he was stunned, he ran around one class and then by the time he got to us he collapsed to the ground, and we had to carry him the rest of the way to the dormitory." There was a long stretched out laughter at my expense.

"Sebati actually collapsed because a girl agreed to go out with him?" one form 4 asked in total amazement.

"Oh yes."

"We're talking about the same Sebati right?"

"Yep, and at supper he could barely eat, that's how excited he was." More laughter followed. I suppose to many of them it was inconceivable that a popular student like me could be just as susceptible to being love struck like everyone else, fortunately Roukes was not one to over extend himself, and in no time the nightmare was over, but I never held it against him. I was still very grateful that he had come up to our huddle, in the academic area on that overcast afternoon - in what now seemed like a lifetime ago.

Our performance that night was good, but nowhere near the show at Madiba a few weeks prior, perhaps a lot of that had to do with the fact that the turnout was not as great as we had hoped it would be, even though it was an evening performance. However, the great part about that particular performance was that somehow Mr. Dan Bhusumane, the producer, who was also a former Students Representative Council (SRC) president at the University of Botswana, secured the services of a video camera operator and his equipment, and we were video tapped for the very first time in the school's history. This was ground breaking, because in 1987 such things were almost unheard of as the technology was still brand new – at least for us students from a school in Palapye. I have a copy of this performance, and one can hear Leruga's timely comments in the background. He was so rowdy that security was forced to throw him out, in spite of the latter's threats of physical violence, but in the end he rode back with us back to the university, and told us how impressed he was with our performance.

"It looks like I taught you well my boy," he said to me before him and Bull left. In spite of all the drama it was good to see him again after a long time, and I instantly missed him. The next day we were on our way back to school, and into fresh rumors that my affair with Faith was now a very badly kept secret.

***

During our trip to Gaborone, it had become apparent that Faith and I just could not keep our hands off of each other, figuratively speaking, and what was worse was that Olivia had come along on this journey, and the fact that she was in a sour mood all throughout gave these rumors even more ammunition. I must admit that I was indeed falling for the girl, and was a bit reckless at times in as far as contact with her was concerned; that MC had to warn me on several occasions to be very careful.

"*No, S.B. le wena o tla zama di blandara ka go bua le cheri ye nako le nako,*" "No, S.B. you are also committing blunders by talking to this girl at every given opportunity," he said time and time again. He was right, because I was doing just as he was saying. For instance, the morning before we left, when we were at the primary school in Gaborone West where we were fed, she was by the fire with a few friends talking, and when I got to them the friends left the two of us alone as though all this had been pre-arranged. I did not notice that as I was captivated by her presence, and as we talked it looked as though there was indeed something going on between us, maybe it was the unspoken attraction between us that everyone including Olivia could see. All this was noticed by MC and the rest.

"Guys, didn't we tell this guy to be as discreet as possible when it comes to making contact with this girl?" MC said, as he and the rest of the guys were watching us from a distance in disbelief. "How then is he going to explain himself to Olivia?" I am told that he was shaking his head as he was saying this. Phatsimo on the other hand had a totally different outtake on things.

"No, I don't think that's the case fellows," he said "the guy just can't help it. He's in love and so is she."

That is why things got really blown out of proportion by the time the news hit the *'Radio Lotsane'* air waves. What was worse, amidst all this, even though nothing had been confirmed between me and Faith as we still had people in our lives, Faith's boyfriend followed the foolish advice of his friends and dumped his girlfriend; a thing he later regretted. I on the other hand had a hard time convincing Olivia that there was nothing going on between me and Faith, which was true at the time, but Olivia seemed set in her belief that I was not telling her the truth. This became somewhat of a scandal among us students, because since I had always been straight as an arrow, and Olivia and I were looked on as the 'it' couple, because we had been together for so long the news of my supposed two timing was sensational; even years later when I ran into Cornmaster he was to recall that incident.

"Man Jones's scandal was the biggest of all scandals at Lotsane, because of the way he allegedly played those two girls," he said to Motse and friends that morning as we were getting ready to head to Universal Studios in Hollywood. That statement still stung a little even after all these years.

After a while though, I was to patch things up with Olivia, and things were back to normal, because in the end people accepted the fact that Faith and I were merely good friends who were obviously attracted to one another, but none of who were willing to cross that line that would most likely break Olivia's heart. And sanity at least for a while prevailed. Before I knew it we were almost the end of the second term, and we had written our midterm exams, which were termed 'mock exams,' and were graded as close as the final exams as possible.

Something then happened toward the end of that second term that I swore would never happen to me for as long as I was alive. One Saturday evening, a friend of mine, and classmate Bose 'Ninja' Moremi, asked if he could show me something in my office. Normally I would object to such a thing, but curiosity got the best of me, and when we got there he produced a bottle of VO Brandy called a nip. He also had with him two Coca Cola cans, and two plastic cups, and instantly mixed the alcohol with coke in the cups, and offered me one. I was stunned.

"Bose, what are you doing man? You know I don't drink," I protested.

"I know, I just wanted you to taste this, trust me you will feel good afterwards," he said with a smile on his face. It was a typical example of casual peer pressure. I swallowed the first helping, it tasted like cow piss, but after a minute or so I felt buoyed, and needed no second invitation for another cup, and in a moment we were both merry.

It was dance night that day, and I was in a joyful mood, but enough to be mindful of the fact that I could not draw unnecessary attention to myself, because any misstep could spell doom; especially for someone like me who was supposed to be leading by example. A little later, I was chatting with Bame by the entrance of the hall when I saw Faith, and without really thinking about it I asked Bame to call her so I could speak to her. By this time a lot of the dust had settled; so we could now speak in public without fear that tongues would start wagging again.

We started chatting about trivial things, and for the first time I was truly getting to know her as a person. She came from a big, loving, and wealthy family, an only girl out of eight children, and the last born and only girl in the family, and thus the true 'daddy's girl' in every respect. She was also the typical example of brains combined with beauty, just like Nametsegang was. She was also like me very ambitious, and was prepared to work hard to do what she had to do to make a good life for herself. And I was falling for her even more, but was careful not to throw the cat among pigeons again. Somehow she sensed that my mood was different that night since I was buzzed.

"Tell me, are you really the Sebati I know tonight?" she asked.

"Yeah, why do you ask?"

"Well you seem ... I don't know ... you seem too happy tonight," she said obviously making a conscious effort of choosing her words carefully.

"I'm always happy when around you," I said.

"Really, why do you say that?" she blushed. She was also flattered I could tell. The next words I said even surprised me, I think it had a lot to do with the fact that I had developed 'Dutch Courage' thanks to the brandy.

"Well the truth of the matter is that I truly, truly love you and very much."

She smiled and paused for a while.

"You know Sebati, I am glad that you said that, because the feelings I have for you I have never had for any other guy. They are much stronger than you may never know so yes I love you too."

I was pleasantly astonished by this bold confession, and immediately understood the repercussions; we had both crossed the line we were a bit hesitant to cross, but in truth it was just a matter of time before we reached that point of no return. I could only imagine the heartache this was going to cause Olivia and the complications I was triggering.

"I'm glad to hear that," I said with a wide smile on my face, "but promise me one thing."

"What?"

"Just promise me that we are going to be very careful until things get sorted out." There was no need to explain what I meant by that. We were to become secret lovers until the right time. I could not believe what I had just done after we went our separate ways. Even though I was happy to get the girl - I hated myself for what I was about to put Olivia through. I felt dirty albeit for a while.

***

The following weekend, a form 4 girl was seen puking her guts out at the girls' public toilets. As her friends were walking her back to her dormitory Anthea Williams, now a prefect as well, who as fate would have it, happened to be in the vicinity, decided to go and investigate, and found out that the girl was totally intoxicated. What was worse was that this was her first experience in hitting the bottle, and instead it hit her hard.

Anthea immediately reported this to the matron who informed Mr. Mahole, and Legoro together with the matron, the head girl Netty Nkala, Lillian, and a few other senior prefects including Olivia, confronted the girl to name who her drinking buddies were. And the young woman in question was not one to go down alone or quietly; so she sang like an African Grey Lourie (the 'Go Away' bird known as *Mokowe* in Setswana). She named all of them, and would have included their grandmothers too, as added bonus, if she had the opportunity. It turns out that there had been a drinking binge that Saturday afternoon; that even involved quite a number of form 4 boys and girls as well, and a couple of form 5 girls. Immediately, a raid was conducted in which all the dormitories were visited, and the culprits ferreted out. Among them was a form 4 girl who made a spectacle of herself, because she was so smashed.

"Oh Mr. Mahole so good to see you, you're such a good looking man and I can kiss you right this moment," she said when she was woken up, and asked to undergo a sobriety test as all the suspects were subjected to. Seeing her in that condition though, there was no need for her to undergo the test so she was left alone to sleep it off; others I heard were throwing up right in front of Legoro. Another girl, a form 5, who was drunk and asleep, actually abused and would have attacked Legoro had she not been restrained, and unfortunately for her she was expelled outright from school when judgment was handed down.

All told there were over 20 people involved in this drinking spree, and heavy suspensions ranging from 15 to 20 school days were handed down, and were set to begin at the start of the third term as this second term was coming to an end. Among those suspended was a girl called Thandi and her friend Moloko. The former was Mpho Rammusi's girlfriend, and he talked about her in earnest and how much he loved her. Moloko I recall was a very good friend of Faith; from what I heard the two were like sisters, and that at times Moloko would say things to Faith like if she died she would always make sure of paying her a visit once in a while.

Around this time as well, Phil was to get himself in trouble again, on an incident similar to one that sparked the fight between him and Hex.

This time he brought a female friend to dorm 20, which at the time was empty and perpetually dark, because the florescent bulb in the room was removed. While in the act, a fellow by the name of Loeto, also known as Shane, saw him, and like Hex did last time began to heckle at Phil and even cat calling. One always wondered why Phil was never totally discreet when engaged in such activities, and always took the great risk of bringing his partners on school premises; something that was strictly prohibited, and as a prefect should have known better.

Phil did not take kindly to Loeto's heckling and beat him up badly. Loeto thereafter immediately went to report the matter to Mr. Molilo, missing nothing in detail, and Mature gladly escalated the matter to Legoro and the rest of the disciplinary committee. Phil was now told that he was to meet the disciplinary committee the following Monday. This time there was no mercy as they intended to throw the book at him. The fact that not too long ago there had been a similar complaint against him did not help matters at all. Later, I was to hear what happened at that encounter with the disciplinary committee, because Phil had wanted me to be brought in as a character witness.

"We have already established that you were with a girl in dorm 20, so please tell us what you were doing in there?" Mr. Mahole asked.

"Sir, there was no girl in the dormitory because I was studying," he denied.

"There is no light in that dormitory," BM declared. "So how is it possible that you could be in there studying at night with no light whatsoever?"

"Well ... you see sir ..."

"No I can't see, just answer the question please," BM pressed on. Everyone knew that any kind of questioning from this man was one of the most uncomfortable things to endure. The crime was committed in his jurisdiction, and thus he was heading the interrogation.

"Actually I was in class and Sebati can attest to that, he saw me." Phil I can imagine was now frantic.

"But you just said you were in the dormitory studying, when the truth is that you were in there with a girl having sexual intercourse and not in class." BM informed him matter of factually. "Why then do we have to drag Sebati into this?"

"W-well he saw me in class."
"What class are you in again?" one of the teachers asked.
"Form 5 zero," he answered.
"And what class is Sebati in?"
"Form 5 three."
"Okay, tell me this how is it possible that you are in form 5 zero, and Sebati in form 5 three, and yet he was able to see you in class when all of us know that you were in dorm 20?" This time Phil knew he had been cornered.
"Okay, maybe Sebati did not see me but …"
"We know Sebati did *not* see you," BM corrected him. "Tell the truth young man, because that's your only chance."
"W-what I was going to say sir is that it is not possible for me to be with a girl because of my condition."
"Your condition?" a few teachers queried at the same time.
"Y-yes sir … I have a problem in that my manhood is swollen to a point that no penetration is possible; so I could not have been doing what you said I was doing in dorm 20." I was told that even some teachers had to laugh in spite of themselves at the ridiculousness of this story. Phil was told to bring proof of this 'condition' and went back to the dormitory, and got his medical card, and forged a doctor's hand writing stating the 'condition'. Some of his dorm mates including States Ndzimumbi admitted that he had done a great job at it nonetheless, because the 'doctor's' diagnosis looked legitimate.
In the end Phil (like Fungwa) was suspended indefinitely, and later expelled with a firm warning that should he as much as threaten Loeto, let alone lay a finger on him, the matter was going to be referred to the police. That was the last I was to see Phil again, and tragically, a brilliant academic life was once again cut short. He was not forgotten though, and once in a while mischievous chaps like Ipha would take advantage of his absence. For instance, one evening Ipha saw Phil's girlfriend (she was not the lady at the center of this fiasco), who was about to enter the hall one night, the entrance was crowded with people as it was entertainment night, and Ipha immediately let loose his tongue.
"Oh, now that Phil is not around I suppose me and you can meet one on one and by that I mean intimately … don't you think?"

Phatsimo was among those people within hearing rage, and was shocked at this bold utterance coming from the small guy. He looked at me and shook his head.

"Can you believe this guy?" he asked, I could but said nothing. Nothing Ipha said could surprise me anymore, and I was to see more of that during the coming second term break.

Chapter 34

Death is always a topic that is regarded as taboo in African culture. It is never talked about if one can help it, because it is believed that by doing so you are without knowing inviting the 'grim reaper' to your fold. For teenagers, death is a far-fetched reality. I would imagine that has a lot to do with the fact that at that point in our lives; we feel that it can never happen to us. This brings us to an incident that to this day still makes the surviving former Dorm 2 dwellers shudder. We were talking about what would happen; *if* one of our dormitory members lost his girlfriend through death.

"Man, I'll be really, really devastated if that would happen to me," Mpho said, and as this uncomfortable topic dragged on he became more and more animated as to how he would react. We would all look back at that fateful day with regret in the not too distant future.

That second term was also when Mr. Mudidi was to come up with a proposal that would rock the country. Earlier that year, there was news about an orphaned boy who was born without limbs named Kabo Matlho. He needed costly prosthetics very badly, and the Botswana Red Cross was appealing to anyone who could, and who would listen, to donate money to this child's cause. This cry for help must have touched Mr. Mudidi in a way that he was to launch a one man crusade in an all out attempt to raise money for this boy. Our play *'The Breaking of Chains'* was to be the vehicle that was to help in this cause. It became known unofficially as the 'Kabo Matlho Campaign.'

As part of our fundraising efforts, one Saturday morning we even went to Palapye with specially designed cans in hand (we had made these from empty soft drink canisters), and went about asking for money from everyone we came across in the name of Kabo. It was fun, going from one business to another and from one stranger to another asking for money for a great cause. There were some individuals though, and I won't say who, who made replica cans, and sought to take advantage of this event to boost their own coffers. Despite all this we raised more money than we would have thought possible. In addition to that our play was being invited to perform at different places, and money earned went toward the Kabo Matlho trust, which Mr. Mudidi had established.

During that time though, I could tell that there was something eating up Bonang Mapolanka in the inside. He would come up to me, look at me in the eye as if he was going to say something, but then at the last minute he would shrug and leave. I did not push him nor did I pry, because I knew that he would tell me what it was in good time. It happened not too long after this thought came to mind. He had me meet him in private behind the 'Block C' building, not too far from the exact spot, where the boot prints matching Fungwa's were last seen, after the window breaking incident involving BM. He was smoking a cigarette, something he never did, and I could only imagine that what he was about to tell me he reached after many conflicting thoughts.

"So Bonang, what's up man talk to me," I said.

He sighed before taking a drag at the cigarette, he was not a smoker, and that much was evident by the way which he held the cigarette, and took the drag.

"Something's definitely on my mind, and I expect that this stays between the two of us for now." There was no need for him to reiterate that he trusted me to the fullest.

"You can count on that B," I said.

"Do you know how much money we have raised?"

"I would say off the top of my head one thousand two hundred and change. Why?"

"Try two thousand one hundred, the trips since Orapa, and the fat cakes have raked in the profits like never before," he said, and I whistled. "The party we can say will cost about 400 Pula at best, and you know that's stretching it, I don't feel comfortable leaving the rest to the form 4's – we will leave them something of course, but remember no one left anything for us except that blanket." I kind of started to see where he was going with this.

"So what are you saying?"

"I say we start giving ourselves a stipend of some sort, maybe 40 Pula every other week."

40 Pula, every other week, for a boarding school student who could stretch a mere 5 Pula for almost an entire term was mind boggling, and that is an understatement.

"What!?!"

"Hear me out Sebati; we shouldered all the work so why shouldn't we reward ourselves in some way?"

"What about the other guys like Cornmaster and the like, won't they smell a rat?" I asked.

"I wanted to talk to you first, and thereafter reel the other guys in, because we are the leaders of this club," he said.

The offer was just too tempting, and I agreed, but was wary about what may happen if this scheme was uncovered. A day later we met with Cornmaster and Motlotlegi, and they were immediately sold on the idea, and so it came to pass that on the second Friday of every month we would meet in my 'office' and Cornmaster would divide 160 Pula evenly among the four of us. Back then we did not think that what we were doing was wrong, nevertheless it was because we were embezzling from the club, even though we felt that we had earned it. From that moment on until I left Lotsane, I never again hit my parents up for money, much to their relief, because they never asked why I had stopped. All of a sudden, I was able to afford a lot of things that I could never have, one of my pride and joy; was buying a school specific track suit that had the name 'Lotsane Senior' printed at the back. I wore that wherever I went and when I could.

That term something unprecedented happened. Mr. Mothei called a meeting of all the boys to the dining hall at a time when we normally had afternoon prep. The purpose of this meeting was for us to air our grievances. As prefects many of us did not have anything to say as all that could have been said came from the floor. Kaelo Gare in particular was in the fore front so were people like Clio Hlanganiso Roy.

"Sir," Kaelo said in his booming voice, "What I want to know is why don't we as students have freedom of speech? This after all is a democratic country; I am raising this point, because whenever we are summoned to the office for some transgression, someone has accused us of, we are never given the chance to defend ourselves or tell our side of the story. Mr. Mothei, I ask again: why don't we have freedom of speech?" A long and loud applause actually threatened to drown the rest of his words, but Moshene's deep voice was equal to the task.

Mr. Mothei, ever the diplomat, and a great one at that had no answer for Kaelo, but in a way skillfully diverted the topic elsewhere. What Kaelo was saying was precedent in those days, and everyone knew it. For instance, if say a girl said something to you that was disparaging and you slapped her or in some extreme cases she actually initiated the attack, and went to tell on you, and while doing that crying hysterically, as girls were known to do, the boy was automatically at fault and subsequently punished. No further questions Your Honor. It was only one day in the future that I saw a situation where two parties were listened to, and the boy was found not guilty, and this time the presiding judge was Mr. Irvine.

However, on this day in question, the boys had a lot to say, some even went as far as accusing the head boy, Kabelo Lebotse, of complicity with the administration in as far as the suspension of Godfrey 'Mafia' Morgan and another classmate named Hendry Chief Monakwe. What had happened is that they had hurled insults not worth repeating at Kabelo, and the latter went on to report them to the authorities, and the two each got a one week suspension from school, and this left the students fuming. Someone even went on to suggest that the head boy secretly snuck food out of the dining hall and into the dormitories, something that was strictly prohibited, but of course this allegation was a travesty. Kabelo was meanwhile taking notes of all this, literally, because he had a pen and paper with him and was writing feverishly.

When Mr. Mothei took a short recess to attend to some matter at the staff room, there was a buzz in the dining hall as everyone was talking among themselves as to what to say next. Everyone it seemed was enjoying the moment; some perhaps more than others, because at that instant Roy stood up to offer his two cents. As a playwright and dramatist way ahead of his time the stage was beaconing, and there was no way he was going to let an opportunity like this one slip through his fingers. When he stood up everyone applauded.

"*Majita le seka la wara, go na le bo Mangope mo go rona*," "Guys don't worry we have Mangopes among us." It was a stinging remark especially to us prefects, but I knew that jibe was directed at one person in particular, I looked at Kabelo, he was seated next to another senior prefect and his best friend named Kenneth Tlou. I could not hear what he was saying from where I was, but I could read his lips clearly even though I am not a lip reader by any stretch.

'*Hee, waitse Roy ke tla mmetsa*," "You know I will beat up Roy," he said to his friend.

Kgosi Lucas Manyane Mangope, (his last name also means 'lumpy porridge 'in Setswana) is the former leader of the Bantustan of Bophuthatswana, and is now as of this writing the current leader of the United Christian Democratic Party, a minor political party based in the North West Province of South Africa. He was born in Motswedi on 27 December 1923 (many people say he was born in Manyana, a small village in Botswana about 40 miles south of Gaborone), he became president of a sovereign state recognized only by South Africa as it was within its borders, and became one of the so called black 'independent' homelands. The rest of the world saw these homelands as 'puppet states', and Mangope himself as a sell out who was despised by everyone. Mangope often referred to liberation movements like the Pan Africanist Congress of Azania (PAC), The United Democratic Front (UDF), and the African National Congress (ANC) as '*mekgatlo*' or 'clubs' - a very reproachful remark, coming from a man who undermined the struggle against one of the most brutal and oppressive system of governments known to men – Apartheid. That is why Kabelo was visibly upset when Roy made that comparison, and stated his anger very clearly when it was finally his chance to speak. Each time when he spoke he would consult the notes on the piece of paper he was holding.

"Mr. Mothei, I am really disturbed by the allegations made today by my fellow students. The question I want to ask is this: does seeing me carry my dish stuffed with rags that I myself wash in the laundry room constitute smuggling food into the dormitories?" He then turned and faced his fellow students before continuing, "Why don't you guys just be man enough, and come up to me and ask me straight up if I'm sneaking food into the dormitories, instead of jumping to conclusions? Another thing concerns the suspension of two of the gentlemen who are my classmates, my duty is to make sure that order is maintained at all times, and after asking these gentlemen to refrain from disrupting the class they insulted my parents in the most crude manner. How many of you would tolerate having your hardworking parents' name desecrated in a manner not worth repeating?" By this time he was getting worked up, and everyone could feel his anger building as he finally tossed the paper aside after taking one last look at it. "In closing sir, and you will have to pardon me on this, I would like to issue a strong warning to people like Roy." He then turned and faced Roy and said almost shouting, "*Monna* Roy, call me Mangope again and I'll beat you up okay? Because I know that silly little remark you made was directed at me." He sat down still fuming, and Mr. Mothei understood his wrath, but mildly reproached him for threatening Roy with impunity even in front of a teacher.

In the end order was restored, and Mr. Mothei made a long and moving speech that reminded us of why we were in school, and the values society expected us to live up to. "You are the leaders of tomorrow", he said time and again, and that this was just the beginning of that long journey called life. Nothing earth shattering was achieved that afternoon by the students, but I could tell that they felt good talking about whatever it is that was on their chests. I did have a chat with Roy about the statement he made in as far as his reference to people whom he called 'Mangopes'. I was after all an Assistant Head Boy and thus part of the 'system'.

"Sebati, just know that it was not you I was referring to," he said and I believed him.

Later Kabelo came to speak to me in private. He was obviously not pleased with the outcome of the meeting, and its purpose in general.

"I think Mr. Mothei is a bit too sympathetic with the students," he said. I on the other hand reserved my opinion, because I was really not sure what to make of the whole thing.

In the end we all had to admit that this was something refreshing, because it was unprecedented. If something like this was done on a regular basis, it would go far in as far as alleviating the school problems; especially among the boys. It would turn out to be the first and last time we were to have a meeting of that nature held at the dining hall. We did have meetings similar to that, but on a much smaller scale at the 'Block A' common room (these excluded the form 4's), where people voiced their opinion that the 9:30PM curfew was too early, since we all wanted to listen to the 9:00PM news bulletin that ended at

10:00PM. This matter was taken into advisement, and later permission was granted that the curfew could be extended by half an hour.

Also studying after lights off was permitted in the 'Block A' common room. No one actually went up to the administration to request that privilege, but people, and one of them Collet Mosudisa, on their own started studying after lights off in this place. This was something that was normally reserved for a time close to the final examinations, but this practice began in the first term and was held on to like a bull terrier; that even MS. Motlotle was to fully endorse this initiative. I would think that the administration was silently pleased that we had taken the ingenuity of studying on our own, after lights off in the common room, even though it was not something that was permitted in the past. What else could they have said – stop studying?

The term finally came to an end. Olivia had informed me that instead of the train she was going to hitch a ride to Francistown that afternoon. It was just as well because Faith was going to catch the train, and even though we were at extreme pains to keep our affair a secret we were wary, and Faith in particular, of letting the cat out of the basket. We were successful in that regard, but promised to keep in touch via mail. I was not expecting any from Olivia since this kind of communication was something she never did, and like I mentioned earlier I was to find out much later the reason why. And just like that the tumultuous second term was over. There was one more trip we were going to make the next term, my very last at Lotsane, and that was another performance at Maitisong for the Kabo Matlho benefit, and this time in front of his Excellency the President of the Republic of Botswana we were told. The thought itself was to give me chills the entire three week holiday.

Chapter 35

The journey back to Gaborone by train was pleasant, I had a great time with Kebagaisitse Mapena, and a few other chaps in the buffet section of the train where I had my very first beer. One was enough for me, however I had more than that, and later on after reaching Mahalapye we were serenaded by a lot of the Madiba students, the girls in particular, when they saw me and Meshack seated together for long periods at a time chatting away.

"Look guys they are headed to the mines," one girl from Madiba said as she ran to call her friends, other boys joined in as well – it was a bit of a spectacle, and Meshack and I enjoyed the attention to the fullest.

"So I bet you guys are going to stir up a revolution when you arrive at your destination," one of the Madiba fellows said. They were of course referring to our characters in our play 'The Breaking of Chains'.

We arrived in Gaborone early the next morning, and immediately my father looked at me and said I looked ill and even thought of taking me to the doctor. I was sick alright, from a hangover, but he had no way of knowing that. My school report arrived a few days later, and my grades were dismal, and that is putting in mildly taking into account the very high standards I had set for myself. From position one in mid 1986 I had fallen 12 places to position 13, and the teacher's comments, in particular that from Mrs. Mbulawa as she was now my class teacher were scathing. *'Sebati has lost interest in his studies this year; his mind is on other things'* the 'other things' she was referring to were my extracurricular activities – drama in particular. I refused to admit it at the time but she was right. My father was not the least bit concerned or worried about the 'impending doom' that was seemingly hanging over my head, and in truth neither was I. For some reason, I just felt that I could turn it on again anytime I wished, like I did last year. The personal disappointment was that I was not going to follow Balisi's footsteps by getting the History prize like I had hoped or even that of English. And the truth of the matter is that I did not deserve them plain and simple.

In retrospect, I think I had studied so hard in 1986 and perhaps sub consciously I felt that I needed to relax a bit, but unfortunately I may have relaxed a bit too much, and became too comfortable. Now with the ultimate examinations looming dangerously close; it was time to get my *mojo* back. The first thing I did those holidays was to purchase booklets of past exam papers. These were for the subjects Mathematics, Physics, Chemistry, and Biology. Also my father had somehow arranged that I do my A' Levels at Maru A Pula school immediately after completing my form 5. His argument, was that it would be a great opportunity for me to build a very strong foundation in Mathematics and Physics, before I headed to the university for a more specialized degree in Engineering. This turned out to be a very unwise plan, and even my uncle Rizzah opposed such a move vehemently. I did not need A Levels if I was heading to the United States, he was of the notion, and so did a lot of people that A Levels were just a waste of time – not so if your plans were to be accepted by a university in the United Kingdom, which was not my plan at all.

I think since Maru A Pula is a very prestigious school, and the very thought of having a son being a part of that institution, may have had a lot to do with my father resisting any attempts to pry me away from this plan he had in mind for me. I also think since the fees were covered by the United Nations, and he would not have to part with a penny weighed favorably on his mind. I was also thrilled at the idea as well at the time, and told everyone who would listen. To be accepted I would have to get grades no less than a 3 (B) in Math and the Science classes. That would prove to be more than extra motivation.

On one of the trips to the mall those holidays I ran into Ipha, and then as we were chatting, we were joined by another Lotsane student named Israel Mosweu Seleka known to everyone as 'Zweks'. Very light skinned, and quite a character in his own unobtrusive way, Zweks was always serenaded in public, because of his *'I am very cool'* mentality, and I found out later that he enjoyed the attention to the fullest. Like Choiza back in 1985, I had known Zweks as far back as 1977, when we were kids when my dad had put Rama and me on a plane from Zambia to Botswana; to visit my uncle Peter 'Daddy' Nthite in Francistown.

As a matter of fact Zweks and I had gotten into a fist fight that was instigated by a fellow also named Bashi, and had resulted in Zweks having a swollen forehead.

When we reunited in 1986, after he was accepted at Lotsane, I was amazed of how much of the stuff he remembered from way back when, and we became very good friends instantly since we also took the same History class.

"By the way, where is that guy Bashi, the guy who made us fight?" I asked him.

"Oh, the chap hung himself a long time ago," he said, and I was saddened to hear about that.

As we were hanging out at the mall, Zweks asked us if we could accompany him to the industrial side of town where his uncle worked. He said that his uncle was to give him some money, and that soon after he would treat us to lunch. The industrial side was a bit of a walk from the mall, but because of his promise we decided to go with him. First there was something we needed to do at the 'African Mall,' the same area where my uncle had his Pharmacy, where I worked that past summer break. On our way there, we saw a group of frolicking white girls headed in the opposite direction, and somehow I just had this feeling that Ipha was going to say something unflattering to them, and thus braced myself as they approached.

"I want to *do* you all," he said calmly in his high-pitched voice. The actual verb he used was more offensive.

"Just try," one of them retorted and we all burst out laughing except Ipha who was entertainingly serious.

The search for Zweks's uncle at the industrial area turned out to be a wild goose chase. For close to two hours we went from one place to another with Zweks saying repeatedly, "oh this is the place, no I think it is that one, oh no I made a mistake it is that one."

In the end Ipha and I lost our patience, and Ipha let him know about it.

"Zweks, it is okay to admit that you have no clue where this uncle of yours works; that is if there is an uncle to begin with."

"Man, I know I am right, it's just that I got my bearings mixed up a bit."

"Zweks, we are not in school man, it's just the three of us so 'cool' does not apply here," Ipha told him matter of factly. This small fellow, could be amazingly level headed, whenever he chose to temporarily discard the high spirited pranks and waywardness he was known for.

"Hey are you saying that I'm not cool?" Zweks asked with no false modesty.

"Good, I'm glad you brought that up, so let's talk about your behavior at school for a moment shall we." A door was opened and Ipha was poised to attack hard and strong. The irony about all this is that it was Ipha of all people about to give a lecture to someone about his behavior at school. "You're cool because everybody serenades you especially when you are the first to head to class from the dormitories after tea break right?"

"Oh yeah, they know what cool is."

"No Zweks, you got it all wrong as you are very misinformed, the guys at school see you as a source of free and cheap entertainment." His actual words were among others: "*Ba go ntshitse entertainment.*" Even I had to laugh even though I was hungry and a bit angry at Zweks for what he was putting us through on a hot sunny day.

"You are the one who's mistaken Ipha, and you know it," Zweks argued.

"The sooner you realize your folly the better Zweks. Don't behave like a trained poodle, just be yourself," Ipha continued as though what Zweks had said was just a breeze of air.

In the end we could not find the place and decided to go back. By this time we were almost starving, and when we got back to the mall Ipha, who almost always seemed to have money, bought us some delicious burgers and chips at a very popular 'Take Away' (fast food) restaurant called '*Kings*'. This place was a landmark and historical site of the main mall, and I was disappointed to hear many years later that it had been torn down.

I guess I should not have been surprised at Ipha, because not only was he generous when it came to sharing, he was also very resourceful. I remember one time at the bus station in Gaborone he was so hungry that he talked a lady who was selling fruits by the wayside into giving him a banana free of charge. These ladies were well known to be very frugal when it came to their goods and their money, as they should, and we were all amazed. After that he walked up to two men who looked to be in their mid 20's, and total strangers mind you, and talked to them obviously asking for something, and soon after we saw one of them whistle at another friend across the street, and signal something to him and then point at Ipha, and then he soon after said something to Ipha who ran to the other man, and the other man subsequently pulled out his wallet and counted a few bank notes into Ipha's outstretched hand. We shook our heads in disbelief.

That is why when we got back to school a few weeks later, and Ipha told the story of Zweks and the wild goose chase, adding embellishments not quiet related to what happened in the process, the tale became an instant hit in the boarding house. Many times I tried to set the record straight concerning some things Ipha said, but no one would listen. Ipha's version was the most entertaining that in the end I was forced to give up and laugh along.

This was also the time when Mr. Geary introduced the *'Ipha notebook'*. Ipha was forever cutting class, among his other misdemeanors, that Mr. Geary had him carry a note book that had to be signed by every teacher of every class he attended that day, there was also a section where they would have to comment on his behavior during the class, they would report whether he was attentive, participating, if he submitted his assignments on time and so forth, and then at the end of the day right after class he would see Mr. Geary, who would go over the whole activities of the day and if satisfied sign off, and the whole process was to be repeated the next day. If the report was in any way unsatisfactory, he would be immediately punished by washing at least 100 chairs at the dining hall, and since manual labor was something Ipha totally abhorred; for now this plan Mr. Geary had him on seemed to work.

It was also said that Ipha was an expert at shaking a *chibuku* box. The kind of *chibuku* sold in Botswana is called *'Shake Shake.'* This is because before opening the carton it had to be shaken thoroughly for optimum taste. Legend had it that whenever Ipha and the guys paid Ma Amogelang a visit, when he shook the carton he would even spin it in the air several times, and catch it before it hit the ground. This was mostly done at the river where chances of being spotted were almost none. The story was so far-fetched and funny that I even told my father about it. And it just so happened that that second term break I ran into

Ipha again this time with my father, and I introduced them. After going our separate ways I decided to remind my father about the 'Shake Shake' schoolboy.

"That is the boy I was telling you about. The boy who shakes the *chibuku* carton in that unique way," I said. My father was astounded.

"Nooo Sebati! ... Him?"

"Yes."

He smiled and shook his head, and I thought that was the end of it, but I was mistaken.

"Thami," my dad called my step mom when we got home, 'Thami' is short for Maithamako. "You have no idea who we met today," he said with a smile on his face.

"Who?" she wanted to know.

"One of Sebati's friends from school ... remember, the young man he was telling us about who can spin a carton of *chibuku* several times in the air without letting it fall."

"Really?" she was smiling too.

"You'd never believe it if you saw the boy ... he is a very sweet and likable young fellow and very respectful." Perhaps that is why Ipha almost always got away with anything, and to some extent enjoyed a special kind of immunity no one could place a finger on.

Chapter 36

That break also marked the first year for Max, and my two other former dorm mates Gilbert and Big Joe, at the University of Botswana. Max was studying Public Administration and Political Science. I had met him at the mall as arranged, and he gave me his room number, and I wasted no time in visiting him the very first chance I got, which happened to be that Saturday. I was dismayed to find that he was not at his room when I got there and left him a note, but as soon as I was at the gate some gut instinct told me to go back, and lo and behold I found him and his roommate, a gentleman I knew only by sight at Lotsane, as he was one of those quiet individuals who kept to themselves back in 1985. His name was Emmanuel Rasisia. We were properly introduced and I liked him instantly.

"Tell me something, weren't you supposed to have completed last year? Why are you just this year doing your form 5? Explain, man explain," he said, and I went on to clarify things to him; something I found myself doing a lot of that year whenever I ran into members of the class of 1985. As we were talking, a strikingly handsome light skinned gentleman entered the room, and settled down like he belonged, and it became apparent that this trio was inseparable. He saw the note that I had left for Max earlier on his table. So he naturally assumed that whoever wrote that note had come and left.

"Oh yes, I know that guy Sebati, I know his father too they call him Bra Mike, yes that is Bra Mike's son I know the guy very well," the gentleman said, his name was Outsa Mokone. I decided to play along.

"Oh so you know him too?"

"Oh yes, oh yes … even his father, great guy that he is."

I smiled and said, "Thanks because that happens to be me."

"Man I was waiting for you to stretch it even further, you let him off the hook easily," Emmanuel said.

I knew he was hell bent on having fun at Outsa's expense, but I did not want to embarrass the guy after he had nothing but nice things to say about me; even though we had never really met. It turns out that Outsa was from Molepolole, and his father who originally was from South Africa, and my dad were very good friends, and since my father made many business trips to Molepolole he got to know Outsa and his siblings very well, and talked about me to them constantly. I was to learn all this from Outsa after we were finally introduced. I became a frequent visitor even long after my Lotsane days were over.

However the biggest news of that break was meeting Big Joe Ntsuke again. He was with his roommate Onkutlwile, whom I had also known by sight way back when we were kids at Lesedi Primary School, and he was to say the same thing about me.

"This is the guy I was telling you about," he told Onkutlwile. I was even flattered that he even mentioned my name to a friend.

He gave me his room number, and the very next weekend when I went to visit them I made sure to bring my photo album with me. As Big Joe and Onkutlwile were looking at the pictures, as I paged through the album, I paused when we got to a page that had Big Joe's picture. I was pretty sure that he had no idea that there was a photo of him in the album, and he was thrilled, but then again he was Big Joe. I still have that photo.

"Ah, ah, ah, ah … have you ever seen such a handsome guy like this guy you are looking at right now? No, no, no, good looking guys like this can get arrested, because it is a crime to be that good looking." We all laughed, it was refreshing for me, because I had always missed Big Joe's wit and humor.

And just like I would visit Max, Emmanuel, and Outsa I was to do the same with these guys, and afterward Sebei, who was now studying for his Bachelor of Science degree, and later on to specialize in Agriculture and Research. This was amazing for a guy who did not even study Agriculture at Junior Certificate level, a time when it was said was crucial if you were to pursue this subject further – Sebei was to break that myth because he now holds a PhD in that discipline, and known now as Dr. Gilbert Kabelo Sebei Gaboutloeloe. The same guy who advised me not to listen to Festus way back in 1985; when I sought to use the latter as my 'go between'.

***

When we were finally back at school for our very last term at Lotsane (form 5's); we were dismayed to find out that there was a bright light that was now fixed at an area near the girls' hostel where lovers hung out. At Lotsane this sort of hanging out was called *'go spota'* ('spotting'), and with this light illuminating the area; that meant that this was going to definitely cramp our style. Within a week though, a well-aimed stone at the light brought things back to normal. There have been many suspects in as far as the breaking of the light was concerned, and just recently I heard that Cornmaster, and a fellow by the name of Damelin 'Om Damen' Kgaodi, were missing for about half an hour from class on the night in question, and to the best of my knowledge; they have not up to this day been able to provide an air tight alibi as to where they were around the time when the light was smashed. A similar light behind the boys' hostel was deemed obsolete I think on the next day. Attempts to replace the bulbs on both lights were futile, because by the next day they were shattered, and finally the school gave up. It was also becoming increasingly obvious too that the patrolling of teachers in these areas was becoming less and less frequent, because of stones that were thrown at them in the dark. The one teacher most afraid of having stones thrown at him was Mr. Molilo.

That third term, I knew that I was going to have to push myself as hard as I possibly could. I had goofed off long enough, and now it was time to get my priorities in order. Faith and I had decided to put things on hold for now, and this was done at her insistence, because her conscience was getting the best of her in as far as Olivia was concerned. It was not easy, but I had to admit that she was right. However, the distance between Olivia and I seemed to widen as the days went by. But really, now was not the time to be wasting valuable time and energy about love issues; when an exam that was to determine my future was drawing all the more closer.

I started waking up early in the morning again, and hitting the books hard. It did not take a while before I started to feel accomplished like I did back in 1986, and this time I was prepared to push myself even further – I was trying to get my *mojo* back. Those early weeks I then, without knowing, established a study group that included my beloved friends all of whom were classmates, and those being Rinah, Margaret, Omponye, and Mabulili. Every night we tested ourselves with the past exam papers from the books I purchased during the break, and with these ladies in the mix, particularly Rinah, words just cannot describe the gratitude I have felt over the years that I had the foresight of studying with them.

The preparations for the 'Kabo Matlho' performance in Gaborone were still underway, and since this was the examinations term, Mr. Mudidi cut us as much slack as possible, when it came to rehearsals and studying, and even made himself available for tutoring in math if the need arose, and I was to take him up on his offer later that term. And life in the dormitory could not have been any more exciting. Whenever possible Ferdinand would bring his parents' truck to school, and we would get permission and all ride in the back of the car, and head to Palapye and have fun in the process. This was a privilege that has yet to be matched during our boarding years that we were the envy of most guys, and the girls took notice, and called us *'the special dorm twoers.'*

Something happened though that landed Ferdinand and Gerald in hot water. One Friday night the two snuck out after lights off, and unfortunately that night BM did his nightly inspection, and found out that the two were missing. He immediately woke me up.

"Sebati where is Gerald and Ferdinand?" he asked.

"Perhaps in the computer room," I said, knowing very well that the likelihood of them being there was slim. Computer Studies students were known to stay up late at night doing their assignments on the computers; this is because at the time '*Windows*' was unknown and the operating system was *DOS* (disc operating system) which was more complicated, long, and tedious. Nevertheless BM was suspicious, and not content with that explanation, he left with the promise that he would return, and I went back to sleep. He did return as he had said he would, but there was still no sign of Gerald and Harare and it was past midnight.

"Okay Sebati," BM said, wake up, and let's head to the Computer Science room, and see if they are indeed there. I am bringing you along because I want to have a witness with me."

I knew now that the situation was becoming more dire by the minute for my two missing dorm mates. We got to the Computer Studies room, and it was dark and by all accounts there seemed to have been no activity since evening studies ended.

"So Sebati as you and I can tell there is no one here. Thank you for coming along, and have those boys see me first thing in the morning," he said. The two were facing suspension from boarding. When I got back to the dormitory the rest of the guys were now up and wide awake. They were keen to find out what had transpired.

"Oh man the guys are in deep doo-doo," I said.

Everyone assumed that Gerald had gone to meet with a girl named Emily in secret; like he normally did at the forbidden grounds behind the girls' dormitories, and that Harare had probably accompanied him as a look out.

"I don't know man, but when Gerald has his mind fixed on that thing between Emily's thighs his brain freezes. Just the mere thought of that coochy drives him insane," said Phatsimo.

In spite of having a steady girlfriend, there was a rumor going around that Gerald was having an illicit affair with another girl on campus, who also happened to be his classmate. There were gossips that the two were always engaged in many sexual encounters whenever the opportunity presented itself. Even Phinda Khame the wag, claimed to have walked in on them in a classroom when he had gone to collect a cup he had forgotten earlier.

"I mean fellows is all this worth getting suspended for?" Phatsimo asked rhetorically.

"Yep, the two are going to be suspended," Itumeleng added. I silently agreed with them; suspension was very likely. And this quite possibly could be fueled by BM's disdain for Harare. The two hated each other, because BM saw Ferdinand as a spoiled brat with a loud mouth, and Harare thought BM was unnecessarily strict.

The two arrived way past midnight talking quietly but excitedly, they later told us that they had heard a gunshot in Palapye, which had them running for dear life. Back in 1987 gunshots were very rare, which is why the two made such a big deal about it. I was to hear the gruesome details regarding that particular gunshot some three years later from a Palapian. What had happened was that a fellow by the name of Jack had the hots for some girl, but she had a boyfriend, and as a result Jack and the gentleman in question had a long lasting feud, and on that fateful night Jack sought the help of his friend, who brought a rifle with him with the intention of threatening the guy into leaving his girl so that Jack could date her unimpeded. A scuffle arose, and the boyfriend was fatally shot in the chest. A shoddy investigation followed, and the police were not able to place the two suspects at the scene at the time of the crime, so they got away with murder, at least for a while, because Jack's accomplice died from a mysterious illness a few weeks later, and Jack himself was driven to near insanity as he was plagued by fear and guilt. It is believed that the demise of the other gentleman was the work of black magic and sorcery.

"BM, was here looking for you guys," I announced to the two guys the moment they arrived. Blood drained from Gerald's face upon hearing the dreadful news. I could tell because he was very light skinned.

"C-c-come again," he stammered with fear. That was the thing about Gerald that used to amaze all those who knew him. He always had a penchant for adventures and high-jinks, and yet he was always wary of the consequences. He was the typical example of someone who liked doing the crime, but extremely scared of doing the time. "BM was here? P-please say you are joking Sebati."

"No I'm not man, ask anyone, we even went to the Computer lab to look for you guys," I affirmed and instantly Gerald's mouth was agape, and his eyes wide open. Harare on the other hand was cool as a cucumber as usual. He immediately got himself a snack and made himself a cup of coffee after boiling it in a kettle that I owned from last year.

"Oh, looks like we are going to have to look for accommodation in Palapye I'm afraid," he said as he stirred his cup, Gerald on the other hand was whimpering like a puppy. A plan however was already hatching in Harare's mind though as I was to soon find out. The next Monday, they were summoned to Mr. Geary's office, where his assistant Mr. Molilo was there as well as the boarding master.

The moment they got to the office, Ferdinand barged in quickly, and before anyone could gather what was happening he said hastily, "Two minutes Mr. Geary, two minutes that's..."

"Okay what are you trying to say Ferdinand? Because from what I hear this will take more than two minutes to resolve," Mr. Geary interrupted, as he quickly recovered from the surprise Harare had initiated.

"BM and Sebati missed us by two minutes, when they went to look for us at the computer room, because by that time we were headed to Mr. Ruf's house to hand him the key," he said even more rapidly.

"Really?"

"Yes sir really, and then on our way to his house we realized how late, rude, and inconsiderate it would be if we knocked at his door at that ghastly hour so we decided to head back to the computer room, and hide the key somewhere in the nearby class, but then when we got there we just felt that it would be folly to leave the keys there instead of taking them with us; the reason being that there is very expensive equipment in that room as you all know, and decided that it would be best to hand the key to Mr. Ruf first thing in the morning which we did, and I suppose that during this time was when BM and Sebati came looking for us. Like I said sir they missed us only by two minutes at the most. I think we missed each other by the tiniest of margins, because they would have smelt our scent in the room." Amazingly they bought this hogwash and the two were set free.

I am certain that Gerald was thanking his lucky stars that Ferdinand was there to bail them out of their predicament. We all agreed to a man; that Gerald would not have been able to withstand the treatment if they had decided to question him in earnest, and separately, as they normally would have done. From that time on the two were very careful.

***

A few weeks later, we started seeing the form 4's who had been suspended last term arriving on the Friday their suspensions were up, and were due to start school the following Monday. From the few that I had seen, and judging by their body language, I could tell that they had learned their lesson.

The following Monday that late September month was a windy one. I remember, as we were headed to assembly, I was looking at the little piles of dust that had gathered into tiny dunes that immediately my imagination started running wild. I was with Gerald and Ferdinand, who seemed engaged in a conversation barely audible to me.

"Guys I suppose if there were people as tall as our pinkies to them this area would be like the Sahara desert wouldn't you agree?" I asked, but the guys totally ignored me as if I was not there. They were still engaged in their conversation. "Hey guys didn't you hear what I just said?" I might as well have been talking to myself. "Eh, fellas ... hello." At last Harare turned to me.

"Shut up Sebati ... something terrible has happened," he said.

"What?"

"Mpho Rammusi's girlfriend and her friend died."

"Hey guys don't play like that man," but the look of Ferdinand's face told me that he was dead serious (excuse the pun). I suddenly felt sick. Was this really happening? After all I had just seen the girl this Friday past, when she had come to drop off her suitcase. Apparently she had gone back home, and was heading back to school that Sunday.

"They were killed in a car accident yesterday, and we are thinking of a way of preventing Mpho from coming to assembly lest he hears it from the headmaster, which will be a disaster as you can imagine." As a matter of fact I could imagine it very well, and suddenly painful memories of Dixie's death came flooding back. I sighed, and immediately hated what I was about to do, but had no choice.

"Okay guys, I'll go and tell him to head back to the dormitory," I said as I immediately turned around, and headed toward the dormitory in a hurry. I saw him coming to the assembly, and I had to fight back tears. "Mpho, please don't ask me why, but head back to the dormitory, don't go to assembly I'll be back in a jiffy and tell you what's going on, but for now please head to the dormitory." I think he must have sensed or had a strange premonition that something was terribly amiss, because he did just like I asked him to, and did not even ask or argue with me. I then headed to assembly hoping and praying that all this was someone's idea of a cruel and sick joke.

It was not a joke apparently, because Legoro made the dreadful announcement, and what was worse was that one of the dead girls was in fact Moloko, Faith's best friend, who had prophesized her own death earlier that year to her friend. If Dixie's death was bad this was terrible, and what was worse is that this time death hit much, much, closer than any of us could have ever imagined, and to one of the nicest people I have ever met, and that being Mpho Rammusi . Why would death do this to us? I asked myself, but then again I had no answer.

I went back to the dormitory to break the news to Mpho, but when I got there I found him lying face down on his pillow sobbing bitterly. Apparently his friend, the other Mpho, and that being Mpho Maposa, broke the news to him before I did. There was nothing I could do, but to try and comfort him as best as I could. And when we all gathered in our dormitory later that day we were all downtrodden. Wasn't it just a few weeks before that we had been talking about death, and how it would affect us if one of us lost a girlfriend? This was too hard to fathom. That is when I understood why the topic of death is such a taboo in African culture.

This was just the beginning, for the next few weeks were the worst. At the dining hall people could not help but look at our table, and at Mpho in particular. We somehow felt it necessary to be strong for our friend. The death of these two young ladies was to have a double blow on me personally, because I now had to deal with Faith in overcoming her grief. And I had to do it in such a way that I did not fluff any feathers in as far as Olivia was concerned. I heard that she was in a state of shock when she heard the news; that for a while people had to leave her alone, because she would become hysterical anytime sympathizers would come to try and comfort her.

Things were not easy for us either. It was hard to look at Mpho's face and not feel terrible, everyone felt that way, but the worst part is that we lived with the guy that was feeling the pain and at nights when he was not crying himself to sleep, he would have terrible nightmares, and he would wake up screaming. In the end I had to call a dormitory meeting at his behest.

"Guys," Mpho said solemnly. "I need your help. I can't sleep, I can't eat, I can't concentrate in class, I just wish I could be away for a few days." We all understood, and it was agreed upon that Ferdinand and I go and see Mr. Mahole, and tell him about the predicament we were in, and plead with him to let Mpho go home for a few days.

Things were even easier than we expected when we went to Legoro. When we got there, we did not mince our words we told him the truth straight up. Also present in his office was Mr. Geary and Mature. But mostly we were amazed by Legoro's response after we presented our case.

"What took you chaps so long?" he asked. Ferdinand and I looked at one another in amazement.

"I'm not sure if we understand Mr. Mahole," I said.

"We were waiting for you guys to come along, because we knew that this young lady had to have had a boyfriend, so yes he can go home for a few days, permission has been granted." Lotsane is one school that to this day has never ceased to amaze me; even when I look back after all these years especially at the type of leadership we had.

After breaking the news, I felt it necessary to call another meeting, I knew what I wanted to say, but I was a bit nervous about how I was going to relay the message, which is why I did not exactly sound as clear as I should have been to the guys.

"Guys, the good news is that Mpho has been granted permission to go home, the administration has helped, but I think the biggest help should come from us. We must try to make the transition as smooth as possible so I hope you understand," I said.

Everybody was silent for a while as they tried very hard to make sense of what I had just said, because the truth is it did not sound sensible to me at all. I was, so goes an old African saying, chewing my food awkwardly because there was sand in it.

"Eish, nna Majita S.B. ga ke mo tlhaloganye," "Guys honestly I have no idea what S.B. is trying to say," Moemedi was the first to break the ice.

"Me too," Archie agreed in his deep voice.

"And me," said another, and another until Bonang 'Stoner' Mosupi came to the rescue.

"Guys, guys, guys, what Sebati is saying is that we can help Mpho by being there for him, and watching our language, unlike what we have done in the past, by talking carelessly about death and other such tragedies." Even I would have not have put it any better, but of course Stoner had a skillful way with words. I could also understand, because Stoner and Mpho were best friends, and he was also hurting just as much as his friend was. The only drawback was that Stoner, Mosimanegape, Phatsimo, and I would not be able to attend the funeral, because that was the weekend when we were to be in Gaborone performing 'The

Breaking of Chains.' And in the process raise more money in the name of Kabo Matlho. That was the performance which we were hoping the president was going to attend, and Mr. Mahole was slated to be the speaker to introduce our play – we were animated.

Chapter 37

A couple of nights before we left, the form 5 girls were in their common room studying after lights off, when one of them was bitten by a bug, and screamed bloody murder as she ran out of the common room. The other girls followed suit, and pandemonium like never before reigned supreme, because all this screaming woke the other girls, who in turn ran out of their dormitories, followed by others, like some terrible evil was about. On hearing all this commotion, a grief stricken Faith immediately woke up from a sleep filled with nightmares, and thought everyone had spotted her dead friend, who had always promised to pay her a visit once in a while from beyond the grave. She told me later, that she thought all this screaming was because people were seeing her spirit heading toward her dormitory.

She tried to get up and run for it, but the horror of it all was too much to handle; that she collapsed and fainted right there and then. Apparently, two other girls who were close friends to the dead ladies suffered the same fate, and had to be rushed to hospital in one of the teacher's cars. When Mr. Mahole found out the cause of this catastrophe he was furious, and would have suspended the girls that very instant. They were publicly castigated at assembly. I on the other hand was very worried about Faith that I felt compelled to cut class, and risk punishment by heading to the Palapye Health Center, where she was being held for observation, without permission. I was glad to find out that she was okay, and was discharged later that day even though she was very weak, and thus could not come with us to Gaborone when we went to perform at Maitisong yet again.

The president was not able to make it to the performance, but Lady Ruth Khama, wife of the very first president of Botswana the late Sir Seretse Khama was in attendance, which was good enough, and also in the audience was my father, Balisi Bonyongo, Motelebane Motelebane wa Mohutsiwa, and Albert Ditlhakeng. The duo (Albert and Balisi) were doing their A Levels at Maru A Pula at the time. Noticeably absent as well that time was Mr. Mahole, who was slated to be the guest speaker before the play, and Mr. Mudidi did the honors. Legoro's absence could be excused, because there were pressing matters at school that needed his presence, and that being the funeral of the two girls. The Kalahari Breweries was kind enough to donate refreshments for the audience after the show.

Our performance this time was great, almost as great as that at Madiba, that in the end I was honored when Lady Khama shook my hand after the play, and called my performance 'superb'. It is a compliment I have always cherished from this great woman, and wife of an even greater husband, and a founding father of a nation way ahead of its time. Among the refreshments provided by the Kalahari Breweries was beer, and having it readily accessible to students was like asking a fox to guard a hen house, because in no time the very many cans of beer disappeared in an instant. My father was to laugh about that incident for many years to come.

When I got the chance to speak to Albert and Balisi, I was again compelled to explain why I was still at Lotsane even though I was supposed to have graduated a year earlier. It was great to see them again nonetheless, and I also informed them of my plan to join them at MAP (as Maru A Pula School is affectionately known) in the not too distant future. They also told me that they were being sponsored by De Beers Botswana, otherwise known as Debswana, and plans were that after A Level, Balisi would be headed to the University of Leeds (where he became only one of two students in his class to graduate with honors), and Albert would be at the Camborne School of Mines, commonly abbreviated CSM, and a specialized department of the University of Exeter.

We had one more performance the next night, and this time it would be at the City hall, where our Setswana play *'Boloi'* was set to perform. We were hosted by St. Josephs College, and by the time we got there we were extremely exhausted. But before we got off the truck Mr. Mudidi had an announcement to make.

"Eh, gentlemen I know that some of you have swiped some of the beer that was at the event, and I ask that you to use caution. We are being gracefully hosted by this great school, and any misbehavior by any of us, no matter how minute, will put our school in a very bad light, having said that have a good night ladies and gentlemen." Mr. Mudidi always treated us like adults and with respect, and thus his instructions were always followed to the letter. He never used force as perhaps Mr. Molilo would have done, and then subsequently met with even greater resistance and defiance.

When we got to their dormitories, we were received by the senior students, who immediately led us to a large dormitory; where there were young students who were fast asleep.

"Hey Form Ones get up, get up, and get out! ... Out!" they ordered them. The youngsters did not even argue, or dare put up a fight, as they silently got their pillows and blankets, and left the room, apparently they were used to this kind of treatment by the look of things, and I could not help but feel a bit sorry for them, but all of us had gone through that, and you can be sure that they were going to do the same when their turn came.

The next morning after breakfast as a token of thanks at the school, we performed the play 'Boloi' for them, and they enjoyed it immensely. And later that night we performed at the city hall, and again Albert and Balisi were in attendance as well, and I promised to keep in touch with them as time went on until I joined them at MAP in September 1988 - I hoped and prayed. We left for Lotsane the next morning - a day after Thandi and Moloko were buried.

I heard that the funeral was a very emotional affair, and my dorm two mates were the center of attention all throughout. What happened was that they all travelled separately in Ferdinand's father's truck, and were the last to arrive at the viewing of the body. Moemedi was to tell me years later that they had strategically positioned Mpho to stand in between them just in case he collapsed, while looking at his girlfriend for the last time. I was glad that I was not there to witness this, but I was also sad that I could not attend the funeral. In the end the healing process was slow but sure.

***

Before long it was early October and time to write the Pre Entry Science Course (PESC) test. This was voluntary and thus not required. The tests were multiple choice, and were to be taken in the dining hall that one afternoon. We were tested in Mathematics, Physics, and Chemistry. I was not sure how I fared after taking the tests. After all, 1987 was not exactly my strongest year in as far as my academics were concerned so I was hoping, but not confident as I should have been had I taken the test in say 1986 for instance. And the irony of it all, was that the studying I was doing in 1986, was also meant to give me a great chance of passing this particular test.

One of the things we enjoyed doing as a dormitory; was challenging other dormitories to a football game. We had a few good players in our team like MC, Zero, Archie, and Kgakgamatso. The rest of us pitched in as best as we could. I for one had not played since 1984 at Itireleng, because Breakdance and Karate had taken over, and in the process eroded whatever rudimentary skills I possessed. But what everyone could count on was my speed with or without the ball, and as a result I was mainly a striker, and was often lucky enough to bang in some goals, because I could outrun my opponents for the most part. This led to an even bigger break. My sub team colleagues at Callies saw that as an advantage they could exploit; especially Kgosietsile 'Horse' Sanka who had been watching our match with one of the dormitories.

"Sebati, from now on you will be playing as well," he said.

And even later that day after the game Archie said to me, "Aha Sebati, the Callies guys saw that you can play so they will be no turning back now." There was a grin on his face as he said this. Archie's team like Stoner and MC was Santos, but lately Archie had been toying with the idea of jumping ship and joining Callies. A most welcome idea as far as I was concerned, because he was a very good defender, and we needed someone stronger at the left back position, currently that position was marshaled by Meshack 'Lani' Mauco, but at times he could be a bit faster than the ball so to speak and commit numerous, and at times costly errors. At sub team level, if a player wanted to join another sub team the team that wanted him had to pay a 5 Pula clearing fee, and for Archie we would have even paid double if we had the opportunity.

I was thrown into the fire the very next weekend in a game against Executive Cosmos. Back in 1984 I could handle the ball easily, and was actually getting to be a very good player, and even had dreams of playing professionally for my childhood team Orlando Pirates, and that was until my father quashed that dream in a way that made it look like I would never be good enough, when really the truth was that he had already decided my future for me, and would have even decided on my future bride as well had I let him. So that first game was a bit too fast for me, the ball might as well have been a ping pong ball, the way it bounced around, and in the end I was taken out of the game in the second half, because I developed a massive cramp on one of my quadriceps.

The next game was a vast improvement compared to my first one, and I was getting more and more comfortable, and getting a little bit of my groove back as far as soccer was concerned. This time we were playing against Santos. During the game there was a disputed corner kick that the referee (a fellow student), correctly adjudged to have been a goal kick for Santos, our player Justice Boemo, who had also developed the reputation of being a fierce goal poacher and a terror to opponents, and a member of the school team, was adamant that the ball was a corner kick instead, and was deliberately holding on to the ball in an attempt to have the referee change his call, which was very unlikely, so I went up to him and pleaded with him to let go of the ball.

"Listen, they can have the damn ball Justice ... we're going to beat them anyway," I said and then at that moment someone on the sidelines, and I believe that was Stoner, but I have never been one hundred per cent certain, said something unbecoming at Justce.

"Just give that ball back you big star you!" It was a stinging remark, and in an instant justice's face that always seemed to have a smile perpetually planted on it suddenly assumed a terrible demeanor. It was like seeing a totally different person take over – literally.

"*Stara ke rrago!*" "No, your father is the star," he said softly at first, and then a little later I saw him actually head to the sideline after giving up the ball. "*Akere wa utlwa monna? Kare stara ke rrago, o ye go mo ra jalo.*" "You heard what I said right? I said your father *is* the star so go and say that to him." He really wanted to make sure that there was no mistake the first time around, when he had made that comment. Later we were to laugh about it, and it was to become our own private joke and catch phrase.

"I saw you too man," he said. "I saw you warning a few guys on the sideline as well." What had happened was that some supporters from the opposing team felt it wise to throw me off my game by calling out nicknames like '*Bolaang*' (the long one), or 'tea break', each time I was in possession of the ball. It stopped only after I threatened them with physical violence, but deep down I knew it would have taken much, much more to get me to that point, I was just a barking dog with no bite, but fortunately they believed me, and all the heckling stopped. Archie later told me that this behavior helped him in making up his mind, and staying with Santos, and not join Callies after all. I always believed that this talk from him of joining Callies was always a facade to test his worth on the market, and spark a bidding war between the two clubs, I have no doubt that he was happy with his decision, because Callies got from bad to worse. I mean if they even had people like me playing regularly; that there tells you the state of affairs our team was in.

I did have my lucky moments though, because I did score in our next game against Chiefs (whom I still detested), and another game against Executive Cosmos. Santos was one team I could not score against, because they were very good at stopping fast runners like me and Justice, which is what happened, when we met them in the first game of the 1987 tournament where we ended up last place again. I was to hear that our team even got worse after we were all gone.

The one great thing that happened that third term, was that the school bought a television set and a Video Cassette Recorder (VCR); we were now able to watch many shows, including live soccer games especially on Saturday afternoons and nights. We had come a long way since the days of scrambling for a signal at the bush behind the staff houses. What was even great was that we could rent movies from a nearby video outlet in Palapye, and thus were able to watch a lot of movies that we otherwise would not have been able to; considering our location. This fell of course under the Entertainment Committee, but somehow Anthea and Gerald wriggled their way into the mix, and Gerald in particular put himself in charge of the T.V. even though he was not a member of the committee, but we did not mind because a new television set and a VCR meant more responsibilities for us, and me in particular as the leader of this group so their unsolicited involvement was welcome. However one night Anthea did something that angered a lot of the students. I was not there when that happened, but arrived soon after the incident in question.

What had happened was that a popular show was on that early Saturday evening, and for some reason Anthea turned off the T.V. when everyone was engrossed in the show. This was rude to begin with, and really she had no grounds to do that and thus everyone was angry, and rightly so. Some I heard made comments not worth repeating especially when it came to remarks about the ownership of the television.

In any case, when I arrived I found everyone seated on the park benches in front of the classroom that substituted as the T.V. room. There was a buzzing around that I could not readily grasp, but I could tell that whatever it was, was about the television that was unceremoniously turned off by a 'bossy' fellow student. At that moment I saw some guys among them a classmate of mine called Daniel 'Fetsi' Sebueng.

They were talking among themselves, minding their own business, when Daniel said something like, "Oh, I don't know I heard the T.V. was turned off, I'm not sure why because I just got here."

As luck would have it, Anthea just happened to be close by, and all she needed was to hear the word 'television', which was enough to drive her off her rocker. She strode over to the guys and immediately confronted Daniel.

"Excuse me, are you talking to me?"

And before a shocked Daniel could answer she slapped him hard right across the face. I too was stunned when I saw this unfold as if in slow motion. Daniel then quickly sprang to his feet.

"*Eish, ngwanyana yo ke tla mmetsa,*" "I will beat up this girl," he said and immediately connected with a right hook to the face. It took a brief moment to sink in, but when the pain set in, Anthea threw her hands to her face, bent forward and started sobbing bitterly. In fact she would have fallen over had some of her friends not come to the rescue. I immediately stepped into the darkness; anxious not to be a party to all this, because as a senior prefect, and an eye witness to the entire thing my word would be heavily relied on in the subsequent investigation that was sure to follow, because a girl had been assaulted in plain view. Harare, was also one of the first few guys at the scene especially since the victim was his sister. The possibility of getting into a fist fight with Daniel for what he had done to her was not even thought of, because Ferdinand was by nature not the fighting type.

"Hey man what do you think you are doing?" he fumed.

"Defending myself what do you think?" Daniel retorted.

Ferdinand had no immediate answer as he looked around, and saw his sister being led to the girls hostel still sobbing, and now hysterically. "You see the mess you've put yourself in?" Ferdinand said to Daniel.

"What mess? I was just minding my own business and your sister just came up to me and slapped me. What am I supposed to do, just sit and take it like a chump? I don't think so." He was right, but I was not sure if that was how the administration was going to look at it, but this time there were witnesses who would be willing to testify on Daniel's behalf, if the need arose, especially witnesses many of who felt scorned when Anthea turned off the T.V. for no apparent reason.

"Oh so you think you can just beat up a girl and get away with it? Think again, you're in big trouble pal."

"So a girl can just come up to a guy slap him for no reason and get away with it, is that what you are saying? No *you* think again"

"We shall see pal," Ferdinand was like a drowning man clutching to straws and he knew it.

"Yeah, we shall see, and don't call me pal, because I'm *not* your pal, what you should be doing is teaching that sister of yours manners." Daniel felt he had a strong case and so did a lot of people.

The teacher on duty that night was Mr. Irvine, and after the assault on Anthea was reported, he went first to her to find out what happened, and when he heard that she had in fact struck Daniel first he had no choice but to dismiss the case. All was settled the next day when the two were asked by Mr. Irvine to kiss and make up, but in a literal sense they shook hands and peace was restored. I was impressed at how Anthea handled the whole thing in the end; even though the bump on her forehead was very noticeable. However, it did little to distort her beautiful face, but I do believe the experience taught her to be in control of her temper in the future. I did tell Ferdinand a few days later that I had made myself scarce because I was not sure I would be a credible witness as far as Anthea was concerned. I liked her that was true, so I was not sure if I was going to be truthful in as far as what had happened, because it did pain me to see her cry like that, but in the end I was glad that the incident was behind us.

Chapter 38

Olivia and I finally called it quits sometime that term. It was just a matter of time, and the writing was already on the wall; as it got to a point where we hardly spoke to one another, which made the break up all the more easier, and I would think more so for me than her, because by that time my affair with Faith could no longer be hidden, even though on one or two occasions; she had wanted to call it off altogether since I was just too impatient in her eyes, because I could not stand the sneaking around, and just loving from a distance. So when Faith brought up the subject again, I felt that I could not stand her wasting my time so I decided to patch things up with Olivia, and then put an end to the secret affair I was having with Faith, I felt that I could not stand the torture anymore.

I made an appointment to meet with Olivia following afternoon prep, and Faith soon after lunch. I had even rehearsed what I was going to say to her. I had chosen my words carefully, because I wanted to let her down gently. I was shocked when she declared her undying love and said that we were not being fair to ourselves. Why should we hide the fact that we are in love? She asked, and I was inclined to agree with her, which now meant that my meeting with Olivia later that day was to now end the relationship. I shuddered to think what would have transpired had I elected to meet Olivia first.

It did turn out much later that Olivia always had a steady boyfriend, who was much older than me, and was a teacher at some Junior Secondary School in Francistown, and that it was to whom she headed every time school closed, and she lived with him during those times when opportunity allowed, which is why I never got a letter from her throughout the holidays when I expected one. What was even more disturbing, was that by the time when we parted, she was actually with child; though it did not show until after we had written our exams and left Lotsane. I was angered mainly by the fact that all this time, I was just the toy boy at school, someone she could not have been serious with. Maybe I am wrong, and had played a huge role in pushing her in another man's arms, but the fact that she was with child, and I easily could have been fingered as the one responsible particularly since blood tests were not common in those days. That issue still once in a while brings a chill at the back of my neck when I get a chance to dream about it. After all, such things as pinning a pregnancy on an innocent guy, whether the two had been intimate in the past or not, was something that did happen once in a while. It had happened to Dakune.

That is the reason why he did not come back in 1986, only for the young lady in question to confess to her parents, months after the baby was born; that Dakune was indeed not the father. The parents of this lady were forced to find a school for Dakune, and pay for all the damages incurred, but in the process Dakune lost an entire year of his life for nothing. Not to mention the mental anguish he had to deal with. But please don't get me wrong, I am not saying that Olivia would have resorted to that, I am just speculating, and stating a fact that was very common those days.

Now with this load off my shoulders, I was happy to concentrate even more on my studies, because I was still struggling a bit to get into the groove I was in last year. I got into that, after something happened that spurned me to even newer heights. It happened one day when we heard that the PESC test results had been released, and that that evening either Mr. Ruf or Mr. Irvine, were going to come to the class to announce those who had been selected. I was numbed with nervousness wondering if I had made the list or not. Mr. Irvine did come to our class as expected.

"Good evening ladies and gentlemen, I have good news for some of you," he said and immediately consulted a list he had in hand. "The following have been accepted into the Pre Entry Science Course at the University of Botswana." He paused before he began reading the names from the list. "Ediretse Nthobatsang ... Hosea Gopalang ... Zibanani Bareki ... Chabaesele Kelibile ... Meshack Ramatshaba ... last and not least ..." I remember thinking *please say Sebati Mafate*, "... Tirelo Katse," he said. And I would be lying if I say I was not thoroughly disappointed, but I had no one to blame but myself, because had I even put half the effort I did like last year I would have definitely made the list. Missing also from that list was Rinah Phoko; for the simple reason that she did not take the test, and Mr. Ruf had admonished her for that, but Rinah's chosen career path did not involve science.

Mr. Irvine went on to say, "Now for all of you, who took the test but did not get selected, please do not feel despondent, because after taking your exams you can still re apply to be reconsidered," he said and left to deliver the good news to the other classes. Even though I had not made the list for reasons I understood very well, I was very disappointed, and determined now to hit the books with a new kind of fortitude that was to make last year seem like a regular reading assignment. I started waking up as early as 2:30 am starting the very next morning. Faith was very sad for me, and she tried to find ways to comfort me, but I told her that perhaps this was a wakeup call for me, and that now what was of paramount importance was to make sure I got the grades that would put me into MAP. I had another goal to strive for that was in my eyes bigger than PESC.

When I told Mrs. Mbulawa that I had not made the list she looked at me, and uttered words that rang in my ears for many years to come, because they were true. "Maybe science is not your line Sebati." It was the God's honest truth, even though I did not agree with her at that very moment.

My study group, with Rinah in the mix, was becoming a daily routine to a point of being a ritual. We consulted one another as far as problems in Math and Physics were concerned, and Rinah proved to be a very great asset. It even got to point where I was even studying on Saturday afternoons of all days, and it did not take long before I hit my stride again. It appears that all that studying I did in 1986 had laid a very strong foundation for me, and thus I was able to catch on real fast, and in no time I was way ahead again like I was before. My *mojo* was back finally, and I could not stop.

As the days to the final exam drew ever so closer, tension and exam fever was beginning to build, whenever the study time siren went off everyone was in class studying; that in time it was not necessary for teachers to patrol the classrooms to make sure that we were doing what we were supposed to. They did not have to, because our futures were very much at stake now. Some had a strange way of dealing with the exam fever. Godfrey Morgan, whom everyone resorted to calling

'Mafia', for instance, one time walked around with a shirt he himself had made, from cloth that we used to apply polish to the floors, and cleaning windows before inspection, and wrote the words *'born to kill'* on the front and back.

He would walk around the classes during study time, and one day he stopped by one of the windows of our classroom to have a chat with us.

"Guys, don't study too hard," he said.

"Why not? Better yet why aren't you studying yourself?" someone asked.

"I suffer from what's called 'displacement reaction syndrome.' What I study today displaces what I studied yesterday, so if I study tomorrow it will displace what I studied today. So I decided to stop." He got laughter from everyone.

That weekend, he shocked the entire boarding school, when he caught two large cat fish; both were as long as a man's arm at the school's sewer pond. How he did it none of us knew, because he did not have a line, fishing pole, hook, and sinker that we were aware of, and what he did with those fish no one knows. Ambi said that he once, without warning, walked through their dormitory urinating on the floor in the process. Stunts like these had a lot of people thinking that Mafia was born with two 'Y' chromosomes. A 'Y' chromosome is what determines that a baby born is male. In extremely rare cases it is said that a male can have two strands of these chromosomes, and people like that are said to be most daring, and thrive on living on the edge as they are known to be adrenaline junkies. Godfrey Mafia Morgan's eccentricities led many to believe that he was that rare creature. In addition to that, he was a very good student; as a matter of fact he had been one of the six in his class who had made the short PESC list.

Back home in Francistown, it was said he was the total opposite to the Mafia we saw in school. They say he was the typical child every parent wished to have, dutiful, and hardworking. It was common to see him running errands for his parents, watering the flowers and the lawn, and even tending to the garden; at school though it was a different story. Some Saturday mornings, he would suddenly run from his dormitory, which was dorm 4, shouting expletives all the way until he got to dorm 20, and the exercise was repeated. It stopped when one morning BM summoned him; apparently he had been hearing these outbursts from his house.

"Hey man, why do you like hurling insults for no reason?" he asked him. And Mafia realizing his indiscretion looked down with shyness, and promised BM that he would not do that again, and he kept his promise.

One morning, without warning, he came into my dormitory fuming, and his wrath was directed mainly at Gerald and Ferdinand.

"Aha you two scumbags!" he screamed, "I tell you what, do that again and you will be sorry, very sorry indeed. Wait a minute do you know who I am, and what I am made of? Don't ever try pulling a stunt like that again." It must be recalled that Mafia was big and strong, and could be scary if he chose too.

At that moment I intervened wanting to know what had happened. "What's going on Godfrey?" I asked.

"Man Sebazim." That's what he always called me. "These guys Sebazim I'm telling you man ... these two guys if they as much as pull what they did last night ..." at that moment he confronted them again, this time pointing a shaking finger at them. "If you as much as do that again ... man you'll be sorry I tell you." I kept wondering what was *'that'* what these two had done to set him off like that since I could not get it from him. It turns out that the dispute was over the T.V. again, and Godfrey had wanted to remind them that the T.V. in fact belonged to the school and not their parents.

***

One thing I must say that was great about that year was that we had very competent and creative people in the Entertainment Committee. Over the years that I was at Lotsane, entertainment always alternated from dance this Saturday, to a movie the next. The routine became predictable, and at times boring, especially on film night if the particular movie was mind-numbing. In this we were very careful in choosing the films that we knew would be popular with students, and this would be mostly action adventure flicks. What our committee did was spice it up a little with variety shows, and competitions that were entertaining like say *'Pick a Box'*. One time there was a beauty contest, and Hex had volunteered to dance on one of the breaks when the judges were tallying up the points, I don't know what I said or maybe somebody misunderstood something, because as we were waiting for the judges to return, and Hex was about to do his dance, Ferdinand who was the master of ceremony spoke into the mike; taking me by complete surprise.

"Sebati Jones Mafate on the dance floor please." In an instant all eyes were on me.

"No, no, no … no way … I never volunteered for this," I protested vehemently. But it was no use because Hex was walking up to me, and I accepted the challenge. We danced well together, and like Two-Two we became sort of dance partners when one day we paired up again during a variety show later that year. The dancing duo was dubbed *'Hex'n Jones'*, and we got great cheering support from our dorm mates. It was fun like that, and I could not help but wonder what my life would be like one day in the not too distant future when Lotsane would be nothing but a memory; the thought was hard to imagine.

Finally, as the days drew all the more closer, the studying intensifying, we were compelled to bring desks into our dormitory and the lockers were turned around to partition them in such a way that they made mini rooms – just as tradition dictated. This led to an encounter with none other than the teacher we called 'Mature' or 'Seoke', because his head was always tilted to the side. One night, he and a few students went from dormitory to dormitory confiscating the desks that were in the dorms, and taking them to the common room, while this was happening, me and a few fellows hid our desks in the toilets, and took them out once the sweep was complete. But unfortunately, Mature came that Saturday morning while we were asleep, and found three desks in our dormitories. He casually asked me who the desks belonged to, and I told him of two not knowing what a big deal it would turn out to be.

Apparently Mature reported this matter to the headmaster saying that we had broken into the common room, which was locked at the time (a total fabrication), and taken the desks. What complicated matters was that only two desks were accounted for as belonging to me and Peter Mafokate, as for the third desk no one knew right away who it belonged to, and Mature fanatical as ever, said the whole dorm was responsible, he even summoned us to his office to deal with the matter. During this encounter we were not allowed to defend ourselves and even ask any questions.

Peter Mafokate I remember said something like, "Now Mr. Molilo in a situation like this what do we …"

"Don't question me!" he howled like a rabid dog. He was the law, in his mind we were guilty and thus we could not say anything, we were denied the freedom of speech that Kaelo had talked so passionately about. However, we had people in our midst like Archie Seemule who were not going to go down without a fight – more especially since really in all honesty they were totally innocent.

"No Mr. Molilo … I cannot accept that, you can't pin that desk on all of us just because no one claims responsibility for it," he said.

"Hey one of you broke into the common room and got it so you are all responsible," Mr. Molilo was adamant as he could be stubborn as a mule as well.

"I did not go anywhere near that common room, I don't know where you could have gotten that," Archie retorted.

"The fact is one of you did and that is why I am holding you all responsible."

"This is not right because I had nothing to do with it, there is no proof that these desks even came from the common room to begin with."

"Yes they did," Molilo insisted.

"No that can't be … unless those desks in the common room told you that fantastic story." We all gasped at the insolence of this statement toward a teacher. It took time for even Mature to come to terms with it, and the fact that he paused that long before responding; told us that there was a chink in his supposed impenetrable armor that he tried very hard to show to the students.

"Eh Archie, you best be careful and know who you are talking to," he said but the damage was done; we had discovered his weak point. And a little later he let us go, but told us that we needed to find out who the third desk belonged to, and later through an investigation of our own we found out that the desk did in fact belong to Phatsimo.

The others were off the hook so Peter, myself, and Phatsimo met with Molilo who had also summoned BM to his office, and promptly told us that we were going to have to answer to Mr. Mahole, and that there was a likelihood that we would be suspended from boarding. I did not for once believe that to be true, and thought Mature was being his usual overzealous self again. BM was quiet all along, and I could tell that he was also wondering what the big deal was.

When we got to Mr. Mahole's office, I could tell that Mature was a bit nervous when he related what had happened to the headmaster. It was clear to me from his manner of speaking to Legoro that he always desperately wanted to be in Legoro's good books. Mature was, after all, an expatriate from Zimbabwe and to keep having his work permit renewed; he would always need Legoro to vouch for him with the immigration authorities. The same held true with another teacher, who could be equally as fanatic as Molilo when he chose to. His name was Mike Chirumbwana and he too was from Zimbabwe.

"Mr. Mahole, I brought these three boys to you because they frustrated our efforts to get the desks back in the common room. When I got there Saturday morning we found the door lock broken and four desks were missing ..."

"Three," I said.

"Excuse me?" Molilo turned around with a sneer.

"When we were in your office you told BM that there were three desks missing, not four," I said.

"Are you saying that I'm lying?" Some African elders liked to use this form of questioning as a means of blackmailing a younger person, and with Molilo such a thing was to be expected, and I was ready for it, because the lies had just gone too far. He just wanted to see us suspended, and I knew that if I did not speak up he might have just gotten his wish.

"No sir, that's not what I said, I was just correcting you."

"Correcting me? In other words, what you are saying is that I am lying," he insisted. I on the other hand felt that he was backing me into a corner.

"That's not what I said ... I was merely pointing out that there were three desks that were unaccounted for, not four, plus we did not break into the common room." I was wondering why BM, or even Legoro for that matter, were not saying anything or intervening as they normally would, but when I glanced at BM I saw a slight smirk on his face (I had an ally) – I did not dare look at Legoro, because that sinister look that he was known for was now plastered on his face.

"Oho, so I'm lying, that is what you are saying … right … right … right?" He now had pushed me far enough, and I could not take it anymore because I was now feeling suffocated.

"Yes sir … you are lying!"

His mouth was agape for a while not knowing what to say next, and I braced myself for the worst. If he had looked at my knees he would have noticed that they were shaking. I was scared stiff.

"Eh, I think I heard my phone ringing Mr. Mahole, I'll be right back," he said and left. I am still waiting for him to come back. We remained in the office for a little while feeling the tension subside a bit, and that was when Peter Mafokate lost his cool and started babbling inanely.

"Mr. Mahole, please sir, understand that we did not do anything wrong as Mr. Molilo implies. I have never been in trouble since I started school, my father knows how well behaved. I am …"

"I know that. That's why I am not in the least bit concerned," Mr. Mahole said. And really that right there should have been the cue for Peter to shut up, but he did not.

"My father knows that I am a good boy sir; from birth I have never given them problems, even my mother still boasts to her friends about what an easy child I was, a baby that only cried when it was hungry, a baby that every mother wished for. So, Mr. Mahole, please sir, you can understand that I would not cause any type of trouble. I never make noise, let alone break doors and get desks from the common room. Please, Mr. Mahole, I am a good boy even my father knows that sir." I could not believe what I was hearing that day.

"Is that all?" Legoro asked. I am sure that if Peter had more to say he would have blabbered on until the Christ's second coming.

"Okay, you're all free to go." And as soon as he said that Peter broke down and wept. Legoro could not help but smile. He had been entertained, no doubt. He looked at me and said, "Sebati, you stay. I need to talk to you."

After Phatsimo and Peter left, Legoro said to me, "Sebati, I want you to quietly find out who it is who has been breaking the windows and tell me who they are." There had been acts of vandalism around campus, specifically by some form 5's since their time at Lotsane was coming to an end, and they resorted to this disgraceful act. I knew a couple of the vandals, and instead of snitching on them I opted to have a chat with them. A suspension or even an expulsion at this time of the year especially; would have been something I did not want to carry around in my conscience. Thus, I decided to do this in private.

"Guys, the headmaster has asked me to tell him who it was whose been committing these acts of vandalism. I know you two are involved so I will advise you to stop right this minute." The two gentlemen agreed, and swore not to do that again. I did inform them that I would keep my eye on them, though.

Days were drawing closer and closer not only to the exam, but to the super party that was to be our farewell. That meant that I needed a suit, so did every other boy in school; it was custom. My father sent word that he needed my measurements for a tailor, and I promptly sort help from the Domestic Science ladies, who did a great job in getting my measurements. At this time Stoner disappeared from school for a few days without permission, and was lucky to escape punishment. Rumor had it that as the days were drawing ever so closer, and with no suit in sight, Stoner was worried, and thus took matters in his own hands, and went home to shake down his parents for the suit. He has always denied that allegation, and maintains that he went home because his dad was very ill, and thus needed to be by his side.

Chapter 39

The week of peace was finally about. We were on our own now, studying twenty four seven. Help was needed whenever required from the teachers. I was so engrossed into my studying that even after classes officially ended, I still consulted Mr. Betridge from time to time. At first there were about ten of us who sought his help, and the number slowly dwindled until I was the only one in the class, which at first was an eerie feeling that I soon got used to. I remember just before classes ended, Mr. Mudidi was going to give his class form 5 two, one final mock exam before the big one, and I asked him if I could take the test as well, and he gladly agreed and I did well on the test. I was as ready as I ever could have been before the exam came around.

Our Completer's Ball (better known as prom) was a huge success, my escort was my class mate Netty Nkala the head girl, and I looked great in my three piece suit that had arrived a few days earlier. I kept that suit for many years, until my very good friend Urban Guava Dabutha asked to borrow it for some event – I have yet to get it back from him. The only glitch to that well-oiled machine that was the Completer's Ball, was that the preacher from Palapye who was supposed to open the ceremony with a prayer, did not for some reason show up, and the honors were handed to a middle aged woman, also from Palapye, who was gratified by this unexpected accolade, and pounced on it with both hands. She prayed I think for close to half an hour asking the Good Lord, amongst other things, to guide and protect us from this hungry beast called life; that was ready to devour us if we did not follow the right track, and went on and on until grunts were heard from almost everyone.

"Amen," someone prompted, followed by another, and another, until the woman finally got the message, and thankfully ended the plea to the Almighty.

We were all dressed our best, except of course Ipha, who chose instead to dress like a vagabond. This year it was Mbumbi who gave a moving speech on behalf of the students, and many times drew quotes from William Shakespeare's *'Julius Caesar'* since he was an English Literature student, and at last it was time to eat, Faith was one of the servers, and as I waited in line she immediately came up to me with a plate well served complete with a fork and knife, and thus I was one of the very first to eat at that 1987 prom. In the end we were all stuffed from the very delicious food, and thereafter danced away to the record night that followed.

The very first paper we wrote, and always seemed to be tradition was the History Paper One, which dealt with South and Central Africa. History Paper Two, European history, was to be written a week or so later, but now the moment had finally arrived. I had all the necessary tools, and the Parker pens I had were a present from the wonderful MS. Angie Modutlwa, who was our neighbor and a great family friend, and very much like a mother to me. The pens were beautiful and comfortable, and like the suit I was to keep them for a very long time.

The first to head to class that day was Moemedi 'Moex' Nthapelelang, and he was serenaded. Since history was one of my favorite subjects, I had a lot of facts many of which I had researched on my own; that it was hard to stay within the one and a half page parameters that were being asked. I always felt for me at least three pages were enough, but then again going over what was instructed meant you were in danger of losing points, and thus I had to be as brief as possible, and stay on point, which was not a very easy thing to do. In the end, I was somewhat satisfied after the exam even though I always felt I could have done better.

One by one, we wrote the papers, and before long everyone got used to the idea that we were writing the ultimate exams. During that time, and the week of peace, we could dress any which way we wanted, but when it came to having lunch at the dining hall we were required to be in uniform. On one of those days, Ipha went to the dining hall dressed in short pants, and a thin raincoat with not even a tee shirt underneath. Mr. Geary saw him the moment he was coming out of the hall casually eating from his plate. It just so happened that right around that time Mr. Geary was headed to his office, something he very rarely did during lunch hours, because right around the time we had lunch the teachers had theirs as well.

"Aha, Ipha come here," he said, much like someone who was already used to the latter's mischief, and thus was always expecting something from him.

"You know you're supposed to be in uniform don't you?" he said as he led the way to his office, followed by Ipha, plate in hand, and eating with affected unconcern.

"Mr. Geary, I was just going by what the weather forecast said."

"What weather forecast?"

"Before lunch I took it upon myself to listen to the news, and at the end they said to expect isolated thunder showers so I put on a raincoat just in case," he said.

"What excellent foresight Ipha, even I would not have guessed," Mr. Geary said sarcastically, before the two disappeared inside his office. Later that day Ipha was seen washing some chairs by the dining hall. Even though school was coming to an end that was not to be the last of his punishment; this kind of thing was to continue to the very end.

Sporadically, at Lotsane, students were treated to a drink that was sweet and made from maize meal known as 'mageu'. Whenever that was brewed, and ready, the announcement would be made at the dining hall during lunch, and later that day particularly following afternoon prep; students would line up and one of the prefects would serve it to the students. This was normally in a huge drum, and was served on a first come first serve basis that in no time the *mageu* would be finished. Sometimes, especially toward the end of the term, there would be so much to go around that the drum would be carried to the hostel, and placed in front of the dormitories for people to come and help themselves as they pleased. For some reason, we had a lot of '*mageu* calls' in 1985 than we did any other year that I was at Lotsane. *Mageu* was not for everyone though, because some students did not like it. I remember one day in 1985, as Sebei and I were drinking some mageu from a drum that had been placed in front of dorm nine, Metric Rathebe the skilled martial artist, who could do the splits easily, and did not drink the *mageu,* decided to be naughty.

"Guys, seriously how do you feel drinking this vomit?" he asked with a smirk on his face.

"Metric stop it man!" Sebei would shout, and we would try to think no further of the remark, because in truth though if you thought about it, and looked at the product, it did resemble what Metric was implying.

When we were writing our final exams that year, a lot of the mageu was brewed that even after our normal share, there were two drums still filled with it, and we were compelled to take one to the boys' dormitories and the girls did the same. We were scheduled to write our Math Paper Two and Physics paper the next day. With all that mageu at our disposal, we had large helpings, and people like Zweks drank more than they could handle, and many of us were to regret it the next day - some more than others.

All that studying and practicing with Rinah and company paid huge dividends. I breezed through the Mathematics Paper Two exam; that I was even smiling to myself as I was taking the test, because many of the problems we had covered and I had practiced so hard that solving them seemed second nature. With math especially, once you are finished it is always wise to go over the problems, because most likely than not there will be some mistakes that need to be fixed. And just as I turned over to the first page to go over the problems once again, I felt the very first sting in my stomach followed by a very sickening growl. It was the unmistakable first signs of the dreaded diarrhea. I tried very hard to suppress it, and concentrate on the task at hand but it was useless. I was in trouble. After just a few minutes, I had no choice but to raise my hand, and Mrs. Geary who was our proctor (invigilator) came up to me, and I indicated to her that I was done. I hated doing that but I had no choice ... the alternative was not even worth imagining. And the *mageu* was fully to blame.

It turns out that I was not the only one; many students who drank a lot of that *mageu* were experiencing the consequences. I heard that Zweks had to be escorted to the public toilets on at least two occasions. Had I known that an escort was provided, I would have requested one, and that would have given me a chance to go over my paper. Escorts were provided, because there was a chance that a student could have answers written on the walls of the toilets. Beside this mishap, I felt really great about the paper, more than I ever did, and by the time I wrote my Principle of Accounts exam, I just knew that I had passed; it was just a question of how well. We then had a week off to recover, before our very last paper, which for most of us was Setswana. The paper was to be written on Wednesday December 2nd 1987.

That weekend, we decided to have our end of year party for the drama club. The previous year we had celebrated that at the beautiful *Masama* rocks off the road to Serowe. Our Karate club had already had its party this year at the same *Masama*, which was a blast, so instead of going back there; we decided to have our drama party as a picnic at the old Palapye ruins.

Before the founding of the village that is now known as Serowe, the capital of the Bangwato people was Palapye (Phalatswe) the actual village itself was some 20 to 30 miles south of where the present village is, the site of the old church, built around 1889, is the most significant of this area, and part of the walls of that building still stand. It was at this site that we were going to have our picnic, but then Mr. Geary almost derailed these plans.

On field trips, no matter the destination, it was standard operating procedure that a teacher accompanies the students. The truck could be secured no problem, but a teacher had to be there with the students, and there was no flexibility when it came to this decree. On the weekend when we were to have our picnic at the old Palapye ruins, Mr. Mudidi let us know way ahead of time that he was going to be somewhere else, and thus could not make it. Nobody complained because the great 'Letsopa' had always been there for us. Mr. Bhusumane on the other hand was a bit indecisive, he told us that he would not accompany us, but would meet us at the site. We were content with this arrangement, and thus went ahead with our preparations.

That Saturday morning as we were getting ready for the trip, somehow Mr. Geary got a whiff of what was going on, so he came up to me, and a few other guys as we were in the midst of the preparations. Food had been cooked the previous night at the Home Economics lab, under the supervision of one of our very active female members, a form 4 whose name was Lesedi. I had even silently earmarked that she be the next chairperson of the Drama club after we left; she had my full backing.

"Sebati," Mr. Geary said. "What is this I am hearing that you people are heading to the old Palapye church without a teacher present?" Mr. Geary over the last month or so had become very temperamental and irritable, something that was totally alien to us, since we were all used to his gentle disposition. And at that moment I was getting a bit of that. Looking back, I think that he was under a lot of stress as a newly elected deputy headmaster, and running the day to day events of the school was an unenvied task at exam time it turns out.

"We will have a teacher present ..."

"Who?" he demanded in a fierce tone that told me that he was going to make it impossible for this trip to happen.

"Mr. Bhusumane ... he is not here right now, but he assured us that he will meet us there and ..."

"No, not good enough that is not going to happen unless a teacher is present." With that he turned around and left. We were speechless. We had wanted to end our incredible year in style, and a picnic at the old Palapye ruins was in our minds an ideal place to do it. We walked back to the Home Economics lab dazed and dejected, because not only were we not going to have this picnic, I was going to have to break the news to the rest of the members. A few weeks before the finals, we had had a chance to have our picnic at *Masama*, just like we did last year, and it was a blast, but we opted instead to head to a different venue, and at a very awkward time and thus we were paying the price.

When word reached the rest of the student body, particularly the girls, I heard, who were not members of the drama club; there was laughter at our expense.

"Haha ... those drama queens have it now. I mean who do they think they are? Now they are going to suffer the ignominy of having their party in a classroom."

The drama club was considered one of the elite in school, and not by mistake. After all, we were recognized in the whole country now, but most importantly we went on field trips more than all the other clubs in the school put together, and this did not sit well with some, and jealousy was abound. What is worse, I heard later after I left Lotsane that some teachers even joined in, and Mr. Mudidi had threatened to manhandle any one of those teachers who joined in this childish trait.

However, the prospect of going back to the truck to unload the food was something that I just could not see myself doing – there had to be a way. And as I strode around campus I saw Mr. Appadoo driving to his house in his small sedan. It was worth a try, and so I decided to give it a shot. I flagged him down, he was accompanied by his oldest son Rudy, who at the time was about eight or nine years old, and a little too smart for his own good.

"Yes Sebati," Mr. Appadoo said, "what can I do for you?"

"Mr. Appadoo, we are in a jam sir, we are supposed to be having a picnic, but unfortunately there is no teacher to come with us, could you please do it sir? ... Come with us to the old Palapye church?"

He thought about it for a moment and said, "Can Rudy come?" *could he ever*? I thought to myself jubilantly.

As we were leaving, I rode with Mr. Appadoo in his car and we followed the truck, but as we were exiting the premises Mr. Geary stopped us. He now could see that we had a teacher with us as he had told us we needed, but I could tell that he was not happy about the whole situation.

"This is bad," he told Mr. Appadoo. "These kids could have done this weeks ago I don't know why they had to force it." For a moment I hated this man, but I stayed still and dared not open my mouth. At last he stepped away from the car and we left.

"He is upset," Mr. Appadoo said, but I was counting my blessings because this trip almost did not materialize.

We took longer than we expected to get to the site, and when we did it was not as exciting as we all thought it would be, but we made the best of it nonetheless. The food was good except for the rice, because at Lesedi's insistence, she had put some type of spicy chilly balls in it that exploded in your mouth, and in the process ruined the taste for all of us. Even Rudy, Mr. Appadoo's son complained.

"You know what," he said to me, "I do not like those round things," he continued as the pointed at them in the rice. I agreed with him, and told Lesedi that next time it would be better if she asked people first about including certain recipes in the food. It did not occur to me at that moment that there was not going to be a next time. This was it, and little did I know that this was to be one of the memories I was going to cherish forever.

When it was time to leave, it turned out that we could not all fit in the truck, a few of us were going to have to stay behind, and wait for the truck to come back for us after it dropped off the rest. I was among the nine or ten of us that remained including Kaelo, and as it got dark we made a fire, and the fact that we were on sacred ground on a pitch black night was not lost to us. We were terrified but tried very hard not to show it. To make matters worse Kaelo started quoting sections from one of Chinua Achebe's classic novels, a book called *'Things Fall Apart'*, which we were all familiar with since we had studied it at some point of our academic lives. I studied the book at Junior Certificate, and others like Kaelo, Mbumbi, and Ferdinand did it at O' Level as well. Kaelo was in his deep voice talking about a scene in the book that was inappropriate at the time; a scene that talked about evil spirits.

"Just imagine Sebati, you come up to a masked spirit that asks as it did in the book *'the body of Uzowulu, do you know me?"* Uzowulu was one of the characters in this Chinua Achebe classic. We laughed nervously not even daring to look around at the surroundings. It was a typical African darkness that whether accompanied by the sounds of wild animals or not is indeed a very scary one. Even to this day I still get chills when I recall that dreadful night. At last we saw the lights in the distance illuminating the trees above, and heard one of the most beautiful sounds I have ever heard - it was the unmistakable sound of the school truck returning to pick us up. It had even arrived much sooner than we had expected, and soon we were back to school – how sweet it was.

When we arrived there was a movie playing, but most of all I was glad and relieved to be back. The next morning after general cleaning, I was supervising the hall this third and last term, Mr. Geary come up to me.

"Sebati, shouldn't you be concentrating on your Setswana paper instead of running around getting picnics organized?" Now I suddenly saw what this whole farce had been all about.

"Mr. Geary, I am as ready as I will ever be, so I don't think one day out will disrupt my quest to pass and pass well," I said. However, I don't quite recall what the actual conversation was, but it got a bit testy that in the midst of all that I turned and walked away.

"Eh, Sebati don't turn your back on me like that and walk away, that's rude," Mr. Geary said, and he was absolutely right. The man had his shortcomings like everybody else, but he was all in all a great man and teacher that I had come to like and respect, and not only that he was always encouraging me in ways no one else did (that is if we exclude the great Emmanuel Mudidi), especially in my acting and writing something that I did not get from my own father. I am glad to say that I did humbly apologize to him for my impudence.

Chapter 40

Reality hit us as dorm members after we wrote our Setswana Paper Two. It was the end of our stay at Lotsane. The night before we talked about how school brought us together, and then scattered us about like wheat in the wind, although this was my last paper I was forced to stay a little longer, because two of things that happened. First we needed to head back to Gaborone, and present the money that we had raised to its recipient Kabo Matlho. Mr. Mudidi had even arranged with the media specifically, *'The Botswana Guardian'* to be present, and secondly Motlotlegi was due to attend his Tirelo Sechaba orientation in Gaborone, and needed a place to stay in Gaborone before the day came, which was a week or so away, and he asked if he could stay with us for a little while which I agreed to. The only hiccup was that Motlotlegi was a Technical Drawing student, and TD students were the very last to write their papers in this case after everybody was gone.

Archie was one of the last few to leave, we escorted him as far as the Palapye/Serowe junction, and he got a ride immediately thereafter, and headed home to Francistown. On our way back we were given a ride back to school by a nice young gentleman, who appeared to be in his mid 20's, we were all sad, and I had to confide in him in a desperate attempt to lessen the impact.

"We've been like brothers for the past year, and all day we had to watch that brotherly bond disintegrate, we've been seeing every one off all day ..."

"And now from happiness it is sadness right?" he finished the sentence for me.

"Yes", we all said with a lump in our throats. I was with Phatsimo, Stoner the other Bonang, and Gerald. Words just cannot describe how we were feeling that day. The next day I loaded my big heavy trunk into the school's small truck. This was the same trunk that the kind security guard had helped me carry when I first arrived at Lotsane way back in

1985. I had not taken it back home since then and this was it. Over the years, what I had done when schools closed, was carry my clothes in a much smaller and portable bag, which I borrowed from Ruth, and this always seemed to suffice. I had arranged with Mr. Mudidi, to have me drop off the trunk at home, after we were done with all that we needed to do that day in Gaborone.

Coming along that day for this historic event was the head girl Netty Nkala, a form 4 named Lekgobo, who was to become one of the pillars of the Drama club after we left, Goabamodimo Mhaladi, and Meshack 'Lani' Mauco. The first stop we made was at Maitisong hall at Maru A Pula School, where I caught a glimpse of Albert and Balisi just outside campus along the main Maru A Pula road; they were of course looking at the van with great curiosity, because it had the Lotsane Senior Secondary School emblem on the sides of the driver and passenger side doors. I tried to get their attention, but they did not see me. I did however remind the guys that next year this time I would be a MAP student – practicing the power of positive thinking.

From MAP we headed to the Save Our Souls (SOS) village in Tlokweng, a village less than 20 miles east of Gaborone at the time. It was here that we were introduced to the man of the moment Kabo Matlho, who at the time was about nine or ten years old. We were all fascinated at how jolly and upbeat he was. His handicap did not seem to bother him at all, if anything he thrived at the attention given him. From there we headed to the *'Botswana Guardian'* offices, here I held Kabo in my arms, a moment I cherish even to this day, and Netty presented him with an envelope with money well over 500 Pula as Lekgobo looked on, and the journalists took the pictures. Unfortunately, Mr. Mudidi did not allow Goabamodimo and Meshack into the picture, because they did not have their full uniforms on.

After we were all done, we stopped by our home where I dropped off the trunk. The advantage I had was that our house was not too far from the main highway that took us to Palapye. All in all, I was very fortunate, because the carrying of a trunk that big and heavy was one of the main inconveniences a student had to deal with; once school was done like it was for us. My father was surprised at seeing us arrive in the school car. He was seated in the shade in front of our house with my youngest sister Baarata on his lap. She was about four months old at the time, and even Mr. Mudidi carried her for a while as he spoke to my father; the two were very well acquainted by now. What I immediately realized was that we finally had a car. It was a light blue VW Golf, a very popular car at the time, but one of its wheels was off because the wheel bearing needed to be replaced.

"So how were the exams?" my father asked anxiously.

"Well, all I can say is that I did my best," which was true. "However one cannot do better than his best."

"Oh, he's philosophizing now," my father said to Mr. Mudidi who merely smiled, and soon after we were on our way back to Palapye. I could not help but brag to my friends how I was going to have a good time in that car over the very long holidays that were now looming.

When we arrived at school Faith, and her friend Kenae, had a hissy fit thinking that I had stayed behind in Gaborone. The school car had dropped us off near the boys hostel, Netty had stayed behind in Gaborone, so when the car pulled into the parking lot, the two ladies had just cause to be alarmed. That day marked the final day of school for the form 4's, so they were waiting for the school truck to drop them at the train station. What a relief it was when she saw me casually walking toward them in the dark.

"Oh Sebati we thought you guys decided to remain in Gaborone, and not come back after all, Kenae and I were actually thinking of ordering the school to go back and pick you guys up." There was no mistaking the fact that she was relieved, and on the other hand not even wild horses could have kept me from heading back to Palapye and be with her.

I was with Gerald, Phatsimo, Motlotlegi and a few other guys who accompanied the form 4's to the station that evening. The prospect of not seeing Faith for over a month at least was tough to bare. We talked about the possibility of me visiting her in her home village of Maun, which was over 700 miles from Gaborone. How and when I was going to do that only the Good Lord knew. While at the station, a north bound goods train made a routine stop, and from the engine driver's section out popped Two-Two. I had not seen him in a year.

"So how have you been?" I asked, as soon as we were done with the brief hugging that always comes after seeing a long lost friend.

"I joined the Botswana Railways, I'm still in training. I'm what you call an 'observer'?"

"Oh," I said as if I had a clue of what he was talking about. He then eyed Faith for a moment.

"Where is Olivia by the way?" he asked.

"I have no idea."

Faith looked at me and said, "tell him."

"Nothing to tell I don't know where she is." Truth is she had gone back home to Francistown, in fact the whole school was gone now except the few of us, and I mean just a handful.

In time he was gone, and it was not too long after the north bound mixed passenger train arrived, and took the rest including Faith with it. In an instant I felt terribly lonely as we walked back to school. It had rained very hard that evening and the weeks before, because December is rainy season in Botswana, if we are lucky enough to avoid the drought, and as such this was one of the very few times when the Lotsane River was overflowing. The sound of the ferocious river reminded Gerald of the great Victoria Falls.

There were only four of us left in dorm 2 that night, the very last night of me being a student at Lotsane Senior Secondary School, and that was the same for the rest. The next day Motlotlegi and others wrote their TD exam, and we went to the hall where we had our very last lunch. Since there were only a handful of us; we were served instead at the back of the hall. There was a lot of food to go around, and we also took with us as much boiled eggs as we could. At last we bid the cooks farewell, many who still reminded me of the play where I was the street urchin, and Mable Maphane the improbable object of my character's desire. We had come a long way, and I was touched that they could remember that far back.

On that slightly overcast Friday afternoon of December 4th 1987, when I walked out of the Lotsane gates, I was not a student of that great school anymore. It would be a long time before I would feel the impact of that loss. We hitched a ride to Gaborone, and we got home later that day, I told my dad about Motlotlegi's dilemma, and the fact that he needed a place to stay. My father, always the people's person, welcomed him with open arms, and in time Motlotlegi was to become a part of the family. That evening, we sat silently at the table, starring at the lantern lamp in the middle of the table. I was in deep thought, and I could tell that Motlotlegi was too. There was no doubt what was in our minds.

"What is it Honorable?" that is what I called him all the time.

"I am just thinking of Catherine," he replied, Catherine was his girlfriend, who like Faith was a form 4. I could relate because I was thinking along the same lines.

"So when do you think you will see her again?"

"I'll see her next year."

The prospect of 1988 seemed far-fetched at the time. 1988 was the beginning of life after Lotsane. I had a lot to look forward to. There were the results that were due either late February or early March that would tell us how we fared in our most recent exams; and on the strength of that if mine were good enough to be accepted at MAP. However, the odyssey that was Lotsane had come to an end. I went outside for a while to digest that fact. I nodded with a smile on my face. It was a great journey and one I was privileged to take, because the memories were enough to last a lifetime. Yes, the sweet memories of Lotsane.

The Aftermath

A week later the *Botswana Guardian* published a picture of me holding Kabo, and Netty giving him the money and Lekgobo looking on. The article was a hit all over the country as everyone kept telling me that they saw me in the papers. However, during these holidays I missed Faith terribly, and decided one day to pay her a surprise visit in Maun. I caught the train, and arrived in Francistown the next morning, and ran into Kabelo Lebotse at the station; we were very pleased to see one another as he was now working part time at an Electronics store while he like me waited for the results. I also sent word out through someone to let my Francistown buddies know that I was in town. The connecting bus to Maun did not depart until 1 PM that afternoon. Guys like Archie, Mosimanegape, Thomas Makwade, Jenamiso Mountain, Ian Makgwakae, and the like got my message, but arrived at the station after I had already left. Word was that I was headed to Maun to do a research on a new novel I was writing, and none of them believed that story to be true.

The results were released at the end of February 1988. We had 81 first class passes and over 200 second class passes, a record that still stands as of this writing. Lotsane was first among the government schools, and second only to perennial best Maru A Pula. I always knew that our group would be great, but not the greatness that I saw when the results were released. I inwardly thanked MS. Motlotle for endorsing that idea of studying after lights off in the boys' common room in 'Block A' from the very beginning of the year, as opposed to waiting for the third term.

I personally did very well. I remember before the results were released, I was always a nervous wreck, and I would tell Max about this whenever I visited him at the university. Max would always say, "Sebati it is not a question of whether you have passed or not, because we both know you have – it is a question of how well."

And when the results were released; he would never have been more proud like he was the day after when I ran into him at the mall. He invited me to go back with him to the university to celebrate in style, but unfortunately I had other pressing plans that prevented that, but we were to celebrate in our own unique way whenever I had the opportunity to visit him at the university. I had gotten the grades I needed to be accepted to do my A Levels at Maru A Pula School, which was 'B' or better in Mathematics, Physical Science (Physics and Chemistry), and English. Many teachers, and myself included, thought I could have fared even better had I not taken too much of a break during the first part of the year. Mr. and Mrs. Mbulawa could not have been any happier when they saw my grades, and the first thing they guessed, and correctly so, was how thrilled my dad was and they were right. My dad was to talk about that accomplishment for many years to come.

Even though I did not do very well at MAP, but that passing grade at O' Level opened many doors for me. I was accepted at one of America's top Engineering universities in Harvey Mudd College, and although I ended up at a different school, that passing grade enabled me most importantly to win the Bishop Desmond Tutu scholarship fund that brought me to the United States where I reside as of this writing.

However, the sad part about life is that as the years have gone by we have lost many ex Lotsane students, and many more I do not know what became of them. Blackie Davis 'Onketsang' Kealotswe is very much alive, and is a top detective with the Botswana Police as of this writing. His son Ras Jecko Scotch Kealotswe has plans of writing a movie about him and playing his father; apparently Blackie's exploits continued even after he left Lotsane. Ballman, Blackie's older brother, passed away I hear in 1996, Andries Hotstix Ryan died in a tragic car accident in 1990. A lot more have since left us namely: Ditshupo Motlhatlhubi, Ishmael Mphela, Gerald Usher, Mbumbi Manyothwane, Oaitse Madume, Loruo Bruce Rakanye, Kaelo Gare, Godfrey Mafia Morgan, Kakambi Bahiti, Chakalisa, Mosimanegape 'MC' Keagile, Israel 'Zweks' Mosweu Seleka, Fredrick 'Congo' Molelekeng, Batisani German, Goabamodimo Mhaladi, Lamech Mamuze, Osborne Twenty, Isaac Mafokate, Joseph Thupe, and many others.

Now as far as Bonang Mapolanka is concerned, I have not been able to get a clear cut answer as to what became of him. There have been nothing but conflicting reports. Some say he is alive and some say he is not, but everyone agreed on one thing and that he was very sickly when they last saw him. The last I did was in 1992, in Francistown, a few months before I came to the United States, and it has been hazy ever since. Mr. Victor Isaac 'Legoro' Mahole left Lotsane after we did, and was transferred to Macha Secondary School. Many believed he took the Lotsane mystique with him, because the school was never the same; he died a few years later. Our great boarding master Mr. Molefi retired I hear in 2000. However, the sweet memories are what I cherish of those alive and those departed - this book is also dedicated to their memory. And I want to thank you very much for taking this journey with me down Lotsane memory lane. I hope it was as enjoyable to you as it has been for me.

The end.